Essentials of
Managing
Stress

Third Edition

Brian Luke Seaward, PhD
Paramount Wellness Institute
Boulder, Colorado

JONES & BARTLETT
LEARNING

World Headquarters
Jones & Bartlett Learning
5 Wall Street
Burlington, MA 01803
978-443-5000
info@jblearning.com
www.jblearning.com

Jones & Bartlett Learning books and products are available through most bookstores and online booksellers. To contact Jones & Bartlett Learning directly, call 800-832-0034, fax 978-443-8000, or visit our website, www.jblearning.com.

Substantial discounts on bulk quantities of Jones & Bartlett Learning publications are available to corporations, professional associations, and other qualified organizations. For details and specific discount information, contact the special sales department at Jones & Bartlett Learning via the above contact information or send an email to specialsales@jblearning.com.

Production Credits
Publisher: William Brottmiller
Editorial Assistant: Agnes Burt
Editorial Assistant: Sean Coombs
Associate Production Editor: Jill Morton
Production Assistant: Stephanie Rineman
Senior Marketing Manager: Jennifer Stiles
V.P., Manufacturing and Inventory Control: Therese Connell
Composition: Paw Print Media
Cover Design: Scott Moden
Rights & Photo Research Assistant: Miranda Rivers
Cover and Title Page Image: © Brian Luke Seaward
Printing and Binding: Edwards Brothers Malloy
Cover Printing: Edwards Brothers Malloy

To order this product, use ISBN: 978-1-4496-9802-7

Library of Congress Cataloging-in-Publication Data
Seaward, Brian Luke.
  Essentials of managing stress / by Brian Luke Seaward. — 3rd ed.
      p. cm.
  Includes bibliographical references and index.
  ISBN 978-1-4496-4631-8
  1. Stress management. 2. Stress (Psychology) 3. Mind and body. I. Title.
  RA785.S43295 2014
  155.9'042—dc23
                        2012031173

6048

Printed in the United States of America
17 16 15 14 13   10 9 8 7 6 5 4 3 2

In honor of the memory and spirit of my grandparents,
Frank and Marie McNulty

Brief Contents

Contents

Contents

Contents

Contents

Contents

Introduction:
One Planet Under Stress

"Modern man is sick because he is not whole."
— Carl Gustav Jung

There is a huge health crisis in the world today that barely gets noticed in the news headlines, even though it underlies nearly every topic of conversation among friends, family, co-workers, acquaintances, consumers, and even young teenagers. The crisis is an epidemic of stress that affects everything in our lives, from our eating habits to the most basic lifestyle behaviors of everyone with whom we interact. Sociologists tell us that stress is one of the few factors that knows no demographic boundaries. As the expression goes, "Stress is the equal opportunity destroyer."

It is no secret that the world itself is currently under a great amount of stress, particularly with the economic collapse. The waves of political issues, environmental problems, and global concerns crash upon the shores of our personal lives in ways that were unimaginable only a few decades ago. Despite the current issues—massive job layoffs, chronic diseases, financial instability, social unrest, global warming, identity theft, terrorism—solutions to these problems are within our grasp if we make the effort to use our inner resources to reach for help.

Before each of us is a fork in the road. The first path may look appealing, even easy at first, but beware: it's an illusion, a lifestyle trap. Many people head down this direction and face years, if not decades, of frustration and possible ill health. The other path looks more challenging at first—very steep and perhaps with unsure footing. Soon, however, this path offers better panoramic views and ultimately a better quality of life. This path is uncrowded because few people choose this direction. Don't let this fact put you off. This book is both a roadmap and a compass to the second path, the path of holistic stress management, the one with the great views and exhilarating experiences.

Holistic stress management is based on the premise of ageless wisdom where the whole is always greater than the sum of the parts. If you were to ask the shamans, sages, mystics, and healers of all times, of all ages, and of all languages regarding the topic of health—"What are the parts that make up the whole?"—you would hear a unanimous voice among these wisdom keepers saying these words: mind, body, spirit, and emotions. When asked to elaborate further, they would explain that holistic health is the divine alchemy derived from the integration, balance, and harmony of these four components.

Today, the voice of ageless wisdom often is drowned out by the dull roar of a scientific community that tends to look for and associate a specific cause with each effect. Rather than looking at the whole picture, Western culture has opted to dissect and study the pieces that make up the whole, yet, curiously, never getting around to putting the pieces back together. Moreover, Western culture often fails to recognize the significance of the unique unifying synergistic force that gives power to the whole being greater than the sum of the parts. Herein lies the danger regarding our current health care system. Symptomatic relief, the capstone of the western medical model, does not honor the code of holistic health, wherein both the causes and symptoms of disease and illness are resolved together. Perhaps most importantly, holistic stress management honors the aspect of spiritual well-being, a component that had been long ignored or neglected entirely.

Paradigms often are slow to change, but, with a newly recognized national interest in various forms of complementary and alternative medicine, new insights into health and healing based on ageless wisdom are taking root in U.S. culture. In his acclaimed book *The Best Alternative Medicine: What Works and What Doesn't*, author Kenneth Pelletier cites that there are more than 600 different modalities of holistic healing, from acupuncture to zero balancing. Despite the plethora of techniques, the purpose (implicit or explicit) of every modality of complementary and alternative medicine (now called CAM by the medical establishment) is to restore a sense of homeostasis through the integration, balance, and harmony of mind, body, spirit, and emotions. It is no coincidence that virtually every modality of holistic stress management is considered a member of this family of 600 healing modalities because the purpose of effective coping skills and relaxation techniques is the same—to return each person to a sense of homeostasis.

To understand, appreciate, and utilize the wealth of knowledge in the realm of holistic health, it is important to realize that the wisdom of mind-body-spirit stress management draws upon the disciplines of psychology, sociology, physiology, theology, anthropology, mythology, quantum physics, cosmology, and several more areas—all of which come together as a means to create the parameters of "the bigger picture." By and large, we live in a society where experts focus their specialty on one discipline rather than on a synthesis of all aspects of the human journey, thus creating a dangerous blind spot. In essence, this fragmented approach creates a very myopic view of life, particularly when trying to deal with the complexities that make up the human condition; none of these are held tightly in the domain of one discipline.

Holistic stress management is more than just a theory, although many people end their journeys there. In support of the premise that the whole is always greater than the sum of its parts, holistic stress management goes beyond theory to include the daily application of this knowledge so that effective coping skills and relaxation techniques become part of one's daily lifestyle, rather than a first aid kit for crises.

I have been a follower of the holistic model of health all my life. Although the premise of the wellness paradigm is clearly intuitive, it is disappointing to me not to see it being more widely embraced. We do not have a healthcare system in this country; we have a sick care system where the focus is on symptomatic relief. In the late 1970s, I made a decision to focus my efforts as a health educator on being an advocate for holistic health. Soon after I completed my master's degree in exercise physiology, a culmination of events opened the door to make this happen with relative ease, not the least of which was the distinct honor of meeting Elisabeth Kübler-Ross, MD. She was the keynote speaker at the American Holistic Medical Association meeting held in La Crosse, Wisconsin, in 1981. Although she was renowned all over the world for her work on the topic of death and dying, she gave a stunning presentation on the nature of holistic healing. Her presentation—as well as my subsequent meetings with her—galvanized the direction of my professional career. The perspective I bring to *Essentials of Managing Stress, Third Edition* is a culmination of the knowledge, wisdom, and experience I have gathered over three decades.

An ancient proverb often quoted in the halls of Wall Street states, "To know and not do is not to know." In simple terms, this means that you can know all of the information that supports a powerful strategy for holistic stress management, yet, by not practicing these techniques and making them part of your daily routine, the knowledge is quite useless. Perhaps in simplest terms, holistic stress management is an adaptation process involving all aspects of mind, body, spirit, and emotions to reach one's highest potential.

Specifically, what is holistic stress management? Here are some insights that collectively shine light on this timeless wisdom:

- Holistic stress management conveys the essence of uniting the powers of the conscious and unconscious minds to work in unison for one's highest potential.

- Holistic stress management suggests a dynamic approach to one's personal energy where one lives in the present moment rather than feeling guilty about things done in the past or worrying about things that may occur in the future.

- Holistic stress management implies using a combination of coping skills to resolve issues that can cause perceptions of stress to linger and relaxation techniques to reduce or eliminate the symptoms of stress and return the body to homeostasis.

- Holistic stress management also can be described as moving from a motivation of fear to a place of unconditional love.

If there is one theme to this text (and, actually, there are many), it is the theme of balance, for without balance in one's life, nothing else is really possible. Every skill and technique described here carries with it the premise of restoring a sense of balance, homeostasis, or inner peace to mind, body, spirit, and emotions.

The contents of *Essentials of Managing Stress, Third Edition* are based on the collective wisdom of a great many 20th- and 21st-century luminaries in the fields of psychology, physiology, sociology, theology, and mythology, including Carl Jung, Abraham Maslow, Ken Cooper, Elisabeth Kübler-Ross, Albert Einstein, Victor Frankl, Joseph Campbell, Carolyn Myss, Richard Gerber, Hans Selye, Wayne Dyer, Dean Ornish, Don Campbell, Norman Cousins, Andrew Weil, Deepak Chopra, Candace Pert, Donna Eden, Jean Houston, and many, many others. The purpose of this text is to increase your awareness regarding the various aspects of wellness through the mind-body-spirit nexus as well as to utilize any and all ideas so that you may fully integrate them into your life. By doing so, you begin to take an active role in the process of cultivating inner peace, rather than feeling like a passive victim in a hostile world.

This new edition includes a new section in Chapter 1, The Sociology of Stress; a new chapter on communication skills (Chapter 12); new insights scattered through additional chapters; and more than ten new exercises to strengthen your internal fortitude for your wonderful life journey of optimal health and well-being.

At the end of each chapter there is a series of exercises based on specific chapter contents, many of which are new or revised for this *Third Edition*. These exercises are designed to be stepping stones to your soul-searching efforts. They have been created specifically to help you process the informational content for the most comprehensive understanding. Although you are encouraged to complete the exercises, you may find it best to read each exercise first and then return to it when you are truly ready. Whereas some exercises were designed specifically for this text, the majority of them were created for workshop participants and college students over a period of two decades. They have proven to be very valuable and, in some cases, life changing. It is my wish that you find them to be equally valuable in seeking that place of inner peace in both your heart and soul.

Best wishes and inner peace,

Brian Luke Seaward, PhD
Paramount Wellness Institute
Boulder, Colorado
http://www.brianlukeseaward.net

To the Instructor

As a benefit/incentive of using *Essentials of Managing Stress, Third Edition* and to save you valuable time in the preparation and instruction of your course, the publisher has provided an enhanced TestBank, an Instructor's Manual, and completely updated and revised PowerPoint presentations all created by the author and available as a free download.

For students, each chapter is designed to aid in the mastery of the material. Features include bolded key terms throughout the text and extensive end-of-chapter exercises to reinforce fundamental concepts. Each chapter concludes with a comprehensive summary of the main points discussed in the chapter along with references for further study. Key terms are clearly defined in a handy glossary at the end of the text, which can be useful when studying for examinations. Also available at the back of each book is a complimentary 60-minute audio CD that provides many relaxation techniques for stress reduction. Mental imagery, meditation, progressive relaxation, and autogenic training are taught with a professional mix of voice and restful music. Through listening to this CD, students are taught how to apply stress-reduction methods to their own lives. These audio files are available for download on the companion Web site for this book and on iTunes.

Managing Stress: A Creative Journal also is available as an optional supplement to the course. The journal contains more than 80 thought-provoking and soul-searching themes designed to engage the student in writing about personal stress, unresolved conflict, and tension-producing emotions. Journal writing has proven to be a formidable coping technique used by psychologists and health educators as an awareness tool for self-exploration and discovery.

Students using *Essentials of Managing Stress, Third Edition* can access the companion Web site at gojblearning.com /seawardessentials for online learning tools and resources such as Web exercises, an interactive glossary, crossword puzzles, flashcards, and practice quizzes.

Acknowledgments

Essentials of Managing Stress, Third Edition contains the wealth of wisdom that I have accrued over several decades of personal growth, discovery, and instruction to thousands of students and workshop participants over my career in the field of stress management. I am deeply indebted to all who have allowed me to share these exercises and meditations as a means for personal growth, soul searching, and mind-body-spirit integration. Your feedback was (and is) greatly appreciated.

A hearty word of thanks goes to my personal assistant, Candace Beck, who repeatedly combed through this manuscript page by page to help me groom it toward excellence and learned much in the process.

Once again, the staff at Jones & Bartlett has proved superlative with their efforts to make this text the best ever. Special thanks go to Shoshanna Goldberg, Agnes Burt, Jill Morton, and everyone else at my publisher— I am eternally grateful, as always, for your support.

Many thanks to all of the stress management instructors and therapists who use this text in their teachings and who reduce the amount of stress in the world by teaching the life skills necessary to navigate the shoals of uncertainty in the challenging time we live in.

Thank you to the reviewers of the *Second Edition*: Nancy A. Barton, MS, ACSM/HFS, Indiana University–Purdue University Indianapolis; Paul Bondurant, MS, Macomb Community College; Regina M. DeGennaro, DNP, RN, AOCN, CNL, University of Virginia School of Nursing; Deborah Gioia, PhD, LCSW-C, University of Maryland; Raeann Koerner, Ventura College; Craig M. Rand, Monroe Community College; Elaine C. Scribner, BSN, RN, MPH, HSMI, Lansing Community College; and Amy Yeates, RN, MSN, Illinois Wesleyan University.

A gracious word of thanks to the people at the National Wellness Institute in Stevens Point, Wisconsin, and the staff of the American Holistic Nursing Association who have supported my efforts to offer holistic stress management instructor training program workshops over the years. Merci beaucoup!

Once again, thanks to my friends, colleagues, and family, too numerous to mention, who have always been such a tremendous support to me and my work over the course of my career.

About the Author

Brian Luke Seaward, PhD, is considered a pioneer in the field of health psychology and is internationally recognized for his contributions in the areas of holistic stress management, human spirituality, and mind-body-spirit healing. The wisdom of Dr. Seaward can be found quoted in PBS specials, college graduation speeches, medical seminars, boardroom meetings, church sermons, and keynote addresses all over the world. Dr. Seaward is highly respected throughout the international community as an accomplished teacher, consultant, motivational speaker, author, and mentor. He is the executive director of the Paramount Wellness Institute and serves on the faculty of the University of Northern Colorado–Greeley in the Department of Community Health and Nutrition. He is the author of several books, including *Stressed Is Desserts Spelled Backward*; *The Art of Calm*; *Health of the Human Spirit*; *Quiet Mind, Fearless Heart*; and the popular *Stand Like Mountain, Flow Like Water*. He can be reached at www .brianlukeseaward.net.

The Wellness Mandala: Holistic Stress Management

The Nature of Stress

"Tension is who you think you should be. Relaxation is who you are."
— Ancient Chinese proverb

Are you stressed? If the answer is yes, then consider yourself to be in good company. Several recent Harris and Gallup polls have noted an alarming trend in the psyche of the American public and beyond—to nearly all citizens of the global village. Across the board, without exception, people admit to having an increasing sense of anxiety, frustration, unease, and discontent in nearly every aspect of their lives. From the aftermath of the Great Recession (and the subsequent economic problems) to mounting environmental reminders of an unsustainable path of human existence, the face of stress can be found just about everywhere. Sadly, episodes of suicides, road rage, school shootings, and personal bankruptcies are so common that they no longer are headline news. Ironically, in a country where the standard of living is considered to be the highest anywhere in the world, the Centers for Disease Control and Prevention estimates that nearly one-quarter of the American population is reported to be on antidepressants. Moreover, economic difficulties persist from the national home foreclosure debacle, and college loan costs continue to escalate. Obesity rates continue to rise dramatically, and current estimates are that one in three people suffers from a chronic disease, ranging from cancer and coronary heart disease to diabetes, lupus, and rheumatoid arthritis. For a country with the highest standard of living, something is very wrong with this picture!

Furthermore, since the start of the Great Recession, a blanket of fear has covered much of the country, if not the world, keeping people in a perpetual, albeit low, state of anxiety. Global problems only seem to intensify our personal stressors. It doesn't make a difference if you're a college student or a CEO of a multinational corporation, where you live, or how much money is in your checking account; stress is the equal opportunity destroyer! But it doesn't have to be this way. Even as personal issues collide with social and planetary problems creating a "perfect storm" of stress, we all have choices—in both our attitude and behaviors. This text will help you connect the dots between mind, body, and spirit to create positive choices that empower you to navigate your life through the turbulent waters of the human journey in the 21st century.

Times of Change and Uncertainty

Today the words *stress* and *change* have become synonymous and the winds of change are in the air. Changes in the economy, technology, communications, information retrieval, health care, and dramatic changes in the weather are just some of the gale forces blowing in our collective faces. By and large, the average person doesn't like change (particularly change they cannot control) because change tends to disrupt one's comfort zones. It appears that the "known," no matter how bad, is a safer bet than the unknown. Change, it should be noted, has always been part of the human landscape. However, today the rate of change has become so fast and furious, without an adequate reference point to anchor oneself, that stress holds the potential to create a perpetual sense of uneasiness in the hearts and minds of nearly everyone. Yet it doesn't have to be this way. Where there is change, there is opportunity.

At one time, getting married, changing jobs, buying a house, raising children, going back to school, dealing with the death of a friend or close relative, and suffering from a chronic illness were all considered to be major life events that might shake the foundations of anyone's life. Although these major life events can and do play a significant role in personal upheaval, a new crop of social stressors has added to the critical mass of an already volatile existence, throwing things further out of balance. Consider how these factors directly influence your life: the rapid acceleration of technology (from software upgrades to downloadable apps), the use of (if not addiction to) the World Wide Web (e.g., Facebook, Instagram, and Twitter), the proliferation of smartphones and WiFi use, an accessible 24/7 society, global economic woes (e.g., gasoline prices, subprime loan foreclosures, rent, food prices), global terrorism, carbon footprints, and public health issues from AIDS and West Nile virus to the latest outbreak of contagious staphylococcus infections. Times of change and uncertainty tend to magnify our personal stress. Perhaps the biggest looming concern facing people today is the issue of personal boundaries or lack thereof. The advances of high technology combined with a rapidly changing social structure have eroded personal boundaries. These boundaries include, but are not limited to, home and work, finances, personal privacy, nutritional habits, relationships, and many, many more, all of which add to the critical mass of one's personal stress. Even the ongoing war on terrorism appears to have no boundaries! Ironically, the lack of boundaries combined with factors that promote a fractured society, where people feel a lack of community and belonging, leads to a greater sense of isolation and this also intensifies our personal stress levels. Believe it or not, life wasn't always like this.

The stress phenomenon, as it is referred to today, is quite new with regard to the history of humanity. Barely a household expression when your parents were your age, use of the word *stress* is now as common as the terms *global warming, iPads,* and *smartphones.* In fact, however, stress in terms of physical arousal can be traced back to the Stone Age as a "survival mechanism." But what was once designed as a means of survival is now associated with the development of disease and illness that claims the lives of millions of people worldwide. The American Institute of Stress (www.stress.org) cites the following statistics:

- 43 percent of all adults suffer adverse health effects due to stress.

- 75 to 90 percent of all visits to primary care physicians are for stress-related complaints or disorders.

Stress has been linked to all the leading causes of death, including heart disease, cancer, lung ailments, accidents, cirrhosis, and suicide. Some health experts now speculate that perhaps as much as 70 to 85 percent of all diseases and illnesses are stress-related.

Government figures compiled by the National Center for Health Statistics in 2004 provide a host of indicators suggesting that human stress is indeed a health factor to be reckoned with. Prior to 1955, the leading causes of death were the sudden onset of illness by infectious diseases (e.g., polio, rubella, tuberculosis, typhoid, and encephalitis) that in most cases have since been eradicated or brought under control by vaccines and medications. The post–World War II era ushered in the age of high technology, which considerably altered the lifestyles of nearly all peoples of every industrialized nation. The start of the 21st century has seen the influence of high technology dramatically alter our lifestyles. The introduction of consumer products, such as the washer, dryer, microwave oven, television, DVD player, laptop computer, and smartphone, were cited as luxuries to add more leisure time to the workweek. But as mass production of high-technology items increased, so too did the competitive drive to increase human effort and productivity, which in turn actually decreased leisure time, and thus created a plethora of unhealthy lifestyles, most notably obesity.

Currently, the leading causes of death are dominated by what are referred to as lifestyle diseases—those diseases whose pathology develops over a period of several years, and perhaps even decades. Whereas infectious diseases are treatable by medication, lifestyle diseases are, for the most part, preventable or correctable by altering the habits and behaviors that contribute to their etiology. Previously, it was suggested that an association existed between stress and disease. Current research, however, suggests that there may, indeed, be a causal factor involved with several types of diseases, particularly heart disease, obesity, and **autoimmune diseases**. Regardless, it is well understood that the influence of stress weakens the body's physiological systems, thereby rapidly advancing the disease process. The most notorious lifestyle disease, coronary heart disease (CHD), continues to be one of the leading causes of death in the United States, far exceeding all other causes. The American Heart Association states that one person dies from heart disease every 34 seconds. Although the incidence of CHD has decreased over the past decade, cancer—in all its many types—continues to climb the statistical charts as the second leading cause of death. According to 2012 statistics from the American Cancer Society (www.cancer.org), cancer claims the lives of one out of every four people in the United States. Alarming increases in suicides, child and spouse abuse, self-mutilation, homicides, alcoholism, and drug addiction are only additional symptoms of a nation under stress. Today, research shows that people still maintain poor coping skills in the face of the personal, social, and even global changes occurring over the course of their lives.

Originally, the word *stress* was a term used in physics, primarily to describe enough tension or force placed on an object to bend or break it. Relaxation, on the other hand, was defined as any nonwork activity done during the evenings or on Sunday afternoons when all the stores were closed. On rare occasions, if one could afford it, relaxation meant a vacation or holiday at some faraway place. Conceptually, relaxation was a value, influenced by several religions and represented as a day of rest. The word *stress* as applied to the human condition was first made popular by noted physiologist Hans Selye in his book *The Stress of Life*, where he described his research: to understand the physiological responses to chronic stress and its relationship to disease (dis-ease). Today, the word *stress* is frequently used to describe the level of tension people feel is placed on their minds and souls by the demands of their jobs, relationships, and responsibilities in their personal lives. Oddly, for some, stress seems to be a status symbol tied to self-esteem.

Relaxation, meanwhile, has been transformed from an American value into a luxury many people find they just don't have enough time for. With the current economic situation, some interesting insights have been observed regarding work and leisure. The average workweek has expanded from 40 to 60 hours. The U.S. Department of Labor and Statistics reports that, with more service-related jobs being created, more overtime is needed to meet the demands of the customers. Not only do more people spend more time at work, they spend more time driving to and from work (which is not considered work time). Moreover, leisure time at home is often related to work activities, resulting in less time for rest and relaxation. Downtime is also compromised. Since 2001, Expedia has conducted an annual survey on vacations (called the Vacation Deprivation Study). The 2009 results revealed that one out of every three Americans don't use all of their vacation time. One in five respondents cited work responsibilities/pressure as the primary reason for canceling a vacation. A new word entered the American lexicon in the summer of 2010; the *staycation*, where people simply stayed home for vacation due to financial and/or work constraints. Those who do head for the mountains or beaches for vacation often take their work (in the form of smartphones, iPads, and laptops) with them—in essence, never really leaving their job. It's no surprise that staying plugged in doesn't give the mind a chance to unwind or the body a chance to relax. In comparison to other countries, Americans take less vacation time than other global citizens. (Germans, on average, take 4–6 weeks/year.) "The stress associated with the current economy makes the need for time away from work even more important than ever, and it's unfortunate that one-third of Americans won't use all of their vacation days this year," said Tim MacDonald, general manager of Expedia.com. The "dividend" of high technology has proven to be an illusion that has resulted in a stressed lifestyle, which in turn creates a significant health deficit.

Definitions of Stress

In contemporary times, the word *stress* has many connotations and definitions based on various perspectives of the human condition. In Eastern philosophies, stress is considered to be an absence of inner peace. In Western culture, stress can be described as a loss of emotional control. Noted healer Serge Kahili King has defined stress as any change experienced by the individual. This definition may be rather general, but it is quite correct. Psychologically speaking, stress as defined by noted researcher Richard Lazarus is a state of anxiety produced when events and responsibilities exceed one's coping abilities. Physiologically speaking, stress is defined as the rate of wear and tear on the body. Selye added to his definition that stress is the nonspecific response of the body to any demand placed upon it to adapt, whether that demand produces pleasure or pain. Selye observed that whether a situation was perceived as good (e.g., a job promotion) or bad (e.g., the loss of a job), the physiological response or arousal was very similar. The body, according to Selye, doesn't know the difference between good and bad stress.

However, with new psychoneuroimmunological data available showing that there are indeed some physiological differences between good and bad stress (e.g., the release of different **neuropeptides**), specialists in the field of **holistic medicine** have expanded Lazarus's and Selye's definitions as follows: Stress is the inability to cope with a perceived (real or imagined) threat to one's mental, physical, emotional, and spiritual well-being, which results in a series of physiological responses and adaptations. The important word to emphasize here is *perceived* (the interpretation), for what might seem to be a threat to one person may not even merit a second thought to another individual. For example, not long ago a raffle was held, with the winning prize being an all-expenses-paid one-week trip for two to a beach resort in Bermuda. Kelly, who won the prize, was ecstatic and already had her bags packed. Her husband, John, was mortified because he hated to fly and he couldn't swim. In his mind this would not be a fun time. In fact, he really wished they hadn't won. Each perceived the same situation in two entirely different ways. Moreover, with the wisdom of hindsight, our perceptions often change. Many episodes that at the time seemed catastrophic later appear insignificant, as humorously stated by Mark Twain when he commented, "I'm an old man and I have known a great many troubles, but most of them never happened." The holistic definition of stress points out that it is a very complex phenomenon affecting the whole person, not just the physical body, and that it involves a host of factors, some of which may not yet even be recognized by scholars and researchers. As more research is completed, it becomes increasingly evident that the responses to stress add up to more than just physical arousal; yet it is ultimately the body that remains the battlefield for the war games of the mind.

The Stress Response

In 1914, Harvard physiologist **Walter Cannon** first coined the term **fight-or-flight response** to describe the dynamics involved in the body's physiological arousal to survive a threat. In a series of animal studies, Cannon noted that the body prepares itself for one of two modes of immediate action: to attack or fight and defend oneself from the pursuing threat, or to run and escape the ensuing danger. What Cannon observed was the body's reaction to acute stress, what is now commonly called the **stress reaction**. Additional observations suggested that the fight response was triggered by anger or aggression and was usually employed to defend territorial boundaries or attack aggressors equal or smaller in size. The fight response required physiological preparations that would recruit power and strength for a short duration, or what is now described as short but intense anaerobic work. Conversely, the flight response, he thought, was induced by fear. It was designed to fuel the body to endure prolonged movement such as running away from lions and bears. In many cases, however, it included not only fleeing but also hiding or withdrawal. (A variation on the flight response is the **freeze response**, often noted with post-traumatic stress disorder, where a person simply freezes, like a deer staring into a car's headlights.) The human body, in all its metabolic splendor, actually prepares itself to do both (fight and flight) at the same time. In terms of evolution, it appears that this dynamic was so advantageous to survival that it developed in nearly all mammalian species, including us. (Some experts now suggest, however, that our bodies have not adapted to the stress-induced lifestyles of the 21st century.)

In simple terms, there are four stages of the fight-or-flight response:

Stage 1. Stimuli from one or more of the five senses are sent to the brain (e.g., a scream, the smell of fire, the taste of poison, a passing truck in *your* lane).

Stage 2. The brain deciphers the stimulus as either a threat or a nonthreat. If the stimulus is not regarded as a threat, this is the end of the response (e.g., the scream came from the television). If, however, the response is decoded as a real threat, the brain then activates the nervous and endocrine systems to quickly prepare for defense and/or escape.

Stage 3. The body stays activated, aroused, or "keyed-up" until the threat is over.

Stage 4. The body returns to **homeostasis**, a state of physiological calmness, once the threat is gone.

It is hypothesized that the fight-or-flight response developed primarily against threats of a physical nature, those that jeopardized the survival of the individual. Although clear physical threats still exist in today's culture, including possible terrorism, they are nowhere near as prevalent as those threats perceived by the mind and, more specifically, the ego. In a theory put forward by a disciple of Selye's, Simeons (1961), and repeated by Sapolsky (1998), it is suggested that, in effect, the fight-or-flight response is an antiquated mechanism that has not kept evolutionary pace with the development of the human mind. Consequently, the **stress response** becomes activated in all types of threats, not just physical intimidations. The physiological repercussions can, and do, prove fatal. The body enters a state of physical readiness when you are about to receive your final exam grades or walk into an important meeting late, just as it does when you sense someone is following you late at night in an unlit parking lot. Moreover, this same stress response kicks in, to the same degree and intensity, even when the threat is wholly imaginary, in reaction to everything from monsters hiding under your bed when you were 4 years old, to the unsubstantiated idea that your boss doesn't like you anymore and is out to get you.

Cannon noted the activation of several physiological mechanisms in this fight-or-flight response, affecting nearly every physiological system in the body, for the preparation of movement and energy production. These are just a few of the reactions:

1. Increased heart rate to pump oxygenated blood to working muscles

2. Increased blood pressure to deliver blood to working muscles

3. Increased ventilation to supply working muscles with oxygen for energy metabolism

4. Vasodilation of arteries to the body's periphery (arms and legs) with the greatest muscle mass

5. Increased serum glucose for metabolic processes during muscle contractions

6. Increased free fatty acid mobilization as an energy source for prolonged activity (e.g., running)

7. Increased blood coagulation and decreased clotting time in the event of bleeding

8. Increased muscular strength

9. Decreased gastric movement and abdominal blood flow to allow blood to go to working muscles

10. Increased perspiration to cool body-core temperature

Unfortunately, the metabolic and physiological changes that are deemed essential for human movement in the event of attack, pursuit, or challenge are quite *ineffective* when dealing with events or situations that threaten the ego, such as receiving a parking ticket or standing in a long line at the grocery store, yet the body responds identically to all types of perceived threats.

Tend and Befriend

Do women respond differently to stress than men? The answer may seem obvious.

Generally speaking, men are prone to act more hostile whereas women have a proclivity to be more nurturing. Yet until recently every source on stress addressed the fight-or-flight response as if it were the only human default response. It was the work of Shelley Taylor and colleagues that filled in the missing piece with regard to the female response to stress. Curious about why only men were studied to formulate the basis for the fight-or-flight response, Taylor hypothesized that the stress response needed to be reexamined, this time including astute observations of the female gender. In 2000 Taylor and colleagues proposed a new theory for the female stress response that they termed **tend and befriend**. Although both men and women have a built-in dynamic for the survival of physical danger, women also have an inherent nurturing response for their off-spring as well as a means to befriend others. This in turn creates a strong social support system, an invaluable coping technique. Taylor suggests that the female response to stress is hardwired into the DNA and revealed through a combination of brain chemistry and hormones. The biological basis for tend and befriend appears to be the hormone oxytocin, now regarded as the "trusting hormone" or the social affiliation hormone. Although oxytocin is found in both women and men (to a lesser degree), estrogen is known to enhance the effects of oxytocin in the brain. Generational social factors may support the tend-and-befriend behavior pattern as well.

Not only do men and women have differences in their stress physiology, but there appears to be gender-specific behaviors for discussing and solving problems as well. Whereas men tend to think their way through by looking for solutions to problems, women like to talk about problems. Women bond quickly by sharing confidences. However, although talking may be beneficial, researchers note that merely talking about stressors tends to perpetuate rather than solve one's stressors. Researchers refer to stress-based conversations as "co-rumination." Although talking may strengthen female friendships, it is also known to increase anxiety and depression if solutions aren't introduced quickly. Experts warn against "unhealthy rumination" and the emotional contagion that results from it (Stepp, 2007).

It is fair to say that the concepts of survival are complex and perhaps not so neatly packaged by hormones or gender. Women are known to back-stab their "friends" and regrettably, on occasion, ditch their new-born babies in dumpsters and run away. Conversely, some men choose peace over violence (Gandhi and Martin Luther King, Jr., come to mind) and, when times get tough, men are known to bond together over a beer or game of golf.

Types of Stress

To the disbelief of some, not all stress is bad for you. In fact, there are many who believe that humans need some degree of stress to stay healthy. The human body craves homeostasis, or physiological calm, yet it also requires physiological arousal to ensure the optimal functioning of several organs, including the heart and musculoskeletal system. How can stress be good? When stress serves as a positive motivation, it is considered beneficial. Beyond this optimal point, stress of any kind does more harm than good.

Actually, there are three kinds of stress: **eustress, neustress**, and **distress**. Eustress is good stress and arises in any situation or circumstance that a person finds motivating or inspiring. Falling in love might be an example of eustress; meeting a movie star or professional athlete may also be a type of eustress. Usually, situations that are classified as eustress are enjoyable and for this reason are not considered to be a threat. Neustress describes sensory stimuli that have no consequential effect; it is considered neither good nor bad. News of an earthquake in a remote corner of the world might fall into this category. The third type of stress, distress, is considered bad and often is abbreviated simply as stress. There are two kinds of distress: **acute stress**, or that which surfaces, is quite intense, and disappears quickly, and **chronic stress**, or that which may not appear quite so intense, yet seems to linger for prolonged periods of time (e.g., hours, days, weeks, or months). An example of acute stress is the following: You are casually driving down the highway, the wind from the open sunroof is blowing through your hair, and you feel pretty good about life. With a quick glance in your rearview mirror you see flashing blue lights. Yikes! So you slow down and pull over. The police car pulls up behind you. Your heart is racing, your voice becomes scratchy, and your palms are sweating as you try to retrieve license and registration from your wallet while rolling your window down at the same time. When the officer asks you why you were speeding you can barely speak; your voice is three octaves higher than usual. After the officer runs a check on your car and license, he only gives you a warning for speeding. Whew! He gets back in his car and leaves. You give him time to get out of sight, start your engine, and signal to get back onto the highway. Within minutes your heart is calm, your palms dry, and you start singing to the song on the radio. The threat is over. The intensity of the acute stress may seem cataclysmic, but it is very short-lived.

Chronic stressors, on the other hand, are not as intense but their duration is unbearably long. Examples might include the following: being stuck for a whole semester with "the roommate from hell," a credit card bill that only seems to grow despite monthly payments, a boss who makes your job seem worse than that of a galley slave, living in a city you cannot tolerate, or maintaining a relationship with a girlfriend, boyfriend, husband, or wife that seems bad to stay in but worse to leave. For this reason, chronic stressors are thought to be the real villains. According to the American Institute of Stress (AIS), it is this type of stress that is associated with disease because the body is perpetually aroused for danger.

A concept called the **Yerkes-Dodson principle**, which is applied to athletic performance, lends itself quite nicely to explaining the relationship among eustress, distress, and health. As can be seen in **Fig. 1.1 ▸**, when stress increases, moving from eustress to distress, performance or health decreases and there is greater risk of disease and illness. The optimal stress level is the midpoint, prior to where eustress turns into distress. Studies

indicate that stress-related hormones in optimal doses actually improve physical performance and mental-processing skills like concentration, making you more alert. Beyond that optimal level, though, all aspects of performance begin to decrease in efficiency. Physiologically speaking, your health is at serious risk. It would be simple if this optimal level was the same for all people, but it's not. Hence, the focus of any effective stress-management program is twofold: (1) to find out where this optimal level of stress is for you so that it can be used to your advantage rather than becoming a detriment to your health status, and (2) to reduce physical arousal levels using both coping skills and relaxation techniques so that you can stay out of the danger zone created by too much stress.

Types of Stressors

Any situation, circumstance, or stimulus that is perceived to be a threat is referred to as a **stressor**, or that which causes or promotes stress. As you might imagine, the list of stressors is not only endless but varies considerably from person to person. Acute stress is often the result of rapid-onset stressors—those that pop up unexpectedly—like a phone call in the middle of the night

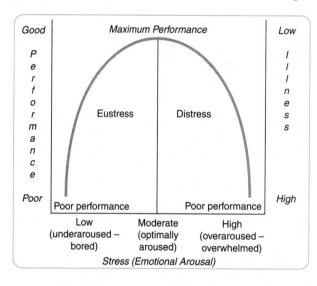

FIGURE 1.1 The Yerkes-Dodson curve illustrates that, to a point, stress or arousal can actually increase performance. Stress to the left of the midpoint is considered to be eustress. Stress beyond the midpoint, however, is believed to detract from performance and/or health status and is therefore labeled distress.

or the discovery that you have lost your car keys. Usually the body begins to react before a full analysis of the situation is made, but a return to a state of calm is also imminent. Chronic stressors—those that may give some advance warning yet manage to cause physical arousal anyway, often merit more attention because their prolonged influence on the body appears to be more significant. Much research has been conducted to determine the nature of stressors, and they are currently divided into three categories: bioecological, psychointrapersonal, and social (Girdano, Everly, and Dusek, 2012).

Bioecological Influences

There are several biological and ecological factors that may trigger the stress response in varying degrees, some of which are outside our awareness. These are external influences, including sunlight, gravitational pull, solar flares, and electromagnetic fields, that affect our biological rhythms. From the field of chronobiology we learn that these factors affect three categories of biological rhythms: (1) circadian rhythms, fluctuations in physiological functions over the course of a 24-hour period (e.g., body temperature); (2) **ultradian rhythms**, fluctuations that occur over less than a 24-hour period (such as stomach contractions and cell divisions); and (3) infradian rhythms, changes that occur in periods longer than 24 hours (e.g., the menses). These biological changes are influenced by such natural phenomena as the earth's orbit and axis rotation, which give us periods of light and darkness as well as seasonal differences. A prime example of a bioecological influence is **seasonal affective disorder (SAD)**, a condition affecting many people who live at or near the Arctic Circle. Many of these people become depressed when they are deprived of sunlight for prolonged periods of time. But technological changes are also included in this category, an example being jet lag as a result of airplane travel through several time zones. Electrical pollution, environmental toxins, solar radiation, and noise pollution are other potential bioecological influences. Genetically modified organisms (GMOs), petrochemicals, synthetic chemicals, and some types of nanotechnology are considered new bioecological threats. In addition, some synthetic food additives may trigger the release of various stress hormones throughout the body. Note that there is a growing opinion among some health practitioners that increased stress levels in the 21st century may be a direct result of our being out of touch with the *natural* elements that so strongly influence our body's physiological systems. In any case, some of these bioecological factors can be positively influenced by lifestyle changes, including dietary habits, exercise, and the regular practice of relaxation techniques, which bring a sense of balance back into our lives.

Psychointrapersonal Influences

Our current understanding is that psychointrapersonal influences make up the greatest percentage of stressors. These are the perceptions of stimuli that we create through our own mental processes. Psychointrapersonal stressors involve those thoughts, values, beliefs, attitudes, opinions, and perceptions that we use to defend our identity or ego. When any of these is challenged, violated, or even changed, the ego is often threatened and the stress response is the outcome. Psychointrapersonal stressors reflect the unique constructs of our personality, and in the words of stress researcher Kenneth Pelletier, represent "the chasm between the perceived self and the ideal self-image." These influences are the most likely to cause stress. For this reason it becomes imperative to intercept the stress response in the mind before it cascades down as a rush of stress hormones into the body to cause potential damage.

Social Influences

Social influences have long been the subject of research to explain the plight of individuals who are unable to cope with their given environment. Most notable is the issue of overcrowding and urban sprawl. Studies conducted on several species have shown that when their numbers exceed the territorial boundary of each animal, despite an abundance of food and water, several seemingly healthy animals die off (Allen, 1983). This need for personal space appears to be universal in the animal kingdom. This includes humans, who likewise begin to show signs of frustration in crowded urban areas, traffic jams, long lines at checkout stands, or whenever their personal space is "invaded." The origin of this particular social influence may be instinctual in nature. Additional social causes of stress include financial insecurity, the effects of relocation, some technological advances, violation of human rights, and low socioeconomic status, to name but a few. New to the list of social influences are global warming concerns and water resource issues as the global population increases, taxing our very lifestyles with regard to scarcity issues.

Social influences related to stress also include major life changes. Two researchers who made significant gains in understanding the relationship between stress and disease through life changes were Thomas Holmes and Richard Rahe. Based on the Life Chart theory of Adolph Meyer, Holmes and Rahe set out to determine what events in people's lives were most stressful. Surveying thousands of individuals, they created a list of circumstances that represent typical life stressors, or events that require some adaptation or readjustment to a situation. Their list, with a total of 43 events, included several life events that, on the surface, appear to be positive, such as vacations, weddings, and outstanding personal achievements, as well as traumatic ordeals such as the death of a child. Then they devised a system to weigh each event according to its stress potential. All events were assigned numerical values based on their degree of disruption of one's life and readjustment following the event. These values were called **life-change units**, or LCUs.

The result of their efforts was an inventory called the **Social Readjustment Rating Scale (SRRS)**, which ranked the 43 life events from most stressful to least stressful. In further research using this assessment tool, Holmes and Rahe gave this inventory to several physicians and then compared their results with major health changes reported by the physicians. There was a significant correlation between life-event scores and personal health histories, with an LCU score of 150 being the point of demarcation between the exposure to major life stressors and health-related problems. With further analysis, they created categories based on LCU scores: 150–199 points suggested a mild life crisis, 200–299 points suggested a moderate life crisis, and any score over 300 points indicated a major life crisis. Based on the work by Holmes and Rahe, this survey and similar ones designed for special populations (e.g., college students) are now used to predict the likelihood of disease and illness following exposure to stressful life events. It is important to note that a high LCU score does not predict illness for all people, and this fact has led to criticism of research. It also shows the complexity of quantifying the stress phenomenon. Evidence indicates that in the face of repeated disasters, some people, by nature of their personalities, appear immune to stress.

Although major life events like getting married or relocating for a new job may be chronic stressors to some, renowned stress researcher **Richard Lazarus** hypothesized in 1984 that the accumulation of acute stressors or **daily life hassles**, such as locking your keys in your car, playing telephone tag, or driving to work every day

in traffic, is just as likely to adversely affect one's health as the death of a spouse. These hassles are often based on unmet expectations that trigger an anger response of some type, whereas stressors of a chronic nature more often than not appear to have a greater association with fear and anxiety. Lazarus defined hassles as "daily interactions with the environment that were essentially negative." He also hypothesized that a balance of emotional experiences—positive emotions as well as negative ones—is necessary, and that people who have no exposure to life's "highs" or emotional uplifts are also susceptible to disease and illness. Further research by Lazarus (1984), Ornstein and Sobel (1990), and others has proved that his hypothesis has significant merit regarding stress and disease. As might be expected, the issue of lifestyle habits, changes, and hassles as social influences has come under attack by those who argue that perception or cognition plays an important role in the impact of stressors. Suffice it to say that all stressors, regardless of classification, are connected to human well-being in a very profound way.

The General Adaptation Syndrome

Following Cannon's lead early in the 20th century, Hans Selye, a young endocrinologist who created a name for himself as a leading researcher in this field, studied the fight-or-flight response, specifically the physiological effects of chronic stress, using rats as subjects. In experiments designed to stress the rats, Selye noted that several physiological adaptations occurred as a result of repeated exposures to stress, adaptations that had pathological repercussions. Examples of these stress-induced changes included the following:

1. Enlargement of the adrenal cortex (a gland that produces stress hormones)

2. Constant release of stress hormones; corticosteroids released from the adrenal cortex

3. Atrophy or shrinkage of lymphatic glands (thymus gland, spleen, and lymph nodes)

4. Significant decrease in the white blood cell count

5. Bleeding ulcerations of the stomach and colon

6. Death of the organism

Many of these changes were very subtle and often went unnoticed until permanent damage had occurred. Selye referred to these collective changes as the **general adaptation syndrome (GAS)**, a process in which the body tries to accommodate stress by adapting to it. From his research, Selye identified three stages of the general adaptation syndrome:

Stage 1: **Alarm reaction.** The alarm reaction describes Cannon's original fight-or-flight response. In this stage several body systems are activated, primarily the nervous system and the endocrine system, followed by the cardiovascular, pulmonary, and musculoskeletal systems. Like a smoke detector alarm buzzing late at night, all senses are put on alert until the danger is over.

Stage 2: **Stage of resistance.** In the resistance stage, the body tries to revert back to a state of physiological calmness, or homeostasis, by resisting the alarm. Because the perception of a threat still exists, however, complete homeostasis is never reached. Instead, the body stays activated or aroused, usually at a lesser intensity than during the alarm stage but enough to cause a higher metabolic rate in some organ tissues. One or more organs may, in effect, be working overtime and, as a result, enter the third and final stage.

Stage 3: **Stage of exhaustion.** Exhaustion occurs when one (or more) of the organs targeted by specific metabolic processes can no longer meet the demands placed upon it and fails to function properly. This can result in death to the organ and, depending on which organ becomes dysfunctional (e.g., the heart), possibly the death of the organism as a whole.

Selye's general adaptation syndrome outlined the parameters of the physiological dangers of stress. His research opened the doors to understanding the strong relationship between stress and disease and the mind-body-spirit equation. In addition, his work laid the foundation for the utilization of relaxation techniques that have the ability to intercept the stress response, thereby decreasing susceptibility to illness and disease. Congruent with standard medical practice of his day (and even today), initial stress management programs were geared toward reducing or eliminating the *symptoms* of stress. Unfortunately, this approach has not always proved successful.

Post-Traumatic Stress Disorder 101

There is stress and then there is STRESS! Although most people claim to live (or even brag about) stressful lives, the truth of the matter is that few people encounter truly horrific events of death and carnage. The repeated horrors of war, however, have notoriously ranked at the top of every list as the most unbearable of all stressors that anyone can endure psychologically—and for good reason. To quote Civil War General William T. Sherman, "War is hell." Exposure to these types of events typically include those that threaten one's life, result in serious physical injury, expose one to horrific carnage, or create intense psychological shock, all of which are strongly influenced by the intensity and duration of the devastation either experienced or observed first hand. The result is an emotional wound embedded in the unconscious mind that is very hard to heal.

Every war seems to have its own name for this type of anxiety disorder. Somber Civil War soldiers were described as having "soldier's heart." Affected military personnel returning from World War I were described as being "shell-shocked," whereas soldiers and veterans from World War II exhibiting neurotic anxiety were described as having severe "battle fatigue" or "combat fatigue." The term *post-traumatic stress disorder*—more commonly known as PTSD—emerged during the treatment of returning soldiers from Vietnam who seemed to lack industrial-strength coping skills to deal with the hellacious memories that haunted them both day and night. This emotional disorder was first registered in the *Diagnostic and Statistical Manual of Mental Disorders* (*DSM*) in 1980 and has been the topic of intense investigation ever since. Sadly, the wars in Iraq and Afghanistan have provided countless case studies for this anxiety disorder today.

Although mortal combat ranks at the top of the list of hellacious experiences, one doesn't have to survive a suicide bomber in the streets of Baghdad to suffer from PTSD. Survivors and rescue workers of the World Trade Center and Pentagon catastrophes are known to still be dealing with this trauma, as are several thousands of people displaced from the wrath of Hurricanes Katrina and Rita. Violent crime victims, airplane crash survivors, sexual/physical assault victims, and occasionally first responders (e.g., police officers, fire fighters, emergency medical technicians) are also prone to this condition. Given the nature of global warming and climate change and terrorism, it is suggested that PTSD may become a common diagnosis among world citizens, with the ripple effect affecting legions of friends, colleagues, and family members alike. Secondary PTSD is a term given to family members, friends, and colleagues who are negatively affected by the ripples of strife from loved ones (even patients) who have had direct exposure to severe trauma.

The symptoms of PTSD include the following: chronic anxiety, nightmares, flashbacks, insomnia, loss of appetite, memory loss, hypervigilance, emotional detachment, clinical depression, helplessness, restlessness, suicidal tendencies, and substance addictions (MayoClinic.com). Typically a person suffering from PTSD has several of these symptoms at one time. Whereas the symptoms for some individuals may last months, for others PTSD becomes a lifelong ordeal, particularly if treatment is avoided, neglected, or shunned. The key to working with PTSD patients is to access the power of the unconscious mind by identifying deep-seated memories so that they may be acknowledged and released in a healthy manner rather than repressed and pushed deeper in the personal unconscious mind.

Specialists who treat patients with PTSD recommend that treatment begin as soon as possible to prevent a worsening effect. Initial treatment (intervention) is referred to as critical incidence stress management (CISM). The purpose of CISM is to (1) significantly reduce the traumatic effects of the incident and (2) prevent further deep-seated PTSD occurrences. Specific treatment modalities include eye movement desensitization and reprocessing (EMDR), counseling, and group therapy as a means to promote emotional catharsis. The Trauma Recovery Institute also cites art therapy, journal writing, and hypnosis as complementary coping skills for emotional catharsis. Many patients are also prescribed medications. Although medications may help reduce anxiety, it should be noted they do not heal emotional wounds.

Stress and Insomnia

Muscle tension may be the number one symptom of stress, but in our ever-present, demanding 24/7 society, insomnia runs a close second. **Insomnia** is best defined as poor-quality sleep, abnormal wakefulness, or the inability to sleep, and it can affect anyone. Overall, Americans get 20 percent less sleep than their 19th-century counterparts. According to a recent survey by the National Sleep Foundation, more than 60 percent of Americans suffer from poor sleep quality, resulting in everything from falling asleep on the job and marital problems to car accidents and lost work productivity. Does your stress level affect your sleep quality? Even if you sleep well, it is hard these days not to notice the proliferation of advertisements

for sleep prescriptions, suggesting a serious public health concern.

Numerous studies have concluded that a regular good night's sleep is essential for optimal health, whereas chronic insomnia is often associated with several kinds of psychiatric problems (Maas, 2001). Emotional stress (the preoccupation with daily stressors) is thought to be a primary cause of insomnia. The result: an anxious state of mind where thoughts race around, ricocheting from brain cell to brain cell, never allowing a pause in the thought processes, let alone allowing the person to nod off.

Many other factors (sleep stealers) detract from one's **sleep hygiene** and can affect the quality of sleep, including hormonal changes (e.g., premenstrual syndrome, menopause), excessive caffeine intake, little or no exercise, frequent urination, circadian rhythm disturbances (e.g., jet lag), shift work, medication side effects, and a host of lifestyle behaviors (e.g., prolonged television watching, alcohol consumption, smartphone use) that infringe on a good night's sleep.

How much sleep is enough to feel recharged? Generally speaking, 8 hours of sleep is the norm, although some people can get as few as 6 hours of sleep and feel fully rested. Others may need as many as 10 hours. New findings suggest that adolescents, including all people up to age 22, need more than 8 hours of sleep (Dawson, 2008).

Not only can stress (mental, emotional, physical, or spiritual) affect the quality and quantity of sleep, but the rebound effect of poor sleep can, in turn, affect stress levels, making the poor sleeper become more irritable, apathetic, or cynical. Left unresolved, it can become an unbroken cycle (negative feedback loop). Although many people seek medical help for insomnia and are often given a prescription, drugs should be considered as a last resort. Many (if not all) techniques for stress management have proven to be effective in promoting a good night's sleep, ranging from cardiovascular exercise to meditation.

The field of sleep research began in earnest more than 60 years ago. Yet, despite numerous studies, the reason why we spend approximately one-third of our lives in slumber still baffles scientists. From all appearances, sleep promotes physical restoration. However, when researchers observe sleep-deprived subjects, it's the mind—not the body—that is most affected, with symptoms of poor concentration, poor retention, and poor problem-solving skills.

Insomnia is categorized in three ways: transient (short term with 1 or 2 weeks affected), intermittent (occurs on and off over a prolonged period), and chronic (the inability to achieve a restful night of sleep over many, many months). Although each of these categories is problematic, chronic insomnia is considered the worst.

All-nighters, exam crams, late-night parties, and midnight movies are common in the lives of college undergraduates, but the cost of these behaviors often proves unproductive. Unfortunately, the population of people who seem to need the most sleep, but often get the least amount, are adolescents younger than age 20.

Although sleep may be relaxing, it is important to remember that sleeping is not a relaxation technique. Studies show that heart rate, blood pressure, and muscle tension can rise significantly during the dream state of sleep. What we do know is that effective coping and relaxation techniques greatly enhance one's quality of sleep.

College Stress

What makes the college experience a significant departure from the first 18 years of life is the realization that with the freedom of lifestyle choices come the responsibilities that go with it. Unless you live at home while attending school, the college experience is one in which you transition from a period of dependence (on your parents) to independence. As you move from the known into the unknown, the list of stressors a college student experiences is rather startling. Here is a sample of some of the more common stressors that college students encounter:

- *Roommate dynamics:* Finding someone who is compatible is not always easy, especially if you had your own room in your parents' house. As we all know or will quickly learn, best friends do not make the best roommates, yet roommates can become good friends over time. Through it all, roommate dynamics involve the skills of compromise and diplomacy under the best and worst conditions. And should you find yourself in an untenable situation, remember, campus housing does its best to accommodate students and resolve problems. However, their time schedule and yours may not always be the same. For those college students who don't leave home, living as an adult in a home in which your parents and siblings are now roommates can become its own form of stress.

- *Professional pursuits:* What major should I choose? Perhaps one of the most common soul-searching questions to be asked in the college years is, What do I want to do the rest of my life? It is a well-known fact that college students can change majors several times in their college careers, and many do. The problem is compounded when there is parental pressure to move toward a specific career path (e.g., law or medicine) or the desire to please your parents by picking a major that they like but you don't.

- *Academic deadlines (exams, papers, and projects):* Academics means taking midterms and finals, writing research papers, and completing projects. This is, after all, the hallmark of measuring what you have learned. With a typical semester load of fifteen to twenty credits, many course deadlines can fall on the same day, and there is the ever-present danger that not meeting expectations can result in poor grades or academic probation.

- *Financial aid and school loans:* If you have ever stood in the financial aid office during the first week of school, you could write a book on the topic of stress. The cost of a college education is skyrocketing, and the pressure to pay off school loans after graduation can make you feel like an indentured servant. Assuming you qualify for financial aid, you should know that receiving the money in time to pay your bills is rare. Problems are compounded when your course schedule gets expunged from computer records because your financial aid check was 2 weeks late. These are just some of the problems associated with financial aid.

- *Budgeting your money:* It's one thing to ask your parents to buy you some new clothes or have them pick up the check at a restaurant. It's quite another when you start paying all your own bills. Learning to budget your money is a skill that takes practice. And learning not to overextend yourself is not only a skill, but also an art in these tough economic times. At some time or other, everyone bounces a check. The trick to avoid doing it is not to spend money you do not have and to live within your means.

■ *Lifestyle behaviors:* The freedom to stay up until 2:00 a.m. on a weekday, skip a class, eat nothing but junk food, or take an impromptu road trip carries with it the responsibilities of these actions. Independence from parental control means balancing freedom with responsibility. Stress enters your life with a vengeance when freedom and responsibility are not balanced.

■ *Peer groups and peer pressure (drugs and alcohol):* There is a great need to feel accepted by new acquaintances in college, and this need often leads to succumbing to peer pressure—and in new environments with new acquaintances, peer pressure can be very strong. Stress arises when the actions of the group are incongruent with your own philosophies and values. The desire to conform to the group is often stronger than your willpower to hold your own ground.

■ *Exploring sexuality:* Although high school is the time when some people explore their sexuality, this behavior occurs with greater frequency during the college years, when you are away from the confines of parental control and more assertive with your self-expression. With the issue of sexual exploration come questions of values, contraception, pregnancy, homosexuality, bisexuality, AIDS, abortion, acceptance, and impotence, all of which can be very stressful.

■ *Friendships:* The friendships made in college take on a special quality. As you grow, mature, and redefine your values, your friends, like you, will change, and so will the quality of each friendship. Cultivating a quality relationship takes time, meaning you cannot be good friends with everyone you like. In addition, tensions can quickly mount as the dynamics between you and those in your close circle of friends come under pressure from all the other college stressors.

■ *Intimate relationships:* Spending time with one special person with whom you can grow in love is special indeed. But the demands of an intimate relationship are strong, and in the presence of a college environment, intimate relationships are under a lot of pressure. If and when the relationship ends, the aftershock can be traumatic for one or both parties, leaving little desire for one's academic pursuits.

■ *Starting a professional career path:* It's a myth that you can start a job making the same salary that your parents make, but many college students believe this to be true. With this myth comes the pressure to equal the lifestyle of one's parents the day after graduation. (This may explain why so many college graduates return home to live after graduation.) The perceived pressures of the real world can become so overwhelming that seniors procrastinate on drafting a resume or initiating the job search until the week of graduation.

For the nontraditional college student, the problem can be summarized in one word: balance! Trying to balance a job, family, and schoolwork becomes a juggling act extraordinaire. In attempting to satisfy the needs of your supervisor, colleagues, friends, spouse, children, and parents (and perhaps even pets), what usually is squeezed out is time for yourself. In the end everything seems to suffer. Often schoolwork is given a lower priority when addressing survival needs, and typically this leads to feelings of frustration over the inadequacy of time and effort available for assignments or exams. Of course, there are other stressors that cross the boundaries between work, home, and school, all of which tend to throw things off balance as well. Exercises 1.1 to 1.5 invite you to reflect on these issues.

The Sociology of Stress

Today's world is a very different place than when Walter Cannon coined the term "fight-or-flight response" and Hans Selye first uttered the words, "general adaptation syndrome." Little did they know just how much stress would become a part of the social fabric of everyday life in the 21st century. Some experts argue that our collective stress is a result of our inability to keep up with all the changes that influence the many aspects of our lives. Simply stated, our physiology has not evolved at a comparable rate as the social changes of the last half-century.

Holmes and Rahe, the creators of the Social Readjustment Rating Scale, were dead-on about various social aspects that can destabilize one's personal equilibrium, even with the best coping skills employed. Yet no matter what corner of the global village you live in, the stresses of moving to a new city or losing a job are now compounded by significant 21st-century issues. We are a product of our society, and societal stress is dramatically on the rise.

Experts who keep a finger on the pulse of humanity suggest that as rapid as these changes are now, the rate and number of changes are only going to increase. It's not just the changes we encounter that affect our stress levels, it's how we engage in these new changes. Increasingly, this engagement is online. Unfortunately, the stress that is provoked is real, not virtual. The majority of interactive Web sites are littered with negative comments, frustrations, expletives, and rants, all of which suggest a malaise in the general public combined with the unparalleled freedom to honestly express oneself anonymously. Being overwhelmed with choices in communication technology for staying in touch with friends, colleagues, and employees leads to a whole new meaning of burnout.

Physiology, psychology, anthropology, theology—the topic of stress is so colossal that it is studied by researchers in a great many disciplines, not the least of which is sociology. Sociology is often described as the study of human social behavior within family, organizations, and institutions: the study of the individual in relationship to society as a whole. Because everybody is born into a family and most people work for a living, no one is exempt from the sociology of stress. Whether we like it or not, we are all connected to each other. Are you a product of your culture? To get a better idea, please complete the survey found in Exercise 1.6.

Perhaps the sociology of stress can best be acknowledged through the newest buzzword, "social networking," with the likes of Facebook, Twitter, Skype, YouTube, Pinterest, Instagram, and new social media and networking outlets taking shape on the cyber-horizon. Technology has even changed how people converse at dinner parties (e.g., one person asks a question and five people pull out their smartphones and Google the answer). Technology, the economy, and the environment have become significant threads of the social fabric.

Techno-Stress

The tsunami of cyber-information has been building for years, yet the first devastating wave seems to have hit the shores of the human mind in earnest about the same time Facebook hit a billion users in 2010, the same year that the Swiss Army Knife included a USB drive for "survival." Although information overload, privacy, ethics, and bandwith are issues for many, deeper problems are coming to the surface in the age of iPads and smartphones. The cyber-alchemy of tweets, Facebook updates, Skype messages, text messages, and the deluge of emails has hit a critical mass of annoyance for some and addiction for a great many people who are fed up with giving their lives over to technology. The growing dependence on technology has even inspired a term: *screen addiction*. If it's not computer screens and smartphones, it's iPads and Bluetooth technology, none of which are bad, but can become problematic if your life is completely centered around being plugged in all the time. The perfect storm of stress is the overwhelming amount of information available, the distractive nature of being plugged in 24/7, a sense of alienation, and the poor boundaries people maintain to regulate this information. The concept of poor boundaries is shown by nearly all college students who text during classroom lectures as well as the scores of people who bring all their technology with them on vacation, thus never separating work from leisure, and possibly compromising both. Similarly, fewer than half of employees nationwide leave their desk/workstation during lunch hour, according to a Manpower survey, leading to higher stress levels and fatigue (Marquardt, 2010).

There are many terms for all the problems associated with the tsunami of information and the convenience to access it, but the one term that sums it all up is *techno-stress*, which is the feeling of being overwhelmed with sensory bombardment from the online technology. Factors contributing to techno-stress include, but are not limited to, privacy issues, identity theft, smartphone radiation, Internet scams, bandwidth, Internet gambling and pornography addiction, and child access to adult content. Perhaps the most widespread stress from technology that most people experience is the perpetual distraction of emails and text messages and the replacement of face-to-face conversation with digital communications.

Research from the University of California at Irvine reveals that the constant interruption of emails triggers the stress response, with the subsequent release of stress hormones affecting short-term memory. And if you ever wondered if people, perhaps even yourself, seem addicted to checking emails, voice mails, or tweets, consider this fact: research shows that the receipt of emails and tweets is accompanied by a release of dopamine. Dopamine, a "feel-good" neurotransmitter, is associated with chemical addictions. In the absence of dopamine release, boredom ensues, until the next fix. Every abrupt shift in the history of societies has had its associated stressors; for example, the shift from agrarian to industrial society was correlated with a dramatic increase in alcoholism, regarded as a "social disease" of its time. In today's abrupt shift to online technology and social media, the online technology is itself the addiction.

Young people today who never knew life without a smartphone or iPad don't understand why older adults seem so concerned about their addictive tech habits. Meanwhile, adults now notice that children and teens raised with screen technology may be well versed in cyber-communication skills, yet socially immature with face-to-face communication skills, including using eye contact.

The boom in the telecommunications industry and computer industry, pillars of the information age, have led to an overnight lifestyle change in U.S. and global society. In their book *Technostress,* authors Weil and Rosen (1998) suggest that the rapid pace of technology will only continue with greater speed in the coming years, giving a whole new meaning to the expression "24/7." Their suggestions have proved quite true. They predict, as do others, that the majority of people will not deal well with this change. The result will be more stress, more illness and disease, more addictions, more dysfunction, and a greater imbalance in people's lives. There is general consensus that the rate of change with technology has far outpaced the level of responsibility and moral codes that typically accompany the creative process. Exercise 1.6 invites you to examine your techno-stress level.

The Rise of Incivility

Have you noticed that people today seem quick-tempered, impatient, cynical, self-centered, and perhaps even rude at times? If you have, you are not alone. Civility, as expressed through social etiquette, refers to the practice of good manners and appropriate behavior. Many consider basic rules of civility to be sorely lacking in today's culture. Experts attribute the lack of civility to an alchemy of narcissism and a national lack of values, contributing not only to social unease, but also to the economic mess that created the Great Recession of 2008. Moreover, a revolution in the way people communicate with each other over the past few years has dramatically changed the social fabric of our culture, particularly how we relate, or fail to relate, to each other in

face-to-face situations. Instant accessibility has sown the seeds of impatience. Politeness has given way to rudeness. Internet rants and talk-radio phone calls carry over into face-to-face shouting matches at sporting events and political rallies. Social manners (e.g., appropriate behavior and thinking of others first) have become minimal if not obsolete for many people, particularly when bursts of anger perpetuate feelings of victimization. Today's self-centered, narcissistic indulgences have hit an all-time high, many of which are directly related to political incivility. Incivility seems to be a global issue as well. Several star athletes were told to pack up and leave during the 2012 London Olympics (some missing their events) for inappropriate "tweets" considered not only rude, inappropriate, and racially offensive, but a violation against the ethics of the International Olympic Committee standards to which these athletes take an oath. How did things go so wrong? Some people blame poor parenting skills. Many cite talk radio and various news media outlets that broadcast incivility. Others point their finger at the proliferation of technology and the constant self-promotion that seems to go along with it (Meyer, 2008). Many say the perfect storm of "uncivil Americans" is a combination of all these factors. Noting the serious issue of American incivility, Rutgers University has initiated a one-credit course called Project Civility for students, with topics ranging from smartphone etiquette and cyber-bullying to civil sportsmanship and social responsibility. It is likely that other colleges will follow this trend.

According to a study by the *New York Times*, the average young American now spends every waking minute (with the possible exception of school classes) using a smartphone, computer, television, or other electronic device. Adults appear to be no different. It is not uncommon to see people texting while at movie theaters, talking on smartphones in restaurants (despite signs prohibiting their use), and texting while driving (despite the growing number of state laws banning this behavior). In 2006, researchers at the University of Utah were curious to see if the distraction of smartphone use while driving was similar to driving while under the influence of alcohol. Using driving simulators it was revealed that people on smartphones show a driving impairment rate similar to a blood alcohol level of 0.08 percent, the demarcation of drunk driving in the majority of states in the United States. Although many people may recognize the dangers of talking and driving, few offer to give up this mode of multi-tasking.

Many people use technology to avoid stressful situations, again adding to a general lack of civility in society. Examples include quitting a job with a tweet, breaking up with a girlfriend/boyfriend on Facebook, or sending a derogatory email and blind-copying everyone in one's address book. The modern lack of civility cannot be blamed entirely on technology, yet the dramatic rise in the use of communication devices has played its part. How would you rate your current level of social etiquette?

Americans may be lacking in the social graces, but in the face of global calamities, such as the 2010 earthquake in Haiti or the 2008 tsunami in Indonesia, Americans are renowned the world over for giving generously to the needy in far-away lands. However, texting a donation during the Superbowl for earthquake relief is far different than face-to-face contact and polite social interactions. It's the direct social contact skills that prove to be sorely lacking in American culture today. How good are your social skills in this age of incivility? You can begin to find out by completing Exercises 1.7 and 1.8.

Environmental Disconnect

Even if you don't listen to the news regularly, it's hard to ignore the impact humanity is having on the state of the planet. With a population exceeding 7 billion people, the word *sustainable* has entered the American lexicon with great regularity, even if the concept is largely ignored by most citizens. Modern society can be said to be suffering from an environmental disconnect, a state in which people have distanced themselves so much from the natural environment that they cannot fathom the magnitude of their impact on it. It was predicted many years ago by a great many experts and luminaries that as humanity distances itself from nature, people will suffer the consequences, primarily in terms of compromised health status. The term *nature deficit disorder* was coined by award-winning author Richard Louv, in *Last Child in the Woods*, to describe the growing abyss between people and the outdoor world. Kids, as it turns out, would rather play video games or surf online than play outside—where there are no outlets or WiFi access.

There is an age-old question that states, "How many angels can dance on the head of a pin?" Today that imponderable question has become, "How many humans can sustainably live on planet Earth?" It's interesting to note that some of the earliest studies on stress

physiology involved placing an abnormally high number of mice in a cage. As their environment, personal space, food availability, and quality of life decreased with each additional occupant, tension significantly increased. The parallels between the environment and behavior of those mice and humans today are unavoidable.

By now everyone has not only heard of the issues on global warming, but also has experienced the preliminary effects first hand: violent storms, warm winters, hotter summers, more intense droughts, and severe weather patterns. The problems of our oil dependence were especially highlighted by the massive 2010 oil spill in the Gulf of Mexico. What has yet to become clear to the average person, however, are the problems with water shortages, an issue that will greatly affect everyone. United Nations Secretary General Ban Ki-moon has repeatedly stated that wars will most likely be fought over water sources in our lifetime. So significant is this stressor that *National Geographic* dedicated an entire issue in April 2010 to the topic of water and our thirsty world. Here are some facts that will impact you now and in the years to come:

- About 97.5 percent of the earth's water is salty, with only 2.5 percent of earth's water considered fresh.

- Two-thirds of all fresh water is frozen.

- Many Western states (e.g., Texas, Arizona, and California) are draining underground aquifers quicker than they can be naturally restored.

- Many fresh-water streams contain hormones and antibiotics from prescription drugs flushed down toilets and agricultural run-off containing petrochemical fertilizers.

- Americans use approximately 100 gallons of water at home each day, compared to 5 gallons/day in developing nations.

- It takes 2,500 gallons of water to make 1 pound of hamburger and 1,800 gallons to grow enough cotton for a pair of blue jeans.

- Clean water is a huge issue in China, so much so that it tried (and failed) to license and export fresh water from the Great Lakes region in the United States and Canada.

- The Three Gorges Dam in central China will cause the earth's axis to tilt by nearly an inch.

Perhaps the most subtle warning about this disconnect from our environment is the news that for the first time it has been noted that Americans are not getting enough vitamin D, as explained by nutritionist and *New York Times* reporter, Jane Brody. Vitamin D deficiency is due to a lack of exposure to sunlight and poor dietary habits. Sunlight is often referred to as the sunshine vitamin because, as sunlight reaches the skin, it reacts to help form vitamin D. Today people spend little time outdoors, denying themselves exposure to adequate amounts of sunlight.

Vitamin D isn't the only nutritional/environmental problem. People who saw the documentary film *Food, Inc.* (or who read the book by Karl Weber) are acutely aware that the move away from family farms to industrial farms in the last few decades has greatly compromised the quality of food, primarily chicken and beef, and encouraged the proliferation of products that use high fructose corn syrup. Changes in the food industry, along with inadequate exercise, help explain the recent dramatic increase in national obesity levels. Genetic engineering of food crops is suggested as a primary reason for the decimation of half of the world's bee population, which is creating a problem regarding the pollination of many crops. But bat and frog populations are being decimated as well. The balance of nature is, in no uncertain terms, out of balance.

Some of the world's leading scientists are not optimistic about the future of humanity, given the stresses we have put on our environment and, in turn, ourselves. Physicist Stephen Hawking's current outlook for humanity is grim at best, unless we learn to change our ways, and quickly. In a 2010 interview with the Huffington Post he stated, "We are entering an increasingly dangerous period in our history. There have been a number of times in the past when survival has been a question of touch and go. We are rapidly depleting the finite natural resources that Earth provides, and our genetic code carries selfish and aggressive instincts." Harvard biologist E. O. Wilson and others now refer to the loss of biodiversity in our modern era as the "sixth mass extinction" on Earth, with hunting and fishing, loss of natural habitat, and pollution as the primary causes (Eldridge, 2001). Meanwhile, sociologist Jared Diamond, author of the best selling book, *Collapse: How Societies Choose to Fail on Success* (2005), has this message: If positive changes are not made with regard to

our use of resources and our relationship to our natural environment, we, too, will face extinction.

Not all views of humanity are so dire or fatalistic. Several, in fact, are quite optimistic—with the caveat that we must act now. Consider that of cell biologist and philosopher Bruce Lipton. In his book *Spontaneous Evolution*, he states: "Society is beginning to realize that our current beliefs are detrimental and that our world is in a very precarious position. The new science (the nexus of quantum physics, psychology, and biology) paves a way into a hopeful story of humanity's potential future, one that promotes planetary healing." Lipton uses the model of holism (where all parts are respected and come together for a greater purpose) as the template for his optimism. Lipton is among a growing group of social luminaries, including Barbara Marx-Hubbard, Jean Houston, Christine Page, Edgar Mitchell, Elizabeth Sartoris, and Gregg Braden, who share this optimistic paradigm of humanity's shifting consciousness (Schlitz, 2010). In the words of the rock musician Sting, "Yes we are in an appalling environmental crisis, but I think as a species, we evolve through crises. That's the only glimmer of hope, really" (Richter, 2010). Exercise 1.9 invites you to evaluate your relationship to the planet's health.

Race and Gender Stress

One cannot address the issue of the sociology of stress without acknowledging the issue of race and gender stress. The United States, a nation of immigrants, has often been described as a melting pot, but recently another metaphor has been used to describe the make-up of its citizens: a tossed salad, where assimilation meets head on with cultural diversity. Race and ethnic issues continually make headline news with regard to illegal alien issues nationwide, disenfranchised black voters in Florida, poverty in New Orleans, and Muslim Americans facing episodes of discrimination, to name a few. Race and gender tensions, however, are not new. It could be argued that they are as old as humanity itself. Since time began, people have been threatened by other people of different skin color, ethnicity, gender, or sexual preference. The 2008 election of the first African American president has helped jumpstart a national discussion on race, but it hasn't resolved the issue of intolerance. Like race issues, gender issues (and to this we can add sexual orientation issues) are also threads in the social fabric once dominated by a white patriarchal society, yet this is changing. Despite the demographic shifts, the dated cultural perceptions of superiority/inferiority persist, and with them the biases that go with them.

Stress, you will remember, is defined as a perceived threat, a threat generated by the ego. These threats manifest in a variety of ways including stereotyping, prejudice, discrimination, harassment, and even physical harm. Race and gender stress may begin early in life, too; many children can attest to being bullied in school, or excluded and teased by social cliques. The emotional stress associated with this type of angst includes low self-esteem, alienation, and anxiety. Everybody wants to be accepted.

How can society help alleviate race and gender stress? Anti-bullying programs are being implemented in many schools nationwide, helping raise awareness among kids and parents to the dangers of bullying. On television, many shows have tried to better reflect the demographics of American society with casts of various ethnicities. Although these are steps in the right direction, school curricula and television shows alone cannot change the world overnight. But they're a start. Remember that when people demonstrate a bias toward race, gender, ethnic background, or anything related to them, they are projecting their fears onto you. A common reaction is to meet stress with stress, but the best answer is to rise above it and take the high road called integrity.

Stress in a Changing World

All you need do is glance at the covers of *Time* or *Newsweek*, or the Internet homepage of MSNBC or Comcast to see and read what we already know: These are stressful times! But the stress we are encountering as a nation is not specific to being a world power. The problem seems to have reached every corner of the planet, permeating the borders of every country, province, and locale. In fact, after conducting several surveys on the topic of stress and illness, the World Health Organization came to the conclusion that stress is hitting a fever pitch in every nation. So alarmed were they by the results of their study that the WHO researchers cited stress as "a global epidemic."

On the home front it appears that stress, like a virus, has infected the American population, and the symptoms are everywhere: Radio talk shows and blogs

have become national forums for complaining; political pundits repeatedly describe voter anger; headlines are filled with stories of people who have gone berserk with hostility, most notably road rage, sports rage, movie theater rage, phone rage, and air rage; television talk shows are reduced to airing personal catharses; workplace violence has escalated to several incidences per month in which co-workers are shot and killed; the American dream is out of reach for many; and psychologists describe a spiritual malaise that has swept the country. Yet where there is despair, there is also compassion. The devastating earthquake in Fukashima, Japan, in 2011 and the devastation of Hurricane Katrina in 2005 brought out the best in some, as countless people came to the aid of their fellow human beings across the globe. The darkest times can bring out our finest hour, if we transition from fear to compassion.

The Power of Adaptation

One of the greatest attributes of the human species is the ability to adapt to change. Adaptation is the number one skill with which to cope with the stress of life. Adaptation involves a great many human attributes, from resiliency and creativity to forgiveness, patience, and many, many more. Given the rapid rate of change in the world today, combined with the typical changes one goes through in a lifetime, the ability to adapt is essential. Those who incorporate a strategy to adapt positively not only will be healthier, but also, in the long run, will be much happier. Adaptation to stress means to make small changes in your personal lifestyle so that you can move in the flow with the winds of change taking place in the world and not feel personally violated or victimized. Sometimes, adaptation to change means merely fine-tuning a perception or attitude. In the best stress management program reduced to 27 words, the following quote attributed to Reinhold Niebuhr speaks to this process: "God, grant me the serenity to accept the things I cannot change, the courage to change the things I can and the wisdom to know the difference." The skills introduced in this text are designed to help you gracefully adapt to the winds of change.

The Premise of Holistic Stress Management

Honoring the premise of this ageless wisdom, holistic stress management promotes the integration, balance, and harmony of one's mind, body, spirit, and emotions for optimal health and well-being. Stress affects all aspects of the wellness paradigm. To appreciate the dynamics of the whole, sometimes it's best to understand the pieces that make up the whole. What follows is a definition of each of the four aspects that constitute the human entity, and the effect that unresolved stress plays on each.

Emotional well-being: The ability to feel and express the entire range of human emotions, and to control them, not be controlled by them. Unresolved stress tends to perpetuate a preponderance of negative emotions (anger and fear), thus compromising emotional balance and causing the inability to experience and enjoy moments of joy, happiness, and bliss.

Physical well-being: The optimal functioning of the body's physiological systems (e.g., cardiovascular, endocrine, reproductive, immune). Not only does unresolved stress create wear and tear on the body, but the association between stress and disease is approximately 80–85 percent. Ultimately, stress can kill.

Mental well-being: The ability of the mind to gather, process, recall, and communicate information. Stress certainly compromises the ability to gather, process, recall, and communicate information.

Spiritual well-being: The maturation of higher consciousness as represented through the dynamic integration of three facets: relationships, values, and a meaningful purpose in life. Most, if not all, stressors involve some aspect of relationships, values (or value conflicts), and the absence of, search for, or fulfillment of a meaningful purpose in one's life.

The circle is a universal symbol of wholeness, often divided into four parts: north, south, east, and west, as well as spring, summer, winter, and fall. Mind, body, spirit, and emotions are also four quadrants that make up the whole, often depicted in a circle. Exercise 1.10 invites you to reflect on the concept of wholeness via this symbol so prevalent in world culture.

The Nature of Holistic Stress Management

With the appreciation that the whole is always greater than the sum of its parts, here are some insights that collectively shine light on this timeless wisdom of the nature of holistic stress management:

- Holistic stress management conveys the essence of uniting the powers of the conscious and unconscious minds to work in unison (rather than in opposition) for one's highest potential. Additionally, a holistic approach to coping effectively with stress unites the functions of both the right and left hemispheres of the brain.

- Holistic stress management suggests a dynamic approach to one's personal energy where one lives consciously in the present moment, rather than feeling guilty about things done in the past or worrying about things that may occur in the future.

- Holistic stress management underlies the premise of using a combination of **effective coping skills** to resolve issues that can cause perceptions of stress to linger and sound relaxation techniques to reduce or eliminate the symptoms of stress and return the body to homeostasis. This is different from the standard practice of merely focusing on symptomatic relief.

- Holistic stress management is achieving a balance between the role of the ego to protect and the purpose of the soul to observe and learn life's lessons.

More often than not, the ego perpetuates personal stress through control and manipulation.

- Holistic stress management is often described as moving from a motivation of fear to a place of unconditional love.

When all of these aspects are taken into consideration, the process of integrating, balancing, and bringing harmony to mind, body, spirit, and emotions becomes much easier, and arriving at the place of inner peace is easier to achieve.

Chapter Summary

- The advancement of technology, which promised more leisure time, has actually increased the pace of life so that many people feel stressed to keep up with this pace.

- Lifestyles based on new technological conveniences are now thought to be associated with several diseases, including coronary heart disease and cancer.

- *Stress* is a term from the field of physics, meaning physical force or tension placed on an object. It was adopted after World War II to signify psychological tension.

- There are many definitions of stress from both Eastern and Western philosophies as well as several academic disciplines, including psychology and physiology. The mind-body separation is now giving way to a holistic philosophy involving the mental, physical, emotional, and spiritual components of well-being.

- Cannon coined the term *fight-or-flight response* to describe the immediate effects of physical stress. This response is now considered by many to be inappropriate for nonphysical stressors.

- There are three types of stress: eustress (good), neustress (neutral), and distress (bad). There are two types of distress: acute (short-term) and chronic (long-term), the latter of which is thought to be the more detrimental because the body does not return to a state of complete homeostasis.

- Stressors have been categorized into three groups: (1) bioecological influences, (2) psychointrapersonal influences, and (3) social influences.

- Holmes and Rahe created the Social Readjustment Rating Scale to identify major life stressors. They found that the incidence of stressors correlated with health status.

- Selye coined the term *general adaptation syndrome* to explain the body's ability to adapt negatively to chronic stress.

- Females are not only wired for fight-or-flight, but also have a survival dynamic called "tend and befriend," a specific nurturing aspect that promotes social support in stressful times.

- The association between stress and insomnia is undeniable. The United States is said to be a sleep-deprived society, but techniques for stress management, including physical exercise, biofeedback, yoga, and diaphragmatic breathing, are proven effective to help promote a good night's sleep.

- Stress can appear at any time in our lives, but the college years offer their own types of stressors because it is at this time that one assumes more (if not complete) responsibility for one's lifestyle behaviors. Stress continues through retirement with a whole new set of stressors in the senior years.

- Sociology is described as the study of human social behavior within family, organizations, and institutions. Societal stress is a force to be reckoned with in today's culture. No one is exempt from the sociology of stress.

- *Techno-stress* is a term used to describe the overwhelming frustrations of sensory bombardment and poor boundaries with the plethora of technological gadgets. Techno-stress began with personal computers but has since evolved with the advent of and addiction to social networking. The body's physiology wasn't designed to be "on" all the time. The result can be burnout and physical health issues.

- Social stress includes a decline in social etiquette. A lack of civility, demonstrated by rude, impatient behavior, is on a dramatic rise in the United States.

- Experts suggest that one aspect of societal stress is an environmental disconnect: a growing disregard of the environment by humanity, such that dramatic changes, from dwindling supplies of fresh water to declining food quality to environmental pollution, will all have a significant impact on each individual's lifestyle and health.

- Race and gender issues have always been part of the social fabric and continue to contribute largely to stress, especially as people express themselves with reckless abandon in the digital age.

- Previous approaches to stress management have been based on the mechanistic model, which divided the mind and body into two separate entities. The paradigm on which this model was based is now shifting toward a holistic paradigm, where the whole is greater than the sum of the parts, and the whole person must be treated by working on the causes as well as the symptoms of stress.

- Effective stress-management programming must address issues related to mental (intellectual), physical, emotional, and spiritual well-being.

Additional Resources

Allen, R. *Human Stress: It's Nature and Control*. Edina, MN: Burgess Intl Group; 1983.

American Heart Association. www.american heart.org.

Beckford, M. Working nine to five is becoming a thing of the past. *The Daily Telegraph*. May 4, 2007.

Bernstein, A. *The Myth of Stress*. New York: Simon & Schuster; 2010.

Brody, J. What Do You Lack? Probably Vitamin D. *New York Times,* July 26, 2010. www.nytimes.com/2010/07/27/health/27brod.html. Accessed July 18, 2012.

Brown, L. *Plan B: Rescuing a Planet Under Stress and a Civilization in Trouble*. New York: Norton; 2006.

Business Management Daily. U.S. Workers Using Less Vacation Time, Survey Says. May 10, 2009. www.businessmanagementdaily.com/articles/18810/1/US-workers-using-less-vacation-time-survey-says/Page1.html#. Accessed October 2, 2012.

Carlson, R. *Don't Sweat the Small Stuff*. New York: Hyperion Books; 1997.

Carr, N. *The Shallows: What the Internet Is Doing to Our Brains*. New York: W. Norton; 2011.

Dawson, P. Sleep and Adolescents. January 2005. http://www.nasponline.org/resources/principals/sleep%20disorders%20web.pdf. Accessed August 1, 2012.

Della Cava, M. Attention Spans Get Rewired. *USA Today*. August 4, 2010, p. 9. http://www.usatoday.com/printedition/life/20100804/netbrain04_cv.art.htm. Accessed August 1, 2012.

Diamond, J. *Collapse: How Societies Choose to Fail or Succeed*. New York: Penguin Books; 2011.

Dossey, L. Plugged In: At What Price? The Perils and Promise of Electrical Communications. *Explore* 5(5):257–262, 2009.

Eisenberg, D., et al. Unconventional Medicine in the United States. *New England Journal of Medicine 328*: 246–252, 1993.

Eisenberg, D., et al. Trends in Alternative Medicine Use in the United States, 1990–1997: Results of a Follow-up National Survey. *JAMA 280*: 1569–1575, 1998.

Eldridge, N. The Sixth Extinction. June 2001. www.actionbioscience.org/newfrontiers/eldredge2.html. Accessed July 18, 2012.

Expedia.com. *2009 International Vacation Deprevation Study Results*. 2009. March 19, 2009. http://media.expedia.com/media/content/expus/graphics/promos/vacations/Expedia_International_Vacation_Deprivation_Survey_2009.pdf. Accessed August 1, 2012.

Gallwey, W.I. *The Inner Game of Stress*. New York: Random House; 2009.

Garrett, T. Lack of Civility in America Brought to Light. *Canyon News*. September 19, 2009. www.canyonnews.com/artman2/publish/Message_to_America_1179/Lack_of_Civility_in_America_Brought_to_Light.php. Accessed August 1, 2012.

Girdano, D., Everly, G., & Dusek, D. *Controlling Stress and Tension*. Upper Saddle River, NJ: Benjamin Cummings; 2012.

Hawking, S. Stephen Hawking to Human Race: Move to Outer Space or Face Extinction, August 6, 2010. www.huffingtonpost.com/2010/08/06/stephen-hawking-to-human_n_673387.html. Accessed July 18, 2012.

Hetler, W. *The Six Dimensional Wellness Model*. The National Wellness Institute. http://www.nationalwellness.org/pdf/SixDimensionsFactSheets.pdf. Accessed October 2, 2012.

Krugman, M. *The Insomnia Solution*. New York: Grand Central Publishing; 2009.

Lallas, N. *Renewing Values in America*. Mill Valley, CA: Artis Press; 2009.

Lanman, S. *Choosing Civility in the Face of Rudeness*. Rutger's Focus, March 2010. http://news.rutgers.edu/focus/issue.2010-03-02.2969546649/article.2010-03-30.3504010889. Accessed August 1, 2012.

Lawlor, M. Take Your Time . . . Vacation Time, That Is. *Signal Connections*. July 17, 2006. www.imakenews .com/signal/e_article000617059.cfm?x=b11,0. Accessed October 2, 2012.

Lazarus, R. Puzzles in the Study of Daily Hassles. *Journal of Behavioral Medicine* 7:375–389, 1984.

Levy, S. Facebook Grows Up. *Newsweek*. August 20, 2007: 41–46.

Lipton, B. Keynote Address: Get Your Shift Together. Loveland, CO, July 18, 2012.

Lipton, B., & Bhareman, S. *Spontaneous Evolution*. Carlsbad, CA: HayHouse; 2010.

Louv, R. *Last Child in the Woods*. Chapel Hill, NC: Algonquin; 2008.

Luskin, F., & Pelletier, K. *Stress Free for Good: 10 Scientifically Proven Life Skills for Health and Happiness*. New York: HarperOne; 2009.

Maas, J. *Power Sleep*. New York: Quill Books; 2001.

Marquardt, K. Take a True Lunch Break. *US News and World Report*. December 2010.

Mayo Clinic. *Post-traumatic Stress Disorder*. www.mayo clinic.com/health/post-traumatic-stress-disorder /DS00246. Accessed October 2, 2012.

McEwen, B. *The End of Stress as We Know It*. Washington, DC: Joseph Henry Press; 2002.

Meyer, D. *Why We Hate Us: American Discontent in the New Millennium*. New York: Crown; 2009.

Mitchum Report on Stress in the 90's. New York: Research and Forecast Inc.; 1990.

Moyers, B. *Healing and the Mind*. Public Broadcasting System; 1993.

Moyers, B. *Healing and the Mind*. New York: Doubleday; 1995.

National Geographic (Special Issue). Water: Our Thirsty World. April 2010.

Ornstein, R., & Sobel, D. *Healthy Pleasures*. Reading, MA: Addison Wesley; 1990.

Overworked Americans Can't Use Up Their Vacation. May 13, 2003. www.hrmguide.net/usa/worklife/unused vacation.htm. Accessed October 2, 2012.

Quintos, N. Vacation-deficit disorder. *National Geographic Traveler*. November/December 2007: 22–27.

Richter, A. Sting, the Yogi Behind the Music. *Energy Times*. October 4–8, 2010. http://www.energytimes .com/pages/features/1010/sting.html. Accessed August 1, 2012.

Rosch, P., president of the American Stress Institute, as quoted in 2003. Reuters Limited. www.msnbc.com /news/950045.asp. Accessed October 2, 2012.

Rubinkam, M. *During Boring Classes, Texting Is the New Doodling*. Associated Press. November 26, 2010. http:// www.boston.com/news/nation/articles/2010/11/26/ during_boring_classes_texting_is_the_new_doodling/. Accessed August 1, 2012.

Sapolsky, R. M. *Why Zebras Don't Get Ulcers*. New York: W. H. Freeman; 2004.

Schlitz, M. *Keynote Address*. 15th Annual Healing Touch International Conference. St. Louis, MO, September 12, 2010.

Seaward, B. L. *Stressed Is Desserts Spelled Backward*. Berkeley, CA: Conari Press; 1999.

Seigler, K. *Tweeting with the Birds: Pitch Tent, Switch to Wi-Fi*. August 3, 2010. www.npr.org/templates /story/story.php?storyId=128697566. Accessed July 18, 2012.

Selye, H. *The Stress of Life*. New York: McGraw-Hill; 1978.

Simeon, A. W. *Man's Presumptuous Brain: An Evolutionary Interpretation of Psychosomatic Disease*. New York: Dutton; 1961.

Simon, S. *Using Your BlackBerry Off-Hours Could Be Overtime*. NPR, August 14, 2010. www.npr.org /templates/story/story.php?storyId=129184907. Accessed July 18, 2012.

Smith, R., & Lourie, B. *Slow Death by Rubber Duck: The Secret Danger of Everyday Things*. Berkeley, CA: Counterpoint; 2011.

Stepp, L. S. Enough Talk Already. *Washington Post*. August 21, 2007. http://forum.psychlinks.ca/relation ships/8854-enough-talk-already-talk-vs-action-in-men-and-women.html. Accessed August 1, 2012.

Swartz, J. Survey Warns of E-mail Stress, July 16, 2010. http://content.usatoday.com/communities/technology live/post/2010/07/e-mail-stress-when-is-too-much -e-mail-too-much/1?loc=interstitialskip. Accessed July 18, 2012.

Taylor, S. *The Tending Instinct*. New York: Owl Books; 2003.

Weber, K. (Ed.). *Food, Inc*. New York; Participant Media; 2009.

Weil, M., & Rosen, L. *Technostress: Coping with Technology @ Work, @ Home and @ Play*. New York: John Wiley & Sons; 1998.

Wong, M. Vacationing Americans Have Given New Meaning to the Advertising Slogan, Don't Leave Home Without It. Associated Press. September 1, 2000.

World Health Organization (WHO). World Health Report, July 31, 2008.

EXERCISE 1.1: Are You Stressed?

Although there is no definitive survey composed of 20 questions to determine if you are stressed or burnt out, or just exactly how stressed you really are, questionnaires do help increase awareness that, indeed, there may be a problem in one or more areas of your life. The following is an example of a simple stress inventory to help you determine the level of stress in your life. Read each statement, and then circle either the word Agree or Disagree. Then count the number of "Agree" points (one per question) and use the Stress Level Key to determine your personal stress level.

Statement	Agree	Disagree
1. I have a hard time falling asleep at night.	AGREE	DISAGREE
2. I tend to suffer from tension and/or migraine headaches.	AGREE	DISAGREE
3. I find myself thinking about finances and making ends meet.	AGREE	DISAGREE
4. I wish I could find more to laugh and smile about each day.	AGREE	DISAGREE
5. More often than not, I skip breakfast or lunch to get things done.	AGREE	DISAGREE
6. If I could change my job situation, I would.	AGREE	DISAGREE
7. I wish I had more personal time for leisure pursuits.	AGREE	DISAGREE
8. I have lost a good friend or family member recently.	AGREE	DISAGREE
9. I am unhappy in my relationship or am recently divorced.	AGREE	DISAGREE
10. I haven't had a quality vacation in a long time.	AGREE	DISAGREE
11. I wish that my life had a clear meaning and purpose.	AGREE	DISAGREE
12. I tend to eat more than three meals a week outside the home.	AGREE	DISAGREE
13. I tend to suffer from chronic pain.	AGREE	DISAGREE
14. I don't have a strong group of friends to whom I can turn.	AGREE	DISAGREE
15. I don't exercise regularly (more than three times per week).	AGREE	DISAGREE
16. I am on prescribed medication for depression.	AGREE	DISAGREE
17. My sex life is not very satisfying.	AGREE	DISAGREE
18. My family relationships are less than desirable.	AGREE	DISAGREE
19. Overall, my self-esteem can be rather low.	AGREE	DISAGREE
20. I spend no time each day dedicated to meditation or centering.	AGREE	DISAGREE

Stress Level Key

Less than 5 points   You have a low level of stress and maintain good coping skills.

More than 5 points   You have a moderate level of personal stress.

More than 10 points   You have a high level of personal stress.

More than 15 points   You have an exceptionally high level of stress.

EXERCISE 1.2: Stimulation Overload

In the early years of our lives, we crave sensory stimulation: Loud music, fast-moving video games, movies, food; the list is nearly endless. All of this stimulation increases our threshold for excitement, and we seek more and more to hit this threshold of excitement. All of this sensory stimulation falls under the category of "good stress," that which motivates us and makes us happy. At some point, however, too much of a good thing can become bad. Too much sensory stimulation can become sensory overload, which then leads to burnout. Burnout is another word for bad stress. This exercise invites you to take an honest look at those things that you would consider good stress and how you manage it to maintain an optimal level of health and performance.

1. What things do you crave for sensory stimulation? Make a list.

2. How do you know when you have had too much sensory stimulation (stimulation overload)? What are the signs/symptoms of personal burnout?

3. How has your threshold of excitement changed over the years? (If you are under the age of 20, consider how your threshold differs from that of your parents and grandparents.)

4. Do you see an association between too much sensory stimulation and your health status (good or bad)? Please explain.

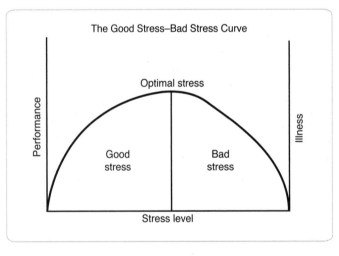

EXERCISE 1.3: Personal Stress Inventory: Top Ten Stressors

It's time to take a personal inventory of your current stressors—those issues, concerns, situations, or challenges that trigger the fight-or-flight response in your body. The first step to resolving any problem is learning to identify exactly what the problem is. Take a moment to list the top ten issues that you are facing at the present moment. Then place a check mark in the columns to signify whether this stressor directly affects one or more aspects of your health (mind, body, spirit, emotions). Then, next to each stressor, chronicle how long it has been a problem. Finally, record whether this stressor is one that elicits some level of anger, fear, or both.

Stressor	Mental	Emotional	Spiritual	Physical	Duration of Problem
1.					
2.					
3.					
4.					
5.					
6.					
7.					
8.					
9.					
10.					

EXERCISE 1.4: Daily Stressors Survey for College Students

It's a safe bet that you will hear the expression "real world" more than once while attending college—the real world being the noncollege world of long hours, hard work, and umpteen responsibilities. Years ago, the college experience was considered a luxury of the wealthy. For many rich kids, going to college was like taking a four-year vacation during which world responsibility could be postponed with the promise of a great job waiting after graduation. Times have changed dramatically since those Ivy League days of long ago. Going to college may not be the same thing as working on Wall Street or in the emergency room of a local hospital, but college constitutes its own real world nonetheless. Being a college student comes with its own list of stressors, big and small. The following worksheet invites you to rank these typical daily student stressors (from 1 being low stress to 5 being high stress). In doing so, you take the first step in recognizing what issues need to be addressed in your current life situation.

Part I: How do these typical college student stressors rank in your life?

	Low				High
1. Coping with roommates, living conditions	1	2	3	4	5
2. Balancing schoolwork with job hours	1	2	3	4	5
3. Making ends meet financially	1	2	3	4	5
4. Academic load (credits, exams, papers, etc.)	1	2	3	4	5
5. Social needs (friends, family, etc.)	1	2	3	4	5
6. Health status, health issues	1	2	3	4	5
7. Food, body image, and weight issues	1	2	3	4	5
8. Transportation (car, traffic, gas, parking/speeding tickets)	1	2	3	4	5
9. Parental issues, childcare issues, etc.	1	2	3	4	5
10. Girlfriend, boyfriend, partner issues	1	2	3	4	5
11. Technology issues (Facebook updates, text messages, bandwidth, cloud issues)	1	2	3	4	5
12. Purpose in life issues (declaring a major, finding a career position)	1	2	3	4	5

EXERCISE 1.4: Daily Stressors Survey for College Students cont....

Part II: Please list any and all additional daily or weekly stressors and rank these as well.

	Low				High
1.	1	2	3	4	5
2.	1	2	3	4	5
3.	1	2	3	4	5
4.	1	2	3	4	5
5.	1	2	3	4	5
6.	1	2	3	4	5
7.	1	2	3	4	5
8.	1	2	3	4	5
9.	1	2	3	4	5
10.	1	2	3	4	5

Part III: Please add any additional comments you wish to make here.

_____

_____

_____

_____

_____

_____

EXERCISE 1.5: Self-Assessment: Poor Sleep Habits Questionnaire

Please take a moment to answer these questions based on your typical behavior. If you feel your sleep quality is compromised, consider that one or more of these factors may contribute to patterns of insomnia by affecting your physiology, circadian rhythms, or emotional thought processing. Although there is no key to determine your degree of insomnia, each question is based on specific factors associated with either a good night's sleep or the lack of it. Use each question to help you fine-tune your sleep hygiene.

1. Do you go to bed at about the same time every night?	YES	NO
2. Does it take you more than 30 minutes to fall asleep once in bed?	YES	NO
3. Do you wake up at about the same time every day?	YES	NO
4. Do you drink coffee, tea, or caffeinated soda after 6 p.m.?	YES	NO
5. Do you watch television from your bed?	YES	NO
6. Do you perform cardiovascular exercise 3–5 times per week?	YES	NO
7. Do you use your bed as your office (e.g., do homework, balance checkbook, write letters)?	YES	NO
8. Do you take a hot shower or bath before you go to sleep?	YES	NO
9. Do you have one or more drinks of alcohol before bedtime?	YES	NO
10. Are you engaged in intense mental activity before bed (e.g., term papers, exams, projects, reports, finances, taxes)?	YES	NO
11. Is your bedroom typically warm or even hot before you go to bed?	YES	NO
12. Does your sleep partner snore, become restless, etc., in the night?	YES	NO
13. Is the size and comfort level of your bed satisfactory?	YES	NO
14. Do you suffer from chronic pain while laying down?	YES	NO
15. Is your sleep environment compromised by noise, light, or pets?	YES	NO
16. Do you frequently take naps during the course of a day?	YES	NO
17. Do you take medications (e.g., decongestants, steroids, antihypertensives, asthma medications, for depression)?	YES	NO
18. Do you tend to suffer from depression?	YES	NO
19. Do you eat a large heavy meal right before you go to bed?	YES	NO
20. Do you use a smartphone regularly, particularly in the evening?	YES	NO

EXERCISE 1.6: Are You a Product of Your Culture?

The following questions are based on various behaviors observed from individuals in society. Please answer each question as you really behave, not how you would like to be, by circling Yes or No where appropriate.

1. I keep my smartphone on throughout the day so I won't miss any calls.　　YES　　NO

2. I use my Facebook account more often than my email account.　　YES　　NO

3. I tend to leave the water running while brushing my teeth.　　YES　　NO

4. I eat more than one meal prepared outside the house each day.　　YES　　NO

5. During the day, I constantly check emails and text messages as they come in.　　YES　　NO

6. I drive rather than take mass transit to and from work/college regularly.　　YES　　NO

7. I typically take my laptop, BlackBerry, etc. on vacation with me.　　YES　　NO

8. I have been known to flush unused medications down the toilet.　　YES　　NO

9. I get more of my news from Comedy Central (e.g., *The Daily Show*, *The Colbert Report*) than newspapers, NPR, TV news, or online news sites.　　YES　　NO

10. I spend less than one hour outside each day in a natural setting.　　YES　　NO

11. I regularly interact (leave comments) on Web sites I visit.　　YES　　NO

12. I find that I rely more and more on the Internet and electronic devices for information (e.g., Garmin GPS, Google, etc.) and less on memory retention.　　YES　　NO

13. More often than not, I Tivo my favorite TV shows and watch them at my preference or watch episodes of my favorite shows on Hulu or other Internet sites.　　YES　　NO

14. I recycle all cans, bottles, newspapers, etc.　　YES　　NO

15. I start to feel antsy if I cannot check my email, text messages, or Facebook account each hour or more often.　　YES　　NO

16. I spend more time playing video games or surfing the Internet inside than outside in nature each day.　　YES　　NO

17. I check my emails, tweets, Facebook updates, etc. within 10 minutes of waking up each morning.　　YES　　NO

18. I have one or more tattoos as a means of self-expression.　　YES　　NO

19. I own more than one smartphone and I use them both at the same time (e.g., phone calls, apps, Google).　　YES　　NO

20. I make more than one purchase online each week.　　YES　　NO

21. I dread answering the onslaught of emails each day.　　YES　　NO

22. I get a bit of a rush or excitement when my smartphone goes off.　　YES　　NO

EXERCISE 1.6: Are You a Product of Your Culture? cont....

23.	I text message my friends and parents more than I call them by phone.	YES	NO
24.	I watch more movies via the Internet or Netflix than in a movie theater.	YES	NO
25.	I make an effort to buy organic produce each week.	YES	NO
26.	I have more than 50 Web sites bookmarked on my computer.	YES	NO
27.	I have more than 250 friends on Facebook.	YES	NO
28.	I purchase plastic water bottles rather than use a stainless steel bottle.	YES	NO
29.	I have more than 25 apps on my iPhone/Android.	YES	NO
30.	I watch at least one YouTube or Socialcam video per day.	YES	NO
31.	The majority of my purchases are via credit card or debit card, not cash.	YES	NO
32.	I post an update to Facebook at least once a day.	YES	NO
33.	I belong to more than one social networking Web site.	YES	NO
34.	I prefer to read books via a Kindle or an iPad than hard cover books.	YES	NO
35.	I post photos and various items on Pinterest and Instagram each week.	YES	NO

Results: The purpose of these questions is to increase your awareness of the influence the current culture has on your behaviors. There is no definitive answer or "score" regarding the impact of cultural influences. We participate in cultural practices primarily as a means of being accepted. Most people are completely unaware of the influence that society has on them, unless they purposely act differently than cultural norms suggest.

EXERCISE 1.7: Living in the Age of Civility

Experts have noticed a dramatic decline in civility, which closely parallels the rise in the use of technology. While it is easy to observe rude and uncivil behavior in other, it's not so easy to see it in ourselves (the ego's ability to rationalize one's behavior is quite powerful). This exercise invites you to take an honest look at your civil behaviors and determine how you stack up with what is culturally expected as good manners in a civil society.

5 = **Always**   4 = **Often**   3 = **Sometimes**   2 = **Seldom**   1 = **Rarely**   0 = **Never**

1.	I hold the door open for people when walking into or out of a store or building.	0	1	2	3	4	5
2.	If I use my smartphone in public, I find a quiet place to talk away from people.	0	1	2	3	4	5
3.	I make a habit of smiling at others including store clerks, postal workers, and restaurant servers.	0	1	2	3	4	5
4.	I only use the express checkout lane in the grocery store when I have the limited number of suggested items, even when in a hurry.	0	1	2	3	4	5
5.	When driving, I allow other drivers to cut in front of me.	0	1	2	3	4	5
6.	If I am at the movies with a friend, I will suspend all conversations during the film.	0	1	2	3	4	5
7.	While on the phone, I give my full attention and don't multitask with checking emails, etc.	0	1	2	3	4	5
8.	I let people finish speaking before I say something or comment.	0	1	2	3	4	5
9.	I say the words please and thank you when requesting something.	0	1	2	3	4	5
10.	I don't use my smartphone while driving.	0	1	2	3	4	5
11.	I will pull a dollar out of my wallet or purse for a homeless person.	0	1	2	3	4	5
12.	If I receive a second call while talking, I will ignore the incoming call.	0	1	2	3	4	5
13.	When listening to my iPod while walking, jogging, snowboarding, or downhill skiing, I acknowledge others' presence with a smile, nod, or comment.	0	1	2	3	4	5
14.	When others express political or religious beliefs that are different than mine, I shift the conversation to a different topic.	0	1	2	3	4	5
15.	I tend to censor the use of swear words in public.	0	1	2	3	4	5
	TOTAL SCORE						

Key: There is no set standard for degrees of civility. Either you are or you are not! This survey is an awareness tool to help you examine your own behavior. If you score less than 30 points, you might consider changing because most likely people see you as lacking in civility.

EXERCISE 1.8: It's All About Me: The Age of Narcissism

"Enough about me. What do you think about me?" — Bette Midler

Consider these facts: Today anyone can publish their own book, record their own song, enter a photo contest, post their own blog, make their own movie, and gain worldwide attention if not millions of fans via YouTube. Reality shows are the rage on TV, from *Jersey Shore* to home improvement shows. Anyone can become a celebrity, specifically a "laptop celebrity." Experts who keep their finger on the pulse of humanity grow increasingly concerned. The "me" generation has now expanded over several decades to include several generations. The self-absorbed, all-about-me, narcissistic, 15-minutes-of-fame culture is nothing more than the ego run amuck. The problems with unbridled egos (multiplied by 7 billion people) cannot be understated! If everyone is only looking out for themselves, many people, perhaps cultures, if not the world, will suffer. Recently the American Psychiatric Association decided to delete the Narcissism Disorder from the *Diagnostic and Statistical Manual of Mental Disorders,* fifth edition, in 2013, suggesting that this behavior is too common now to be recognized as a disorder. Granted, you have to have some interest in yourself. After all, that's what self-esteem is all about. Balance is the key. At what point is the line crossed? That is the million-dollar question. The opposite of narcissism is altruism—doing something for others without any expectation of reciprocation; in essence, random acts of kindness.

1. Have you noticed that, in general, people are self-absorbed, perhaps even clueless about others eclipsed by their own stature and in denial about their inflated egos?

2. Have you been accused of being narcissistic, or simply full of yourself? Please explain.

3. How would you best describe your "presence" in the world? Do you have a Web site? A blog? Multiple YouTube video postings? Tweets on a Twitter account? Books on Amazon? How many Facebook updates do you post per day? How many minutes have you used up on your 15 minutes of fame allotment (or have you gone over this limit)?

4. Why do you suppose people are over the top with being self-righteous or simply fascinated with themselves? Is it a need for approval? Is it a need for acceptance? Is it a question of insecurity? What is your take on this new normal of the "me" generation?

5. If indeed altruism is the polar opposite of narcissism, what actions do you take on a regular basis to seek balance? What do you do to domesticate your ego?

EXERCISE 1.9: The Environmental Disconnect

How tuned in to the environment are you? Let's find out. Take this quick True/False quiz.

1. The majority of the ocean's coral reefs are dying due to agricultural runoff, poor fishing practices, and formaldehyde used to capture tropical fish.   TRUE   FALSE

2. Over 60 percent of food in your local grocery store is genetically modified.   TRUE   FALSE

3. About one half of the world's population does not have drinkable water in their house.   TRUE   FALSE

4. The acidity of the world's oceans is increasing at an alarming rate.   TRUE   FALSE

5. Wild salmon has much less PCBs than that raised in fisheries.   TRUE   FALSE

6. Mercury found in coldwater fish comes from coal-burning plants used to make electricity for everyday use.   TRUE   FALSE

7. Hormones and antibiotics dumped into toilets are not filtered out in water treatment plants.   TRUE   FALSE

8. Experts predict that the ocean's natural fisheries will collapse in your lifetime.   TRUE   FALSE

9. It takes 2,500 gallons of water to produce one hamburger.   TRUE   FALSE

10. On average, there are over 16 million new cars on the road every year.   TRUE   FALSE

11. Ethanol fuel still requires petrochemicals (oil) for fertilizers to grow the corn.   TRUE   FALSE

12. Farm-raised salmon must take beta carotine pellets so its flesh is pink/orange.   TRUE   FALSE

13. City light pollution is thought to be a contributing factor to the increase in insomnia across the United States.   TRUE   FALSE

14. The majority of food in your local grocery story has been transported over 1,500 miles to rest on those store shelves before being purchased.   TRUE   FALSE

15. Droughts in the Amazon rainforest contribute to global warming.   TRUE   FALSE

The answer for all of these questions is *true*. But don't get too stressed out. Being aware of each problem is half of the solution. Knowledge is power. Environmental disconnect is based largely on ignorance and apathy. Although some people choose to stick their head in the sand, others are taking an active role towards living a sustainable life by changing their behaviors to become in sync with the environment. One person's life may seem insignificant to the big picture, but nothing could be further from the truth. What can you do? Plenty!

EXERCISE 1.9: The Environmental Disconnect cont....

List ten things that you do (or can start doing) to live a more sustainable lifestyle and reconnect with the biosphere we live on called planet Earth.

1. _____

2. _____

3. _____

4. _____

5. _____

6. _____

7. _____

8. _____

9. _____

10. _____

EXERCISE 1.10: The Circle: The Universal Symbol of Wholeness

The circle is a universal symbol of wholeness, as expressed in the American Indian medicine wheel, the Tibetan mandala, and many other symbols recognized worldwide. Typically these symbols depict four aspects such as spring, summer, winter, and fall; mind, body, spirit, and emotions; or north, south, east, and west. This exercise invites you to increase your awareness of the power of this symbol.

1. List ten objects, found in nature, that symbolize wholeness (e.g., full moon, sun, etc.).

    a. _____

    b. _____

    c. _____

    d. _____

    e. _____

    f. _____

    g. _____

    h. _____

    i. _____

    j. _____

2. List ten objects or designs that are used in American culture (or world culture) to convey a sense of wholeness to the unconscious mind (e.g., Starbucks logo, dinner plates, Christmas wreaths, the peace symbol, etc.).

    a. _____

    b. _____

    c. _____

    d. _____

    e. _____

    f. _____

    g. _____

    h. _____

    i. _____

    j. _____

The Body: The Battlefield for the Mind's War Games

"The immune system does not reside solely in the body."
— Patricia Norris, PhD

Here is a startling statistic: More than 80 percent of patients' visits to physicians' offices are associated with stress (unresolved issues of anger and fear). Moreover, 80 percent of worker's compensation claims are directly related to stress. Here is another statistic: Researchers in the field of psychoneuroimmunology (PNI) and energy healing not only suggest that as much as 85 percent of illness and disease is associated with stress, but also note a direct causal link, giving a new perspective on the word *dis-ease*. Anyone who has ever suffered a tension headache knows intuitively how strong the mind-body connection really is.

Rest assured the dynamics of disease and illness are quite complex and yet to be fully understood. This chapter combines the best aspects of both Western and Eastern wisdom for a more comprehensive understanding of mind-body-spirit health and well-being.

Today, it is well documented that stress aggravates several health conditions, particularly Type II diabetes and rheumatoid arthritis. Furthermore, many diseases, such as lupus, fibromyalgia, Epstein-Barr, rheumatoid arthritis, and Type I diabetes, are now thought to have an autoimmune component to them. The list of stress-related illnesses continues to grow, from herpes and hemorrhoids to the common cold, cancer, and practically everything in between. Pharmaceuticals and surgery are the two tools of the trade used in Western (allopathic) medicine, yet the trade-offs can include severe side effects. This is one reason why so many people are turning to complementary forms of alternative healing for chronic health problems.

Prior to the discovery of vaccinations and antibiotics, the leading cause of death was infectious diseases. Today the leading causes of death are chronic lifestyle diseases (e.g., most cancers, diabetes, obesity, strokes, coronary heart disease), all of which have a strong stress component to them. Moreover, an increasing number of people suffer from chronic pain that ranges from bothersome discomfort to complete immobility. The Western model of health care (which some people label as "sick care") places a strong focus on symptomatic relief rather than prevention and healing restoration. As we are now learning, the most advantageous approach appears to combine the best of allopathic and holistic healing to address both the causes and symptoms of stress that will return one back to homeostasis, turning the battleground into a peaceful landscape. Exercise 2.1 is a personal stress inventory to help you determine any association between stress and symptoms of stress in your body.

Stress and Chronic Pain

In addition to issues related to chronic disease, an increasing number of Americans suffer from debilitating chronic pain. Muscular pain associated with the lower back, hips, shoulders, and neck is a constant nightmare, so much so that it steals your attention from practically everything else. The connection between stress and chronic pain cannot be ignored. Neither can the connection between stress and obesity. All of these factors are tightly integrated. It may come as no surprise that many of the coping and relaxation techniques in the cadre of holistic stress management used to maintain health and well-being are well-documented as a means to help restore a sense of homeostasis as well.

Your Human Space Suit

Renowned inventor and philosopher Buckminster Fuller once said that the human body is our one and only space suit in which to inhabit the planet Earth. It comes with its own oxygen tank, a metabolic waste removal system, a sensory detector system to enjoy all the pleasures of planetary exploration, and an immune defense system to ensure the health of the space suit in the occasionally harsh global environment. This specially designed space suit also is equipped with a unique program for self-healing. Factors associated with this self-healing process include the basic common health behaviors associated with longevity: regular physical exercise, proper nutrition, adequate sleep, the avoidance of drugs, and a supportive community of friends and family. Unfortunately, most people don't take good care of their space suits and many have forgotten the means to activate the program for self-healing.

Fight-or-Flight with a Bite

The fight-or-flight response may begin with a perception in the mind, but this thought process quickly becomes a series of neurological and chemical reactions in the body. In the blink of an eye, the nervous system releases epinephrine and norepinephrine throughout the body for immediate blood redistribution and muscle contraction. At the same time, a flood of hormones prepares the body for immediate and long-term metabolic survival. Similar to the cascade of a waterfall, hormones are secreted from the brain's pituitary and hypothalamus glands as messengers moving quickly downstream to the adrenal gland (cone-shaped organs that sit atop each kidney). Upon command, cortisol, aldosterone, and other glucocorticoids infiltrate the bloodstream to do their jobs, all in the name of physical survival.

What works well for acute stress can cause serious problems with chronic stress. Repeated synthesis and release of these stress hormones day after day (the consequence of prolonged bouts of unresolved stress issues) can literally wreak havoc on the physical body. In essence, the body becomes the battlefield for the war games of the mind.

Gross Anatomy and Physiology

Your body is composed of a network of several amazing systems that work together as an alliance for the necessary functions of all daily life activities. For centuries, these aspects were identified as nine separate systems living under the anatomical structure of the human body. Now most health experts agree (through the wisdom of PNI) that this is truly one system, with the whole always being greater than the sum of the parts. The parts are the musculoskeletal system, nervous system, cardiovascular system, pulmonary system, endocrine system, reproductive system, renal system, digestive system, and immune system. If you have a health problem with one of these systems initially, eventually all other systems become directly affected. In union with this "one system" are the many anatomical organs responsible for the integrity of its work, including, but not limited to, the heart, lungs, kidneys, liver, stomach, pancreas, brain, and lymph nodes. Physical well-being is often described as the optimal functioning of all of these physiological systems. What comes to mind when you hear the expression "the picture of health"? For most people this conjures up an image of a physically fit person enjoying some rigorous outdoor activity well into their later years. Sadly, this has now become an image few can relate to. Stress not only can affect the optimal functioning of all of these physiological systems to destroy the picture of health, but also can literally shut down the entire body. Simply stated: Left unresolved, stress kills! Exercise 2.2 is a questionnaire that brings to your attention the health habits that make a composite of your current health picture.

Subtle Anatomy and Physiology

Equally important, yet often less obvious than gross anatomy, are three other systems critical to the operations of the human space suit. These are more commonly known as **subtle anatomy** and physiology, and they are the human energy field, the meridian system, and the

chakra system. A holistic perspective of health would be incomplete without mentioning this aspect of health. The following sections provide a more detailed look at the aspects of our subtle anatomy and physiology.

The Human Energy Field

Western science has recently discovered that the human body has a unique field of electromagnetic energy that not only surrounds, but also permeates the entire body. Often called the "human aura" by mystics, it is the basis of Kirlian photography and the diagnosis of disease through magnetic resonance imaging (MRI). Ageless wisdom notes that there are many layers of the **human energy field**, with each layer associated with some aspect of consciousness (e.g., instinct, intellect, intuition, emotions). This and other findings support the timeless premise that our mind isn't located in our body. Instead, our body is located in our mind!

Each layer of consciousness in the human energy field is considered a harmonic vibration. Like keys on a piano keyboard, the frequency of the body's vibrations, and that of the emotional, mental, and spiritual fields, are set at different octaves, yet are within the harmonic range of each other. If a thought coupled with an emotion is left unresolved, it can cause dissonance or imbalance within the layers of energy in the aura. Distortion first appears in the aura outside the physical body. When left unresolved, these emotional frequencies cascade through the layers of energy (which include the chakras and meridians) to pool within various cell tissues. The end result is dysfunction in the corresponding area in the physical body. Dissonance (the opposite of resonance) eventually appears at the cellular level, and the once harmonic vibration is no longer tuned to homeostasis, hence, setting the stage for disease and illness. Medical intuitives including Mona Lisa Schulz, MD; Judith Orloff, MD; Caroline Myss; Donna Eden; Mietek Wirkus; and others describe the initial stage of illness and disease as unresolved emotions (e.g., anger or fear). Through this model of well-being, disease develops outside the body and filters down through the layers of energy. Ironically, physical symptoms in the body are not the first signs of illness, but the last. The body indeed becomes the battlefield for the war games of the mind.

The Meridian System

First brought to the world's attention through the ancient Chinese culture, the physical body holds 12 bilateral rivers (**meridians**) of energy or *chi*. Each meridian connects to one or more vital organs (e.g., heart, lungs, liver, kidneys). When energy is blocked or congested in any meridian, the health of the associated organ will suffer. Acupuncture is the primary modality used to ensure the free flow of energy through these meridians, by placing tiny bulblike needles at various gates (acupuncture points) along the meridian pathways to unblock energy congestion. Acupressure (also known as shiatsu) is another method used for energy regulation. Although Western medicine doesn't quite acknowledge the concept of chi or meridians, it does recognize many remarkable outcomes of acupuncture (without side effects) in the treatment of chronic illnesses, in which Western medicine itself has proven less than effective.

The Chakra Energy System

The human body is said to have seven major energy portals. The ancient Sanskrit word for these energy portals is *chakra*, which translates to mean "spinning wheel," and looks like a small tornado attached to the body. Like the meridian energy system, each **chakra** is associated with the health of vital organs specific to the region to which it's attached. When the chakra shows signs of congestion or distortion, then the life force of energy through the chakra cannot be maintained in its specific region, and the health of those organs is compromised. Each chakra is associated with not only a body region, but also a layer of consciousness in the human energy field, directly linking mind, body, and spirit. Exercise 2.3 explores the concept of chakras and your health status.

The science behind subtle energy provides valuable insight into a problem that has vexed Western health experts who study the area of stress and disease: Why is it that two people who go through a similar stressful experience can contract different chronic illnesses? The answer may appear to be strongly associated with the dynamics of the chakra energy system. The following is a brief summary of the seven primary chakras.

First Chakra. The first chakra is commonly known as the root chakra and is located at the base of the spine. The root chakra is associated with issues of safety and security. There is also a relationship with our connectedness to the earth and feelings of groundedness. The root chakra is tied energetically to some organs of the reproductive system, as well as the hip joints, lower back, and pelvic area. Health problems in these areas, including lower-back pain, sciatica, rectal difficulties, and some cancers (e.g., prostate), are thought to

correspond to disturbances with the root chakra. The root chakra is also known as the seat of the Kundalini energy, a spiritually based concept yet to be understood in Western culture.

Second Chakra. The second chakra, also known as the sacral chakra, is recognized as being associated with the sex organs, as well as personal power in terms of business and social relationships. The second chakra deals with emotional feelings associated with issues of sexuality and self-worth. When self-worth is viewed through external means such as money, job, or sexuality, this causes an energy distortion in this region. Obsessiveness with material gain is thought to be a means to compensate for low self-worth, hence a distortion to this chakra. Common symptoms associated with this chakra region may include menstrual difficulties, infertility, vaginal infections, ovarian cysts, impotency, lower-back pain, prostate problems, sexual dysfunction, slipped disks, and bladder and urinary infections.

Third Chakra. Located in the upper stomach region, the third chakra is also known as the solar plexus chakra. Energetically, this chakra feeds into the organs of the GI tract, including the abdomen, small intestine, colon, gallbladder, kidneys, liver, pancreas, adrenal glands, and spleen. Not to be confused with self-worth, the region of the third chakra is associated with self-confidence, self-respect, and empowerment. The wisdom of the solar plexus chakra is more commonly known as a gut feeling, an intuitive sense closely tied to our level of personal power, as exemplified in the expression, "This doesn't feel right." Blockages to this chakra are thought to be related to ulcers, cancerous tumors, diabetes, hepatitis, anorexia, bulimia, and all stomach-related problems. Issues of unresolved anger and fear are deeply connected to organic dysfunction in this body region.

Fourth Chakra. The fourth chakra is affectionately known as the heart chakra, and it is considered to be one of the most important energy centers of the body. The heart chakra represents the ability to express love. Like a symbolic heart placed over the organic heart, feelings of unresolved anger or expressions of conditional love work to congest the heart chakra, which in turn has a corresponding effect on the anatomical heart, as noted by renowned cardiologist Dean Ornish. The heart, however, is not the only organ closely tied to the heart chakra. Other organs include the lungs, breasts, and esophagus. Symptoms of a blocked heart chakra can include heart attacks, enlarged heart, asthma, allergies, lung cancer, bronchial difficulties, circulation problems, breast cancer, and problems associated with the upper back and shoulders. Also, an important association exists between the heart chakra and the thymus gland. The thymus gland, so instrumental in the making of T cells, shrinks with age.

Fifth Chakra. The fifth chakra lies above and is connected to the throat. Organs associated with the throat chakra are the thyroid and parathyroid glands, mouth, vocal cords, and trachea. As a symbol of communication, the throat chakra represents the development of personal expression, creativity, purpose in life, and willpower. The inability to express oneself in feelings or creativity or to exercise one's will freely inevitably distorts the flow of energy to the throat chakra and is thought to result in chronic sore throat problems, temporomandibular joint dysfunction (TMJD), mouth sores, stiffness in the neck area, thyroid dysfunction, migraines, and even cancerous tumors in this region.

Sixth Chakra. The sixth chakra is more commonly known as the brow chakra or the third eye. This chakra is associated with intuition and the ability to access the ageless wisdom or bank of knowledge in the depths of universal consciousness. As energy moves through the dimension of universal wisdom into this chakra it promotes the development of intelligence and reasoning skills. Directly tied to the pituitary and pineal glands, this chakra feeds energy to the brain for information processing. Unlike the solar plexus chakra, which is responsible for a gut level of intuition with personal matters, the wisdom channeled through the brow chakra is more universal in nature with implications for the spiritual aspect of life. Diseases caused by dysfunction of the brow chakra (e.g., brain tumors, hemorrhages, blood clots, blindness, comas, depression, schizophrenia) may be caused by an individual's not wanting to see something that is extremely important to his or her soul growth.

Seventh Chakra. If the concept of chakras is foreign to the Western mind, then the seventh chakra may hold promise to bridge East and West. Featured most predominantly in the Judeo-Christian culture through paintings and sculptures as the halo over saintly beings, the seventh chakra, also known as the crown chakra, is associated with matters of the soul and the spiritual quest. When the crown chakra is open and fully functioning, it is known to access the highest level of consciousness. Although no specific disease or illness may be associated with the crown chakra, in truth, every disease has a spiritual significance.

Although not everyone can see or sense the human energy field, meridians, or the chakras, you can be trained to do so. Exercise 2.4, "Energy Ball Exercise," is an introductory session to the perceptions of the human energy field. Exercise 2.5 includes several ideas for maintaining a healthy flow of personal energy or chi.

Stress and the Immune System

It's no surprise to learn that under chronic stress, the immune system is greatly compromised, beginning with the immunoglobulins in the saliva down to the natural killer cells that scan the body for unwanted pathogens and mutant cancer cells. Chances are if you were to look back to the most recent time you became ill, right before it (days, even weeks) you'll find a stressful experience that triggered a cascade of unresolved stress emotions, in turn washing a flood of stress hormones through your body.

What physiological factors are responsible for a suppressed immune system? At first, the finger was pointed at the central nervous system (e.g., epinephrine, norepinephrine). Then attention soon turned to **cortisol**, the stress hormone secreted by the adrenal glands responsible for a host of metabolic survival activities. Apparently, when cortisol gets done with its fight-or-flight duties, for some unknown reason, it has a nasty habit of attacking and destroying white blood cells, the front-line defense of the immune system. Research suggests that cortisol is not the only culprit when it comes to an immune system compromised by stress. Landmark research by Candace Pert (1997) and others determined that various neuropeptides, secreted by the brain and other cells in the body, are triggered by emotional responses. Pert calls these "molecules of emotion," and they can either enhance or detract from the efficacy of the immune system. In essence, thoughts are energy—they can kill or heal.

Through the lens of holistic wellness, it is important to realize that the immune system does not reside solely in the body. The aspects that comprise your subtle anatomy also constitute your immune system.

The Stress and Disease Connection

Through the eyes of Western science, which views each human being as a machine, stress is often described as "wear and tear" on the physical body. Like a car that has more than 200,000 miles, the body has parts that typically break down and need to be fixed or replaced.

In this paradigm, these parts are often called "target organs," because they seem to be specifically targeted by neurochemical pathways produced by chronic stress. Any organ can be a target organ: hair, skin, blood vessels, joints, muscles, stomach, colon, and many others. In some people one organ may be targeted, whereas in others many organs can be affected. First, we'll take a look at disease and illness from a Western perspective and then conclude with a holistic view of the healing system. Western science has categorized stress-related disorders into two classifications: **nervous system–related disorders** and **immune system–related disorders**. The following is a brief listing of chronic diseases from each of these two categories.

Nervous System–Related Disorders

- *Tension headaches:* Tension headaches are produced by contractions of the muscles of the forehead, eyes, neck, and jaw. Increased pain results from increased contraction of these muscles. Lower back pain can also result from the same process. Although pain relievers such as ibuprofen or Advil are the most common source of relief, tension headaches have also been shown to dissipate with the use of meditation, mental imagery, and biofeedback.

- *Migraine headaches:* A migraine headache is a vascular headache. Symptoms can include a flash of light followed by intense throbbing, dizziness, and nausea. Migraines are thought to be related to the inability to express anger and frustration. Although several medications are prescribed for migraines, biofeedback, mental imagery, and the herb feverfew can be equally effective and used with fewer side effects.

- *Temporomandibular joint dysfunction:* Excessive contraction of the jaw muscles can lead to a phenomenon called temporomandibular joint dysfunction (TMJD). In many cases, people are unaware that they have this illness because the behavioral damage (grinding one's teeth) occurs during sleep. Like migraines, TMJD is often associated with the inability to express feelings of anger. Relaxation techniques, including biofeedback and progressive muscular relaxation, have been shown to be effective in decreasing the muscular tension associated with TMJD.

- *Bronchial asthma:* This is an illness in which a pronounced secretion of bronchial fluids causes a swelling of the smooth-muscle tissue of the large air passageways (bronchi). The onset of asthmatic attacks is often associated with anxiety. Currently drugs (e.g., prednisone) are the first method of treatment. However, relaxation techniques, including mental imagery, autogenic training, and meditation, may be just as effective in both delaying the onset and reducing the severity of these attacks.

- *Irritable bowel syndrome (IBS):* IBS is characterized by repeated bouts of abdominal pain or tenderness, cramps, diarrhea, nausea, constipation, and excessive flatulence. One reason IBS is considered so directly related to stress is that the hypothalamus, which controls appetite regulation (hunger and satiety), is closely associated with emotional regulation as well. Relaxation skills, including thermal biofeedback, progressive muscular relaxation, mental imagery, and reframing, can help to reduce existing levels of anxiety with promising results.

- *Coronary heart disease (CHD):* Elevated blood pressure (hypertension) is a significant risk factor for CHD. Stress hormones are often responsible for increasing blood pressure. When pressure is increased in a closed system, the risk of damage to vascular tissue due to increased turbulence is significantly increased. This damage to the vessel walls appears as small microtears, particularly in the intima lining of the coronary heart vessels, which supply the heart muscle (myocardium) itself with oxygen. As a way of healing these tears, several constituents floating in the blood bind with the damaged vascular cell tissue. Paradoxically, the primary "healing" agent is a sticky substance found floating in the blood serum called cholesterol, resulting in atherosclerosis, which can eventually lead to a heart attack.

Immune System–Related Disorders

- *The common cold and influenza:* Stress hormones (specifically cortisol) tend to destroy members of the white blood cell family, suppressing the immune system, hence leaving one susceptible to cold and flu.

- *Allergies:* An allergic reaction is initiated when a foreign substance (e.g., pollen, dust spores) enters the body. However, in some people, allergic reactions can occur just by thinking about a stimulus that provoked a previous attack. Allergic reactions are also more prevalent and severe in people who are prone to anxiety. Over-the-counter medications containing antihistamines and allergy shots are the most common approaches to dealing with allergies. Relaxation techniques also help minimize the effects of allergy-promoting substances.

- *Rheumatoid arthritis:* Rheumatoid arthritis, a joint and connective tissue disease, occurs when synovial membrane tissue swells, causing the joint to become inflamed. In time, synovial fluid may enter cartilage and bone tissue, causing further deterioration of the affected joint(s). The severity of arthritic pain is often related to episodes of stress, particularly suppressed anger. The treatment for this disease varies from pain relievers (e.g., ibuprofen or Advil) to steroid injections (e.g., cortisone), depending on the severity of pain and rate of joint deterioration. Relaxation techniques offer a complementary modality to help reduce these symptoms.

- *Ulcers and colitis:* More than 75 percent of ulcers are caused by the bacteria known as *Helicobacter*, creating an open wound that stomach acids only worsen. Treatment with antibiotics is now shown to be highly effective for a large percentage of people who have ulcers, yet two questions remain: What makes some people more vulnerable to *Helicobacter* than others? Why are antibiotics effective in only 75 percent of the cases of people with ulcers? Stress is thought to be the answer.

- *Cancer:* Cancer has proved to be one of the most perplexing diseases of our time, affecting one out of every three Americans. The body typically produces an abnormal cell once every 6 hours, but the natural killer cells of the immune system roam the body to search for and destroy these mutant cells. Stress hormones tend to suppress the immune system, allowing some mutant cells to become cancerous tumors. The treatments for cancer include chemotherapy, radiation, and surgery. However, coping skills involving cognitive restructuring, art therapy, and relaxation techniques including mental imagery and meditation are being used as complementary healing methods. Although these methods are not a cure for cancer in themselves, in some cases they seem to have a pronounced effect when used in combination with traditional medicine.

The Dynamics of Self-Healing

All things being equal, the body craves homeostasis and will do all it can to maintain a sense of balance. The body has a remarkable ability to heal itself, when given the chance to do so. Exercise, nutrition, and sleep play an essential role in the healing process, but so do our thoughts and feelings. Ultimately, disease, in all its many forms, is a sign that something is clearly out of balance among mind, body, and spirit. Chronic illness suggests that the body's attempt to regain that inner balance is compromised, most likely by lifestyle behaviors that don't support the healing process.

In his acclaimed book *Spontaneous Healing*, Dr. Andrew Weil documents the unique **self-healing** process of the human body, from the body's wisdom to kill germs by raising the body's core temperature clear down to the role of a specific enzyme to repair DNA. Deepak Chopra approaches the topic in a similar way in his book, *Quantum Healing*. For instance, Chopra explains that every cell in the body regenerates itself; some regenerate within a matter of days, others take years. The life span of red blood cells, for instance, is approximately 37 days. Nerve cells, it seems, take the longest. We know now that even brain cells have the capacity to regenerate. Consequently, within a 7-year time period, you have a completely new body of cells.

Most cancerous tumors take years, even decades, to grow. So why is it, then, that with a new body we have old tumors? Perhaps the answer resides in the vibrations of consciousness that surround and permeate each and every cell and that get passed on from generation to generation of cells through a process called entrainment. Entrainment is a physics term used to describe sympathetic resonance between two objects. It's commonly known in physics circles as the law of conservation of energy. The classic example of human entrainment is observed when women who live or work together begin to see a synchronization of their menstrual periods. Where there are neighboring energies, there is entrainment as well. Every cell vibrates with energy, as do tumors.

Unlike conventional wisdom that states that only brain cells hold some level of consciousness, it now appears that every cell in the body contains a vibration of consciousness. It is suggested that this imprint of conscious frequency is then transferred via entrainment from cell to cell, thus allowing a tumor to develop and keep growing, long after the original aberrant cells have died off. Can changes in one's thoughts change the vibration of cells? The answer appears to be yes, in a critical mass of people—those who demonstrate "spontaneous remission" of cancerous tumors.

Which emotions are prone to compromise the integrity of the immune system? In simplest terms, any lingering unresolved emotion associated with the fight-or-flight response. It would be too hard to single out anger and fear as the only culprits; however, both of these serve as umbrella emotions for literally hundreds of other emotions, which along with joy, love, and happiness constitute the full spectrum of feelings. As was mentioned earlier, when used properly, none of these emotions are bad, not even anger or fear. However, when left unresolved, anger or fear and all the many ways in which these two survival emotions manifest, over time, will suppress the immune system. In doing so, they open the door wide to a multitude of health-related problems.

Just as a preponderance of unhealthy emotions can suppress the immune system, positive thoughts and feelings can enhance it. Although all aspects of the inherent self-healing program are not fully understood, one thing is clear: Effective coping skills that help to resolve the causes of stress in tandem with effective relaxation skills that strive to return the body to homeostasis offer the best opportunity to engage the healing process to its fullest potential.

Chapter Summary

- An extended stress response beyond "physical survival" creates wear and tear on many physiological systems of the human body including the cardiovascular, digestive, and endocrine systems.

- Just as there is gross anatomy, there is also subtle anatomy, specifically the human energy field and the meridian and chakra systems, all of which are connected to the mind-body-spirit continuum.

- Prolonged (chronic) stress definitely has an impact on the immune system—in essence, suppressing it—thus making one more vulnerable to disease and illness.

- The stress and disease connection is very real. Chronic stress is now related to a number of health-related problems from the common cold to cancer.

- The body actually needs some stress (e.g., exercise), but also craves homeostasis. Many, if not all, stress management techniques promote self-healing dynamics by helping the body return to homeostasis.

Additional Resources

Anodea, J. *Eastern Body, Western Mind*. Berkeley, CA: Celestial Arts; 2004.

APA Online. Stress Affects Immunity in Ways Related to Stress Type and Duration, As Shown by Nearly 300 Studies. Media Information. July 4, 2004. http://www.apa.org/releases/stress_immune.html. Accessed October 2, 2012.

Arntz, W., Chasse, B., & Vicente, M. *What the Bleep Do We Know!?* Deerfield Beach, FL: Health Communications; 2005.

Chopra, D. *Quantum Healing*. New York: Bantam; 1990.

Dale, C. *The Subtle Body: An Encyclopedia of Your Energetic Body*. Boulder, CO: Sounds True; 2009.

Dispenza, J. *Evolve Your Brain: The Science of Changing Your Mind*. Deerfield Beach, FL: Health Communications; 2007.

Eden, D. *Energy Medicine*. New York: Tarcher/Putnam; 2008.

Gerber, R. *Vibrational Medicine* (3rd ed.). Rochester, VT: Bear & Co.; 2001.

Lipton, B. *The Biology of Belief: Unleashing the Power of Consciousness, Matter, and Miracles*. Santa Rosa, CA: Mountain of Love/Elite; 2008.

Mate, G. *When the Body Says No: Exploring the Stress and Disease Connection*. New York: Wiley; 2011.

McTaggart, L. *The Field*. New York: Harper Collins; 2008.

Ornish, D. *Love and Survival*. New York: Harper Collins; 1998.

Pert, C. *Molecules of Emotion*. New York: Scribner; 1997.

Powell, D., & Institute of Noetic Sciences. *The 2007 Shift Report: Evidence of a World Transforming*. Petaluma, CA: Institute of Noetic Sciences; 2007, pp. 28–36.

Segerstrom, S. C., & Miller, G. E. Psychological stress and the Human Immune System: A Meta-Analytical Study of 30 Years of Inquiry. *Psychological Bulletin* 130(4):601–630, 2004.

Swanson, C. *Life Force: The Scientific Basis* (2nd ed.). Tucson, AZ: Poseidia Press; 2009.

Weil, A. *Spontaneous Healing*. New York: Knopf; 2000.

EXERCISE 2.1: Physical Symptoms Questionnaire

Please look over this list of stress-related symptoms and circle how often they have occurred in the past week, how severe they seemed to you, and how long they lasted. Then reflect on the past week's workload and see if you notice any connection.

	How Often? (number of days in the past week)	How Severe? (1 = mild, 5 = severe)	How Long? (1 = 1 hour, 5 = all day)
1. Tension headache	0 1 2 3 4 5 6 7	1 2 3 4 5	1 2 3 4 5
2. Migraine headache	0 1 2 3 4 5 6 7	1 2 3 4 5	1 2 3 4 5
3. Muscle tension (neck and/or shoulders)	0 1 2 3 4 5 6 7	1 2 3 4 5	1 2 3 4 5
4. Muscle tension (lower back)	0 1 2 3 4 5 6 7	1 2 3 4 5	1 2 3 4 5
5. Joint pain	0 1 2 3 4 5 6 7	1 2 3 4 5	1 2 3 4 5
6 Cold	0 1 2 3 4 5 6 7	1 2 3 4 5	1 2 3 4 5
7. Flu	0 1 2 3 4 5 6 7	1 2 3 4 5	1 2 3 4 5
8. Stomachache	0 1 2 3 4 5 6 7	1 2 3 4 5	1 2 3 4 5
9. Stomach/abdominal bloating/distention/gas	0 1 2 3 4 5 6 7	1 2 3 4 5	1 2 3 4 5
10. Diarrhea	0 1 2 3 4 5 6 7	1 2 3 4 5	1 2 3 4 5
11. Constipation	0 1 2 3 4 5 6 7	1 2 3 4 5	1 2 3 4 5
12. Ulcer flare-up	0 1 2 3 4 5 6 7	1 2 3 4 5	1 2 3 4 5
13. Asthma attack	0 1 2 3 4 5 6 7	1 2 3 4 5	1 2 3 4 5
14. Allergies	0 1 2 3 4 5 6 7	1 2 3 4 5	1 2 3 4 5
15 Canker/cold sores	0 1 2 3 4 5 6 7	1 2 3 4 5	1 2 3 4 5
16. Dizzy spells	0 1 2 3 4 5 6 7	1 2 3 4 5	1 2 3 4 5
17. Heart palpitations (racing heart)	0 1 2 3 4 5 6 7	1 2 3 4 5	1 2 3 4 5
18. TMJD	0 1 2 3 4 5 6 7	1 2 3 4 5	1 2 3 4 5
19. Insomnia	0 1 2 3 4 5 6 7	1 2 3 4 5	1 2 3 4 5
20. Nightmares	0 1 2 3 4 5 6 7	1 2 3 4 5	1 2 3 4 5
21. Fatigue	0 1 2 3 4 5 6 7	1 2 3 4 5	1 2 3 4 5
22. Hemorrhoids	0 1 2 3 4 5 6 7	1 2 3 4 5	1 2 3 4 5
23. Pimples/acne	0 1 2 3 4 5 6 7	1 2 3 4 5	1 2 3 4 5
24. Cramps	0 1 2 3 4 5 6 7	1 2 3 4 5	1 2 3 4 5
25. Frequent accidents	0 1 2 3 4 5 6 7	1 2 3 4 5	1 2 3 4 5
26. Other (please specify) _____	0 1 2 3 4 5 6 7	1 2 3 4 5	1 2 3 4 5

Score: Look over this entire list. Do you observe any patterns or relationships between your stress levels and your physical health? A value over 30 points may indicate a stress-related health problem. If it seems to you that these symptoms are related to undue stress, they probably are. Although medical treatment is advocated when necessary, the regular use of relaxation techniques may lessen the intensity, frequency, and duration of these episodes.

EXERCISE 2.2: Your Picture of Health

We all have an idea of what ideal health is. Many of us take our health for granted until something goes wrong to remind us that our picture of health is compromised and less than ideal. Although health may seem to be objective, it will certainly vary from person to person over the entire aging process. The following statements are based on characteristics associated with longevity and a healthy quality of life (none of which considers any genetic factors). Rather than answering the questions to see how long you may live, please complete this inventory to determine your current picture of health.

	3 = Often	2 = Sometimes	1 = Rarely	0 = Never

	3	2	1	0
1. With rare exception, I sleep an average of 7 to 8 hours each night.	3	2	1	0
2. I tend to eat my meals at the same time each day.	3	2	1	0
3. I keep my bedtime consistent every night.	3	2	1	0
4. I do cardiovascular exercise at least three times per week.	3	2	1	0
5. My weight is considered ideal for my height.	3	2	1	0
6. Without exception, my alcohol consumption is in moderation.	3	2	1	0
7. I consider my nutritional habits to be exceptional.	3	2	1	0
8. My health status is considered excellent, with no pre-existing conditions.	3	2	1	0
9. I neither smoke, nor participate in the use of recreational drugs.	3	2	1	0
10. I have a solid group of friends with whom I socialize regularly.	3	2	1	0
TOTAL SCORE				

Score: 26–30 points = Excellent health habits
20–25 points = Moderate health habits
14–19 points = Questionable health habits
0–13 points = Poor health habits

EXERCISE 2.3: Subtle Anatomy Energy Map

The accompanying figure is an outline of the human body highlighted with the seven primary chakras. Note the body region associated with each chakra and then take a moment to identify any health issues or concerns associated within this specific region of your body. Write your observations on the following pages. Once you have done this, refer back to earlier in this text and ask yourself honestly if you happen to recognize any connection between the important aspects of the chakra(s) associated with the region(s) in which you have indicated a specific health concern.

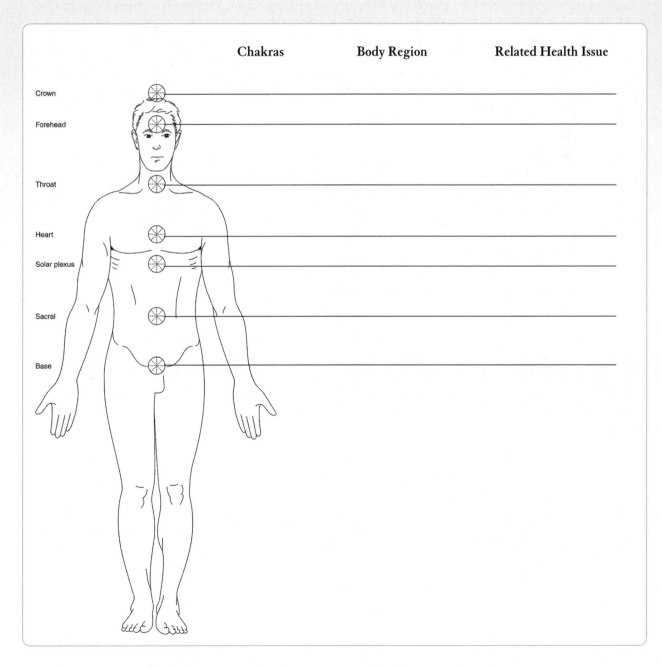

EXERCISE 2.4: Energy Ball Exercise

This is a relaxation technique taught to me by the renowned bioenergy healers Mietek and Margaret Wirkus. I have adapted and taught this technique many times in classes and workshops throughout the country with great success. Although it was introduced to me as the first of many healing techniques in bioenergy healing, first and foremost, this is a relaxation exercise. This technique is done through the following steps:

1. Begin by sitting comfortably with your legs crossed and your back straight. You may wish to sit up against a wall. In this exercise, it really helps to keep your back straight. Close your eyes and focus your attention on your breathing. Take a moment to clear your mind of distracting thoughts and feelings. Place your attention on your breathing. If it helps to have some soft instrumental music in the background, then try this as well. Sometimes, to set the tone, it helps to think of a happy moment in your life, when you were filled with utter joy. Allow this feeling to resonate within every cell in your body. Then take a couple of comfortably slow deep breaths to let it be absorbed.

2. Unlike belly breathing, which is typically taught in relaxation workshops, this particular exercise requires that you focus your attention on the upper lobes of your lungs. Take a moment to place your hands on your upper chest to become fully conscious of your upper lungs. Then take five breaths, breathing comfortably slow and deep into your upper lungs.

3. Once you have completed this, then place your hands on your knees and repeat this breathing style by taking five slow deep breaths. As you exhale, repeat this phrase to yourself, *"My body is calm and relaxed."* As you say this, feel a deep sense of relaxation throughout your body with each exhalation.

4. Next, being fully conscious of your hands resting on your knees or thighs palms up, take five more deep breaths, but this time as you exhale, repeat this phrase to yourself, *"I am my hands."* With each breath, place all of your concentration, all of your attention, on your hands. Sense what your hands feel like. Are they warm? If so, where? On the palms, fingertips, or backs of your hands? Where? Again, remind yourself of the phrase, *"I am my hands."*

5. Using your imagination, picture a small window in the center of each palm, about the size of a dime. Imagine now that as you breathe, air comes not only into your nose or mouth, but also into your hands. If you prefer, you may use the image of light coming into your palms. Imagine that as you inhale, air or light enters your palms and moves up your arms, to the center (heart space) of your upper chest. As you exhale, feel the energy return from where it entered through your hands. Try repeating this several times, again taking several slow deep breaths and again repeating to yourself, *"I am my hands."*

6. Next, slowly lift your hands off your knees or thighs so that they rest comfortably in the air, suspended in front of your chest, with the palms facing up, toward the ceiling.

EXERCISE 2.4: Energy Ball Exercise cont....

7. Next, fully conscious of your hands, take five more deep breaths. As you exhale each breath, repeat the phrase, *"I am my hands."* With each breath, place all of your concentration, all of your attention, on your hands. Again sense what your hands feel like. Are they warm? If so, where? On the palms, the fingertips, the backs of your hands? Do your hands feel heavy? If so, how heavy? What other sensations do you feel? Again, remind yourself as you exhale, *"I am my hands."* As you do this, notice if you see any colors.

8. Now, keeping your hands about 10–12 inches apart, allow the palms of each hand to face each other. Again using your imagination, picture or sense that between your hands is a large sponge ball. As you hold this ball, slowly press in and then release. What do you feel as you do this? Again, bring your hands closer together without touching, then begin to separate them farther apart. Ask yourself, what do you feel? At what distance is the sensation the strongest?

9. Now, placing the palms of your hands about 6–12 inches apart, imagine that there is a beam of light from palm to palm, window to window. Take a slow deep breath and as you exhale, slowly compress the beam by slowly bringing your palms together without touching. Then, during the next inhalation, allow your hands to separate again slowly. What do you feel as you do this? Is the sensation between your hands stronger when you inhale or exhale?

10. Again, return to the sensation between your hands. Between your hands is a ball of energy, the healing energy ball. Take this ball of energy and place it into a region of your body that feels stressed or desires healing. If you are completely relaxed, try placing this energy in your heart. Take five slow deep breaths and repeat the phrase, *"My body is calm and relaxed."* Feel a sense of relaxation throughout your entire body. Take one final slow deep breath and enjoy this sensation again.

11. When you are done, slowly place your hands back on your knees or thighs. Recognize that although you feel relaxed, you feel energized. When you are ready, open your eyes to a soft gaze in front of you. Then make yourself aware of your surroundings so that you may continue on with your daily activities.

EXERCISE 2.5: Subtle Energy System "Vitamins"

Donna Eden is a renowned energy healer with a gift for not only observing subtle energies, but also teaching others how to regulate their subtle energy for enhanced health and well-being. Integrating the flow of energy through the human aura, chakras, and meridians, Donna combines a variety of self-help techniques so that, in her words, "You keep your energies humming and vibrant." The following are ideas and suggestions that Donna teaches in her energy medicine workshops, exercises that she calls energy system vitamins. She recommends that you do this short routine daily.

Three Body Taps: There are various acupuncture/acupressure points that, when stimulated, will help direct the flow of energy, and thus increase your vitality and help boost your immune system.

1. *Chest bone tap:* Known to acupuncturists as KD-27 (from points on the kidney meridian), gently tap on the top of your chest bone just below the medial ends of the two clavicles for about 15–20 seconds. This should open your breathing, relax the chest, and tonify the immune system.

2. *Thymus gland tap:* Your thymus gland (an important gland of the immune system) resides between your throat and your heart, but the point to tap is in the center of your chest bone about 2 inches below KD-27. Once you have found this point, tap on it with your fingertips for about 15–20 seconds.

3. *Spleen points tap:* The spleen is also an essential organ to your immune system. The spleen points are located on the rib cage, directly below your nipples. Once you have found these two points, tap vigorously with your fingers for about 15–20 seconds.

Cross Crawl Movements: To do the cross crawl, first you must understand that the left side of the brain controls the right side of the body, and vice versa. Many people's energies are not vibrant or harmonized due to stagnation from the lack of neural energy from the right to left or left to right sides of the brain. Poor energy movement is referred to as a homolateral pattern, and this will affect thought processes, coordination, and vitality. Sitting or standing, raise your right knee and your left arm (you can touch knee to elbow if you'd like). Follow this by raising your left knee and your right arm. Twist your torso so that your arms cross the mid-point of your body. Try this movement pattern for about 30–60 seconds.

The Crown Pull: Placing your hands on top of your forehead and crown of the head, imagine that your fingers are pulling from the center down to your ears, in a motion starting from the front of your head and working to the back of your skull. The purpose of this exercise is to move stagnant energy from the top of your head, and it helps to open the crown chakra. This exercise can be helpful in relieving headaches, too.

Zip Up: The central meridian (in the front of your body), also known as the conception vessel, can easily become congested, open, or exposed to others' energy. This technique invites you to close your auric field as a means of health and protection. Start by tapping the KD-27 point again and then reach down to the top of your thighs with your right (or left) hand, take a deep breath, and pull up as if you were pulling up a zipper, clear up to your chin. Repeat this three times. By pulling up, you trace the directional flow of the central meridian and strengthen the flow of energy. This technique is recommended before making speeches or dealing with someone who is very angry.

The Emotions: From a Motivation of Fear to a Motivation of Love

"Until you extend the circle of compassion to all living things, you will not find inner peace."

— Albert Schweitzer, MD

Love. Anger. Grief. Happiness. Anxiety. Bliss. Sorrow. Guilt. Mirth. Compassion. Despair. Joy. Emotional well-being can best be described as the ability to feel and express the entire range of human emotions, and to control them, not be controlled by them. This may sound like a tall order, but it's not impossible. The spectrum of human emotions spans the continuum from anger to love, and everything in between. Humans are thought to be unique among all the earth's creatures in our capacity to exhibit such an array of emotions. This gift comes with a price. We also seem to be the only species on the planet that can become a slave to our emotions and spiritually immobilized in the process.

Healthy Emotions

Given this definition of emotional well-being, all emotions are considered part of the spectrum, yet the question begs to be asked: What constitutes a **healthy emotion**? From a holistic perspective, the expression of all emotions is considered healthy, because to deny the ability to feel and express any emotion suggests a serious emotional imbalance. Each sensation in the spectrum of human emotions is included in the software of the human mind for a reason—to feel and express ourselves in every possible way. The expression of each emotion also allows a release of feelings, or what is more commonly known as a "catharsis."

Many people consider joy, bliss, euphoria, and love to be the healthy emotions, whereas anger and fear are labeled as unhealthy. In truth, anger and fear are also considered to be healthy emotions, when they are used specifically for their intended purpose—to get out of harm's way. Both anger and fear are considered to be survival emotions and therefore essential for human life. Each is only meant to last long enough to get out of physical danger. Healthy emotions quickly become unhealthy when they last longer than the intended purpose for which they serve. Unhealthy emotions appear like a black cloud hanging over our heads. Left unresolved, they can cause serious problems in the mind-body-spirit dynamics of optimal health.

Unhealthy Emotions

Ideally, anger, fear, and all the many ways in which they manifest in the spectrum of human emotions serve to protect you. Upon the slightest inkling of danger, they summon an alarm to move rapidly into a state of physical survival. Both anger and fear are only meant to last long enough to get us out of physical danger, which typically takes seconds, perhaps minutes, but not much longer. When feelings of anger and/or fear linger longer than the amount of time needed to reach a place of safety, then we do not control our emotions, they control us! As such, our emotional well-being is greatly compromised.

When we hang on to feelings of anger or fear, rather than letting them go, we literally give our power away. To feel "emotionally drained" is the hallmark of when a healthy emotion becomes unhealthy. Prolonged anger, fear, grief, and depression are not only classic, but also all too common examples of unhealthy emotions reflected on the faces of Americans everywhere today.

The Stress Emotions: Anger and Fear

Stated simply, anger and fear are the two primary stress emotions. Anger is the fight response. Fear is the flight response. Anger is exhibited in a great many ways, including impatience, guilt, envy, indignation, intimidation, intolerance, frustration, rage, prejudice, and hostility. Like anger, the color of fear also comes in many hues, including doubt, embarrassment, anxiety, apprehension, insecurity, and paranoia, to name a few. A quick glance at the news headlines on any given day reveals the extreme level of stress in the world, with anger and fear underscoring nearly every news story. From school shootings and suicides to road rage, global financial problems, and acts of international terrorism, anger has increasingly become part of the human landscape. For this reason it merits attention.

Mismanaged Anger Styles

Every episode of anger is the result of an unmet expectation. On average, the typical person gets angry about 15 to 20 times per day. When one realizes how anger can manifest, from impatience to rage, this number begins to make more sense. Given the number of expectations one has in the course of a day, this number may appear quite low. Although anger can be felt and expressed in a great many ways, there are four specific patterns in which people from all global cultures tend to mismanage their anger. Typically, we tend to exhibit all of these, but it has been noted that one mismanaged anger style seems to dominate our personality. Please read through this list and note any signs of familiarity.

- *The somatizer:* The **somatizer** is best described as a person who doesn't express his or her anger; instead, the person suppresses it. Unexpressed emotions carry a price, and in this case the body (soma) pays this price with serious physical problems, including migraine headaches, temporomandibular joint dysfunction (TMJD), ulcers, liver problems, hypertension, and rheumatoid arthritis. Women, more than men, tend to be somatizers.

- *The self-punisher:* **Self-punishers** feel guilty about feeling angry; hence, they tend to substitute feelings of anger for some obsessive behavior including excess eating, drinking, exercise, shopping, and sex. Sadly, self-mutilators (cutters) also fall into this category.

- *The exploder:* The **exploder**'s main outlet of anger is intimidation. Like a volcano, exploders erupt, spewing their hot lava in the direction of the perceived threat. Road rage, foul language, acts of violence, bullying, and hostility top the list of this mismanaged anger style. Explosive behavior is more common in men, but women can exhibit it as well.

- *The underhander:* Revenge is a motive for **underhanders** in what they perceive to be considered socially acceptable behavior, particularly at the worksite. Sarcasm is the most common form of underhanded behavior, but there are other passive–aggressive behaviors in this style of mismanaged anger as well.

In each of these **mismanaged anger styles**, prolonged anger results in the person trying to control him- or herself (somatizer and self-punisher) or others (exploder and underhander). Instead, they are being controlled by their anger and giving their power away. We now know that if we wish to change our behavior, we first have to identify what we are doing so we can then learn to behave differently. These mismanaged anger styles are merely labels to help you identify undesirable behaviors associated with unresolved issues. Exercises 3.1 and 3.2 are inventories to help you identify which mismanaged anger style dominates your personality. Exercise 3.3 invites you to think up ways to creatively manage your anger, so that you can begin to control it, and not have it control you. Grieving also is a part of anger. Exercise 3.5 invites you to explore any unresolved issues through the Mandala of Healthy Grieving exercise.

Depression: The Black Cloud of Stress

It's no secret that **depression** is a huge problem in U.S. culture. Some estimates suggest that as much as one quarter of the population takes prescribed antidepressants. Although many factors are involved with depression, including an imbalance of the neurochemicals seratonin and dopamine, a holistic approach to stress suggests that there is a strong relationship between an emotional imbalance and a chemical imbalance. Is there a connection between depression and anger? Most holistic practitioners believe so. As the joke goes, "Depression is anger without the enthusiasm." Although pharmaceuticals may assist in bringing balance to one's brain chemistry, medications don't heal emotional wounds. As the Food and Drug Administration (FDA) announced, in some cases, medications may actually make things worse, including increasing suicidal urges.

Facing Your Fear

Simply stated, fear is a response to physical danger. Rarely in this day and age, however, do we encounter physical danger that requires us to run away and hide. However, the emotion of fear is there in case we do. Self-promoted feelings of fear and worry are extremely prevalent in today's society, and the reasons have more to do with a perceived sense of failure, rejection, and the unknown than any real physical danger. Credit card debt, struggling relationships, loss of a job, and terminal illnesses tend to top a long list of common chronic stressors associated with fear and anxiety.

If rational fears are triggered by physical danger, then one might assume that fear under any other prolonged circumstance is irrational. In truth, any fear that is not quickly resolved is often referred to as unwarranted or **irrational fear**, and this type of fear can certainly become emotionally draining. Unlike anger, which is a very energizing emotion, fear is energy-depleting. However, like unresolved anger, over time, chronic fear, and the stress hormones associated with it, can be very toxic to the body.

For fear to be fully resolved, it must be confronted diplomatically. This means that each circumstance where fear surfaces must be faced, without a loss of self-esteem. As the expression goes, "Face your fear and it will disappear." If other people are involved, then the confrontation must not make them defensive or angry, beccause this will only perpetuate the problem. Diplomacy is essential with each confrontation. Exercise 3.4, "Confrontation of a Stressor," addresses this issue of making peace with fear.

From a Motivation of Fear Toward a Motivation of Love

One of the primary areas of study in the field of psychology is the aspect of motivational behavior—why we do the things we do. A conclusion by many is that, by and large, most of our behaviors are fear-based thoughts and actions (anger being considered an aspect of fear). This perspective suggests that humans operate from a fight-or-flight response the majority of time. Although this may sound preposterous, a quick glance through the annals of human history supports this theory. From a personal perspective, consider making a habit of observing your thoughts and behaviors to determine the source of motivation behind these actions. You may be surprised at the outcome.

Moving from fear to love means responding rather than reacting to stress. It means showing tolerance rather than anger, patience rather than hostility, forgiveness rather than resentment, and humor rather than arrogance. Ultimately, it means not placing yourself first all the time and viewing the bigger picture with an open heart rather than a closed mind. All humans are capable of this endeavor!

Joy and Happiness: The Other (Eustress) Emotions

Not all stress is bad. Good stress is a necessary part of life, as are all the emotions associated with it. Joy, happiness, love, compassion, and all the feelings that hearty laughter brings are essential to optimal health. These emotions, now known as positive psychology, generate a whole pharmacopia of beneficial neuropeptides that enhance the immune system. Emotional well-being is truly a balance of emotional experiences. By not seeking a balance to the full emotional spectrum with frequent exposure to the emotions associated with good stress, all aspects of our personal wellness paradigm are affected. Therefore, it's in our best interest to seek out the peak experiences, the joyful moments, and the comic relief that give balance to our lives. Moreover, it is these emotions that, when combined with a host of coping skills and relaxation techniques, create very powerful results.

The Pursuit of Happiness

What do scientific studies tell us about happiness? Researchers have looked at all kinds of indices, from stress hormones to neuropeptides, cardiac activity, facial coding (smiles per day), creative pursuits, nutritional diets, and spending habits. Here are some conclusions from the current research on joy and happiness, known in research circles as *subjective social well-being*:

- Until people's basic needs are met (food, clothing, shelter, income), happiness is elusive. (Graham, 2010)

- There is a strong correlation between happiness and trust. If trust is lacking, happiness is nonexistent. Trust is a prerequisite for happiness. (Robinson, 2008)

- Serotonin, a neurotransmitter, seems to be a chemical by-product of feeling happy. A lack of serotonin is associated with depression, hence serotonin's nickname of the "happiness hormone." Carbohydrates may increase serotonin levels, but carbohydrates do not necessarily make one happy. (Sommers, 1999)

- If serotonin is the happy hormone, then oxytocin is considered to be the "love hormone," and love often makes people feel happy.

- Having choices (freedom) makes people happy to a point, after which too many choices make people feel overwhelmed and eventually stressed. (Nauert, 2006)

- Money does not equate with happiness, but poverty can promote stress. (Deaton, 2008)

- There is a strong correlation between happiness and the ability to be creative, according to findings by Harvard researcher Teresa Amabile. (2005)

- Fulfilling relationships are the cornerstone to lifelong happiness. (Buettner, 2010)

- The happiest people aren't always found living on tropical islands. Eric Weiner, the author of the bestseller, *The Geography of Bliss*, states that people in Iceland, Denmark, Sweden, Holland, and Switzerland rank as some of the happiest people on the planet. (The people of Moldova ranked last.) (Weiner, 2008)

First and foremost, happiness is a perception—a thought combined with an emotion generated from within. Money, cars, clothing, food, or vacations in Tahiti may seem to promote happiness, but the real measure of happiness is your attitude—your ability to appreciate these things. In the words of Abraham Lincoln, "People are about as happy as they make their minds up to be." How would you rate your level of happiness? You can find out more clearly by completing Exercise 3.6, "The Key to Happiness Survey."

Exercises 3.6 and 3.7 offer you a chance to explore the emotions of joy, love, and compassion.

Chapter Summary

- The emotional spectrum ranges from fear to love. All emotions are thought to have a reason. They are considered healthy emotions when they are used for their intended purpose. They are consider unhealthy when they last longer than needed for their purpose.

- There are two stress emotions, anger (fight) and fear (flight). They are considered to be survival emotions for physical threats.

- Prolonged anger is considered a negative emotion. There are four mismanaged anger styles in which people hang on to anger: the somatizer, exploder, self-punisher, and underhander.

- Depression and anger are deeply entwined. Some suggest that depression is rooted in unresolved anger issues (depression is anger turned inward).

- Holistic stress management can be described as moving from a motivation of fear to a motivation of love and compassion.

- Two emotions associated with good stress (eustress) are joy and happiness.

Additional Resources

Amabile, T., et al. Affect and Creativity at Work. *Administrative Science Quarterly 50*:367–403, 2005.

Bradbury, T., & Graems, J. *Emotional Intellegence 2.0*. San Diego, CA: Talentsmart; 2009.

Buettner, D. *Thrive: Finding Happiness the Blue Zone Way*. Washington, DC: National Geographic; 2010.

Cox, D., Bruckner, K., & Stabb, S. *The Anger Advantage*. New York: Broadway Books; 2003.

Deaton, A. Income, Health, and Well-Being Around the World: Evidence from the Gallup World Poll. *Journal of Economic Perspectives 22*(2):53–72, 2008.

Emmons, R. *Thanks: How the Science of Gratitude Can Make You Happier*. New York: Houghton Mifflin; 2007.

Fleeman, W. *Pathways to Peace: Anger Management Workbook*. Alameda, CA: Hunter House; 2003.

Gilbert, D. *Stumbling on Happiness*. New York: Vintage Press; 2007.

Graham, C. *Happiness Around the World: The Paradox of Happy Peasants and Miserable Millionaires*. Oxford: Oxford University Press; 2012.

Lerner, H. *The Dance of Anger* (20th anniv. ed.). New York: Harper & Row; 2005.

Naiman, L. *Happiness at Work*. May 2007. http://www.creativityatwork.com/blog/2007/05/28/creativity-at-work-newsletter-happiness/. Accessed October 2, 2012.

Nauert, R. *Does Freedom of Choice Ensure Happiness?* July 18, 2006. http://psychcentral.com/news/2006/07/18/does-freedom-of-choice-ensure-happiness/101.html. Accessed July 18, 2012.

Robinson, J. Happiness Flows from Trust. *National Post*. October 24, 2008. http://www.nationalpost.com/story.html?id=906300. Accessed July 18, 2012.

Seligman, M. *Authentic Happiness: Using the New Positive Psychology to Realize Your Potential for Lasting Fulfillment*. New York: Free Press; 2003.

Seligman, M. *What You Can Change and What You Can't: The Complete Guide to Successful Self-Improvement*. New York: Ballantine Books; 2007.

Skog, S. *Depression: What Your Body Is Trying to Tell You*. New York: Wholecare; 2001.

Sommers, E. *Food and Mood*. New York: Henry Holt & Co.; 1999.

Sriparna. *Serotonin—The Molecule of Happiness*. May 30, 2012. http://hubpages.com/hub/Serotonin-The-Molecule-of-Happiness. Accessed October 2, 2012.

Tavris, C. *Anger: The Misunderstood Emotion*. New York: Touchstone; 1989.

Warren, N. C. *Make Anger Your Ally*. New York: Simon & Schuster; 1999.

Weiner, E. *The Geography of Bliss*. New York: Twelve Books; 2009.

Williams, R. *Anger Kills*. New York: Harper Collins; 1998.

Witvliet, C. Surprised by Happiness. *Huffington Post*. November 25, 2010. http://www.huffingtonpost.com/charlotte-vanoyen-witvliet-phd/surprised-by-happiness-wh_b_787126.html. Accessed July 18, 2012.

EXERCISE 3.1: Anger Recognition Checklist

"He who angers you, conquers you."— Elizabeth Kenny

The following is a quick exercise to understand how anger can surface in the course of a normal working day and how you *may* mismanage it. Please place a check mark in front of any of the following that apply to you when you "get angry" or "feel frustrated or upset." After completing this section, please refer to the bottom right-hand corner and estimate the number of anger episodes, on average, you experience per day.

When I feel angry, my anger tends to surface in the following ways:

_____ anxious

_____ depressed

_____ overeat

_____ start dieting

_____ trouble sleeping

_____ excessive sleeping

_____ careless driving

_____ chronic fatigue

_____ abuse alcohol/drugs

_____ explode in rage

_____ cold withdrawal

_____ tension headaches

_____ migraine headaches

_____ use sarcasm

_____ hostile joking

_____ accident prone

_____ guilty and self-blaming

_____ smoke or drink

_____ high blood pressure

_____ frequent nightmares

_____ tendency to harp or nag

_____ intellectualize

_____ upset stomach (e.g., gas, cramps, IBS)

_____ muscle tension (neck, lower back)

_____ swear and/or name call

_____ cry

_____ threaten others

_____ buy things

_____ frequent lateness

_____ never feel angry

_____ clenched jaw muscles, TMJD

_____ bored

_____ nausea, vomiting

_____ skin problems

_____ easily irritable

_____ sexual difficulty

_____ sexual apathy

_____ busy work (clean, straighten)

_____ sulk

_____ hit, throw things

_____ complain, whine

_____ cut/mutilate myself

_____ insomnia

_____ promiscuity

_____ help others

_____ Other? _____

* My average number of anger episodes

per day is _____.

EXERCISE 3.2: Mismanaged Anger Style Indicator

Part I: Check the statements that are true for you the majority of the time.

_____ 1. Even though I may wish to complain, I usually don't.

_____ 2. When upset, I have a habit of slamming, punching, or breaking things.

_____ 3. When I feel guilty, I have been known to contemplate self-destructive behaviors.

_____ 4. I can be really nice to people, but then back-stab them when they're not around.

_____ 5. I have a habit of grinding my teeth at night.

_____ 6. When I am really irritated or frustrated by others, I tend to intimidate them.

_____ 7. When I am frustrated, I feel like going shopping and spending money.

_____ 8. I can manipulate people without them even knowing it.

_____ 9. It's fair to say that I rarely, if ever, get angry or mad.

_____ 10. I have been known to talk back to people of authority.

_____ 11. Sleeping in is a good way to forget about my problems and frustrations.

_____ 12. Watching TV or playing video games offers a good escape from my frustrations.

_____ 13. If I complain, I feel people won't like me as much, so I usually don't.

_____ 14. When driving at times, I feel like I want to run over people with my car.

_____ 15. When I get mad or frustrated, I have been known to eat to calm my nerves.

_____ 16. I plan a script or rehearse what I am going to say to win a conflict.

_____ 17. It's hard/uncomfortable for me to say the words "I am angry."

_____ 18. I usually try to get the final say in situations with others.

_____ 19. I have been known to use alcohol and/or drugs to deal with my anger feelings.

_____ 20. By and large, I tend to agree with the statement, "Don't get mad, get even."

_____ 21. I tend to keep my feelings to myself.

_____ 22. When I get angry, I have been known to swear a lot.

_____ 23. I usually feel guilty about feeling angry, frustrated, or annoyed.

_____ 24. It's OK to use sarcasm to make a point.

_____ 25. I am the kind of person who calms the waters when tempers flare at home or work.

_____ 26. It's easy to say the words "I am angry" or "I am pissed" and really mean it.

_____ 27. On more than one occasion, I have imagined taking my own life.

_____ 28. I think of various ways to put people down.

_____ 29. Typically, I place the needs of others before myself.

_____ 30. I suffer from migraine headaches, TMJD, rheumatoid arthritis, or lupus.

EXERCISE 3.2: Mismanaged Anger Style Indicator cont....

Part II: Score Sheet

Write down the numbers of the statements that you have checked off:

_____

As a rule, we tend to engage in all of these behaviors at some time; however, some behaviors are very common whereas others are more occasional, suggesting that when certain predominant behaviors are grouped together they reveal a specific style of mismanaged anger. Mismanaged anger leads to a host of serious problems for both ourselves and others. By learning to recognize series of behaviors that fall into one or perhaps two categories, we can more easily identify this behavior and then make a strategy to change or modify it so that stress is reduced rather than perpetuated. Labels are good to identify behaviors, but they are not meant to serve as a mismanaged scarlet letter.

- If you have four or more answers from these choices—1, 5, 9, 13, 17, 21, 25, 29, 30—your mismanaged anger style suggests you might be a somatizer.

- If you have four or more answers from these choices—3, 7, 11, 12, 15, 19, 23, 27—your mismanaged anger style suggests you might be a self-punisher.

- If you have four or more answers from these choices—2, 6, 10, 14, 18, 22, 26—your mismanaged anger style suggests you might be an exploder.

- If you have four or more answers from these choices—4, 8, 16, 20, 24, 28—your mismanaged anger style suggests you might be an underhander.

EXERCISE 3.3: Creative Anger Management Skills Action Plan

Dealing with anger effectively means working to resolve the issues and expectations that surfaced from the anger episode. There are many ways to creatively resolve anger so that you reclaim your emotional sovereignty. The following is a synthesis of suggestions from a variety of sources. Read through each suggestion and below it write a description of what steps you can implement to creatively manage your anger and keep each episode of anger within a healthy time period.

1. Know your anger style: What is your most predominant mismanaged anger style?

_____

2. Learn to self-monitor your anger: Reflect on the past day's events (including listening to the news) and estimate the number of times you felt anger.

_____

3. Learn to de-escalate your anger: List three ways to let off steam (e.g., leave the room, take a big sigh, count to 10, etc.).

a. _____   b. _____   c. _____

4. Learn to out-think your anger: Many times anger results from insufficient information. Identify an anger situation and reprocess the information to neutralize your anger feelings.

_____

5. Get comfortable with all your feelings: Some people have a hard time saying the phrase "I am angry" or "I feel angry." Are you one of them? Please explain.

_____

6. Plan in advance: Although avoidance is not advocated, making plans to work around a problem is known as the path of least resistance. Identify a current frustration and then list three things you can do as an action plan to rise above the occasion.

a. _____   b. _____   c. _____

7. Develop a strong support system: List three people to whom you can turn to vent your frustrations as well as provide an objective voice about your stressful situation.

_____

8. Develop realistic expectations for yourself and others: Pick one anger situation you have had today (or yesterday), identify the expectation that wasn't met, and then refine the expectation.

Unmet expectation: _____

Refined expectation: _____

9. Turn complaints into requests: As the expression goes, you catch more flies with honey than vinegar. Script a phrase that you can use to incorporate the magic of request.

_____

10. Make past anger pass: Letting go of anger begins with forgiveness. List three people you feel have violated you in some way, with whom the steps of forgiveness need to be taken.

a. _____   b. _____   c. _____

EXERCISE 3.4: Confrontation of a Stressor

It happens to us all the time. Someone or something gets us frustrated, and we literally or figuratively head for the hills, either avoiding the person or thing altogether or ignoring the situation in the hope that it will go away. But when we ignore situations like this, they typically come back to haunt us. In the short run, avoidance looks appealing, even safe. But in the long run, it is bad policy. Really bad policy! We avoid confrontation because we want to avoid the emotional pain associated with it, the pain our ego suffers. Handled creatively, diplomatically, and rationally, the pain is minimal, and it often helps our spirits grow. After all, this is what life is all about: achieving our full human potential.

The art of peaceful confrontation involves a strategy of creativity, diplomacy, and grace to ensure that you come out the victor, not the victim. In this sense, confrontation doesn't mean a physical battle, but rather a mental, emotional, or spiritual battle. Unlike a physical battle where knights wear armor, this confrontation requires that you set aside the shield of your ego long enough to resolve the fear or anger associated with the stressor. The weapons of this confrontation are self-assertiveness, self-reliance, and faith. There is no malice, spite, or deceit involved. Coping mechanisms that aid the confrontation process include, but are not limited to, the following strategies: communication, information seeking, cognitive reappraisal, social engineering, and values assessment and clarification.

We all encounter stressors that we tend to run away from. Now it is time to gather your internal resources and make a plan to successfully confront your stressor. When you initiate this confrontation plan, you will come out the victor with a positive resolution and a feeling of accomplishment. First, reexamine the list of your top ten stressors. Then, select a major stressor to confront and resolve. Prepare a plan of action, and then carry it out. When you return, write about it: what the stressor was, what your strategy was, how it worked, how you felt about the outcome, and perhaps most important, what you learned from this experience.

EXERCISE 3.4: Confrontation of a Stressor cont....

The Stressor: (State the stressor you plan to confront here.)

_____
_____
_____
_____
_____
_____
_____
_____

Action Plan: (State your plan of diplomatic confrontation here.)

_____
_____
_____
_____
_____
_____
_____
_____
_____

Emotional Processing: (After you have faced your fear, describe here what happened and how you now feel having done this. Also, what did you learn from this experience?)

_____
_____
_____
_____
_____
_____
_____
_____

EXERCISE 3.5: Mandala of Healthy Grieving

"I felt sorry for myself because I had no shoes, till I met a man who had no feet." — Anonymous

Description: Grieving is a natural part of the human condition; however, new insights suggest that loss (big or small) is a metaphor of our own personal death—something most people tend to avoid. Everyone grieves in their own way, yet the most important aspect of grieving is not to get stuck in a prolonged (unhealthy) grieving process.

First consider an experience of loss. Using the template of the circle (mandala or medicine wheel), draw in four quadrants (north, south, east, and west) on a blank sheet of paper. Take a moment to reflect on and then write answers to these questions. Start with the quadrant of the east and move through to the south, followed by the west, and conclude with the north.

East (Past):

- What are your best memories of this loss experience?
- What issues, if any, are left unresolved?
- What emotions do you associate with this loss?
- What regrets, if any, do you have about this loss?

South (Lessons):

- What lesson did you learn from this experience?
- What do you feel you can share with others about this experience?
- What fears hold you back from similar experiences?
- What frustrations misdirect your next leg of the human journey?

West (Future):

- List three things you would like to do that you have never done before.
- List two personal goals you wish to accomplish in the next 6 months.
- List one new activity that you can do to meet/make a new friend.
- List three lifetime wishes or dreams.

North (Inspiration):

- What is your gift(s) to the world?
- How can you best offer this gift to the world?
- List three way to volunteer (provide service) to your community.
- What is the best way to pay tribute to your loss?

EXERCISE 3.6: The Key to Happiness Survey

There are several inventories, questionnaires, and surveys on personal happiness. Some are based on momentary happiness (how you feel right now) whereas others are based on happiness as a part of who you are (state vs. trait characteristics). Although some surveys are measured for reliability and validity, by and large, happiness is very subjective, meaning that you, not a questionnaire, are the only one who can tell if you are really a happy person. Following are several questions based on the ideals of happiness as viewed from the Oxford Happiness Question-naire and the Authentic Happiness work of Martin Seligman. Although those questions are measured on a scale of 1–5, these are Yes/No statements. This survey has not been measured for validity, but by reading and answering the questions, you can get a pretty good idea if happiness is a part of who you are. If, after taking this survey, you feel that the happiness quotient is low in your life, reread these statements and ask yourself what you can do to shift your perceptions to balance your scale of emotions.

1. By and large, I see myself as a happy person.   YES   NO

2. Overall, I am pretty satisfied with the direction of my life.   YES   NO

3. Usually, I wake up excited about the day ahead of me.   YES   NO

4. I tend to surround myself with happy, creative, and confident people.   YES   NO

5. Overall, my level of confidence is rather high with most everything I do.   YES   NO

6. Without a doubt, my life has a meaningful purpose.   YES   NO

7. I take delight in new adventures and discovering life's little surprises.   YES   NO

8. I find myself laughing several times a day, even to myself.   YES   NO

9. When things go badly, I am able to quickly shift my expectations.   YES   NO

10. Even when I am low on money, I can still find exciting things to do.   YES   NO

11. I have very few, if any, regrets with how I have lived my life.   YES   NO

12. I have many positive memories of my life.   YES   NO

13. It's pretty easy to see the good in people and the beauty in things.   YES   NO

14. Overall, I have positive thoughts and feelings about most things.   YES   NO

15. My future is bright and full of potential.   YES   NO

16. I can and do laugh at my own mistakes.   YES   NO

17. I can find time to do the things I really wish to do.   YES   NO

18. Overall, I feel that I have a sense of control/direction in my life.   YES   NO

19. I can be as happy in the company of others as I can be by myself.   YES   NO

20. I have a good amount of physical, mental, and spiritual energy.   YES   NO

EXERCISE 3.6: The Key to Happiness Survey cont....

Key: This survey is not a validated measure, but if you responded Yes to over half of the statements, consider yourself to be a happy person. If you responded No to over half of these statements, and you would like to have more happiness in your life, ask yourself what steps you can take to shift the perceptions highlighted in this survey to balance your scale of emotions.

Additional thoughts on your level of happiness:

_____

_____

_____

EXERCISE 3.7: Creative Altruism: The Power of Unconditional Love

Love, it is said, is the glue that holds the universe together. The expression of love can be made manifest in a great many ways. The following questions encourage you to explore the concept of unconditional love as an alternative to the motivation of fear.

1. Write your best definition of love.

_____

_____

2. If love is the energy that moves the human spirit, then fear is the metaphorical brake that stops love in its tracks. How does fear impede your ability to express love?

_____

_____

3. The slogan "random acts of kindness" was coined by a woman who was searching for a way to make the world a better place in which to live. She created this catchphrase as a means to express heartfelt altruism. The idea of performing a random act of kindness means to give anonymously without the expectation of receiving anything back. Compose a list of five ways to "give" altruistically and identify at least three ways that don't involve money.

a. _____

b. _____

c. _____

d. _____

e. _____

4. Service! One cannot speak on the topic of altruism without speaking of the concept of service. Although there are many stories in the news about acts of service (e.g., Habitat for Humanity), examples are not as common as one might expect. It's hard to feel sorry for yourself when you are helping others who are less fortunate. For more than a decade, the Institute of Noetic Sciences has given the Temple Awards for Creative Altruism to those unique individuals who demonstrate the spirit of selfless service. If you could create an altruistic nonprofit organization to help others, what would you do? Explain it here:

_____

_____

_____

_____

_____

_____

_____

The Mind: The Psychology of Stress

"And yet the mind seems to act independently of the brain in the same sense that the programmer acts independently of the computer."

— Wilder Penfield,
The Mystery of the Mind

For eons, philosophers, scientists, theologians, psychologists, as well as countless planetary citizens have all wondered, hypothesized, and speculated on the topic of the human mind. What is it? Where is it? How does it work? Why do identical twins have different minds and personalities? Where does the mind go when we die? What is a premonition? Can the mind be trained? What is intelligence? What is conscience? How fast can the mind travel? What is a thought?

As we begin the dawn of the 21st century, scientists are now beginning to confirm what the mystics stated long ago: The mind is a reservoir of conscious energy that surrounds and permeates the human body. From a holistic perspective, the mind and the brain are not the same thing. The mind, the quintessential seat of consciousness, merely uses the brain as its primary organ of choice. With new revelations from organ transplant recipients (some of whom exhibit changes in personality), apparently the mind uses other organs as well. In fact, new research suggests that every cell has consciousness, giving rise to a new term, *cell memory*.

The study of the mind (and the brain) has led to a deeper understanding of human consciousness, yet it's fair to say that through this vast exploration of dreams, cognitive inventories, hypnosis, meditation, DNA, EEGs, and MRIs, our knowledge, at best, is still embryonic. Current research in the field of consciousness reveals interesting insights about a phenomenon that only grows more fascinating with further study. For example, distant healing, remote viewing, premonitions, synchronicities, near-death experiences, out-of-body experiences, spontaneous healings, and much more only begin to substantiate that mind, as consciousness, is certainly not a simple consequence of brain chemistry, though there are many who still believe this.

This much we do know: Much like a laptop computer, mental well-being is the ability to gather, process, recall, and communicate information. We also know that stress compromises the mind's ability to do all of these functions. Information is constantly gathered and processed through the portals of the five senses for a variety of reasons (from threats to simple curiosity). Yet it's no secret that information comes into the conscious mind in other ways, including intuition, meditation, and what can only be explained as "extrasensory perception." Just as we know that the mind can generate stress without any outside stimulus, the power of the mind to heal the body is also well documented. Although no one book can begin to elaborate on the psychology of stress or the secrets to mental well-being, the following offers some keen insights into the psychology of stress, as observed by renowned leaders in the field who have shared the greatest wisdom to date on the mysteries of the mind.

The Anatomy of Ego

When it comes to the mind, one cannot look at stress without first examining the role of the mind's censor, the **ego**. Many claim that the ego is the cause of both personal and worldly problems, and although this may not be far from the truth, it must also be recognized that the ego is not always bad either. A healthy ego generates high self-esteem. As **Freud** accurately pointed out, the ego serves a role of protection. It also constitutes one's identity (or as Freud stated, Id-entity). Perhaps more accurately, the ego is the mind's bodyguard and censor. In an effort to protect one from harm, the ego sounds the alarm of imminent danger for mental, emotional, and physical threats. Stated simply, it is the ego that trips the fight-or-flight response when one feels threatened. Sometimes the ego goes overboard in its role as the mind's bodyguard and tends to make mountains out of molehills. Experts in the field of psychology call this **cognitive distortion**.

The ego has many tricks up its sleeve for protection. Freud called these **defense mechanisms**—thoughts and behaviors that act to decrease pain and perhaps even increase pleasure to the mind and body. He said that, by and large, we use more than one at a time, and for the most part we are not even aware of it. Here is a quick overview of some of the more common defenses of the ego:

- *Denial:* I didn't do it!

- *Repression:* I don't remember doing it!

- *Projection:* He did it!

- *Displacement:* He made me do it!

- *Rationalization:* Everyone does it!

- *Humor:* I did it and a year from now maybe I'll laugh about this!

At its best, the ego serves as the bodyguard for the soul. At its worst, the ego tries to manipulate everything (and perhaps everybody) through control dramas. When ruled by fear and anger, the ego transitions from a place of power to control, or what some people refer to as the unhealthy ego. Freud might have been the first person in the West to study this aspect of the mind, but he certainly wasn't the first to acknowledge it. Philosophers as far back as ancient Greece, India, China, and Tibet often spoke of the mind's shadow side. In Eastern culture, the ego is called the small mind (also called the false self), and ancient traditions suggest that the best means for mental well-being is to domesticate the small mind so that it can work in harmony with the larger mind of the universe. Psychologist Carl Jung described this process as "embracing the shadow." Ultimately, this means moving beyond a motivation of fear toward a motivation of love and compassion, a process that is not impossible but requires much discipline.

In terms of coping with the perceptions of stress rather than using a defense mechanism to avoid it, the holistic approach to stress management suggests following advice from the Eastern tradition by learning to domesticate the ego. Meditation is the premier skill to accomplish this goal. Exercise 4.1 can also help you start with this process.

The Power of Two Minds

Metaphorically speaking, you have not one, but two minds: the conscious mind and the unconscious mind. The conscious mind is best described as an awareness, like that which appears on your computer screen, and it receives nearly all of the attention of the ego. The unconscious mind is analogous to not only that which appears on your hard drive, but also some would say the entire Internet as well. Like an iceberg with nearly 90 percent of its entirety below water, the total mind is vast. It contains a wealth of information that often is never realized, yet is the model for today's typical computer. Unlike the conscious mind, which shuts down when you sleep, the unconscious mind works 24 hours a day, every day of your life. It, too, offers a sense of awareness. It is a reservoir of endless wisdom as well as a container of all your personal memories **Fig. 4.1 ▶**.

It would be simple if these two minds spoke the same language, but unfortunately this is not the case. Whereas the conscious mind is fluent in verbal skills, linear thinking, rational thinking, and many, many other cognitive functions that are now associated with the left hemisphere of the brain, the unconscious mind is fluent in intuition, imagination, and acceptance, cognitive skills associated with the right brain. Like a virus scanner on your computer, the ego serves the role of censor and gatekeeper, making sure nothing bubbles up to the surface of the conscious mind that might prove to be a threat. Unfortunately, much of this wisdom never passes through the gates of the ego. In no uncertain terms, stress can be defined as the conflict between the conscious and unconscious minds.

It was **Carl Jung**, one-time protégé of Sigmund Freud, who began, in earnest, to study the workings of the unconscious mind, particularly through dream analysis, but also through artwork and other nonverbal means of communication. Jung was of the opinion that if people took the time to learn the language of the unconscious mind, often expressed in archetypal

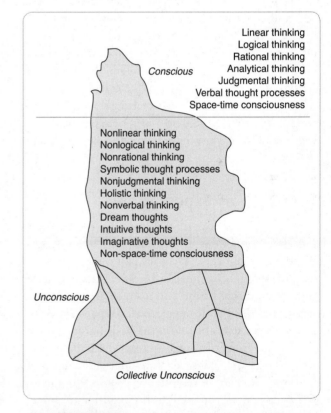

FIGURE 4.1 The metaphor of an iceberg is often used to describe the complexities of the mind, with the conscious mind (10 percent) above the water and the unconscious mind (90 percent) below; each aspect of the mind employs different thought processes.

symbols, and, in turn, gathered the wisdom that is there for the asking, then as a whole we would have a lot less stress in our lives.

Jung was also of the belief that the mind was a gateway to the soul. Anxiety, he suggested, was not merely a consequence of physical survival but the evolution of the human spirit. In other words, when we take the time to learn from our life experiences, then stress offers an opportunity for spiritual growth. The mind and the soul share a common space in the landscape of the human spirit. The word *psyche*, from which the word *psychology* is derived, means soul, and it goes without saying that there is tremendous overlap between the quadrants of mental well-being and spiritual well-being. Carl Jung was quick to note this association when he stated that every crisis over the age of 30 is a spiritual crisis. It was Jung who also noted that although we each have a personal unconscious composed of personal thoughts and memories, we are each connected to a larger reservoir of wisdom that he called the "collective unconscious," where time and space play by different rules. In fact, it was a conversation with Albert Einstein about the theory of relativity that seeded the idea of the collective unconscious in Jung's mind. Much of Jung's work can be found in the roots of many stress management therapies, including dream therapy, mental imagery, and art therapy.

The Death of Expectations

Anger (fight) and fear (flight) make up the two primary stress emotions from which all other stress-related emotions derive. Over the past century, anxiety stole the spotlight, primarily because Freud thought this was the easier of the two instinctual emotions to work with. Meanwhile anger, in all its many manifestations, began to boil over on the back burner on the world stage, from road rage and the Columbine massacre to child and spouse abuse to international acts of terrorism. First and foremost, every episode of anger, no matter how big or small, is the result of an unmet expectation. Behind every episode of anger awaits the feelings of remorse and grief.

Death is perhaps the hardest concept for the ego to reconcile. In an effort to maintain control, the ego does everything in its power to keep the upper hand. The work of Elisabeth Kübler-Ross, who observed the

progression of thoughts and behaviors one experiences through one's own personal death and dying process, has now become such common knowledge that it can be found everywhere from greeting cards to cereal boxes. The stages are the following: denial, anger, bargaining, withdrawal, and acceptance. Grieving is a natural part of the human experience. All of these stages constitute the fine art of grieving. (It should be noted that the stage after acceptance is adaptation.) Prolonged grieving, however, is not healthy and serves only to perpetuate chronic stress, yet many people never move beyond anger to acceptance, a crucial step in the resolution of all stressors.

You don't have to come down with terminal cancer to experience this progression of thought processes. Most likely you experience this same linear process with the death of each expectation, no matter how big or small, whether it's a dent in your new car or the breakup of your marriage. The next time you find yourself angry, ask yourself what expectation wasn't met, and therein may lie the answer to your problem.

Finding the Meaning of Life

There is a wise proverb that states: "Pain is inevitable, suffering is optional." *Suffering* is another word for stress, and chronic stress proves to be quite common with those who find themselves in an existential vacuum—a life that seems to have no purpose or meaning. Angst is a common plight among those who find themselves retired from a lifelong career, roaming an empty house made vacant by the last teenager leaving home, experiencing the sudden loss of a loved one, or even among Olympic athletes who walk off the podium with a bronze medal. Angst is also common among people who dislike their jobs. Interestingly, more heart attacks occur on Monday mornings than at any other time of the week, suggesting a link between the meaning of life and one's health. Depression, the hallmark cry of the soul, is a common malady in our stress-filled world. Despite the magic bullet of modern medicine, a chemical cure through prescribed pharmaceuticals does nothing to treat the trauma of emotional wounds. In some cases, it only masks these wounds and makes them worse by doing so.

How can suffering be optional? The voice of ageless wisdom, as echoed by Nazi concentration camp survivor Viktor Frankl in his classic book *Man's Search for Meaning*, suggests that to ease the angst of suffering, one must create a new meaning in one's life. To do this, one must find a new passion, make a new goal or goals, and make a commitment in deciding how to spend one's life energy, rather than letting it drain away. The voice of ageless wisdom advises the weary traveler to acknowledge the past, but not dwell on it. Rather, one must set one's eyes on the future, one day at a time, one step at a time, till one regains balance and can move forward on the human journey.

Energy Psychology

Perhaps because the field of psychology has worked so hard to establish credibility as a science, it has stayed clear of all things metaphysical, including all things categorized as paranormal. However, a handful of maverick scientists and luminaries in the field of psychology has taken the initiative to integrate various aspects of ageless wisdom with many theoretical principles of modern psychology. The result forges a path to different offshoots of this discipline, starting with humanistic psychology, health psychology, and transpersonal psychology and moving on to the emerging field of **energy psychology**: a field of study that honors the mind-body-spirit dynamics and techniques to help counsel patients and clients through a wide range of psychological conditions. The premise of energy psychology is based on the ageless wisdom of the human energy matrix of subtle anatomy, including the auric field (layers of consciousness), chakras, and meridians. By using the human energy grid to detect congestion and distortions associated with mental and emotional disturbances, great gains can be made at the spiritual, mental, emotional, and physical levels to restore one to optimal health.

In the field of energy psychology, just as each layer of the auric field is associated with a specific layer of consciousness, each of the primary chakras is associated with one or more aspects of one's personality. By recognizing the various aspects of each chakra, one can begin to process and resolve issues that tend to manifest as physical symptoms. One of the techniques used in energy psychology is body tapping, also known as the emotional freedom technique (EMT), which is very similar to energy vitamins.

Stress-Prone and Stress-Resistant Personalities

No topic of mental well-being would be complete without some discussion of personality types that make up the collective persona of the human species. It's fair to say that the topic of personalities is as complex as it is popular to discuss and demystify. Personality is composed of attitudes, behaviors, values, philosophies, opinions, belief systems, and perhaps much, much more. Character, a component of one's personality, is often said to be how you behave when no one else is looking. The Myers-Briggs personality type inventory (based on the work of Carl Jung) is one of many personality profiles used to determine and predict how people will get along with each other. The Enneagram personality type inventory is another. Perhaps because there are so many variables, personality assessments still remain more of an art than a science. Nonetheless, they offer keen insight into the complexities of the mind and how we deal with stress.

Whereas hard science points to genetic aspects (nature) that comprise aspects of one's personality, the softer sciences suggest a host of environmental factors (nurture) associated with the make-up of one's thoughts, attitudes, behaviors, and beliefs. Still others add a third dimension, ranging from astrological aspects to spiritual (karmic) considerations—all of which, to some extent, play a part in the complexities of the personality of each individual.

Although using a questionnaire to determine one's personality may be limiting, observations of character traits under stressful conditions can be quite revealing. Based on several decades of work, the following personality types have been assessed as being either stress-prone or stress-resistant.

Stress-Prone Personalities

These personality types not only do poorly in stressful situations, but with low self-esteem, they also actually tend to attract more stress into their lives. Exercise 4.2 offers an assessment of possible **stress-prone personality** traits.

- *Type A:* Once labeled as the impatient personality, the **Type A personality** is now regarded as someone with latent anger issues that manifest in explosive, competitive, and impetuous behaviors.

- *Type D:* New research reveals that symptoms of chronic depression (suppressed anger) may also play a primary role in coronary heart disease, and perhaps other chronic illnesses. As such, Type D, like Type A, is now considered a stress personality in the category of stress-prone personalities.

- *Codependent:* This personality is composed of many traits that coalesce as a collective defense mechanism to cope with problems such as alcoholic parents or loved ones. The codependent personality is also known in rehab circles as the enabler. Approval seeking, being a super overachiever with poor boundaries, and living with a constant level of fear (primarily the fear of rejection) are common traits of this personality. Exercise 4.2 is an example of a survey to help identify traits associated with this stress-prone personality.

- *Helpless-hopeless:* This personality style best describes someone who, for whatever reason, has met failure at every turn (e.g., child abuse, sexual abuse). Self-esteem is at rock bottom and the individual feels a lack of personal resources to help cope with problems, both big and small. Depression and feelings of helplessness and hopelessness are often associated with each other, in what sometimes can be described as a downward spiral.

Stress-Resistant Personalities

These people tend to let small things roll off their back and deal with big problems in a very positive way. Exercise 4.3 offers an assessment of your **stress-resistant personality** traits.

- *Hardy personality:* Marked by three distinct characteristics, people who exhibit the hardy personality demonstrate commitment to see a problem through to resolution, challenge themselves to accomplish a goal or resolve a crisis with honor, and control their emotions in a balanced way.

- *Survivor personality:* These people are true heroes who exhibit a balance of right and left brain skills so that problems can be approached creatively and solutions executed with confidence. Aron Ralston (celebrated rock climber) is one example of the survivor personality.

- *Calculated risk taker:* This person approaches life with courage rather than fear. The calculated risk taker sees danger and may even thrive on it, but only after surveying all options and choosing the most level-headed approach. People who do extreme sports would fall in this category.

The evidence is quite clear that changing one's personality is impossible, yet we can begin to change our thoughts, attitudes, beliefs, and perceptions that either influence or negate various personality traits. Although you may demonstrate traits associated with the Type A or the codependent personality, it doesn't mean that you cannot change your thinking patterns to stop those behaviors and begin to adopt stress-resistant traits instead.

The Power of the Mind

Holistic stress management honors the ageless wisdom of the power of the mind—the collective spirit of both conscious and unconscious minds to work in unison, as partners rather than rivals. History is punctuated with unfathomable stories of men and women who have harnessed the power of their minds to perform truly remarkable human feats. Ernest Shackleton, the captain of the *Endurance*; Rosa Parks, civil rights leader; and Aron Ralston, mountain climber, are but a few examples of people who have harnessed the power of their minds to overcome adversity. Their secret of success is no secret. You, too, have the means within you to harness the power of your mind. Meditation, music therapy, visualization, mental imagery, humor therapy, and positive affirmations are just a few of the many ways that the power of the mind can be disciplined and utilized to not only cope with the stress of life, but also rise to our highest human potential. Exercise 4.4 offers you a unique opportunity to begin to cultivate the powers of your mind.

Chapter Summary

- According to Freud, the ego includes several defense mechanisms: denial, repression, projection, displacement, rationalization, and even humor.

- The power of two minds includes the unconscious mind, often forgotten in stress management courses. It is said that the unconscious mind controls many of our behaviors.

- Many unresolved anger issues result in prolonged grieving (the death of expectations), as explained by Elisabeth Kübler-Ross in her death and dying model, which has five stages: denial, anger, bargaining, withdrawal, and acceptance.

- The psychology of stress includes a meaningful purpose in life, as described by Viktor Frankl. When meaning is missing, stress ensues.

- Energy psychology combines the concepts of the human energy system (e.g., chakras) with states of consciousness and the resolution of stress.

- Some people seem prone to stress whereas others seem to be immune from it. The concept of stress-prone and stress-resistant personalities invites us to examine our personality and change behaviors that promote stress while enhancing factors that resist it.

Additional Resources

Beattie, M. *Codependent No More.* Center City, MN: Hazelden; 1986.

Bernstein, A. *The Myth of Stress.* New York: Simon & Schuster; 2010.

Craig, G. *The EFT Manual: Emotional Freedom Technique* (2nd ed.). Fulton, CA: Energy Psychology Press; 2011.

Eden, D. *Energy Medicine.* New York: Tarcher/Putnam; 2008.

Frankl, V. *Man's Search For Meaning.* Boston, MA: Beacon Press; 1959, 1992.

Kübler-Ross, E. *On Death and Dying* (rev. ed.). Berkeley, CA: Celestial Arts; 2008.

Miller, M. C. The dangers of chronic distress. *Newsweek.* pp. 58–59. October 3, 2005.

Peirce, P. *Frequency: The Power of Personal Vibration.* New York: Atria; 2011.

Seligman, M. *Authentic Happiness.* New York: Free Press; 2002.

Shackleton, E. *South: The Last Antarctic Expedition of Shackleton and the Endurance.* New York: Lyons Press; 1919, 2008.

Siebert, A. *The Resiliency Advantage.* San Francisco, CA: Berrett-Koehler Publishers; 2005.

Siebert, A. *The Survivor Personality.* New York: Perigee; 2010.

EXERCISE 4.1: Domestication of the Ego

Renowned psychologist Carl Jung once said, "The conscious mind rejects that which it does not understand." What he meant by that statement is that the ego acts as a powerful censor to the wealth of information residing just below the surface of conscious thought. The ego not only makes no attempt to understand the unconscious mind, but also reacts to all unfamiliar ideas as enemies at the gate, ready to be shot down on a whim. Like an overactive security system that twitches at the hint of a threat, the ego defends us not only against real danger, but also against illusionary dangers that it creates itself. The net result is that we lose out on a lot in life by having an overprotective ego, always trying to maintain control, rather than empowering us to new heights.

In Eastern culture, there is an expression that reminds us to beware of an overprotective ego. It is said that we need to learn to "domesticate our ego," or else run the risk of having "poop" all over the place. What can one do to start this domestication process? First, you have to admit that, indeed, your ego can be the source of problems, if nothing else, holding you back and limiting your human potential. To do this, you have to observe your thought processes on a regular basis, repeatedly catch yourself in the act, and stop this limiting ego process in mid-air enough times so that this new behavior takes root, becomes second nature, and replaces the old and useless thought processes of an overreactive and self-defeating ego.

Carl Jung often used the term "embracing the shadow," an expression he is credited with coining to represent the dark side of the ego. But before you embrace (vs. exploit) your dark side, you must first tame it by being conscious of thoughts that are fear-based.

Domesticating the ego requires more than easing up on the suppressing role of the censor. It also means not seeing people, things, and opportunities as a threat to one's existence. Furthermore, it means engaging in acts of forgiveness, tolerance, patience, and compassion.

The following are some questions to ponder about things that might push buttons, but with a little bit of thought, might also allow you to house-train your ego.

1. What types of people do you feel a sense of prejudice toward/against? List them here, and next to each answer write a short reason why you harbor these feelings.

a. _____

b. _____

c. _____

2. What stereotypes do you find yourself labeling people with? What is the basis for these thoughts?

_____

_____

_____

_____

_____

3. Name three people you find yourself trying to control or manipulate.

a. _____

b. _____

c. _____

EXERCISE 4.1: Domestication of the Ego cont....

4. If you had to list three insecurities you have, what would you identify?

a. _____

b. _____

c. _____

5. Describe in a few words your most common recurring dream.

_____

_____

_____

_____

_____

6. List three of the deepest fears that you can identify.

a. _____

b. _____

c. _____

7. What three people are you holding grudges against? Next to each name write the duration of time you have been holding this sense of resentment, and why the grudge still exists.

a. _____

b. _____

c. _____

Additional Thoughts: _____

_____

_____

_____

_____

_____

EXERCISE 4.2: Stress-Prone Personality Survey

The following is a survey based on the traits of the codependent personality. Please answer the following questions with the most appropriate number.

3 = Often   **2 = Sometimes**   **1 = Rarely**   **0 = Never**

1. I tend to seek approval (acceptance) from others (e.g., friends, colleagues, family members).	3	2	1	0
2. I have very strong perfection tendencies.	3	2	1	0
3. I am usually involved in many projects at one time.	3	2	1	0
4. I rise to the occasion in times of crisis.	3	2	1	0
5. Despite problems with my family, I will always defend them.	3	2	1	0
6. I have a tendency to put others before myself.	3	2	1	0
7. I don't feel appreciated for all the things I do.	3	2	1	0
8. I tend to tell a lot of white lies.	3	2	1	0
9. I will help most anyone in need.	3	2	1	0
10. I tend to trust others' perceptions rather than my own.	3	2	1	0
11. I have a habit of overreacting to situations.	3	2	1	0
12. Despite great achievements, my self-esteem usually suffers.	3	2	1	0
13. My family background is better described as victim than victor.	3	2	1	0
14. I have been known to manipulate others with acts of generosity and favors.	3	2	1	0
15. I am really good at empathizing with my friends and family.	3	2	1	0
16. I usually try to make the best impression possible with people.	3	2	1	0
17. I like to validate my feelings with others' perceptions.	3	2	1	0
18. I am an extremely well-organized individual.	3	2	1	0
19. It's easier for me to give love and much more difficult to receive it.	3	2	1	0
20. I tend to hide my feelings if I know they will upset others.	3	2	1	0
TOTAL SCORE				

Score: A score of more than 30 points indicates that you most likely have traits associated with the codependent personality, a personality style known to be stress-prone.

EXERCISE 4.3: Stress-Resistant Personality Survey

The following survey is composed of statements based on the hardy, survivor, and risk-taking personality traits—all of which share common aspects that resist rather than attract or promote stress in one's life. Please answer the following questions with the most appropriate number.

4 = Always   3 = Often   2 = Sometimes   1 = Rarely   0 = Never

1. I wake up each morning ready to face a new day.	4	3	2	1	0
2. I tend not to let fear run my life.	4	3	2	1	0
3. I would consider myself to be an optimist.	4	3	2	1	0
4. I tend to see "problems" as opportunities for personal growth and success.	4	3	2	1	0
5. Although I like to be in control of my fate, I know when to go with the flow when things are out of my control.	4	3	2	1	0
6. Curiosity is one of my stronger attributes.	4	3	2	1	0
7. Life isn't always fair, but I still manage to enjoy myself.	4	3	2	1	0
8. When things knock me off balance, I am resilient and get back on my feet quickly.	4	3	2	1	0
9. My friends would say that I have the ability to turn misfortune into luck.	4	3	2	1	0
10. I believe that if you don't take risks, you live a boring life and won't get far.	4	3	2	1	0
11. I like to think of myself as being a creative person.	4	3	2	1	0
12. I believe in the philosophy that "one person truly can make a difference."	4	3	2	1	0
13. I am both organized and flexible with my life's day-to-day schedule.	4	3	2	1	0
14. Sometimes having nothing to do is the best way to spend a day.	4	3	2	1	0
15. I trust that I am part of a greater force of life in the universe.	4	3	2	1	0
16. I believe in the philosophy that "you make your own breaks."	4	3	2	1	0
17. I approach new situations with the idea that I will learn something valuable, regardless of the outcome.	4	3	2	1	0
18. When I start a project, I see it through to its successful completion.	4	3	2	1	0
19. I am strong willed, which I see as a positive characteristic to accomplish hard tasks.	4	3	2	1	0
20. I am committed to doing my best in most everything in life.	4	3	2	1	0
TOTAL SCORE					

Score: A score of more than 30 points indicates that you most likely have traits associated with the hardy, survivor, and calculated risk-taker personalities—personality types known to be stress-resistant.

EXERCISE 4.4: Mind over Matter: Harnessing the Power of Your Mind

Spoon bending may seem to be in a different league than the spontaneous remission of a cancerous tumor, but in reality, the premise of each is the same. Most likely you've heard the expression "mind over matter," yet few people actually put this philosophy into play. Mind over matter simply means using the power of your mind (both conscious and unconscious minds) to accomplish a task. Mind over matter isn't a means to control others. It's a means of becoming empowered rather than giving your power away. Those who teach mind power often use the spoon-bending exercise as the first stepping stone toward the goal of other, seemingly larger but no less challenging goals. Mind over matter isn't magic, an illusion, or a cute parlor trick. It's merely the manifestation of an inherent power that we each hold in the center of our own minds. The process of mind over matter involves the following three distinct steps.

Step 1: Focus Your Mind. The first step of mind over matter requires your mind to be focused completely and entirely on the task at hand. A wandering mind is analogous to irritating static on your favorite radio station making the transmission inaudible.

Step 2: Believe. Once the mind is clear of distracting thoughts and is completely focused on the task at hand, the heart and mind (conscious and unconscious minds) must be aligned. This means that all doubt must be cast aside and faith must galvanize you with a sense of absolutely knowing that you will, indeed, accomplish the deed (whatever it happens to be). To reinforce the belief process, use the power of your imagination to picture the event as having already occurred. Feel the exhilaration of completing this task.

Step 3: State the Command. State the command to complete the desired action. To bend a spoon, you might simply state, "Bend!" To dissolve a tumor, state the command, "Dissolve away!"

Spoon Bending 101

Locate an old spoon (or fork) from the silverware drawer (one that you don't intend to use again). Hold the base of the utensil in one hand and with a slight effort with the free hand apply a little pressure simply to test the strength of the metal. Follow steps 1–3 above. After stating the command "Bend!" once again hold the top of the utensil and bend it at the neck. If possible, bend the neck of the spoon or fork into a loop. Sometimes it helps to visualize the neck of the spoon as molten red, right before you apply pressure to bend the spoon. Once the utensil is transformed, consider keeping it in a place where you can see it often as a symbol to remind you of the power of your mind.

Spoon bending is really nothing more than a simple metaphor of the power of mind over matter. Once you have mastered this task, consider trying this technique in other areas of your life.

The Spirit: Health of the Human Spirit

"We are at this moment participating in one of the very greatest leaps of the human spirit—to a knowledge not only outside but also our deep inward mystery—the greatest leap ever."

— Joseph Campbell

How does one describe the indescribable? The topic of human spirituality has been pondered, discussed, and argued for eons. Yet even though many libraries are filled with volumes of books pontificating on the nature of spirituality, this unique concept defies a clear-cut definition or explanation through the limitations of human language. It is safe to say that we as a human race don't possess the vocabulary to give the concept of spirituality an adequate definition or description. This, in turn, has led to frustration and confusion among a great many people around the world, who desire something tangible to comprehend. Undoubtedly, spirituality includes the aspects of higher consciousness, transcendence, self-reliance, love, faith, enlightenment, community, self-actualization, compassion, forgiveness, mysticism, a higher power, grace, and a multitude of other qualities.

In reality, no one word alone is sufficient to describe the essence of human spirituality, and herein lies the dilemma. To define a term or concept is to separate and distinguish it from everything else long enough to gain a clear focus and understanding of its true nature. However, it appears that human spirituality encompasses so many factors—possibly everything—that to separate anything out, if only momentarily, denies a full understanding of this unique phenomenon.

This we do know: Spirituality is not the same thing as religion, though these two concepts do share some common ground, specifically a union with the divine **Fig. 5.1 ▼**. Spirituality is inclusive, whereas religions tend to be exclusive (e.g., you cannot be Jewish and Baptist at the same time). Spirituality is a unique experience with a force greater than oneself. Religions are based on rules and dogma, whereas spirituality has no dogma. Religions are based on faith. Spirituality is

based on a personal knowledge. In the words of theologian Houston Smith, "Religions are very organized, spirituality is a mess."

In nearly every culture around the globe, the words *spirit* and *breath* are synonymous, suggesting that spirit is a life force of energy that circulates through us and around us. Mystics say that this life force of energy is greatly affected by our thoughts and feelings. In essence, joy, happiness, and love keep the spirit vibrant, whereas unresolved issues of anger and fear can literally choke the human spirit. Health of the human spirit therefore is a metaphorical expression for keeping the spirit free-flowing, balanced, and vibrant.

Although the words of English, Arabic, Chinese, Navajo, and all other languages come up short when describing the nature of human spirituality, there is one language that begins to do justice to this topic. It is the language of metaphor. We use the language of metaphor and simile to help explain the unexplainable, to make the intangible tangible, if only long enough to gain a better glimpse of it. It's no exaggeration to say that the language of human spirituality is loaded with metaphors; journeys, mountaintops, roadblocks, and distractions are but a few of these metaphors. Perhaps by no coincidence, these archetypal metaphors are similar in all languages and cultures.

Sometimes, in order to understand a concept you just have to experience it, and experiences will certainly vary, as will the interpretation of these experiences. As the expression goes, there is no substitute for direct experience. Typically, people tend to describe their collective experiences of this nature as a "journey" or "path." Most important, for a path to enhance the maturation or evolution of your spiritual well-being, it must be a creative, not destructive, path; a progressive, not regressive path. It must stimulate and enhance the human spirit, not stifle spiritual well-being. From this premise, remember too that there are many paths to enlightenment and no one path holds dominance over the others. It matters not which path you take, but only that you keep moving forward (growing) on the path you have chosen. In the words of Carlos Castaneda from *The Teachings of Don Juan*, "Look at every path closely and deliberately. Try it as many times as you think is necessary. Then ask yourself, and yourself alone one question. Does this path have a heart? If it does, the path is good; if it doesn't it is of no use."

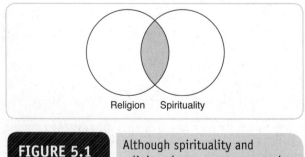

Religion   Spirituality

FIGURE 5.1   Although spirituality and religion share common ground (gray area), they are not the same concepts.

The Neglect of the Human Spirit

Perhaps because spirituality is impossible to define and even harder to measure, it has taken a back seat in the paradigm of health in Western culture. For the past 370 years, due in large part to the influence of René Descartes, creator of the Cartesian principle or paradigm in which things that could not be measured through the five senses were often ignored, the focus of human spirituality has largely been ignored in Western health care. Ignoring the aspects of human spirituality, however, only leads to an incomplete picture of the human experience. To ignore the role of spirituality as a means to cope with stress tends to create a sense of victimization and helplessness rather than empowerment. In the past decade, theologians, scientists, teachers, physicians, and scores of other professionals have come together to take a stance that the spiritual component can no longer be ignored or neglected in terms of the wellness paradigm. Today there is a clarion call for a new paradigm (which is actually a very old paradigm) that honors the integration, balance, and harmony of mind, body, spirit, and emotions, where the whole is always greater than the sum of its parts.

The Dance of Stress and Human Spirituality

At first glance, it might appear that stress and human spirituality are mutually exclusive. Indeed, there are many people who believe that these two words cannot be used in the same sentence. In reality, stress and spirituality combine to form a unique alchemy. Quite literally, they are partners in the dance of life. When we are willing to learn from each human experience, stress provides an opportunity for spiritual growth. Like a precious gemstone with rough edges, the wisdom gained from each experience, both good and bad, smoothes the rough edges to bring out our inherent beauty. Stressors are resolved when spirit is allowed to help you move through the situation rather than become stuck in it.

Through the perspective of ageless wisdom, stress is defined as "a perceived disconnection from our divine source," whatever we conceive this to be. In truth, we are never disconnected or separated from the divine source. Moreover, we are never betrayed by it either. Yet unresolved issues of anger and fear begin to cloud our vision so that we feel as though we have been cut off, abandoned, or betrayed. Despite our greatest fears, we can never be separated from our divine source. If you are still unsure if stress and human spirituality are partners in the dance of life, consider filling out Exercise 5.1.

Times of Spiritual Hunger

There comes a time in everyone's life when he or she begins to search for answers to life's most difficult questions. What begins as soul searching for life's meaning quickly grows into a **spiritual hunger**, a search for truth that often lies well beyond the reach of each individual at a much larger perspective of the universe and our role in it. The goal of this quest is to seek answers that help guide us further along our own life journey.

In past generations, people often sought spiritual refuge in their religious traditions. However, today many people have become a little disenchanted with their standard religious practices, perhaps because they don't seem to offer insights and answers to problems looming on the horizons of humanity. With an appetite greater than that which can be satisfied by existing institutions, people have begun to look beyond their own backyards to seek the answers to life's questions. The advent of the Internet has been only one of many means to satisfy this hunger. Books, workshops, and *Oprah* all become stepping stones on this quest. Spiritual hunger leads to spiritual exploration. Ageless wisdom notes that setting out to appease this hunger is an essential part of the spiritual journey, for we each must question truth to fully understand it.

Spiritual Materialism

Simply stated, the spiritual path is one of egolessness, yet reaching such a state is far easier said than done. To achieve emotional and material detachment is a daily challenge. Many Eastern spiritual leaders who have migrated West to share their perspectives on human spirituality and spiritual well-being, including Tibetan Buddhist leader Chogyam Trungpa Rinpoche, have encountered a phenomenon: an oxymoron they now call **spiritual materialism**. Spiritual materialism reveals itself among people with the best intentions, but with egotistical trappings; people who pride themselves on attending countless spiritual retreats, workshops, or pilgrimages to distant holy lands. They drop the names of their yogis, spiritual teachers, healers, and ashrams like the names of popular movie stars. Nowhere is this more prevalent than in the practice of hatha yoga (an egoless activity) that is now laden with certifications, wardrobes, and workout props. Spiritual materialism, a status of falsely claiming to be highly spiritual or enlightened, misses the boat when it comes to really understanding the balance of ego and soul.

I Don't Believe It!

Since humans first walked the earth, the search for truth—the meaning of human existence, divine consciousness, creation, miracles, and so forth—has taken many roads. Until we actually experience something directly (and even then doubt may arise), it is hard to accept everything at face value, let alone on the faith of someone else's word. In fact, it is not uncommon to reject as fact some, if not all, of what we encounter.

For some people, this rejection may be the result of a bad experience with church leaders or parents who try to limit or force a particular "truth." It is a consensus among those who study the field of human spirituality that divine truth comprises several paradoxes and ironies, all of which can make anyone scratch his or her head in confusion. Whether one claims to be an **agnostic** (someone who doesn't know if there is a higher power) or an **atheist** (someone who doesn't believe in a higher power), doubt and disbelief are actually part of the spiritual path as well. Doubts can certainly appear once a person leaves home and discovers other people with differing beliefs. As with a child who eventually grows up to leave home and discover the world on his or her own, questioning life's answers is a healthy part of the human journey, which is why a period of not knowing, or not believing, is considered a stage of spiritual development. But if a person finds him- or herself stuck in this phase out of fear (doubt) or anger (arrogance), this can lead to an unhealthy spirit. The inventor, philosopher, and global citizen Buckminster Fuller said it best: "God, to me, is a verb, not a noun (proper or improper)." Implied in his message is that the verb is *love*, something we can (and perhaps should) all believe in. Renowned architect Frank Lloyd Wright said it a bit differently, "I believe in God, only I spell it Nature."

Windows of the Soul

If you were to take the time to listen to the shamans, sages, mystics, and healers, the wisdom keepers of all times, all cultures, and all languages, you would hear them say that a circle is a universal symbol of wholeness; all parts come together to form the whole, yet the whole is always greater than the sum of its parts. Implicit in this message is that divinity resides in the power of the circle. We see this in the Taoist *taiji*, or yin-yang symbol. We are reminded of this in the Tibetan mandala, in the

beauty of the American Indian medicine wheel, Stonehenge, the Mayan calendar, the peace symbol, and yes, even a Christmas wreath. In the words of Hermes Trismegistus, "God is a sphere whose center is everywhere and whose circumference is nowhere."

In a stress-filled world, it is easy to become distracted and forget the sacredness of the circle. Moreover, we often forget our own inherent connection to the divine. In the event that you ever forget your wholeness, your divine connection, all you need to do is take a look in the nearest mirror, in the reflection of your own eyes. There, in the iris of each eye, is a beautiful sacred circle to remind you of your own divinity. Indeed, as Shakespeare once said, "The eyes are the windows of the soul."

Within the power of the circle **Fig. 5.2 ▾**, the number four is very significant (e.g., the four corners of the earth, the four seasons, the four chambers of the heart, and the four parts that make up the human entity: mind, body, spirit, and emotions). If you were to converse once again with the shamans, sages, and mystics of all times and ask them to share their wisdom on the concept of human spirituality, you would hear them mention four aspects that unite to create a formidable essence. All four components transcend the boundaries of all religions and cultures. The first three, relationships, values, and a meaningful purpose in life,

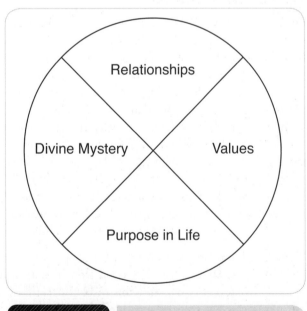

FIGURE 5.2 Although it is difficult, if not impossible, to define human spirituality, wisdom keepers agree that its four pillars are relationships, values, a meaningful purpose in life, and the divine mystery.

can be linked directly to every stressor you will encounter on the human odyssey. The fourth pillar speaks to the appreciation of the divine mystery of life. Exercise 5.2 invites you to walk through the mandala of the human spirit to gain a full perspective of the power of the whole being greater than the sum of the parts in all aspects of your life.

Relationships, Values, and a Meaningful Purpose in Life

A short prayer from the Lakota nation states, *"mitakuye oyasin."* The translation means "all my relations." Nearly all the indigenous cultures around the world have a similar prayer, honoring the connectedness of life. Indeed, all life is relationship, and the health of the human spirit honors this connection. Two types of relationships coexist in this pillar of human spirituality to form the cornerstone of this paradigm. The first is an internal relationship that each individual has with him- or herself and one's higher self. The second is called external relationships, the connection to all people and things outside of oneself. Many stressors involve the relationship we hold with ourselves as well as those we maintain among family, friends, peers, and colleagues.

The second pillar of human spirituality involves a personal value system. Values are abstract concepts of importance that we tend to make tangible through symbols. For instance, wealth is a value. Money is a symbol of wealth. Education is a value. A degree or diploma is a symbol of this value. It is believed that we each hold a strong set of core values and a larger set of supporting values that support the core values. Tension often arises when shifts occur in our value system, such as the tension between freedom and responsibility.

A meaningful purpose in life constitutes the third pillar of human spirituality. It represents who we are and why we are here. There is a general consensus that over the course of one's existence, a person will begin and complete many purposes. Yet, in between the completion of one and the start of another resides the potential for suffering. Exercises 5.3 through 5.5 take you through these pillars as a means to gain a better understanding of them.

Roadblocks on the Spiritual Path

Metaphorically speaking, every stressor we encounter on the human journey holds the potential to obstruct our passage, if we let it. Some stressors are nothing more than potholes on the road of life and can be easily sidestepped. Others seem like insurmountable roadblocks. The common tendency upon reaching a huge roadblock is to turn around and find another route. This behavior tends to promote avoidance, which can prove to be an extremely ineffective coping skill. Although the path of least resistance is often encouraged, avoidance is not. Wisdom reminds us that when we avoid roadblocks, we will most certainly see the same obstacle (perhaps with a different name) 5, 10, or 20 miles down the road waiting for us. On the human journey, roadblocks are meant to be dismantled, circumnavigated, or transcended, but never avoided completely. Exercise 5.6 invites you to look at any roadblocks you may have in your life. The first step to dismantling roadblocks is to recognize them for what they are—obstructions on life's journey.

Distractions on the Spiritual Path

Everyone has heard the expression, "Stop and smell the roses." By and large this is wonderful advice. Life was never meant to be a sprint to the finish line. Taking time to enjoy the simple things in life, as well as resting to enjoy the view, is considered by many to be as much a part of the journey as the arduous trek itself. There are many attractions along the road of life, but when attractions become distractions, then problems soon develop. Distractions pull one off the path, sometimes indefinitely. Today distractions are some of our biggest health problems, from drugs and alcohol addiction to an obsessive need to answer voice mail and email. Distractions begin as attractions, and like Rip van Winkle who pulled off the side of the road for a drink one night and slept for 20 years, we too can fall victim to the lure of attractions if we are not careful. Falling asleep on the spiritual path is a common metaphor in literature. Moreover, stress tends to cast a spell that lures one farther off the path. Exercise 5.7 invites you to look at any distractions you may have in your life, so that they can be identified and resolved.

The Divine Mystery

Although relationships, values, and a meaningful purpose in life constitute the framework for human spirituality, shamans, sages, mystics, and wisdom keepers will also tell you that there is a fourth aspect to human spirituality. In many circles, this aspect is called the **divine mystery**, and it speaks to all the things that can never possibly be explained rationally or scientifically. Sadly, Western culture not only ignores this aspect, but also often ridicules it. Until recently, most people who had a mystical experience kept it to themselves for fear of looking stupid (embarrassment is a form of stress). More recently, though, there has been a greater acceptance of mystic experiences in American culture. Moreover, some brave souls in the academic disciplines have tried to create a scientific methodology that begins to elucidate a clearer understanding of the divine and widen the perspective of human understanding. Studies on prayer, subtle energies, and spontaneous remissions are just some of these areas of current research.

Indeed, there are many things that remain outside the domain of the five senses. Renowned philosopher and inventor Buckminster Fuller once said that 80 percent of reality could not be observed or detected through the five senses. Western culture subscribes to the Cartesian principle or mechanistic paradigm of reality, and as such, ignores all things outside the realm of the five senses. Oddly, things that it cannot ignore are often labeled as the "ghost in the machine." What are some examples of these unexplained ghosts? The list is rather long, but some examples include spontaneous healings, bizarre synchronicities, angelic encounters, near-death experiences, faith healings, and legitimate crop circles. Wisdom keepers never try to explain these events and happenings in rational terms; rather, they simply suggest that it is better to become a mystic, meaning that one merely appreciates the mystical nature of the universe rather than deny its existence. To be a good mystic doesn't mean you understand unexplained phenomena. It simply means you have come to appreciate the mystery!

Another aspect of the divine mystery is the feeling of exuberance upon experiencing a sense of oneness with the world. Abraham Maslow called this a "peak experience," a unique type of eustress that takes your breath away, where feelings of euphoria cannot be put into words. So much emphasis is placed on distress these days that we tend to forget the other side of the coin: good stress. Some people call this experience a natural high, where the culmination of all five senses, perhaps in tandem with a sixth sense, provides a unique, exhilarating, ineffable sensation of a loving oneness. Everyone has had this experience at least once in his or her life. Maslow was of the opinion that peak experiences would be more common if basic needs were met (e.g., food, clothing, shelter, companionship), hence allowing

for a quicker pace toward self-actualization where peak moments are commonly experienced. Not only do we all have the potential to experience these peak moments, but we also hold the consciousness to be a good mystic. To be a good mystic means to simply appreciate the mystical aspects of the divine universe. Exercise 5.8 invites you to share your thoughts and feelings on this unique aspect of human spirituality.

Of Ego and Soul

The relationship between stress and spirituality is a lifelong dance. The dancers found within each individual are composed of the ego and the soul. The partnership between ego and soul is as wonderful as it is baffling. The soul, the spark of divine creation that resides in the core of our being, has but one purpose—to learn to give and receive love. With all due respect to Freud, the real purpose of the ego is to serve as a bodyguard for the soul. Problems arise when the agenda of the ego (e.g., to control and dominate) overrides the soul's purpose, leading to an inherent tension within the mind and heart of the individual. Although all issues of unresolved stress can be traced to the ego, the ego is not the bad guy. Self-esteem and self-worth are very much tied to the purpose of the ego as well. Without an ego, the soul would be unprotected to do its work. The tension between ego and soul is often called a dance. At best it's a romantic tango, at worst, a continual body slam. Like anyone taking dance lessons, the ego can be trained to step in a coordinated rhythm.

Seasons of the Soul

The planet Earth is a large mandala distinguished by four unique seasons: autumn, winter, spring, and summer. Like the planet Earth, of which we are very much a part, we too go through four specific seasons of the soul growth process, much like the earth's seasons. Wisdom keepers from all corners of the earth speak of four distinct phases of the soul growth process. These seasons go by many names, yet their similarities are undeniable. The **seasons of the soul** are the centering, emptying, grounding, and connecting processes. Let's take a closer look at each.

The Centering Process (Autumn)

The **centering process** is a time of soul searching and introspection. It is a time to go inside and cultivate the relationship you have with yourself and your higher self. The centering process is identified with autumn because as the earth spins on its axis allowing less light in the course of each day, we too go inside earlier. The centering process is an invitation to turn off the sensory stimulation from the outside world and go within. The word *center* contains the word *enter,* and the purpose of the centering process is to enter the heart.

The Emptying Process (Winter)

Once the centering process has been initiated, the **emptying process** begins. The emptying process is a time to clear out, let go of, and release any and all thoughts, attitudes, behaviors, and perceptions that at one time may have helped you but now only hold you back. In no uncertain terms, the emptying process is the void. It's a time to let go, release, or detach and then step into the unknown, unencumbered by the things that you have accumulated along the journey. The purpose of the emptying process is to make room for new thoughts, insights, and ideas that will guide you further along on the human journey.

Due to our emotional attachments, letting go can seem quite painful in some cases. The emptying process goes by a few different names: *the winter of discontent* and, perhaps most notably, *the dark night of the soul.* Although this season isn't meant to be torturous, it can seem like that for many people who have a hard time letting go of things. With letting go comes grieving. Sadly, many people get stuck in this season and see no way out. The void can seem like a lonely place; however, it's not meant to be a final destination. Rather, it is merely a necessary transition to the next season.

The Grounding Process (Spring)

Once room has been made for new insights, then the **grounding process** begins by attracting those things that are necessary to continue along the human journey. Just as winter turns to spring, so too does the clearance of space allow for new insights and shades of enlightenment. Nature abhors a vacuum! Surely, when room is made, something new will come to fill the space. New insights come in small pieces of information. It might be an intuitive thought. It might be a coincidence. Or it could be something that you hear mentioned by several different people in the course of a few days. In the custom of the American Indian, the grounding process is the vision in the vision quest. This season is called the

grounding process because when a nugget of insight arrives, it provides a sense of security and stability.

The Connecting Process (Summer)

When you think of summer it's likely that you think of family reunions, picnics, family barbecues, and social get-togethers. Summer is a time of coming together and being together with friends and family. It is a time of bonding, nurturing old connections and ties and creating new ones. At a spiritual level, the **connecting process** is much the same. It's a time of sharing whatever insights you picked up in the grounding process so that everyone can benefit, because greed is not a spiritual value. The premise of the connecting process is nurturing our connections through unconditional love. This season is often compared to Disney World and, indeed, this season is as glorious as the emptying process seems daunting. It's compelling to want to stay here forever, but the rhythm of the seasons never allows for anyone to stay in one place too long.

What makes life interesting if not complicated is that, in truth, we have many seasons going on at one time. We could be in the emptying season with regard to a relationship and the connecting process in our professional lives. Moreover, friends and family going through similar stressors tend to rotate through the seasons of the soul at different times, making it hard to relate to each other, and hence possibly causing more stress. Exercise 5.9 invites you to reflect on the seasons of your soul at this time.

Muscles of the Soul

There are two ways to get through a stressful experience. The first is to become a victim. This is where you constantly remind yourself and others of how bad you have suffered from whatever ordeal you have encountered. Rather than letting go and moving on, you hang on to feelings of resentment, and this only perpetuates the feelings of victimhood. The second (and best) way to emerge from a bad situation is to come through gracefully. People who do this show no sign of anger, animosity, or resentment from their ordeal. They have learned whatever they can from the experience and have moved on with their lives. When asked how they got through their situation, these people often have a similar answer. They say it was a sense of faith, a sense of courage, or a sense of humor. Some mention that it was their sense of patience, others speak of a sense of optimism. These inner resources, which include but are not limited to humor, intuition, patience, honesty, imagination, integrity, forgiveness, humbleness, and compassion, are not gifts for a chosen few; they are birthrights for everyone.

In his study of several hundred remarkable people, renowned psychologist Abraham Maslow searched for personality traits that culminated in what he called the *self-actualized* person—an individual who was able to rise above the stressors of everyday life and reach his or her highest human potential. In recent years, the term *hardy personality* has been used to explain those people who deal with life's changes in the ever-changing workforce. Researchers Salvatore Maddi and Susan Kobasa reduced Maslow's characteristics of self-actualization to three traits: challenge, control, and commitment. In my own research, I have found that there are several more traits than those three that allow one to stand tall, yet go with the flow, particularly after experiencing a life-threatening event that can best be described as "a trip to hell and back."

There are two ways to emerge from a proverbial trip to hell. The first is as a victim, where one carries a sense of remorse or resentment for a very long time—sometimes forever. The second is as an individual who emerges gracefully (with neither animosity nor resentment). These people shine! In doing so, they serve as role models for the rest of us. In my research to understand just how these people emerged gracefully, I found they describe a collection of inner resources that I have now come to call **muscles of the soul**. More often than not, when called to action, people use many of these muscles in a unique combination; however, one muscle seems to shine above the rest. Exercise 5.10 invites you to focus on these muscles to be exercised as you work to dismantle your roadblocks. The following is a brief description of several muscles of the soul for this exercise:

Compassion: To love without reciprocation, to care for someone or something without recognition or reward constitute the hallmarks of compassion. Compassion is the ability to feel and express love when fear is an easier choice. Mother Teresa was compassion personified. You don't have to be a saint to feel compassion. Love is the fabric of our souls.

Courage: The word *courage* comes to the English language via two French words, meaning "big heart."

Courage often brings to mind the idea of bravery, and this is certainly a hallmark of courage. Courage can be thought of as the opposite of fear, for it is courage that allows one to go forward, whereas fear holds one back. Courage is a brave heart.

Creativity: Creativity is two parts imagination, one part organization, one part inspiration, and one part perspiration. Creativity is not a right brain function; it is an inner resource that requires both hemispheres of the brain. Creativity starts with imagination and then makes the ideas happen. Creativity is the synthesis of imagination and ingenuity.

Curiosity: In the effort to learn, the soul has a wide streak of curiosity. Some may call this an inquiring mind, whereas others call it information seeking. Either way, seeking options, answers, and ideas to learn makes life's journey more interesting.

Faith: Faith is one part optimism, one part love, and two parts mystery. Faith is more than a belief that things will work out OK—it is an innate certainty that all will end well. Faith is an inherent knowing that we are part of a much bigger whole and that the whole has a loving divine nature to it.

Forgiveness: **Forgiveness** is the capacity to pardon those who we feel have violated us, as well as the capacity to forgive ourselves for our mistakes and foibles. Forgiveness is not letting someone off the hook when we feel violated or victimized. Forgiveness is a gift of compassion we give ourselves so that we can move on. If someone else benefits, great, but forgiveness isn't done for someone else. It is done for ourselves. Moreover, we must learn to forgive ourselves as well.

Humbleness: The ego begs to go first. The soul is content going last. Humbleness is a trait that is called upon when we are reminded to serve others by allowing them to be served first. Humbleness is manifested in acts of politeness, yet it never undermines self-esteem. Humbleness is based on the Golden Rule, where you treat others as you would have them treat you. In a fast-paced world where rudeness prevails, acts of humbleness are so greatly appreciated.

Humor: Humor is often described as a perception or insight that makes us giggle and laugh. Humor isn't a mood, but it certainly can promote a positive mood of happiness. Between parody and irony, between double entrendres and slapstick humor, there are literally hundreds of things to make our lips curl and faces laugh. Mark Twain once said that humor is humankind's greatest blessing. There are many people who insist that a sense of humor is what truly saved their lives in times of stress.

Integrity: When you meet someone with integrity, the first thought that comes to mind is honesty. Although this is certainly the cornerstone of integrity, there is more. Integrity is honesty over time. It is a code of conduct with a pledge to the highest ideals in the lowest of times. Integrity means taking the high road when the low road looks easier. In truth, integrity means the integration of many muscles of the soul.

Intuition: This muscle of the soul may not help you win the lottery, but it is useful in sensing good from bad, right from wrong, and up from down. Research delving into the lateralization of left and right brain hemispheres suggests that intuition is a right brain function. Intuition is an inherent knowing about something before the ego jumps in to confuse things. Premonitions, sudden insights, intuitive thoughts, inspiration, and pure enlightenment are examples of how this level of consciousness surfaces in everyday use if we let it.

Optimism: Optimism is an inherent quality of being positive. This is not to say that every stressor is meant to be a Pollyanna moment. Rather, it is seeing the best in a bad situation, learning from each lesson offered. A great definition of an optimist is someone who looks at a pessimist and sees hope.

Patience: This is the ability to wait and wait and wait until some sign acknowledges that it is time to move on. Just as there is strength in motion, there is power in stillness. Western culture is big on immediate gratification, the antithesis of patience. Impatience often leads to intolerance and anger. Patience quells an angry heart.

Persistence: A persistent person is someone who doesn't take "no" for an answer until he or she has exhausted every conceivable option. (There are variations on this theme. Some people stretch the meaning of persistence to what is now called aggressive, in-your-face tactics.) The spiritual approach is one of being pleasantly persistent (not aggressive), like flowing water that ever so slowly softens the hardest rock.

Resiliency: Some people call this the ability to bounce back; specifically, bouncing back from horrendous adversity. Resiliency is a trait that combines self-reliance, faith, optimism, and humor, yet resiliency is undeniably greater than the sum of these parts.

Unconditional love: To extend love and compassion from your heart without conditions or expectations is the hallmark of this muscle of the soul. There are some who say that humans are not capable of unconditional love, but just ask any mother of a newborn baby and you will learn quite quickly that indeed we possess this attribute. Unconditional love is egoless.

Spiritual Potential and Spiritual Health

Within the heart and soul of each person lies the means to solve any problem and move beyond any roadblock, no matter what size. Just as everyone has the muscles to flex their arms and bend their knees, so too do we have spiritual muscles that are ready to be used to dismantle roadblocks of any size, whenever called upon to do so. **Spiritual potential** is the potential that resides in each one of us to use these muscles of the soul when needed. Sadly, many people never meet their potential; instead, they allow these muscles to atrophy with disuse as they circle continuously in the whirlpool of stressful currents. When individuals do begin to flex these muscles of the soul and make the effort to break down, circumnavigate, or transcend the roadblocks in front of them, they have moved from a place of spiritual potential to **spiritual health**.

The Hero's Journey

From all four corners of the earth, the spiritual path is described as a journey or lifelong right of passage. It is an odyssey that can be measured in neither years nor miles. Certainly not possessions. Some say that this journey can be measured in experiences, whereas others say that it cannot be measured at all. Sages will tell you that the spiritual journey is no more than 12 to 14 inches, the distance from one's head to one's heart. Most likely, this is very true!

One wisdom keeper who dedicated his life to understanding the nature of the spiritual journey is **Joseph Campbell**. Leaving no stone unturned, Campbell compared the myths, legends, and fables of all cultures only to find that regardless of the culture, one story-line is consistent: A person leaves the known to venture into the unknown, he or she encounters all kinds of problems, with rare exception these problems are resolved successfully, followed by a return home to a hero's welcome. In his classic book, *Hero with a Thousand Faces*, Campbell referred to this template as "the **hero's journey**." These classic stories serve not only as reminders, but also as guides for our human sojourn, when we take the time to listen to the wisdom. It was Campbell's opinion that each and every one of us is on the hero's journey, and that every life span encompasses many, many journeys within the grand journey.

The template of the hero's journey involves three distinct stages, the departure, the initiation, and the return home. Let's take a closer look at each stage, and I'll provide some classic examples that illustrate the parts of the hero's journey theme.

The departure: In the departure stage, the character leaves the familiar (usually home) and enters the unknown. Sometimes there is a call to adventure; other times there is great reluctance to venture out into the unknown. It was Campbell's belief that every hero is called to adventure, even if he or she is pushed unwillingly out the door. Examples include Frodo Baggins leaving the Shire or Dorothy leaving Kansas. In contemporary times, departure can occur each time you step out the front door to go to work. Simply stated, the departure can be any change in your life.

The stage of initiation: Initiation can be considered another word for stressor. Initiations are tests that the hero must pass or overcome so that he or she can move on to complete the quest. This stage goes by many names, including rites of passage, baptism by fire, or the road of trials. In this stage, every hero faces a challenge and is called upon to complete the challenge. If he or she fails, another challenge will appear until it is mastered successfully. Frodo had to get rid of the ring, and Dorothy had to get the Wicked Witch's broom. Every hero must fulfill a task, accomplish a mission, or resolve a stressor because this apparently thickens the plot. The stage of initiation also includes what Joseph Campbell calls "spiritual aids," a helping hand from the divine source, whether it be angels, fairies, wizards, or the culmination of inner strength found within the soul of each individual. Dorothy had the help of the

Good Witch of the North, Frodo had Gandalf, and you have assistance, too.

The return home: Upon completing the challenge, the character returns home to be recognized as a hero. Often, but not always, the hero returns with a symbol of his strength such as the golden fleece or the Medusa's head. Also called incorporation, the return home is a point where the hero becomes a master of two worlds, the world she conquered and the world she returns to. Sometimes returning home doesn't mean a literal return but rather a symbolic return, in essence, coming to a place of inner peace or homeostasis. Ulysses made it home, as did Jason and the Argonauts; so did Frodo and Dorothy. The promise of the hero's journey is that you will, too.

If you look closely, you will see the storyline of the hero's journey as the foundation for every great story, from Ulysses, King Arthur, and Dorothy to Frodo Baggins and Harry Potter. Through the same eyes you can see that the hero's journey also is told through countless stories of real-life heroes like Rosa Parks and Maria von Trapp. Whether you know it or not, you are the central character in the hero's journey of your life.

Campbell did note this word of caution: On rare occasion, the hero may lose sight of his or her goals and ultimately fail to return home. Greed, apathy, lust, or some other aspect of the ego overrides the soul's intention, derailing the journey's completion. Metaphorically speaking, the character becomes distracted and falls asleep on the spiritual path. Rip van Winkle is a classic example of this. There are many others. Please consider using Exercise 5.11 as a means to view your life through the template of the hero's journey.

Health of the Human Spirit

Taking steps to ensure the health of the human spirit is as important as taking steps to ensure physical health. In some people's minds, it's even more important because spiritual well-being is the cornerstone of the entire wellness paradigm. Health of the human spirit ensures a continuous healthy flow of the life force of universal energy, unencumbered by unresolved feelings of anger or fear. Moreover, at best, health of the human spirit fully acknowledges a relationship with the divine, however you choose to call this. Actions to ensure the health of the human spirit honor the sacredness of life and our connection to it. Ultimately, health of the human spirit means moving from a motivation of fear toward a motivation of unconditional love. Exercise 5.12 invites you to consider ways to enhance the health of your human spirit.

Chapter Summary

- Spiritual well-being is considered to be an essential component of the wellness paradigm, and as such needs to be addressed with regard to coping with stressful aspects of one's life.

- Stress and human spirituality are not mutually exclusive. They are considered to be partners in the dance of life.

- Spiritual hunger describes a search for answers to life's difficult problems.

- Spiritual materialism refers to people who run down the spiritual path led (and often misdirected) by the ego, hence missing the point entirely.

- Those people who claim to be atheists are no less spiritual with regard to relationships, values, and purpose in life.

- Relationships, values, and purpose in life are the three primary aspects of human spirituality. Most every stressor involves one or more of these aspects.

- Divine mystery (the fourth and subtle quadrant of human spirituality) describes all that cannot be explained through the Cartesian method of scientific investigation and the use of the five senses.

- The delicate balance between the ego and soul becomes unbalanced when the ego moves beyond its role as bodyguard.

- There are four seasons of the soul, which metaphorically speaking are akin to the earth's seasons: centering (autumn), emptying (winter), grounding (spring), and connecting (summer). The emptying process is considered to be the most stressful.

- The muscles of the soul are one's inner resources for coping effectively with life's stressors both big and small. They include, but are not limited to, humor, optimism, forgiveness, patience, and love.

- Spiritual potential explains the inherent muscles of the soul. Spiritual health is a concept that explores the cultivation and utilization of these muscles.

- Renowned mythologist Joseph Campbell described each life in terms of what he called "the hero's journey." There are three stages: the departure, the initiation, and the return home. The first two stages can be very stressful.

- In simplest terms, unresolved anger and fear compromise the health of the human spirit.

Additional Resources

Bolen, J. S. *The Tao of Psychology.* New York: Harper & Row; 1979.

Burch, J. *The New Trinity.* Camarillo, CA: DeVorss Publications; 2011.

Campbell, J. *Hero with a Thousand Faces.* Princeton, NJ: Princeton University Press; 1968.

Castaneda, C. *The Teaching of Don Juan.* New York: Pocket; 1968.

Dossey, L. *Recovering the Soul.* New York: Bantam New Age; 1989.

Frankl, V. *Man's Search for Meaning* (rev. ed.). New York: Pocket; 1997.

Peck, M. S. *The Road Less Traveled* (25th anniv. ed.). New York: Touchstone; 2003.

Roman, S. *Spiritual Growth.* Tibirion, CA: HJ Kramer; 1989.

Ruiz, D. M. *The Four Agreements.* New York: Amber Allen; 1997.

Seaward, B. L. *Health of the Human Spirit: Spiritual Dimensions for Personal Health.* Burlington, MA: Jones & Bartlett; 2012.

Seaward, B. L. *Managing Stress: Principles and Strategies* (7th ed.). Sudbury, MA: Jones & Bartlett; 2011.

Seaward, B. L. *Quiet Mind, Fearless Heart: The Taoist Path of Stress and Spirituality.* New York: John Wiley & Sons; 2004.

Seaward, B. L. *Stand Like Mountain, Flow Like Water: Reflections on Stress and Human Spirituality.* Deerfield Beach, FL: Health Communications; 2007.

Tolle, E. *The Power of Now.* Novato, CA: New World Library; 1999.

Zukav, G. *The Seat of the Soul.* New York: Fireside; 1989.

EXERCISE 5.1: Stress and Human Spirituality

It may seem as though stress is the absence of human spirituality, but where there is stress, there is a lesson to enhance the soul's growth process. Take a moment to make a list of your top ten stressors. If you have less than ten, that's fine. If you have more than ten, simply list the top ten concerns, issues, or problems that are on your mind at this time. When you get done, place a check mark next to each stressor that involves issues with yourself or other people. Next, place a check mark next to all stressors that involve values or values conflict (e.g., time, money, privacy, education). Finally place a check mark next to all stressors that involve or are related to a meaningful purpose in life (e.g., family, education, career, retirement). It is fine to have a stressor with more than one check mark. We'll come back to this theme in upcoming exercises.

Stressor	Relationships	Values	Purpose in Life
1.			
2.			
3.			
4.			
5.			
6.			
7.			
8.			
9.			
10.			

Additional Thoughts:

_____

_____

EXERCISE 5.2: Mandala of the Human Spirit

A *mandala* is a circular object symbolizing unity with four separate quarters that represent directions of the universe, seasons of the years, or four points of reference. The origin of the mandala can be traced back to the dawn of humankind. Mandalas vary in size, design, colors, and symbolism. They are often used in meditation as a focal point of concentration. In addition, they are used as decorations in many cultures, from the Native American medicine wheel to art depictions from Asia.

The mandala of the human spirit is a symbol of wholeness. It is a tool of self-awareness to allow you the opportunity to reflect on some of the components of the human spirit: a meaningful purpose in your life, personal values, and the implicit chance to learn more about yourself in precious moments of solitude. Each quadrant represents a direction of your life with a symbol of orientation. The east is the initial point of origin. It represents the rising sun, the point of origin for each day. The focus of the mandala then moves southward, then to the west, and finally to the north.

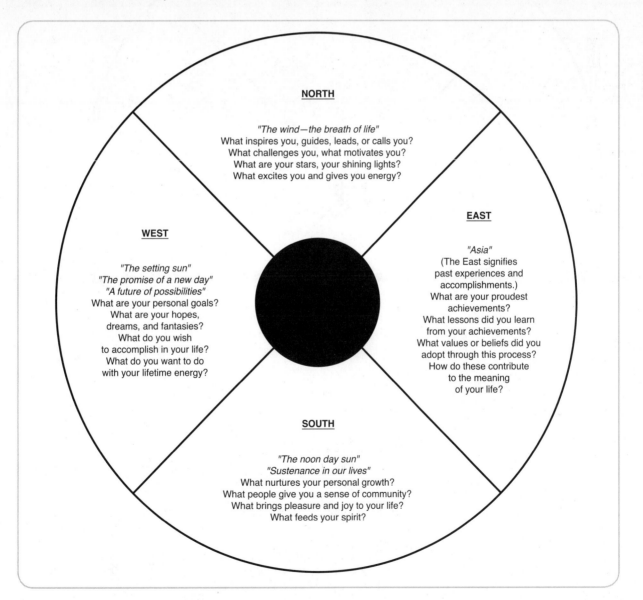

NORTH

"The wind—the breath of life"
What inspires you, guides, leads, or calls you?
What challenges you, what motivates you?
What are your stars, your shining lights?
What excites you and gives you energy?

EAST

"Asia"
(The East signifies
past experiences and
accomplishments.)
What are your proudest
achievements?
What lessons did you learn
from your achievements?
What values or beliefs did you
adopt through this process?
How do these contribute
to the meaning
of your life?

WEST

"The setting sun"
"The promise of a new day"
"A future of possibilities"
What are your personal goals?
What are your hopes,
dreams, and fantasies?
What do you wish
to accomplish in your life?
What do you want to do
with your lifetime energy?

SOUTH

"The noon day sun"
"Sustenance in our lives"
What nurtures your personal growth?
What people give you a sense of community?
What brings pleasure and joy to your life?
What feeds your spirit?

EXERCISE 5.2: Mandala of the Human Spirit cont....

Each focal point of the mandala of the human spirit provides questions for reflection. Take a few moments to reflect on the directions of the mandala to get a better perspective on the well-being of your human spirit. Using the circle provided, fill in the answers to the respective questions, creating a mandala of your very own human spirit.

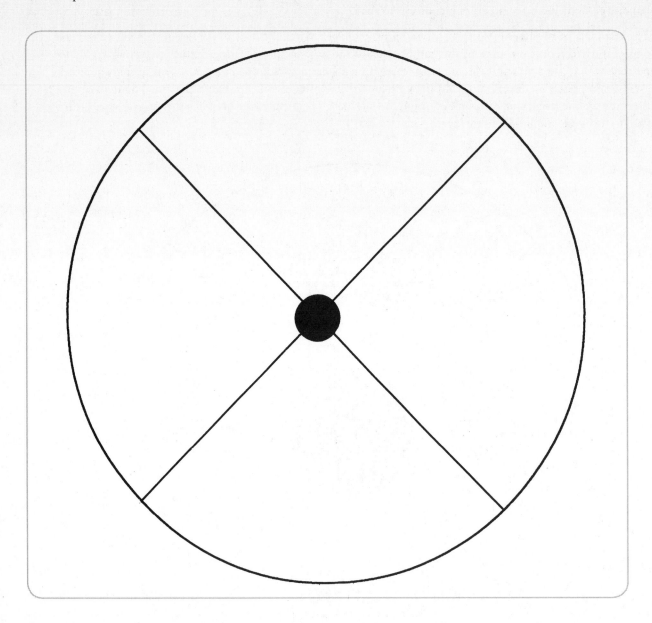

EXERCISE 5.3: The Pillars of Human Spirituality

"Every crisis over the age of 30 is a spiritual crisis. Spiritual crises require spiritual cures." — Carl Gustav Jung

The shamans, healers, sages, and wisdom keepers of all times, all continents, and all peoples, in their ageless wisdom say that human spirituality is composed of three aspects: relationships, values, and purpose in life. These three components are tightly integrated so that it may be hard to separate them from each other. But if this were possible, take a moment to reflect on these aspects of human spirituality to determine the status of your spiritual well-being.

I. Relationships

All life is relationship! In simple terms, there are two categories of relationships: internal (domestic policy)—how you deal with yourself, how you nurture the relationship with yourself and your higher self—and external (foreign policy)—how you relate, support, and interact with those people (and all living entities) in your environment. How would you evaluate your internal relationship and what steps could you take to cultivate it? Moving from an aspect of "domestic policy" to "foreign policy," how would you evaluate your external relationships?

_____

_____

_____

II. Your Personal Value System

We each have a value system composed of core and supporting values. Core values (about four to six) are those that form the foundation of our personal belief system. Supporting values support the core values. Intangible core values (e.g., love, honesty, freedom) and supporting values (e.g., education, creativity, and integrity) are often symbolized in material possessions. Quite regularly our personal value system tends to go through a reorganization process, particularly when there are conflicts in our values. What are your core and supporting values?

Core Values	Supporting Values
1.	1.
2.	2.
3.	3.
4.	4
5.	5.

III. A Meaningful Purpose in Life

A meaningful purpose in life is that which gives our life meaning. Some might call it a life mission. Although it is true that we may have an overall life mission, it is also true that our lives are a collection of meaningful purposes. Suffering awaits those times in between each purpose. What would you say is your life mission, and what purpose are you now supporting to accomplish this mission?

_____

_____

EXERCISE 5.4: Personal and Interpersonal Relationships

It is often said that all life is relationship—how we deal with ourselves and how we relate to everything else in our lives. It's no secret that relationships can cause stress. For this reason alone, all relationships need nurturing to some degree. Reflect for a moment on all the many relationships that you hold in your life, including the most important relationship—the one you hold with yourself. Relationships also constitute the foundation of your support system. Relationships go further than friends and family. This core pillar of human spirituality also includes our relationship with the air we breathe, the water we drink, and the ground we walk on. How is your relationship with your environment? Write your name in the center circle in the drawing, and then begin to fill in the circles with the names of those people, places, and things that constitute your relationship with life. Finally, place a star next to those relationships that need special nurturing, and then make a strategy for starting this process.

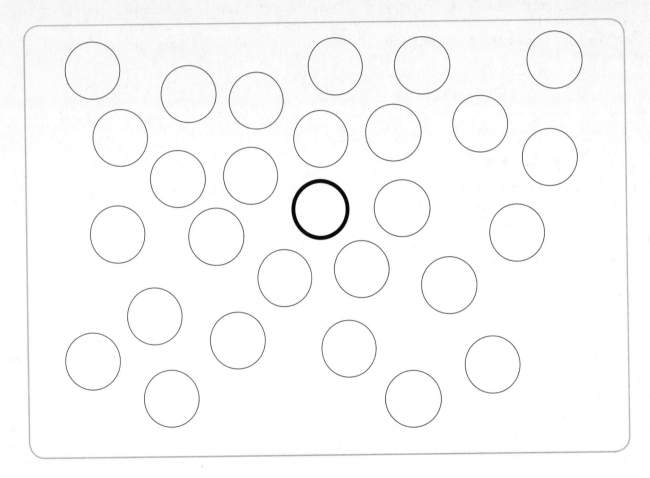

EXERCISE 5.5: Your Personal Value System

We all have a personal value system—a core pillar of the human spirit that is constantly undergoing renovation. What does your value system currently look like? Perhaps this diagram can give you some insights and, in turn, help resolve some issues that might be causing stress. The circle in the center represents your core values—abstract or intangible constructs of importance that can be symbolized by a host of material possessions. It is believed that we hold about four to six core values that constitute our personal belief system, that like a compass guide the spirit on our human journey. Give this concept some thought, and then write in this circle what you consider to be your current core values (e.g., love, happiness, health). The many circles that surround the main circle represent your supporting values—those values that lend support to your core values (these typically number from 5 to 12). Take a moment to reflect on what these might be, and then assign one value per small circle. Also inside each small circle include what typically symbolizes that value for you (e.g., wealth can be symbolized by money, a car, a house). Finally, consider if any stress you feel in your life is the result of a conflict between your supporting and core values.

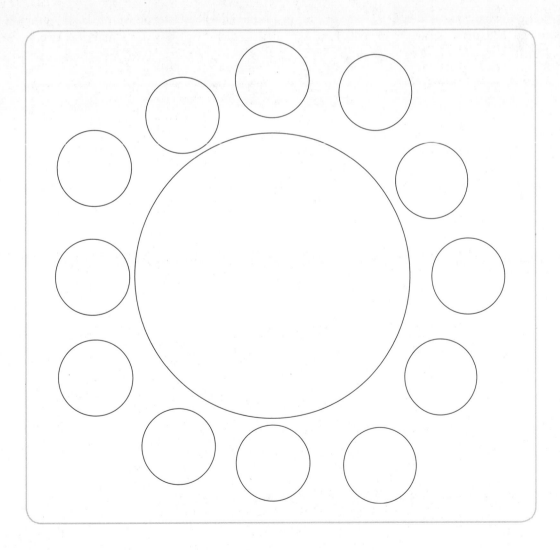

EXERCISE 5.6: Roadblocks on the Human Path

If our experience on the human path is, indeed, the evolution of our soul growth process, then roadblocks can metaphorically be used to describe a temporary halt to this evolutionary process. Roadblocks on the human path are not necessarily aspects in our lives that separate us from our divine source or mission—even though they may seem like this at times. Rather, roadblocks *are* part of the human path. And although they may initially seem to stifle or inhibit our spiritual growth, this only occurs if we give up or give in to them and do nothing. In the words of a Nazi concentration camp holocaust survivor, "Giving up is a final solution to a temporary problem."

Roadblocks take many forms, including unresolved anger or fear, greed, apathy, laziness, excessive judgment, and denial, just to name a few. More often than not, these obstacles manifest symbolically as problems, issues, concerns (and sometimes people). Although the first thing we may want to do when coming upon a roadblock is retreat and do an about-face, avoidance only serves to postpone the inevitable. Miles down the road, we will encounter the same obstacles. Roadblocks must be dealt with.

First, make a list of what you consider to be some of your major (tangible) obstacles on your human journey (e.g., the boss from hell, the ex-spouse from hell). Take a moment to identify each with a sentence or two.

1. _____

2. _____

3. _____

4. _____

5. _____

Next, begin to ask yourself and identify what emotions are associated with each roadblock listed above. What emotions do they elicit and why do you suppose these emotions surface for you as these obstacles come into view?

1. _____

2. _____

3. _____

4. _____

5. _____

EXERCISE 5.7: Distractions on the Human Path
"Remember—distractions begin as attractions."

Distractions can best be described as those things that pull us off the spiritual path—indefinitely. Distractions begin as attractions, but the allure can often cast a spell of slumber on the soul growth process. Although a respite on the human journey is desirable, even necessary at times, a prolonged distraction will ultimately weaken our spiritual resolve. The human spirit, like energy, must flow, never stagnate.

The lessons of distractions are quite common in fairy tales. Whether it is the story of Pinocchio or Hansel and Gretel, the warnings of distractions are as plentiful as the distractions themselves. The lessons of distractions are common in the great spiritual teachings as well. Here they are called "temptations." Not always, but often, attractions that become distractions have an addictive quality to them as well.

What happens when we become distracted? Metaphorically speaking, we fall asleep on the human path. Like Dorothy and her friends on the way to Oz, who stepped off the yellow brick road to smell the poppies and fell fast asleep, we too lose our direction and our mission, and our energy stagnates. The end result is never promising.

Unlike roadblocks, distractions are not so much meant to be circumvented, dismantled, or even transcended. Rather, they are meant to be appreciated—perhaps from afar, perhaps enjoyed briefly and then left behind. Fairy tales aside, what are contemporary distractions? Common examples of everyday distractions might include social contacts, alcohol, television, and the Internet.

Take a moment to reflect on what might be some distractions in your life. Make a list and describe each one in a sentence or two. Upon recognition of these, what steps can you take to "wake up" and get back on the path?

1. _____

_____

_____

2. _____

_____

_____

3. _____

_____

_____

4. _____

_____

_____

5. _____

_____

_____

EXERCISE 5.8: On Being a Good Mystic

In a recent Harris Poll, more than 70 percent of those questioned admitted to having a mystical experience. It's likely the number is even higher. There are many types of mystical experiences, many of which defy description, but by not attempting to articulate them into a comprehensible language, we begin to forget details of fragments that initially lingered in the mind. By writing them down we make the intangible slightly more tangible, the supernatural a little more natural, and the ordinary a little more extraordinary.

1. Beyond the five senses: What experiences have you had that you consider to be of a mystical, divine nature? Please take a moment to describe two or three of the most memorable ones here.

_____

_____

_____

2. Carl Jung spent the better part of his professional career exploring the mystical nature of the mind. Much of his research involved dreams and dream analysis. He was of the opinion that not only are we capable of precognitive dreams and premonitions, but these are common occurrences. Do you recall any dreams that foretold future events? Please explain them here.

_____

_____

_____

3. The word *synchronicity* was coined by Carl Jung as a means to describe two seemingly random events that come together with great significance. More than just a coincidence, synchronistic events are often thought to be divine messages, when we take the time to decode them. As the expression goes, "There is no such thing as a coincidence. It's God's way of remaining anonymous." What unusual coincidences have you had that are worth noting?

_____

_____

_____

4. Abraham Maslow coined the term *peak experience* to convey a sense of oneness with the universe. People who experience this sensation describe it as touching the face of God. Although these experiences are often beyond description, as best you can, describe in words through metaphor, simile, or analogy what this experience was like.

_____

_____

_____

EXERCISE 5.8: On Being a Good Mystic cont....

5. To be a good mystic means to appreciate the mystery of life. M. Scott Peck, author of the acclaimed book *The Road Less Traveled*, stated that the highest stage of spiritual growth was to explore the mystery of life but never lose one's appreciation for it. To some, the mystical side of life, those things that cannot be explained rationally through the framework of Western science, is baffling. It leads to a sense of frustration rather than a sense of appreciation. Where do you fall on this continuum?

_____

_____

_____

6. Please include any other thoughts you wish to share here.

_____

_____

_____

EXERCISE 5.9: Your Seasons of the Soul

Centering, emptying, grounding, and connecting constitute the four seasons of the soul. Now is the time to take stock of your life. Are you in the midst of one particular season at the present time? Like the planet Earth, we can have many seasons occurring at the same time. There is a normal procession of these seasons; however, it is easy to get stuck in one particular season of the soul. The emptying process is one season most people try to avoid, only to remain stuck there the longest. Based on the concepts explained earlier in this chapter, take a moment to identify where you feel you are at this time in your life. Please identify what you normally do in each season to get the most out of it. Is there a season you choose to skip? If so, why? Do you take periodic time to do some quality soul searching? Of these four seasons, is there one that seems to hold the most importance for you? If so, why? How would you describe your connecting process?

The Centering Process (Autumn)

_____

_____

_____

_____

The Emptying Process (Winter)

_____

_____

_____

_____

The Grounding Process (Spring)

_____

_____

_____

_____

The Connecting Process (Summer)

_____

_____

_____

_____

_____

EXERCISE 5.10: Muscles of the Soul

"Giving up is a final solution to a temporary problem." — Nazi Concentration Camp Survivor

Just as a circle is a universal symbol of wholeness, the butterfly is a symbol of wholeness. Given the fact that butterflies, unlike the lowly caterpillar, have wings to fly, butterflies also are considered a symbol of transformation. They can rise above what was once considered a limiting existence. There is a story of a boy who, upon seeing a young butterfly trying to emerge from its chrysalis, wanted to help by pulling apart the paper cocoon that housed the metamorphosis. The boy's mother, who saw what he was about to do, quickly stopped him by explaining that the butterfly strengthens its young wings by pushing through the walls of the cocoon. In doing so, its wings become strong enough to fly.

If you were to talk with people who have emerged gracefully from a difficult situation, they would most likely tell you that the muscles they used to break through their barrier(s) included patience, humor, forgiveness, optimism, humbleness, creativity, persistence, courage, willpower, and love. Some people call these inner resources. I call these "muscles of the soul." These are the muscles we use to dismantle, circumnavigate, and transcend the roadblocks and obstacles in life. Like physical muscles, these muscles will never disappear; however, they will atrophy with disuse. We are given ample opportunity to exercise these muscles, yet not everyone does.

Using the butterfly illustration, write in the wings those attributes, inner resources, and muscles of the soul that you feel help you get through the tough times—with grace and dignity, rather than feeling victimized. If there are traits you wish to include to augment the health of your human spirit, yet you feel aren't quite there, write those outside the wings and then draw an arrow into the wings, giving your soul a message that you wish to include (strengthen) these as well. Finally, if you have a box of crayons or pastels, color in your butterfly. Then hang it up on the fridge or bathroom mirror—someplace where you can see it regularly, to remind yourself of your spiritual health and your innate ability to transcend life's problems, big and small.

EXERCISE 5.11: The Hero's Journey: Exploring the Wisdom of Joseph Campbell

An ancient proverb states, "It takes a brave soul to walk the planet Earth." In the eyes of God, we are all heroes. The role of a hero is not an easy one. To depart from home can promote feelings of insecurity and even abandonment. Initiations, and there are many in one lifetime, are demanding and arduous; the phrase "baptism by fire" comes to mind. Yet through it all we are assured a warm reception upon our return, no matter the outcome of our journey.

The hero's journey is a mythical quest. Myths are clues to the spiritual potential of the human life. They offer meaning and significance as well as values. A myth is a source of truth, which often becomes exaggerated, but still holds its own essence. According to Campbell, a myth does four things to assist us on this remarkable journey:

1. A myth brings us into communion with the transcendent realms and eternal forms.

2. A myth provides a revelation to waking consciousness of the power of its sustaining source.

3. A myth tell us that no matter the culture, the rituals of living and dying have spiritual and moral roots.

4. A myth fosters the centering and unfolding of the individual in integrity with the ultimate creative mystery that is both beyond and within oneself and all things.

Campbell was of the opinion that the greatest danger of the hero's journey is to fail to use the power of myth as a guide on the spiritual path. He was keenly aware that contemporary American culture has abandoned its association with myths, a clear and present danger to any society.

The Spiritual Quest: Your Mythical Journey

The plot of every myth includes a beginning, a middle, and an end. In this case, the beginning is a departure from the known and familiar, the middle is a set of trials (called initiations), and the end is the return back home. In truth, we engage in this process of the hero's journey many times during the course of our lives.

1. *The Departure:* Are you in the process of moving out of the familiar into the unknown? What are you departing from? Typically, there is a refusal of the call. Are you ignoring a call to move on?

_____

_____

_____

_____

2. *The Initiation:* The initiation is the threshold of adventure. Mythically speaking, the initiation is to slay a dragon or monster. In real life, initiations come in many forms, from rites of passage to issues, problems, and stressors. What is the single major life issue, concern, or problem that you are facing at the present moment?

_____

_____

_____

_____

EXERCISE 5.11: The Hero's Journey cont....

How would you describe your "spiritual aids"?

_____

_____

_____

_____

3. *The Return Home:* The return is symbolized by coming home to the old, but with a fresh perspective. The return home bears a responsibility to share what you have learned on the journey. What have you learned from your most recent journey?

_____

_____

_____

_____

4. *A Working Myth:* What myth do you hold as a compass on your spiritual quest? Where did you learn of this myth, and how has it helped you?

_____

_____

_____

_____

EXERCISE 5.12: Health of the Human Spirit

Imagine, if you will, that there is a life force of divine energy that runs through your body. This life force is what we call the human spirit. We are a unique alchemy of humanity and divinity. Like a river, spirit runs through us with each breath. It is spirit that invigorates the soul. A lack of spirit can literally starve the soul, as a lack of oxygen can starve each cell. The ways to nurture the soul are countless, yet each ensures a constant flow of this essential life force. Unresolved anger and fear are the two most common ways to choke the human spirit, yet whenever the ego dominates the soul, then the health of the human spirit is diminished. The following are just a few of the many ways to enhance the health of your human spirit. As you read through these ideas, write down, in the form of lists, some ideas that you can use to engage in these activities and, in doing so, engage in the health of your human spirit.

1. *The Art of Self-Renewal:* Self-renewal is a practice of taking time to recharge your personal energy and reconnect to the divine source of life. List three ways in which you can find time to renew your personal energy—alone. Select the activity, the day, and the time of day.

a. _____

_____

b. _____

_____

c. _____

_____

2. *The Practice of Sacred Rituals:* Sacred rituals are traditions that we do to remind us of the sacredness of life. They include any habit we engage in to which we attribute a sense of the divine. List three rituals you partake in on a regular basis to remind you of the sacredness of life.

a. _____

_____

b. _____

_____

c. _____

_____

3. *Embracing the Shadow:* The shadow is a symbol of our dark side, when the ego rules our lives. The shadow appears in the behaviors of prejudice, arrogance, sarcasm, and other less than desirable attributes. To embrace the shadow doesn't mean to exploit these traits, but rather to acknowledge them and work to minimize them. List three aspects of yourself that you find less than flattering. How can you begin to come to peace with these aspects of yourself?

a. _____

_____

b. _____

_____

c. _____

_____

EXERCISE 5.12: Health of the Human Spirit cont....

4. *Acts of Forgiveness:* Forgiveness is the antidote for unresolved anger. Every act of forgiveness is an act of unconditional love. When you forgive someone, don't expect an apology. Forgiveness is not the same thing as restitution. Forgiveness is a means of letting go and moving on with your life. A large component of forgiveness is learning to forgive yourself as well. List three people who currently have made it to the top of your "s" list. First write down why you feel violated, and then write down how you can let it go and move on with your life—forgive and start moving freely again.

a. _____

_____

b. _____

_____

c. _____

_____

5. *Living Your Joy:* You cannot live your joy till you name it. So, name your joy. What things in life give you pleasure, real unconditional happiness, without any sense of regret afterward? Name three things that make you happy and bring a smile to your face. Unresolved stress can inhibit the feelings of joy. List your top three pleasures. When was the last time you did each one of these? How soon can you do them again?

a. _____

_____

b. _____

_____

c. _____

_____

6. *Compassion in Action:* Compassion in action is pure altruism. It is doing for others without any expectation of reciprocation. Putting compassion in action is putting the work of the soul above the priorities of the ego. Compassion in action begins as random acts of kindness, but doesn't end there. List three things you can do to express your compassion in action. Is it a random act of kindness? Is it a generous gesture? Or perhaps it is just being there—without feeling a sense of obligation—really being there. Next, set out to do all three of these.

a. _____

_____

b. _____

_____

c. _____

_____

Effective Coping Skills

Reframing: Creating a Positive Mind-Set

"Attitude is the paintbrush with which we color the world."
— Ancient proverb

Chapter 6

The Ageless Wisdom of Positive Thinking

There are those who say the world is composed of two kinds of people: optimists and pessimists. Ageless wisdom reveals that within the mind of each person there are at least two voices, a positive and a negative influence, suggesting that each of us contains the potential for both mind-sets. Since the days of Plato and perhaps much earlier, it has been observed that the direction of one's life, by and large, is a product of one's thoughts and attitudes. To be sure, we cannot avoid life's problems; however, our attitude about each situation tends to reveal the outcome. Changing one's attitude provides the impetus to change the direction of one's life. As the old adage goes, "Attitude is the paintbrush with which we paint the world."

In his critically acclaimed book, *Man's Search for Meaning*, Viktor Frankl credited his survival in the most notorious Nazi concentration camp, Auschwitz, to his ability to find meaning in his suffering, a meaning that strengthened his willpower and choice of attitude. Frankl noted that despite the fact that prisoners were stripped of all their possessions and many essential human rights, the one thing concentration camp officials could not take away was their ability to choose the perceptions of their circumstances. To quote another adage, "Each situation has a good side and a bad side. Each moment, you decide."

If you listen to the news much these days you might notice several references to the Great Depression with regard to the economy. As it turns out, the period of the Great Depression was a study not only in the economy, but also in psychology. Although many people struggled day by day, several people thrived in the face of adversity. We are already seeing that same dichotomy emerge once again in these troubled economic times.

The phrase *self-fulfilling prophecy* was used long before Freud coined the word *ego*. Ageless wisdom confirms the idea that negative thoughts tend to create and often perpetuate negative circumstances. Likewise, positive thoughts do the same. Current research regarding the power of intention upholds this timeless wisdom. Our thoughts, attitudes, perceptions, and beliefs unite as a powerful source of conscious energy. Therefore, it makes sense to use this energy for the best means possible.

The Influence of the Media

Current estimates suggest that the average person is bombarded with more than 3,000 advertisements a day from television, radio, T-shirts, billboards, and the Internet—all of which constantly inundate us with messages that strike at our insecurities. In marketing circles it is known as aggressive, in-your-face tactics. The desired result leaves one with an underlying sense of inadequacy if not an inferiority complex. There is no doubt this method works, otherwise marketers would move on to a different strategy.

Corporate marketing is only part of the fear-based media equation. As was so poignantly illustrated in the 2002 Academy Award–winning documentary *Bowling for Columbine*, both local and national news broadcasts have discovered that the addictive nature of fear sells. Even the Weather Channel has changed its focus to broadcast weather-related disasters between forecast updates just to keep viewers' attention. Moreover, the federal government was accused of using the media to fan the flames of anxiety with hypervigilant color-coded terrorism alerts. One of the best ways to increase your tolerance to negative media is to reduce your exposure to it, limiting the time you spend watching television, if not getting rid of it altogether.

An Attitude of Gratitude

Although it's true that it is difficult, if not impossible, to give sincere thanks for a crisis the moment it appears (that's called denial), continuously dwelling on a problem only tends to make things worse. A shift in consciousness toward those things that are blessings tends to balance the negative thoughts that persist from personal stressors. In doing so, an attitude of gratitude provides a perspective that helps resolve the problem at hand. In the midst of stress, regardless of the size of the problem, it is easy to take things for granted.

The preferred option is to count your blessings by seeing even the smallest things as gifts. One aspect of **reframing** suggests to do just that—adopt an attitude of gratitude for all the things in life that are going right, rather than curse all the things that seem to be going wrong. In a society where only 1 day out of 365 is dedicated to giving thanks, the regular practice of an attitude of gratitude may not seem to be encouraged, but remember, this is the same society that promotes fear-based television programming. Buck the tide and make a habit of giving thanks regularly.

In hindsight, what appears to be a curse may actually be looked upon as a blessing. Many people caught in the midst of a crisis utter the words, "This is the worst thing that ever happened to me," only to reframe this perspective later to say, "This was the best thing that ever happened to me."

The Art of Acceptance

Clearly, there are some things in life we cannot change, nor can we change the people involved with these situations. Attempting to do so becomes a series of control dramas that only perpetuate the cycles of stress. The ability to accept a situation for what it is, rather than exerting (and wasting) your energy to alter what you cannot change, is a unique human resource, and a valuable component of reframing. Acceptance isn't a sense of resignation or defeat. Rather, it is a sense of liberation that allows you to release any emotional baggage and move on with your life. Acceptance may be an overnight epiphany for some, but for most people it's an attitude that takes several days, weeks, or months to adopt.

The Power of Positive Affirmations

If you were to eavesdrop on the continuous stream of your conscious thoughts, you might be surprised to hear whispers of sabotage. The overbearing voice of the ego is constantly striving to dominate the passionate voice of the soul. By the time most people reach their late teens, the ego has practically declared victory! Sometimes the voice of the ego sounds like background static. Other times it sounds like blaring headline news. The ego best communicates throughout the landscape of the mind by providing a steady stream of negative or fear-based thoughts, attitudes, beliefs, and perceptions that, over time, begin to cloud almost everything you see.

Renowned psychologist Carl Jung referred to the constant mental chatter of the ego as "psychic tension." Many people suffer from this type of stress; however, there is a way to break this cycle and redirect your thoughts toward a positive direction. Jung called this "psychic equilibrium," and the balance of this mind-set is within the grasp of each individual—including you!

Using an apt metaphor, the negative voice of the ego that feeds subliminal (and perhaps obvious) messages of fear is similar to the broadcast of a local radio station. The good news is that there is a better choice of quality programming to listen to, primarily the optimistic voice that provides a clear message of your highest qualities, your inner resources (e.g., humor, creativity, faith), to reach your highest human potential.

If you were to talk to those people who have groomed themselves for success, from Olympic athletes and Grammy-winning musicians to the countless untold heroes of every age, you would find that they have learned to switch the mind's radio dial from the nagging voice of the ego to the passionate, grounded voice of the soul. In doing so, they have become the master of their destiny on the voyage of their highest human potential. You can do this too! People like Rosa Parks and Google.com creator Sergey Brin have learned that confidence is not the same thing as arrogance. **Positive affirmations** become the mind's compass, leading the way toward humble success.

Developing Your Mastery of Reframing and Optimism

Grooming your mind's thoughts is a skill that takes practice, but it's not impossible. A quick study of elite athletes and Broadway actors reveals that they didn't get to the top by listening to the negative voice in their head. They redirected their thoughts toward an optimistic belief system.

1. The first step of reframing a situation is to gain an awareness of your thoughts and feelings. When you encounter a difficult situation, get in the habit of asking yourself how you feel, and why you feel this way. If you need validation of your perceptions, consider asking a friend for his or her honest opinions.

2. Once you have become familiar with the recurring pattern of your thoughts and feelings, the next step is to match each negative thought with a positive thought. In essence, find something positive in the negative situation—and there is always something positive in every bad situation. Every situation, good, bad, and ugly, offers a valuable life lesson, and when this is acknowledged, something good can be gleaned from it.

3. Negative thoughts about a situation act like a mirror image to our own thoughts about ourselves, and they can have an immense negative impact on our self-esteem. Another step in the reframing process is to take an inventory of your personal strengths. By doing so, you begin to focus on your positive attributes rather than aspects that contribute to low self-esteem.

4. The last suggestion for adopting a positive mind-set is to include the ageless wisdom of counting your blessings. Rather than focusing on what's not right, shift your attention to all that *is* right. There is a concept known as the self-fulfilling prophecy. Others call it the law of universal attraction. It states that the more you think about negative things, the more negative things come into your life to think about. The same is true for positive things. In essence, to a large extent, you attract into your life that which you think most about.

Remember, negativity and the repeated thought processes that produce it can become a downward spiral of consciousness.

Tips to Incorporate the Practice of Reframing

There are many ways to shift the focus of your attention from a negative mind-set to a neutral or positive frame of mind. Remember that reframing isn't a denial of the situation; rather, it is a positive twist that acts to first recognize, and then neutralize the sting of a potentially bad situation. Try these suggestions:

1. When you find a situation to be stressful, ask yourself what can be learned from the situation.

2. When you find yourself in a stressful circumstance, take a moment to grieve for the situation and then try to come up with between three and five things for which you are grateful.

3. When things don't go as planned (unmet expectations), rather than focusing on your negative attributes, come up with three positive aspects about yourself that you know are your personal strengths. Then pick one and start to use it. Examples might include creativity, humor, and faith.

4. To cultivate a positive mind-set in nonstressful times so that you have it to use during stressful times, place a short list of positive affirmations on your bathroom mirror or computer monitor.

Exercise 6.1 invites you to try your hand at the reframing process.

Tips to Incorporate the Practice of Positive Affirmation Statements

Effective positive affirmation statements have a few things in common:

1. The use of the words "I am" to begin each statement (e.g., "I am a wonderful human being," or "I am confident of my abilities to succeed in this endeavor")

2. Scripting the phrase in the affirmative (e.g., "I am going to make it" vs. "I am not going to make it")

3. Scripting the phrase in the present tense (e.g., "I am succeeding in this endeavor" vs. "I am going to succeed in this endeavor")

4. Try to combine the use of your affirmation phrase with visualizing a symbolic image to combine the dynamic efforts of the conscious and unconscious minds

The following are empowering affirmations to awaken the often slumbering human spirit; suggestions offered for *your* internal radio station. The purpose is for you to consciously reprogram and incorporate these thoughts into the perpetually running tapes of your conscious and unconscious minds, so that you may achieve what Carl Jung called psychic equilibrium, or mental homeostasis—the foundation for all success.

The ultimate goal in this process is to reclaim your mental and spiritual sovereignty, which in turn allows you to transition from inertia to inspiration, from victim to victor on the path of what Joseph Campbell called "the hero's journey."

Please feel free to embellish, edit, and adapt any or all of these affirmations to best suit your needs. Keep in mind that, as with any new skill, listening to these might seem awkward at first, yet after a few sessions, it will begin to feel quite normal, in fact, second nature. Soon you will notice that these thoughts, these affirmations, will become integrated into your normal thinking process, particularly in times of personal challenge, and brightly color everything you do with confidence and grace.

1. I am calm and relaxed. (or, My body is calm and relaxed.)

2. I am grateful for all the many blessings in my life, even those that appear to be less than desirable.

3. I seek a balance in my life by bringing an optimistic perspective to everyday challenges, big and small.

Exercise 6.2 asks you to think of all that is going "right" in your life.

Best Benefits of Reframing

The benefits of reframing and positive affirmations are amazing. With a new focus on life through an optimistic lens, your world will transform from black and white to full color. This is not to say that you are fooling yourself into thinking that life is a continual vacation at Disney World or in denial with a Pollyanna perspective. Rather, reframing and positive affirmations become one of many resources to strengthen your resiliency during stressful times.

Chapter Summary

- Positive thinking, one form of reframing, isn't a denial of reality; rather, it is an approach to balance the ego's constant running commentary of negativity.

- The ego can generate negative thoughts, but it has been suggested that it is influenced by the media in very subtle ways to chip away at one's self-esteem.

- One aspect of reframing suggests focusing on what we have rather than what we don't have: an attitude of gratitude, because it's hard to be stressed when you are grateful.

- Reframing invites us to look at the big picture and not see ourselves as victims. Some things we cannot change. Acceptance is a coping technique that empowers us to deal with that which we cannot change and move on with our lives.

- The power of positive affirmations suggests that unless we employ both the conscious and the unconscious minds, no amount of positive self-talk will change anything.

- To master the art of reframing and optimism one needs to cultivate the skills of the mind.

Additional Resources

There are many great books on the topic of positive affirmations and reframing, a selection of which is listed here. There also are many wonderful guided mental imagery CDs with tracks that include positive affirmations.

Books

Armstrong, L. *It's Not About the Bike*. New York: Putnam; 2000.

Dyer, W. *The Power of Intention*. Carlsbad, CA: Hayhouse; 2004.

Frankl, V. *Man's Search for Meaning*. New York: Pocket; 1974.

Frederickson, B. *Positivity*. New York: Crown; 2009.

Maltz, M. *The New Psycho-Cybernetics*. New York: Prentice Hall Press; 2001.

Murphy, J. *The Power of Your Subconscious Mind* (rev. ed.). New York: Bantam; 2001.

Ornstein, R., & Sobel, D. *Healthy Pleasures*. Reading, MA: Addison-Wesley; 1989.

Peale, N. V. *The Power of Positive Thinking*. New York: Simon & Schuster; 2005.

Ryan, M. J. *Attitude of Gratitude*. Berkeley, CA: Conari Press; 2000.

Seligman, M. *Learned Optimism*. New York: Knopf; 1991.

CDs

Naparstek, B. *General Wellness*. Time Warner Audiobooks; 1993. 800.800.8661

Seaward, B. L. *Sweet Surrender*. Boulder, CO: Inspiration Unlimited; 2003. 303.678.9962

Shamir, I. *A Thousand Things Went Right Today*. www.yourtruenature.com.

EXERCISE 6.1: Reframing: Seeing from a Bigger, Clearer Perspective

Anger and fear that arise from encountering a stressful situation can narrow our focus of the bigger picture. Although the initial aspects of dealing with these situations involve some degree of grieving, the secret to coping with stress is to change the threatening perception to a nonthreatening perception. This exercise invites you to identify one to three stressors and, if necessary, draft a new "reframed" perspective (not a rationalization) that allows you to get out of the rut of a myopic view and start moving on with your life.

1. Situation: _____

_____

_____

Reframed Perspective: _____

_____

_____

2. Situation: _____

_____

_____

Reframed Perspective: _____

_____

_____

3. Situation: _____

_____

_____

Reframed Perspective: _____

_____

_____

EXERCISE 6.2: 1,000 Things Went Right Today!

In a stress-filled world, it becomes easy to start focusing on the negative things in life. Pretty soon you begin to attract more negative things into your life. Breaking free from this thought process isn't easy, but neither is it impossible. There is an expression, coined by Ilan Shamir, that states, "A thousand things went right today."® The concept behind this expression suggests that by beginning to look for the positive things in life, you will start attracting these as well, and let's face it, we can all use more positive things in our lives.

Rather than taxing your mind to come up with 1,000 things, or even 100, try starting with ten things that went right today, and then see if you can begin to include this frame of mind at the midpoint of each day to keep you on course. Remember, in a world of negativity, it takes just a little more effort to be happy!

1. _____
2. _____
3. _____
4. _____
5. _____
6. _____
7. _____
8. _____
9. _____
10. _____

After having written these things, is there any lesson that you can learn from completing this exercise?

_____
_____
_____
_____
_____

Comic Relief: The Healing Power of Humor

"*Against the assault of laughter, nothing can stand.*"
— Mark Twain

The Ageless Wisdom of Comic Relief and Humor Therapy

There is a cute three-panel cartoon of a caveman holding his club. In the first panel he is walking along holding his club. In the second panel, he stops and laughs. The third panel shows him walking again. The caption below reads, "The first private joke!"

Humor has been very much a part of the human landscape as a means to cope with the most grueling problems, even before recorded history. Although there were no cartoons or jokes written on the walls of caves in southern Europe, it's safe to assume that, indeed, prehistoric humans could produce a good belly laugh. Ancient Greek theater balanced tragedies with comedies. One of the most quoted passages from the Old Testament comes from the book Proverbs (17:22), "A merry heart does good like medicine, but a broken spirit drieth the bones." No sooner were radio and television invented than comedy hours were broadcast over the airwaves. Families would huddle around the new Zenith radio listening to George Burns and Amos and Andy, and more than 60 years after the first *I Love Lucy* show was broadcast, it can still be seen in syndication all over the planet. Humor has been and always will be a tool of the mind to combat stress.

Despite the intuitive sense that humor was good for both body and soul, it wasn't until Norman Cousins used humor to heal himself from a debilitating chronic disease that the medical establishment sat up and took notice. By creating his own prescription of watching several comedies each day, from Charlie Chaplin to the best of *Candid Camera*, Cousins was able to lessen his pain and eventually reverse his condition and restore his health. Cousins planted a seed of wisdom that took root to become the foundation of the field of **psychoneuroimmunology** (PNI): Our thoughts and feelings affect our state of health, for better or worse.

The word *humor* comes from a Latin word of the same spelling that means fluid or moisture. Today that definition is translated to mean "go with the flow," and given the chance to laugh at one's own foibles, humor eases the embarrassments in life to do just that. Humor is a human magnet. People love to listen to jokes just as much as they like to share them, particularly over the Internet.

Humorous Insights

As a psychological phenomenon, humor is a little more complicated than simply telling a joke. There are many different types of humor, and there is more than one reason why we laugh and smile. Just as two people can hear the same joke and only one person laughs, two people can hear the same joke and laugh for different reasons. Moreover, there are humor styles that reduce stress, just as there are a few types of humor that actually promote it. By first understanding some of the nuances of humor, the healing power of humor takes on a more profound effect. To avoid the trap of the scholars who write about humor in a dry style, humorous examples are included where possible to lighten things up.

Reasons Why We Laugh and Smile

There is a small group of academics who spend their time studying and writing on the topic of the psychology of humor. Sadly, their work is devoid of humor, but a synthesis of this information reveals that there seem to be four distinct reasons why people laugh and smile. Perhaps by no coincidence, individually each mirrors one of the four components of holistic wellness.

- *Superiority theory:* In ancient Greece, it was Plato who first suggested that people laugh and smile at the expense of others' misfortune. When someone puts him- or herself above others it gives a sense of superiority, hence the name **superiority theory**. Plato noted that the higher the position of authority, the greater the laugh. The superiority theory is an emotion-based theory, and examples abound everywhere in contemporary culture, from poking fun at politicians to snickering at the unforgettable exploits of Tiger Woods or Prince Harry.

- *Release/relief theory:* Sigmund Freud is credited with creating the **release/relief theory**. Freud was of the opinion that all thoughts and behaviors are instinctual. He also proposed that all thoughts and behaviors have a hidden sexual component to them. So perhaps it should come as no surprise that Freud believed not only that humor is a defense mechanism, but also that the reason why we laugh and smile is a physical means to release sexual tension. This may be the reason why sexual jokes never fade in popularity.

- *Incongruity theory:* The **incongruity theory** is a cognitive-based theory suggesting that laughter and smiles result from the mind's inability to make rational sense of something. In the failure to find the logic of a situation, one either thinks, Huh? or, Ha, ha. Much of the humor described as irony and quick-witted humor serve as examples of this theory. Example: Why are hemorrhoids called hemorrhoids and not asteroids?

- *Divinity theory:* Could humor be a gift from God? Some scholars think so. A strong component of human spirituality is the aspect of connection, and when two people laugh at the same joke, a connection is made, no matter how brief. Chaucer, the author of the *Canterbury Tales*, once said that many a truth be told in jest, suggesting that there is a divine quality in the ability to use humor to make a point. In some cultures tribal shamans (witch doctors, healers) were not only healers, but also jokesters in a sense. The original derivation of clowns is a personification of the divine, and if the make-up is right, one shouldn't be able to tell if the clown is male or female.

Types of Humor

There are many different types of humor, just as there are many different venues in which humor can be staged. Sometimes these styles can be combined to add even greater depth to the field.

- *Parody:* **Parody** is best defined as making fun of something. Perhaps the most famous current examples are *The Colbert Report* and *The Daily Show* that parody everything, and nothing is sacred. Self-parody is the unique ability to make fun of yourself without compromising your self-esteem. For this reason, parody is ranked at the top of the list.

- *Satire:* **Satire** is often defined as a written form of humor with a strong aspect of parody running through it. American satirists, including Dave Barry, Louis C. K., and P. J. O'Rourke, are highly esteemed and appear in newspapers and on Web pages.

- *Slapstick:* Pies in the face, slipping on banana peels, and slaps across the face are just a few of the examples of **slapstick**. Slapstick humor is based on early-20th-century vaudeville. The word *slapstick* conveys a sense of physical farce, where it looks like someone is getting hurt, but really isn't (that's the farce). Slapstick humor has an aggressive nature to it, but it is really a way to diffuse anger, like getting an egg dropped on one's head.

- *Black humor:* **Black humor** isn't ethnic humor, as some people think. Black humor, also called gallows humor, is morbid humor that relieves the stress of death and dying. It's the most common type of humor among nurses, physicians, police officers, EMTs, and anyone who works on the front lines of death. The popular show *M*A*S*H* was based on black humor, as was the cult classic movie *Zombieland*.

- *Absurd/nonsense humor:* **Absurd humor** dates back to medieval times, and perhaps much earlier. This kind of humor is very creative but leaves many people scratching their heads. When cartoonist Gary Larson introduced his single-panel *Far Side* cartoon decades ago, he set a new standard for absurd humor. Although Larson has officially retired, he has spurred a whole new generation of cartoonists to carry the absurd humor torch in strips such as *Bizarro*. About the time that the *Far Side* was making waves in newspapers across the country, comedian Steven Wright brought absurd humor to a whole new level in his stand-up acts.

- *Double entendre:* When a joke has two meanings, it is called a **double entendre**. Many sexual jokes fall into this category, but not all double entendres are sexual in nature. Many of the early Disney cartoons were written with both child and adult humor, and thus are loaded with double entendres. More often than not, so is the dialogue in James Bond movies. Example: Sometimes I wake up grumpy, and sometimes I let him sleep in.

- *Quick-witted humor:* Clever humor that makes you stop and think falls under the domain of **quick-witted humor**. NPR's show *Car Talk*, now syndicated in its rebroadcasts, is an example of this type of humor, as is the humor of Jerry Seinfeld.

- *Dry humor and puns:* Mark Twain used **dry humor**. Garrison Kellor of *Prairie Home Companion* also uses it, and there are people who really like this style of humor. An example is a sign on a music shop door, "Bach in a minuet!" Some people call this style of humor the lowest form of humor, but there are two styles even lower.

- *Bathroom humor:* Body functions performed behind closed doors, like farts, burps, and things that cannot be mentioned here, have always been the subject of jokes. With the threshold of acceptability being lowered by Hollywood in movies such as *Dumb and Dumber, There's Something About Mary, Bridesmaids, Borat,* and *The Hangover,* **bathroom humor** has become a fixture of American culture.

- *Sarcasm*: If you were to look up the word **sarcasm** in any dictionary, you would see it derives from a word meaning to tear flesh. Sarcasm is often called biting humor, and there is a good reason. Sarcastic comments that hit the intended target hurt. The use of sarcasm represents one or more underlying, unresolved anger issues. It doesn't resolve stress, it promotes it. This style of humor should be avoided at all costs.

How to Incorporate Humor Therapy into Your Life Routine

Here's a short list of tips that people have found extra helpful as a means to provide emotional balance to a stress-filled life. I call it "in search of the proverbial funny bone." Whether you have a headache, cancer, or a lousy day at the office, these are some ideas to boost your laughter quota to a healthy level.

1. *Learn not to take yourself too seriously.* Have you ever had a bad day and said to yourself, "A year from now, this is going to be funny, but right now, it's not funny!" Why wait a whole year and miss out on the fun? Whether it's the Puritan curse or just plain human ego, we tend to take ourselves way too seriously. This bit of sage advice reminds us to loosen up. Remember that the word *humor* actually means moisture, as in going with the flow. Try doing one thing a day to prove you can take yourself lightly. Exercise 7.1 challenges you to give this a try.

2. *Look for one humorous thing a day.* Humor is like a magnet. The more you pull in, the more you attract. So set out to find one humorous thing

a day, and you will be surprised what comes your way. Now, be prepared that what you find funny may be completely "geographic jokes," as in "you had to be there." But don't let this stop you. If you're looking for a place to start, try the greeting card section of the grocery store. Move on to *Calvin and Hobbes* or the *Bizarro* cartoon books or the *National Enquirer,* and round out the day with www.jokes.com, www.jokes gallery.com, or www.ahajokes.com. When you're driving, look for funny bumper stickers (but don't rear-end somebody) like these: "My son is inmate of the month at the state penitentiary," "Clean up the earth, it's not Uranus!" or "My Other Car Is a Nimbus 2000." Pretty soon, you will find that you don't have to look too hard. Humorous moments are everywhere.

3. *Work to improve your imagination and creativity.* Humor and creativity go hand in hand like peanut butter and jelly. You don't have to be a heavyweight like Walt Disney to be creative. Anything will do. Write a funny poem or limerick. Take candid snapshots of people picking their nose at the nearest mall—anything! Create

Bizarro (2007) © Dan Piraro. King Features Syndicate.

funny captions for your photo scrapbook so that anyone who reads it will be entertained. Exercise 7.3 invites you to be creative by completing a set of proverbs through the eyes of a child.

4. *Seek and find a host of humorous venues.* You can find humor in books, movies, plays, magazines, television shows, and comedy clubs. Make a list of places you can go to get a good laugh. Then start going to them. The more venues you can have at your disposal, the stronger your funny bone will become.

5. *Learn to exaggerate when describing a story.* Many people think that to have a good sense of humor you have to be good at telling jokes. Not true! Having a good sense of humor means you appreciate funny jokes. Telling jokes, however, doesn't hurt either. Exaggeration brings out the ironic and incongruous aspects of life (and there are many!). Comedians have perfected the exaggeration theme to the fullest. Example: Rodney Dangerfield told this joke: "Boy did I have it rough. A rough childhood, even a rough infancy. My mother was Jewish, my father was Japanese. I was circumcised at Benihana's."

6. *Build a humor (tickler) notebook.* Rather than have my students write a term paper in my healing power of humor course, I have them make a scrapbook. Not just any scrapbook! It's called a **tickler notebook** (Exercise 7.2). They are instructed to collect cartoons, photos, birthday cards, funny Dear Abby columns, email jokes, JPEG printouts, and photocopies of anything that brings a smile to their face. A few alumni of the course have contacted me to tell me that this turned out to be the saving grace during their stay in a hospital. To this day I still have students and workshop participants contacting me to tell me they are on their fourth tickler notebook. Give it a try! It will become one of your best friends. Speaking of friends . . .

7. *Call on a good friend(s) to lift your spirits.* We all have days when we are down in the dumps. That's when you use the secret weapon: a good friend. Norman Cousins had Alan Funt, the producer of *Candid Camera*, who spliced together the best of *Candid Camera* for his sick buddy. We all have friends. The people to call on are the former class clowns who, to

be honest, are still looking for an audience. Don't deny them this opportunity. Call them today.

Humor is not only a muscle of the soul, but also nutrition for the spirit. It might not cure cancer or solve world hunger, but it certainly makes every life challenge more bearable.

Best Benefits of Comic Relief

If chronic emotional stress is considered to be a preponderance of negative thoughts and feelings, then humor is the means to break up the continuity of this negativity. Humor has the ability to decrease fear and diffuse anger. Although humor isn't an emotion, it certainly elicits positive emotions that are sorely needed in times of chronic stress. Humor serves to diminish the ill effects of stress in two ways: First, humor acts as a mental diversion from the cares and worries that tend to plague a busy mind. Second, the physical effects of humor appear to have a number of physiological benefits, from reducing muscle tension to promoting the release of beta endorphins that, in turn, create a sense of euphoria and block pain. In short, humor decreases pain and increases pleasure, and we can all do with more of that.

Chapter Summary

- Humor is not an emotion. Humor is a perception that can create a positive emotion (eustress).

- Humor has been used for millennia as an effective coping technique.

- There are four accepted reasons why we laugh and smile: the superiority theory (Plato), the incongruity theory, the release/relief theory (Freud), and the divinity theory.

- There are many types of humor, including parody, satire, slapstick, black humor, absurd humor, double entendres, quick-witted humor, puns, dry humor, bathroom humor, and sarcasm. Of these, sarcasm (latent anger) promotes stress rather than relieving it.

- There are several ways to incorporate humor and strengthen your funny bone, from searching for one funny thing a day and creating a tickler notebook to augmenting your circle of friends.

Additional Resources

Cousins, N. *Anatomy of an Illness*. New York: Norton; 1969.

Funny Times. 888.386.6984. www.funnytimes.com.

Funny Times. *The Best of the Best American Humor. Funny Times*. New York: Three Rivers Press; 2002.

The Humor Project. Saratoga Springs, NY. 518.587.8770. www.humorproject.com.

Klein, A. *The Healing Power of Humor*. Los Angeles: Tarcher; 1989.

La Roche, L. *Life Is Short—Wear Your Party Pants*. Carlsbad, CA: Hay House; 2003.

La Roche, L. *Relax—You May Only Have a Few Minutes Left*. New York: Villard; 1998.

Martin, R. *The Psychology of Humor*. New York: Academic Press; 2006.

Morreall, J. *Comic Relief: A Comprehensive Philosophy of Humor*. New York: Wiley-Blackwell; 2009.

Provine, R. *Laughter: A Scientific Investigation*. New York: Penguin; 2001.

EXERCISE 7.1: Working the Funny Bone

1. It's time to create a new voice mail message. Most likely your message is the same as everyone else's. Here is an example of a "winning" voice mail message. See if you can come up with something equally funny:

Hi, you've reached the home of Bob and Jill. We can't come to the phone right now, because we are doing something we really enjoy. Jill likes doing it up and down. I like doing it sideways. Just as soon as we get done brushing our teeth, we'll call you right back.

Your new voice mail message: _____

_____

_____

2. The word *humor* means "fluid" or "moisture," so let the juices flow! Complete the following sentence by filling in the blank. Combine your talents of creativity and exaggeration to come up with something funny.

You know you're having a bad day when _____

_____

_____

3. You (or a good friend) are new in town and are looking for a new romantic relationship. The problem is shyness, so the solution is a personal ad. Remember that a sense of humor is one of the first things people look for in a "mate."

_____

_____

_____

4. Make a list of your top five movie comedies (with the intention of seeing them again soon).

a. _____

b. _____

c. _____

d. _____

e. _____

EXERCISE 7.2: Making a Tickler Notebook

Consider this: Estimates suggest that the average child laughs or giggles about 300 times a day. The typical adult laughs about 15 times a day. Research reveals that the average hospital patient never laughs at all. This assignment invites you to begin to make a tickler notebook (three-ring notebooks work best) composed of favorite jokes, photographs, JPEG printouts, birthday cards, love letters, Dear Abby columns, poems, or anything else that brings a smile to your face. Keep the tickler notebook on hand, so if you are having a bad day, you can pull it out to help you regain some emotional balance. And, if you ever find yourself in the hospital for whatever reason, be sure to bring it along so that you can at least get your quota of 15 laughs a day. The following are a few jokes to help you form a critical mass of funny things to include in your notebook.

Tickler Notebook Starter Page

The New Boss

An established corporation, feeling it is time for a shakeup, hires a new CEO. This new boss is determined to rid the company of all slackers. On a tour of the facilities, the CEO notices a guy leaning on a wall. The room is full of workers, and he wants to let them know he means business! The CEO walks up to the guy and asks, "And how much money do you make a week?" Undaunted, the young fellow looks at him and replies, "I make $200 a week. Why?"

The CEO hands the guy $1,000 in cash and screams, "Here's a month's pay, now GET OUT and don't come back!"

Surprisingly, the guy takes the cash with a smile, says, "Yes sir! Thank you, sir!" and leaves.

Feeling pretty good about his first firing, the CEO looks around the room and asks, "Does anyone want to tell me what that slacker did here?" With a sheepish grin, one of the other workers mutters, "Pizza delivery guy from Domino's."

The Bell Curve of Life

At age 4, success is . . . not peeing in your pants.

At age 12, success is . . . having friends.

At age 16, success is . . . having a driver's license.

At age 20, success is . . . having sex.

At age 30, success is . . . having money.

At age 50, success is . . . having money.

At age 60, success is . . . having sex.

At age 70, success is . . . having a driver's license.

At age 75, success is . . . having friends.

At age 80, success is . . . not peeing in your pants!

EXERCISE 7.2: Making a Tickler Notebook cont....

Have a Little Faith

A little girl was talking to her teacher about whales. The teacher said it was physically impossible for a whale to swallow a human because even though they were very large mammals their throats were very small.

The little girl stated that Jonah was swallowed by a whale. The teacher reiterated that a whale could not swallow a human; it was impossible.

The little girl said, "When I get to heaven I will ask Jonah."

The teacher asked, "What if Jonah went to hell?"

The little girl replied, "Then you ask him."

The Good Son

An old man lived alone in Idaho. He wanted to spade his potato garden, but it was very hard work. His only son, Bubba, who always helped him, was in prison for armed robbery. The old man wrote a letter to his son and mentioned his predicament:

"Dear Bubba, I'm feeling pretty low because it looks like I won't be able to plant my potato garden this year. I've gotten too old to be digging up a garden plot. If you were here, my troubles would be over. I know you would dig the plot for me.

Love, Dad"

A few days later the old man received a letter from his son:

"Dear Dad, For HEAVEN'S SAKE, DAD, don't dig up the GARDEN! That's where I buried the GUNS and the MONEY!

Love, Bubba"

At 4:00 a.m. the next morning, a dozen FBI agents and local police officers showed up and dug up the entire area. After finding nothing they apologized to the old man and left. That same afternoon the old man received another letter from his son:

"Dear Dad, Go ahead and plant the potatoes now. It's the best I could do under the circumstances.

Love, Bubba"

The Conversation

God is sitting in Heaven when a scientist says to Him, "Lord, we don't need you anymore. Science has finally figured out a way to create life out of nothing. In other words, we can now do what you did in the beginning."

"Is that so? Tell me about it," replies God.

"Well," says the scientist, "we can take dirt and form it into the likeness of You and breathe life into it, thus creating man."

"Well, that's interesting. Show Me."

So the scientist bends down to the earth and starts to mold the soil.

"No, no, no. . . ." interrupts God, "Get your own dirt."

EXERCISE 7.3: Good Vibrations: Proverbs by First Graders

A first grade teacher in Virginia had 25 students in her class. She presented each child in her classroom the first half of a well-known proverb and asked them to come up with the remainder of the proverb. It's hard to believe these were actually done by first graders. Their insight may surprise you. While reading, keep in mind that these are first graders, 6-year-olds, because the last one is a classic!

1. Don't change horses . . .	until they stop running.
2. Strike while the . . .	bug is close.
3. It's always darkest before . . .	Daylight Savings Time.
4. Never underestimate the power of . . .	termites.
5. You can lead a horse to water but . . .	how?
6. Don't bite the hand that . . .	looks dirty.
7. No news is . . .	impossible.
8. A miss is as good as a . . .	Mr.
9. You can't teach an old dog new . . .	math.
10. If you lie down with dogs, you'll . . .	stink in the morning.
11. Love all, trust . . .	me.
12. The pen is mightier than the . . .	pigs.
13. An idle mind is . . .	the best way to relax.
14. Where there's smoke there's . . .	pollution.
15. Happy the bride who . . .	gets all the presents.
16. A penny saved is . . .	not much.
17. Two's company, three's . . .	the Musketeers.
18. Don't put off till tomorrow what . . .	you put on to go to bed.
19. Laugh and the whole world laughs with you, cry and . . .	you have to blow your nose.
20. There are none so blind as . . .	Stevie Wonder.
21. Children should be seen and not . . .	spanked or grounded.
22. If at first you don't succeed . . .	get new batteries.
23. You get out of something only what you . . .	see in the picture on the box.
24. When the blind lead the blind . . .	get out of the way.

And the WINNER and last one!

25. Better late than . . .	pregnant.

EXERCISE 7.3: Good Vibrations: Proverbs by First Graders cont....

Tickling the Funny Bone Part II

Taking a hint from the wisdom of first graders, please complete the following proverbs with 21st century pearls of wisdom. Be creative, but most of all, be funny.

1. Don't get mad . . . _____

2. A rolling stone . . . _____

3. A bird in the hand . . . _____

4. Out of sight . . . _____

5. Blood is thicker than . . . _____

6. Fish or . . . _____

7. Don't throw the baby . . . _____

8. Easy come . . . _____

9. Feed a cold . . . _____

10. Good fences make . . . _____

11. Here today . . . _____

12. If you can't beat 'em . . . _____

13. If you can't stand the heat . . . _____

14. Once bitten . . . _____

15. Scratch my back and . . . _____

16. You made your bed, now . . . _____

17. Speak softly and . . . _____

18. It takes a village to . . . _____

19. The rich get rich and . . . _____

20. A friend in need is . . . _____

21. Half a loaf is . . . _____

22. He who laughs last . . . _____

23. The grass is always greener . . . _____

24. Two heads are . . . _____

25. When in Rome . . . _____

26. Too many cooks . . . _____

Simple Assertiveness and Healthy Boundaries

"Even if you're on the right track, you'll get run over if you just sit there."
— Will Rogers

The Ageless Wisdom of Assertiveness

Within the paradigm of wellness lies a paradox. On the one hand, there is no separation between mind, body, spirit, and emotions. They all combine to form one dynamic package. All efforts to separate them are done purely for academic and theoretical purposes. Ageless wisdom acknowledges that separation of anything is, in fact, an illusion. At some level everything is connected. Quantum physics supports this fact. On the other hand, borders between subjects and objects are necessary to clearly identify one thing from another. Moreover, boundaries are important to ensure that everything doesn't merge together as one big mess. This is particularly true with people. On one level, boundaries lead to confusion, on another level they provide security. It is a wise person who knows the difference.

Setting clear boundaries in one's life is a part of the great learning process of the human journey. Knowing when to say yes versus when to say no can mean the difference between inner peace and emotional anguish. In terms of day-to-day situations, boundaries are structures of the mind, based on a set of values, that provide a sense of security and guidance in which to live a balanced life. In today's world, personal boundaries include everything from how may hours of television you watch per day to keeping your checkbook balanced by spending within your financial means. Relationships involve boundaries just as the use of technology (e.g., smartphones and laptops) does. It's fair to say that all aspects of life involve personal boundaries.

Boundaries have become *the* issue of the the 21st century. At no time in the history of humanity has the permeability of boundaries become so weak or nonexistent, whether it's with the use of technology, poor finances, eating habits, television habits, whining, relationships, or most any human behavior. In a 24/7 society where everything and practically everyone is accessible, there is a very strong correlation between poor boundaries and high stress levels. Moreover, poor boundaries pave the path toward inappropriate behaviors, which then further erode one's boundaries.

Sociologists, those people who keep their fingers on the pulse of humanity, are quite concerned, if not alarmed, about the many factors affecting the integrity of the human condition. Consider these facts:

- Not long ago retail stores were closed Sundays (and often on Mondays). Now most stores are open 7 days a week, and many stores are open 24 hours a day.

- There was a time when television programming was scheduled from 6 a.m. to 12 midnight. This, too, is now running on a 24/7 schedule.

- Less than two decades ago, most homes had only one or two TVs in the house. Now there are often more televisions than people living in each house, with each child having a TV in his or her bedroom.

- Less than a decade ago, most homes had one phone number. Today many people have several phone numbers and make themselves accessible 24/7 as well.

- Most people had one job (and many wives stayed home to raise the children). Today wives work, and many husbands and wives work more than one job to make ends meet.

- Less than a decade ago, the nightly news was information based. Now it's hard to distinguish between news and commercials, because both are sensationalized to gain the highest ratings.

- Eating out at restaurants used to be considered a treat, but with the advent of fast-food restaurants people now cook less at home. Super-size meals and beverages are just one of the many reasons cited for the obese population, but consuming mass amounts of calories falls under the domain of poor eating habits, which is a boundary issue.

- Although loans have been a stable practice in banking, credit cards are a new creation. The danger of buying on credit is that it gives one the illusion of wealth, until the bills come in. Americans are infamous for huge amounts of credit card debt, suggesting very poor financial boundaries.

It's no exaggeration to say that trends in society, from corporate stock expectations to rapid advances in technology (e.g., smartphones, email) have undermined many boundaries, which in turn sets the stage for personal boundaries to be less stable. The end result of boundary violations, no matter how big or small, is stress! One of the most important issues facing Americans today, and some sociologists feel it is *the* most important issue concerning balance, is the issue of **healthy boundaries,** or the lack thereof. Today there is no shortage of poor boundary issues between home and work, eating habits, personal finances (credit card debt), and personal relationships (e.g., infidelity, sexual abuse). The consequence of poor boundaries is mental, emotional, and spiritual stress through feelings of victimization.

The Art of Healthy Boundaries

Healthy boundaries are nothing more than rules and guidelines that you establish as the basis for a preferred lifestyle. Based on a set of values that you have adopted (consciously or unconsciously), healthy boundaries provide structure and integrity so you don't feel victimized by the invading forces of life's situations and other people's inappropriate behaviors. Setting clear, healthy boundaries and enforcing them is empowering.

There is a cautionary note about healthy boundaries: Just as poor boundaries can lead to feelings of victimization and stress, rigid boundaries can cause stress as well. Healthy boundaries are organic, meaning that they grow and change based on present conditions. Healthy boundaries can become unhealthy when there is no flexibility, so that the established boundaries become a prison of sorts. Moreover, although friends, family members, colleagues, and strangers can certainly approach the edge of our personal boundaries and even cross the line at times, so too can we ignore our own personal boundaries and victimize ourselves. Without a doubt, establishing and maintaining healthy boundaries are essential for optimal health and well-being.

Developing a Mastery of Healthy Boundaries

The first step to creating healthy boundaries involves developing an awareness of your values and personal goals. As an example, if one of your values is privacy, yet you answer your phone every time it goes off, then a conflict arises and boundary violations run rampant. Employing steady but humble assertiveness is essential to maintaining healthy boundaries. Exercise 8.1 invites you to take a closer look at your personal boundaries to determine which, if any, need attention and

reinforcements. Exercise 8.3 addresses the topic of personal values. By completing this exercise, you no doubt will have a better idea of the relationship between values and boundaries.

Benefits of Healthy Boundaries

The benefits of solid, yet flexible boundaries are immeasurable. First, they give structure and stability to your life. In times of uncertainty, which we are certainly living in, structure and stability are assets worth striving for and maintaining. Second, healthy boundaries provide a sense of empowerment over potential feelings of victimization; in essence, they prevent you from feeling as if you are being walked all over all the time. Additionally, high **self-esteem** is a critical factor in maintaining healthy boundaries, yet the maintenance of healthy boundaries can, in turn, promote a greater sense of high self-esteem as well. The two go hand in hand for optimal wellness.

The Anatomy of High Self-Esteem

Self-esteem plays a critical role in how we handle day-to-day stress. Low self-esteem becomes a bull's-eye for problems and issues to target, whereas high self-esteem allows small problems to roll off our back and bigger problems to be divided and conquered. The secrets of high self-esteem have been studied for ages and no longer are deemed secrets. As odd as this may seem, the ego is essential to high self-esteem, for without it one's sense of self-worth would be nothing. Conversely, too strong of an ego tips the scales of high self-esteem out of balance, from confidence to cockiness.

Although there are many things that comprise the totality of self-esteem, five key aspects seem to be regarded as the pillars of this essential human attribute necessary to navigate the shoals of life's waters successfully. These five characteristics are uniqueness, role models, connectedness, the ability to take calculated risks, and empowerment. Let's take a closer look at each:

- *Uniqueness:* This aspect of high self-esteem is based on the concept of attributes that we see in ourselves that we deem unique or special and that distinguish us from others. Attributes are both tangible and intangible and include everything from the color of your hair to your sense of humor. **Uniqueness** also includes the combination of inner resources (the muscles of the soul).

- *Role models:* Heroes, mentors, and **role models** include those people we admire and who have certain characteristics that we wish to emulate and incorporate as aspects of our own personality.

- *Connectedness:* Having a sense of **connectedness** and belonging is essential for health and well-being. Friends, family members, peers, and colleagues constitute what is now called a personal "support group." Friends not only make us feel accepted, but also tend to buffer the effects of stress when we are feeling low.

- *Calculated risks:* Fear is an immobilizing emotion that holds one back from a multitude of life's experiences and adventures. Taking a **calculated risk** involves a number of inner resources, not the least of which is courage—a unique alchemy of confidence and faith that allows you to move through the barriers of fear to enjoy the rewards of life's best moments. Calculated risks allow you to be an active participant in life rather than a passive victim in it.

- *Empowerment:* **Empowerment** is best described as a sense of personal energy or vitality. Some even call it inspiration. Empowerment is a sense of keeping one's personal power rather than giving it away to one's job, significant other, possessions, sports team, or even celebrities. Giving away personal power is a drain of personal energy, which can ultimately lead to disease and illness.

The Importance of Empowerment

From a holistic perspective, empowerment is vital not only to one's self-esteem, but also to one's life force of energy. It appears to be human nature to give our power away. In some cases it appears as an exchange for something, such as restored health from a team of physicians. In other cases there is no exchange or benefit whatsoever. Healers who observe the human energy field around their clients explain that a loss of power is an energy leak analogous to a water tank with a crack at the bottom.

People tend to confuse empowerment with control, yet these are two entirely different concepts. At its best, empowerment is the exhibition of one's highest potential manifested as grace. Control is an attempt to manipulate oneself, others, or both. Control has an addictive quality to it in that no matter how much one has, it never seems to be enough. Empowerment is the realization that control is an illusion, at which point the leak is fixed and the tank becomes filled up again. Exercise 8.4, "Giving Your Self-Esteem a Healthy Boost," helps you integrate these ideas in your life.

The Anatomy of Assertiveness

To be walked all over, taken advantage of, or not appreciated for one's talents and abilities are the first stages of victimization. Conversely, to be arrogant, rude, manipulative, and self-centered constitutes the hallmark of aggressiveness. Like so many aspects of holistic stress management where balance is the key to inner peace, **assertiveness** resides between passiveness and aggressiveness. Assertiveness means standing up for your rights, yet not controlling or manipulating others. To be assertive means to act with a conscience. It means to balance freedom with responsibility by taking what is yours without taking away from anyone else. The epitome of assertiveness is the display of a well-balanced ego.

Acts of assertiveness require a fair amount of diplomacy, humbleness, and grace; anything less will come across as aggressive behavior and will immediately draw a defensive reaction from others. Examples of assertiveness range from asking the waiter for a better table to asking someone to turn off their smartphone at the cinema. Assertiveness is also essential for establishing healthy boundaries, because without the means to make these known and honored, feelings of victimization may ensue.

One final note about empowerment: It's best to know the subtle difference between rights and entitlements. Rights fall under the domain of being treated with respect. Entitlements are privileges that may or may not be extended to everyone. Confusion between these two constructs can promote stress, particularly with the expectations of receiving entitlements when there may be none to be had. As our vast world becomes a small global village, many expectations go unmet and tempers flair as a result. The anatomy of assertiveness includes humbleness.

How to Incorporate Assertiveness into Your Life Routine

Developing a mastery of assertiveness lies in the wisdom of knowing when to say yes (advocating for your rights) and knowing when to say no (knowing your limitations so as not to feel victimized with too many responsibilities). This mastery also includes fine-tuning the inherent balance between freedom and responsibility. As a rule, people tend to take on too many responsibilities.

- *Learn to say no.* When others ask for your time, learn and practice saying no if you really don't have the time (avoid the co-dependency trap). Even if you say yes initially, you can always come back and say no as long as you are diplomatic.

- *Use "I" statements.* By using the word *I*, you claim ownership of your thoughts and feelings (e.g., I am angry you did this!).

- *Use direct eye contact.* When speaking to people, look them directly in the eye to make your point understood.

- *Use assertive body language.* How you stand and position your arms can come across as defensive, weak, or strong. Stand equally on two feet and use your hands to express your point.

- Exercise 8.2 invites you to practice (mentally rehearse) some hypothetical situations where your assertiveness will come in handy.

Best Benefits of Assertiveness

The best benefits of engaging in acts of assertive behavior are restoring and maintaining a sense of self-worth and self-esteem. Self-worth is easily defeated by negative **self-talk**. Incorporating an attitude of assertiveness and taking proactive steps to make assertiveness a key inner resource allays the feelings of victimization and helplessness so that you can live your life in balance.

Chapter Summary

- Healthy boundaries are guidelines you live by that provide a sense of structure to your life. Poor boundaries often get violated, resulting in feelings of victimization.

- Enforcing healthy boundaries includes having an assertive attitude to ensure that personal security is maintained.

- The benefits of healthy boundaries include everything from feelings of security to a sense of empowerment to accomplish whatever you wish.

- High self-esteem is composed of several aspects, including uniqueness, role models and mentors, connectedness, empowerment, and calculated risks.

- Some people categorize human behavior into three areas: passiveness, assertiveness, and aggression. The first can lead to feelings of victimization. The last tends to promote feelings of anger. Experts advocate the middle road: assertiveness.

Additional Resources

Branden, N. *The Six Pillars of Self-Esteem*. New York: Bantam; 1994.

Burns, D. *The Feeling Good Handbook*. New York: Plume; 1999.

Cloud, H., & Townsen, J. *Boundaries*. Grand Rapids, MI: Zondervan; 2008.

Duhigg, C. *The Power of Habit*. New York: Random House; 2012.

Katherine, A. *Where to Draw the Line*. New York: Fireside; 2000.

Maltz, M. *The New Psycho-Cybernetics*. New York: Prentice Hall Press; 2001.

McKay, M., & Fanning, P. *Self-Esteem* (3rd ed.). Oakland, CA: New Harbinger; 2000.

Shiraldi, G. *The Self-Esteem Workbook*. Oakland, CA: New Harbinger; 2001.

EXERCISE 8.1: Healthy Boundaries: Building and Maintaining Personal Stability

We are living in an age when the average person has very poor boundaries in his or her life. Technology may be a factor, but it's not the only reason. People bring their work home, while at the same time problems from home invade their professional lives. It seems that most everyone has poor financial boundaries, with the average person carrying $5,000 annually in credit card debt. People think nothing of bringing their smart-phones into restaurants and movie theaters, and what begins as just an hour in front of the television ends up being a whole evening. Poor personal boundaries result in feelings of being overwhelmed, annoyed, and victimized, all of which contribute to a critical mass of stress.

Healthy boundaries first require an insight into what's appropriate in each and every setting in which you find yourself, in essence, creating the boundaries you need and want in order to maintain a sense of personal balance. Next, healthy boundaries require courage to assert your boundaries so that they are not violated. Finally, healthy boundaries require willpower and discipline to honor what you yourself have established to give you better structure and stability in your life.

1. List four areas in your life that you feel have weak boundaries (or perhaps no boundaries). Examples might include finances, alcohol intake, use of technology, eating habits, or television watching.

a. _____

b. _____

c. _____

d. _____

2. Now, please list four boundaries that you would like to create in your life to bring about a sense of balance. Then add a few words about what you can do to have these boundaries honored.

a. _____

_____

b. _____

_____

c. _____

_____

d. _____

_____

EXERCISE 8.2: Assertiveness Training 101

Please write your initial reaction to each of the following situations, followed by a more assertive response, if necessary.

Part I

Situation 1: A Failed Exam

You receive a failing grade on the first exam in a course for your major, and you are devastated. You feel as if the grade is not a true reflection of your knowledge of the subject.

Initial Reaction:

_____

_____

_____

Assertive Response:

_____

_____

_____

Situation 2: Poor Boundaries

You come home from class or work starved, only to discover that one of your roommates has eaten your food (again). You are on a limited budget and cannot feed the world.

Initial Reaction:

_____

_____

_____

Assertive Response:

_____

_____

_____

Situation 3: Strong Back Favors

One of your best college friends has to move out of his apartment at the end of the month and has found a new place to live a few miles away. He tells you that he really needs some help moving and needs to borrow a car like yours. He asks for both your time and your car. You have two term papers due the same weekend.

Initial Reaction:

_____

_____

_____

EXERCISE 8.2: Assertiveness Training 101 cont....

Assertive Response:

_____

_____

_____

Any Additional Response:

_____

_____

_____

_____

_____

_____

Part II

1. Select an undesirable behavior you are aware that you perform (e.g., drinking expensive designer coffee).

_____

_____

2. Ask yourself how motivated you are to change this behavior. (Remember, as with any change, there might be sacrifices involved.) Ask yourself whether the costs of making this change will outweigh the benefits.

_____

_____

3. Think about what changes in your perceptions and attitudes must accompany this behavioral change, and how you can adopt these new perceptions as your own to become second nature.

_____

_____

4. Specify what new behavior you wish to adopt. It is best not to state that you want to stop the old behavior (a negative thought process). The new behavior should be expressed as a positive goal (e.g., I would like to have long fingernails).

_____

_____

5. After trying the new behavior, ask yourself how you did. Was your first or second attempt successful? Why or why not? If not, what other approaches can you take to accomplish this goal?

_____

_____

EXERCISE 8.3: Value Assessment and Clarification

Values—those abstract ideals that shape our lives—are constructs of importance. They give the conscious mind structure. They can also give countries and governments structure. The U.S. Declaration of Independence is all about values, including "life, liberty, and the pursuit of happiness." Although values are intangible, they are often symbolized by material objects or possessions, which can make values very real. Some everyday examples of values are love, peace, privacy, education, freedom, happiness, creativity, fame, integrity, faith, friendship, morals, health, justice, loyalty, honesty, and independence.

Where do values come from? We adopt values at a very early age, unconsciously, from people whom we admire, love, or desire acceptance from, like our parents, brothers and sisters, schoolteachers, and clergy. Values are often categorized into two groups: *basic* values, a collection of three to five instrumental values that are the cornerstones of the foundation of our personalities, and *supporting* values, which augment our basic values. Throughout our development we construct a value system, a collection of values that influences our attitudes and behaviors, all of which make up our personality.

As we mature, our value systems also change because we become accountable for the way we think and behave. Like the earth's tectonic plates, our values shift in importance, causing our own earth to quake. These shifts are called *value conflicts*, and they can cause a lot of stress. Classic examples of value conflicts include love versus religious faith or social class (*Romeo and Juliet*), freedom versus responsibility, and work versus leisure (the American dream). Conflicts in values can be helpful in our own maturing process if we work though the conflict to a full resolution. Problems arise when we ignore the conflict and avoid clarifying our value system. The purpose of this exercise is for you to take an honest look at your value system, assess its current status, and clarify unresolved issues associated with values in conflict. The following are some questions to help you in the process of values assessment and clarification:

1. Make a list of the core values you hold (values come from things that give you meaning and importance, yet they are abstract in nature).

2. See if you can identify which of these values are *basic*, or instrumental, at this point in your life and which *support* or augment your basic values.

3. How are your values represented in your possessions (e.g., a BMW may represent wealth or freedom)?

4. Describe how your values influence your dominant thoughts, attitudes, and beliefs.

5. Do you have any values that compete for priority with one another? If so, what are they, and why is there a conflict?

6. What do you see as the best way to begin to resolve this conflict in values? Ask yourself if it is time to change the priority of your values or perhaps discard values that no longer give importance to your life.

EXERCISE 8.3: Value Assessment and Clarification cont....

EXERCISE 8.4: Giving Your Self-Esteem a Healthy Boost

Self-esteem is thought to be composed of five components: uniqueness, role models, empowerment, connectedness, and calculated risk taking. With this in mind, let's take a look at your level of self-esteem with respect to these five areas. Try to answer the following questions as best you can.

1. Uniqueness

List five characteristics or personal attributes that make you feel special and unique (e.g., a sense of humor, being a great cook, a passion for travel, a sense of patience):

a. _____

b. _____

c. _____

d. _____

e. _____

2. Empowerment

List five areas or aspects of your life in which you feel you are empowered (e.g., ways you regain your personal power rather than give it away):

a. _____

b. _____

c. _____

d. _____

e. _____

3. Mentors and Role Models

Who are your role models? Name five people (e.g., heroes, mentors, role models) who have one or more characteristics that you wish to emulate or include as a part of your own personality. Please describe each person and his or her trait or traits:

a. _____

b. _____

c. _____

d. _____

e. _____

EXERCISE 8.4: Giving Your Self-Esteem a Healthy Boost cont....

4. Social Support Groups

Friends and family are now thought to be crucial to one's health status. To have a sense of belonging is very important in your life. With whom (or what) do you feel a sense of belonging? Please describe each in a sentence:

a. _____

b. _____

c. _____

d. _____

e. _____

5. Calculated Risk Taking

List five good risks that you have taken in the past year that your feel have augmented your sense of self-worth and courage:

a. _____

b. _____

c. _____

d. _____

e. _____

Additional Thoughts: Now that you have looked at self-esteem through the context of these aspects, what is your assessment of your level of self-esteem, both overall and from day to day?

_____

_____

_____

_____

_____

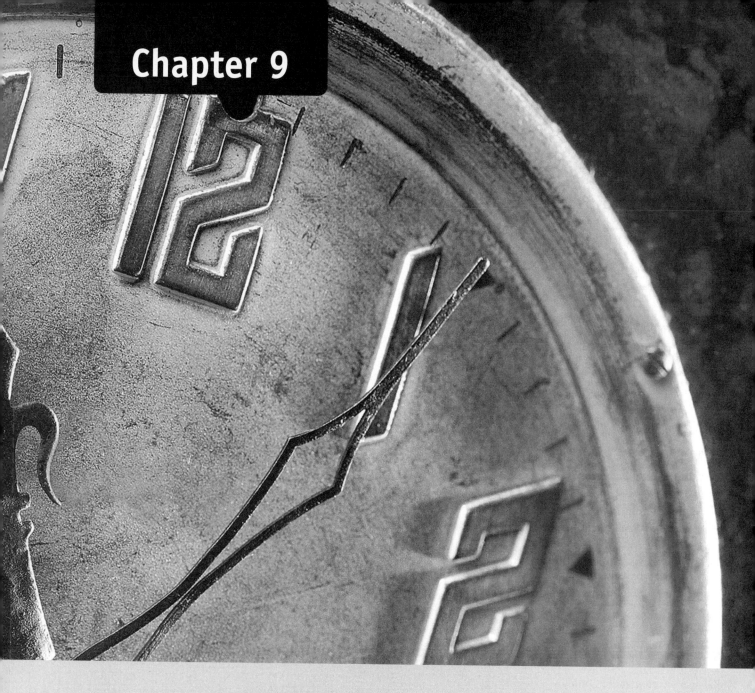

Time and Money: Effective Resource Management

"The best way to double your money is to fold it in half and put it back in your wallet."

— Anonymous

The Ageless Wisdom of Time and Money as Important Resources

Time and money. Time and money. For most people it seems like every stressor involves time and money, because these are two resources that are constantly in high demand, and often squandered. Would you agree? If so, you are in good company. A great many people think that most problems would simply vanish if there were a few more hours in the day and a few extra thousand dollars tucked away in a private bank account. The sad truth is that old habits die hard. Unless a change of attitude is adopted, more time and more money will only result in more responsibilities and more purchases (and possible debt). Consider these sobering facts: The average American typically pays off his or her December Christmas shopping the following June. The average American has 2.5 credit cards with approximately $5,000 of credit card debt and little or no savings.

If there is one lesson to be learned from the economic mess of 2008–2009, it's that greed for some produces a lot of stress for everyone. Both fear and anger are rampant. It's also fair to say that most people have been living outside their financial means for some time and now it's time to tighten our belts. Consider these sobering facts: Foreclosures, layoffs, and fiscal irresponsibility in the accumulation of huge credit card debt and no savings to speak of have added to the downward spiral of economic disaster. Perhaps it's true that Americans have "champagne taste on a beer budget," but these habits start early in life. The average college student holds as many as four credit cards and about $3,000 of debt, according to several news sources, and this amount doesn't even include tuition or school supplies.

This chapter first looks at the topic of finances, and then examines the essentials of budgeting your time so that you can begin to utilize these two resources for your best interest. Before you continue reading, please consider completing the survey in Exercise 9.1 to help you determine what your relationship is with money.

The Art of Money Matters

One would think that maintaining one's personal finances, including keeping a checkbook balanced, would be rather easy with these four simple rules:

1. Make a budget and follow it.
2. Don't spend what you don't have.
3. Pay all your bills on time.
4. Put away at least 10 percent of your monthly income into a savings account (and don't touch it).

If only it were this easy. There are many temptations, big and small, that can add up significantly over a short period of time. For example, the cost of a high-end cup of coffee priced at $4 each day equals approximately $1,400 a year—enough for a spring break vacation. It is good to live in the present moment, but don't squander it! The key to managing your money is balance. On the one hand, you don't want to be a neurotic, penny-pinching Scrooge, yet on the other hand, you cannot afford to be fiscally flamboyant. People never get rich throwing their money away. Today, it appears there are a lot of people who are squandering their income, spending their paychecks as if it were all discretionary income, or worse, living on credit cards.

The relationship between finances and stress has always been dubious, ever since the first coin was exchanged for goods millennia ago. However, with the advent of credit cards, it becomes easy to spend what you don't have, making financial debt all too common a stressor, and for most a way of life. Although it's true that buying now and paying later with a credit card provides a sense of power, the truth is, it's an illusion of power. Remember, the ego (whose purpose is to decrease pain and increase pleasure) also loves power, even if it's a delusion.

Marketing to Your Insecurities: Mass Marketing to *Your* Ego

Are you one of the countless Americans who lives outside your means? Do you spend your money eating at restaurants, buying lots of nice brand-name clothes? Do you purchase expensive coffee and entertain yourself with a huge flat-screen television? Does shopping give you a sense of power? Do you purchase material possessions to fill a spiritual emptiness? Do your mood swings mirror the daily stock report? Are you swayed by instant gratification? Do you make purchases (retail therapy) to allay your anxieties and frustrations? Do you buy items that your friends have, like iPods or satellite radio? Keeping up with the Joneses is a full-time job, and sadly one that never pays a dividend. Rather, it takes hard-earned money away. The next time you watch television, pay close attention to the lifestyles of the characters. There are few if any shows about living in poverty—this doesn't make good viewing! Actors in TV sitcoms and crime shows alike portray upper-middle-class people striving to become upper-class people. According to researchers, the subtle advertising in television programming is akin to an intravenous tube delivering a desirable lifestyle that most people cannot afford (and this doesn't even include the commercials). The ego, looking for pleasure (and a quick fix), is easily manipulated by slick corporate marketers eager to sell you anything and everything. (Remember P. T. Barnum's philosophy, "There's a sucker born every minute!") Take a quick look around you at the clothes people are wearing. How many people do you see walking around as unpaid billboards for corporate America? Take a look around your house or apartment. How many purchases have you made on impulse that are now collecting dust? Marketing to the insecurities of the ego has become an art form in corporate America. With the proliferation of magnetic resonance imaging (MRI) studies to determine the brain's neural code for each thought and behavior, scientists have now teamed up with marketing experts to unlock the code for greater purchasing power, soon bypassing the ego altogether. The term is called *neuromarketing*. Harvard marketing professor Gerald Zaltman has received a patent (#5,436,830) for his technique to market goods and services to your unconscious mind using Jung's theory of archetypal images. Please complete Exercise 9.3 "The Time Crunch Questionnaire."

The Psychology of Poverty

Not long ago, a world-class economist theorized that if you took all the money in the world from the wealthiest people and distributed it evenly among all the global inhabitants, in less than 2 years it would all be back in the hands of the people who initially held it. Why? Because human nature is prone to act on fear (and laziness). As such, people's attitudes are very hard to change. Most people would quickly spend their portion, some would simply lose theirs, the gamblers would gamble their money away, yet very few would save or invest. As odd as it might sound, many people have a fear of money, or simply stated, a fear of the lack of money, often called "poverty consciousness." Ironically, the fear of poverty becomes a self-fulfilling prophecy that repels money rather than attracts it to you, and this thought process becomes a never-ending cycle played out in daily behaviors, according to Joe Dominguez and Vicki Robin, authors of the best-selling book, *Your Money or Your Life*.

How to Incorporate Sound Financial Management into Your Life Routine

The causes of money problems are as varied as the amount of money found in each person's checking account. Stated in simple economic terms, demand for goods and services always exceeds supply of cash on hand. Regardless of what the expenses are, the result begins with fiscal hemorrhaging and ends up with undeniable debt. Catastrophic medical bills and huge car repair bills are one thing, but frivolous spending is another, and currently in this country it's hitting epidemic proportions. There is no shortage of suggestions regarding ways to pull the reins of one's financial spending. Here are some time-tested tips to consider:

1. *Make and follow a budget.* If you don't already have a budget, then now is the time to start one. If you do have one, when is the last time you fine-tuned it? Exercise 9.2 is an example of a typical personal budget sheet. You should know, within a few dollars, how much you have each month to spend as discretionary income.

2. *Live a sustainable lifestyle.* Life isn't a sprint; rather, it's more like an ultra-marathon. As such, spending money should be well paced, yet some people spend like there is no tomorrow. A sustainable life means living a conscious life where purchases are made consciously rather than frivolously. It also means enjoying the present moment, yet keeping an eye on the future as well. Living a sustainable life also means buying only what you will use and not wasting precious natural resources. Behaviors include using reusable cloth grocery bags or driving a hybrid car.

3. *Freeze your credit card.* Credit cards are nothing more than expensive loans. Every time you pull out a credit card you are borrowing money and paying a high interest rate (13 percent to 23 percent). Get in the habit of going cold turkey with your credit card. One suggestion is to cut up all but one card and stick the remaining card in a glass of water and place it in the freezer. This ensures that you will use it only for emergencies.

4. *Keep a spending journal.* If your money burns a hole in your pocket or debit card and you are not sure where it really goes, start keeping a

spending journal to see where money is wasted. You may be quite surprised at how frivolous spending adds up and reflects a habit of hard-earned money going down the drain.

5. *See each purchase as an investment.* What are your assets? Your house, your car, your stock portfolio? Every purchase you make is an investment, yet most of these depreciate to nothing quickly, including clothes. Here is a question to ask yourself: Will I want or use this item a year from now? If the answer is no, then walk away.

6. *Consolidate your debt.* Do you have several credit card bills and other loans? Talk to your bank manager about consolidating your debt into one loan payment, and pay this off as soon as possible.

Michelle Singletary is a syndicated columnist for the *Washington Post* and author of *Spend Well, Live Right*. The following are some of her tips for achieving financial stability.

1. *Remove yourself from temptation.* If you don't have money to spend (or waste), then don't hang around people who go shopping to spend lots of money, because this can become a trap of sorts: adult peer pressure. Also, before you go shopping, make a list of what you really need and maintain the willpower to buy only what's on your list.

2. *Ask "why" before you buy.* Do you really need the item you're about to purchase? Underwear and toothpaste are necessities. Lattes, appetizers, weekly DVD rentals, and new shoes are not.

3. *Don't buy on impulse.* If you find something you like, hold off from buying it that day. Sleep on it. If it's still something you think you need, go back the next day.

4. *Be wary of bargains.* You may save money on sales, but many people end up spending more money than they expected by purchasing more items than they need. Rather than saving money, they spend money they don't have.

5. *Clean your house.* One of the best incentives to harness uncontrolled spending is taking stock of what you already have. There is no need to buy something only to find out you already own it. Additionally, follow the 2-year rule: If you haven't used an item or article of clothing in 2 years, donate it to a charity before it collects more dust.

6. *Learn to say no to your kids, spouse, friends, and marketers.* Don't allow other people to spend your money for you. Have good boundaries with your money and be assertive with these boundaries.

Suze Orman is a best-selling author on the topic of financial planning and is also a syndicated television financial expert. Her tips for financial freedom include the following. Read these first and then try completing Exercise 9.2.

1. *Adopt a healthy attitude about money.* What is your relationship to money? Do you have poverty consciousness? Do you waste money? Do you repel money? Do you carry the fiscal poverty attitude of your parents? Your attitude about money has a lot to do with how little or how much you have, and will have over time.

2. *Make sound financial goals.* Do you intend to work the rest of your life? Do you have a retirement account? Can you see beyond your next paycheck? Do you wish to take a yearly vacation? Financial goals are guidelines to help you achieve financial security. What are your goals? What is your long-term strategic plan for financial security?

3. *Put your money to work for you.* Even if you think you have no money to invest, you really do, even if it's only $100/year. There are mutual funds, IRAs, shares of stock, Treasury bills, and savings accounts. Talk to a financial advisor (usually the first consultation is free) to discuss your options and make a plan to have your money make money for you.

4. *The best financial advisor is you.* Having a financial advisor is good, but remember, they are making money off *your* money. Get sound advice and then do your homework by reading books on this topic. Check out information on the Internet. Learn how to budget your money, how to invest your money, and how to make your money work for you.

Best Benefits of Financial Management

Having oodles of money tucked away in various portfolios does not ensure a stress-free life. Many rich people are anything but happy and stress free. Conversely, having little or no money can be equally stressful. Living within your financial means, including putting a little away each paycheck, acts as a buffer against the huge burden of financial stress that many people suffer.

By all accounts financial concerns top the list of many people's stressors, but it doesn't have to be that way. Among the best benefits of financial management are a sense of empowerment (knowing that you have the ability to spend money responsibly, as well as getting a good night's sleep not worrying about every last nickel and dime). Spending your hard earned money wisely is truly an investment in your health and well-being.

The Ageless Wisdom of Time Management

One of the biggest complaints heard over the ages is simply not having enough time to do what needs to get done in the course of any given day. Perhaps since time began, humans have done everything in their power to manipulate time, from tinkering with daylight savings to numerous revisions to the yearly calendar. Did you ever wonder why the annual lunar cycle is 13, yet the monthly calendar only has 12 months?

Nearly everyone wishes they had more time for leisure and less hours of the day devoted to earning a paycheck. Ironically, the promise of technology made decades ago to allow more leisure time never materialized. Although technology has provided a plethora of wonderful gadgets (e.g., smartphones, answering machines, laptop computers, microwave ovens, washers, dryers, dishwashers, and word processors), few if any people are sitting back comfortably with hours upon hours of leisure time on their hands these days. If anything, people seem to have less leisure time, not more, than they did decades ago. For this reason, people are continually seeking out ideas and suggestions to better organize their time and enjoy the time they have. Day planners and iPads are effective, but there are literally hundreds of other ways to streamline your day for higher efficiency and productivity, none of which compromise your integrity. Exercise 9.4 is a worksheet that can be used in group situations to help brainstorm for new ideas to manage time. Remember that if you get one good idea that you can use, it's worth it.

Time management is best defined as the prioritization, scheduling, and execution of responsibilities to personal satisfaction. Let's take a closer look at each of these aspects so that you can begin to manage your time even better:

- *Prioritization:* **Prioritization** first requires one to identify specific tasks and responsibilities to be accomplished. To prioritize one's to-do list means knowing the difference between what's essential and what's not. In the business model, it's imperative to know the difference between what's urgent and what's not, and what's important and what's not. Human nature tends to make us want to gravitate toward things that are of high interest and low priority, leaving the things of high urgency and low interest until last.

- There are several ways to identify the urgency of responsibilities. The first includes the ABC rank-order method (A = highest priority, B = moderate priority, and C = low priority). The second, based on the work of Steven Covey, is the important vs. urgent grid, where, by writing down tasks into one of four grid boxes, you gain clarity regarding what needs to get done first. Exercise 9.5 includes both of these methods.

- *Scheduling:* Once tasks and responsibilities are identified, then comes the need to set each task with a time schedule to get it accomplished. **Scheduling** involves the skills of organization to know when is the best time to get things done and the means to do so. Experts in the field of time management suggest various techniques for the most efficient means of scheduling tasks and responsibilities. *Clustering* is the name for grouping tasks. Examples include clustering errands (e.g., post office, dry cleaners, and video store) so that time is not wasted driving all over the place. *Boxing* is the term given to designating large segments of the day when big chunks of uninterrupted time are needed. *Dismantling* refers to breaking down large projects into smaller, more manageable tasks. Examples might include large projects, term papers, wedding plans, or backyard landscaping. **Time mapping** is a technique used to designate specific parts of each hour for scheduling purposes. Exercise 9.6 is an example of time mapping.

- *Execution (action plan):* To be able to prioritize responsibilities and schedule them into your day is good, but it's not enough to get the job done. Rolling up your sleeves and actually doing the work is the lion's share (70 percent) of effective time management. **Execution** is the act of carrying out, completing, or finishing each and every task you set out to accomplish. A large part of time management's execution is sheer willpower—the drive to get things done and done well.

One way to add some inspiration to your willpower is to consider assigning a reward for each large task looming on your horizon. Whether the reward is large or small, tangible (a Hawaiian vacation) or intangible (sheer happiness), having an incentive is often helpful. It's important to remember, however, in this age of instant gratification, the reward comes after, not before, the task is completed. Exercise 9.7 provides a template for matching various personal tasks with possible rewards that may serve as a motivation to get each task accomplished. Although rewards don't work for everyone, they might be an idea worth considering. One caution about carrying out an action plan: Avoid multi-tasking!

The Art of Subtraction

It may be human nature to accumulate things, but as anyone knows, too much of anything is not good. By and large, Americans are very good at honoring the art of addition, by accumulating more and more stuff. Not all stuff carries with it endless responsibilities, but a lot of possessions do. Effective time management honors the inherent concept of balance. To achieve balance, one must occasionally let go of things that one has accumulated.

Technology, consumerism, and many American values promote a lifestyle of addition. Holistic stress management requires living life in balance, meaning that the art of subtraction must be practiced as well. How does one engage in the art of subtraction? Ideas include, but are not limited to, bringing clothes to Goodwill, recycling newspapers and bottles, and watching less television. The overriding premise of the **art of subtraction** is making life simpler by having less things and people in your life that waste time. Exercise 9.8 invites you to make a list of things and people who either clutter your life or pull badly needed energy from you and ultimately serve as a distraction to getting things done.

Time Robbers

Have you ever spent hours cleaning the house, garage, or car when you really should have been finishing a project or paying bills? If so, know that you're in good company. You are also in the company of one of life's many **time robbers**. Time robbers are things that steal your valuable time away from what really needs attention. Experts agree that one of the biggest time robbers today is the Web, and specifically Facebook. What might start as a few moments to check messages becomes hours of scrolling through your friends' updated posts. Time robbers are things that literally suck the life energy right out of you. Although procrastination, in all its many forms, comprises a large percentage of time robbers, things that steal minutes or hours out of your life include more than just little things you do to avoid necessary responsibilities. People can be time robbers, too! For this reason, having healthy boundaries is essential when setting out to start and complete things on your to-do list.

If you think that you waste time in the course of each day, or like sand slipping through an hourglass your time slips away, consider using Exercise 9.6 (time mapping) to chronicle the time robbers in your life.

Time-Honored Time Management Tips

Do you wish you had more leisure time to enjoy life's simple pleasures? The following are tips and suggestions of how to use your time more effectively so that you may enjoy your leisure time more peacefully.

1. *Put a healthy boundary on social media outlets (e.g., Facebook, Twitter, Pinterest, etc.).* Checking on friends' updates can become quite addictive, and waste a lot of valuable time. Consider going to Facebook at the end of the day, when all of your other work and family responsibilities are complete.

2. *Do one activity at a time (no multi-tasking)!* There are few people who can do two things at once and do them well. The best the rest of us can do is accept mediocrity, which does not support the premise of holistic stress management. Multi-tasking may be the in thing, but it never results in a quality job.

3. *Let technology serve you, rather than you serving it!* Smartphones, laptops, and iPads are wonderful tools to increase efficiency, yet they are not meant to be used every hour of the day. There is a strong addictive quality to technology (e.g., constantly texting, using new apps), which soon reverses the relationship so that people become slaves to the very thing that is supposed to serve them. Good boundaries are essential with the ever-changing face of high technology. This fact cannot be overstated!

4. *Get a good night's sleep!* People have the odd belief that shaving off hours of sleep on either end of the day will allow them to get more done. Poor sleep compromises mental acuity, thus compromising your quality of work. Get a good night's sleep every night.

5. *Be assertive!* Learn to say no when others ask you to do work for them or activities with them that impede the progress of your own work schedule. By not being assertive, you may begin to feel victimized, which leads to feelings of anger.

6. *Schedule personal time each day (and use it)!* Your health is essential to ensure the best quality of life. If you neglect personal time for exercise, healthy eating, and nurturing relationships, then your health becomes compromised, adding more stress to your life.

7. *Cultivate your networking skills!* Many tasks can be done by yourself, but others require help. Make it a practice to cultivate relationships with friends, neighbors, family members, and professional colleagues who can assist you by offering anything from sound advice to a helping hand when needed.

8. *Watch less television!* The average person watches between 20 and 30 hours of television a week. This is nearly a full-time job! Although there are a few good programs on television these days, most people agree that the rest is mindless junk. For most people, television is human Kryptonite! It sucks your power away. Establish a healthy boundary with television and consider removing it altogether.

How to Incorporate Time Management into Your Life Routine

There is an adage that states: To know and not to do, is not to know. You can know all the right tips and suggestions for time management, but until you actually put these into play, not much will really change. The following are some tips to help you not only know, but do.

1. The first step in incorporating effective time management skills into your life routine is to observe where your time robbers are.

2. Do a quick survey and determine how to apply the art of subtraction—what things can you delete from your life that are taking up valuable time or draining your personal energy?

3. Identify and prioritize daily responsibilities (your to-do list) from larger goals to personal goals (e.g., buying a house, taking a vacation, writing a book). Remember to include in your daily responsibilities time for exercise, meditation, adequate sleep, healthy meals, social time, and even a few unscheduled interruptions.

4. After clearing all distractions, sit down and get to work on the things of highest priority and urgency. Remember that big projects need to be broken down into smaller pieces so that the end result can be accomplished successfully.

5. At the end of each day, take a quick inventory to see what got done and what needs to roll over into the next day. Before you call it a day, consider spending a few minutes doing some organizational prep work so that you can start the next day without a huge adrenaline rush.

Effective time management requires moment to moment corrections of your personal daily schedule because life is dynamic, not static, and changes can and will occur. Perhaps the biggest obstacle to effective time management is the ego, which has a tendency to want to step in and control everything. Remember, there are many people who could work 20 hours a day and still not get everything done. At some point you have to resign yourself to the fact that the quality must be balanced with the quantity of tasks and responsibilities.

How to Develop Your Mastery of Time Management

Effective time management skills involve both a sense of discipline and flexibility. Discipline is essential with regard to healthy boundaries so that you know when not to take on additional responsibilities, thus feeling overwhelmed and possibly victimized. Flexibility is critical in terms of moving through the course of each day, shifting with new priorities without feeling stressed about other things that also need to be accomplished. Your mastery of effective time management is a skill that must be continually refined because the dynamics of one's life quickly change.

Ultimately, time management becomes the most important coping skill for holistic stress management, because if one doesn't make the time for the other coping and relaxation techniques to fully integrate, balance, and harmonize mind, body, spirit, and emotions, then even the best efforts for inner peace are ultimately compromised, if not abandoned altogether.

Best Benefits of Time Management

The benefits of effective time management are many. Rather than running around in a state of frenzy, you feel a sense of empowerment from getting things done and having the time to enjoy life's simple pleasures. A large part of effective time management includes setting healthy boundaries and having the willpower to enforce these boundaries. There is simply no way to add more time to a 24-hour day, which means that spending your time wisely is the greatest benefit of all.

Chapter Summary

- The art of money matters suggests that we live responsibly within our means, not on credit or debt. Suggestions include: make a budget and follow it, spend only what you have, pay your bills on time, and always include your savings as an expense.

- Corporate America knows how to get you to spend your money on things you don't need with money you don't have. They market to your ego directly through your unconscious mind. Don't let them.

- The psychology of poverty describes people who have a fear of not having enough, which becomes a self-fulfilling prophecy.

- There are countless ways to live within your means without being a Scrooge.

- Benefits of fiscal management include a sense of empowerment and assuredness that you are not a victim to your money (or lack of it).

- The anatomy of time management includes three aspects: prioritizing, scheduling, and execution.

- The art of subtraction describes the philosophy that less is more, which when adopted helps you manage your time (and perhaps your money) better.

- There are many things that tend to steal our time away. Time robbers include procrastination,

television watching, the Web, and virtually anything that wastes precious time.

- There are many ways to effectively manage your time better.

- Development of your mastery of time management is a skill that, with practice, will serve you well over the years.

Additional Resources

Allen, D. *Getting Things Done*. New York: Penguin; 2003.

Dodd, P., & Sundheim, D. *The 25 Best Time Management Tools and Techniques*. New York: Peak Performance Press; 2005.

Dominguez, J., & Robin, V. *Your Money or Your Life*. New York: Penguin; 1999.

Flyte. *Web Marketing Advice*. 2012. http://www.flyte .biz/resources/newsletters/09/05-social-media-time-management.php. Accessed October 2, 2012.

Jasper, J. *Take Back Your Time: How to Regain Control of Work, Information and Technology*. New York: St. Martin's; 1999.

Knaus, W. *The Procrastination Workbook*. Oakland, CA: New Harbinger Publications; 2002.

Koch, R. *The 80/20 Principle: The Secret of Achieving More with Less*. New York: Bantam Doubleday Dell; 1998.

McPeak, M. 19886: Living it Up, Paying it Down. *National Geographic*. February 2005, pp. 124–130.

Morganstern, J. *Time Management from the Inside Out*. New York: Henry Holt; 2000.

Orman, S. *Suze Orman's Financial Guidebook*. New York: Three Rivers Press; 2002.

Rubin, V. *Your Money or Your Life*. New York: Penguin; 2008.

Rubleski, J. *The 10 Steps to Financial Wellness*. Omaha, NE: WELCOA; 2007.

Schlosser, E. *Fast Food Nation*. Boston: Houghton Mifflin; 2001.

Sherman, S. *The Cure for Money Madness*. New York: Broadway; 2009.

Singletary, M. *Spend Well, Live Right*. New York: Ballantine; 2004.

Szegedy-Maszak, M. Mysteries of the Mind. *U.S. News and World Report*. February 28, 2005, pp. 52–61.

Twist, L. *The Soul of Money*. New York: W.W. Norton; 2003.

EXERCISE 9.1: Your Relationship with Money Survey

The following are some thought-provoking questions to help you examine your beliefs, attitudes, and behaviors regarding money. There are no wrong answers to these questions. They are merely listed to help you reflect on your fiscal relationship.

1. Do you continually stress out about not having enough money? YES NO
2. Do you make purchases for things that you really don't need? YES NO
3. Do you spend money on others to make them like you? YES NO
4. Do your friends always seem to have things that you wish you had. YES NO
5. Do you put 10 percent of your monthly income away in a savings account? YES NO
6. Do you know how much it costs you to live each month? YES NO
7. Do you typically buy things only to find when you get home you already have them? YES NO
8. Do you eat out more than twice a week? YES NO
9. Do you pay to keep things in a storage facility? YES NO
10. Are you the kind of person who typically buys on impulse? YES NO
11. Do you pay off your credit card each billing cycle? YES NO
12. Do you have more than one credit card (e.g, Visa, MasterCard, Discover, AMEX)? YES NO
13. As a child, did your parents make you work for an allowance? YES NO
14. Look around your house/apartment; do you really use the items you purchase? YES NO
15. Do you spend more than $50/month on phone calls? YES NO
16. When eating out, do you split the check evenly or count pennies to determine who owes what? YES NO
17. Do you only withdraw money from your bank's ATM? YES NO
18. Regardless of how much you make, do you give money to charity? YES NO
19. Do you tend to frequently borrow money from friends? YES NO
20. Do you frequently buy lottery tickets or gamble in the hopes of winning big bucks? YES NO
21. Do you occasionally bounce checks or borrow from your line of credit? YES NO
22. Do you use coupons for items you might not otherwise purchase? YES NO
23. Do you pay yourself a salary (to be placed in a retirement account)? YES NO
24. Do you know your net worth? YES NO
25. Do you know your monthly disposable income amount? YES NO

EXERCISE 9.2: My Personal Budget Worksheet

The following is a monthly budget worksheet to help you better see how your personal funds are directed between income and expenses. If your expenses exceed your income, ask yourself what changes can be made to bring these back into balance. Note that personal savings is a necessary expense.

Month _____

Income

1. Monthly paycheck(s) $ _____
2. Stock dividends $ _____
3. Gifts (e.g., from parents) $ _____
4. Other $ _____

                               Total $ _____

Necessary Expenses

1. Rent/mortgage $ _____
2. Food $ _____
3. Utilities (e.g., power/gas) $ _____
4. Phone $ _____
5. Car loan payment $ _____
6. Transportation (e.g., gas, car maintenance) $ _____
7. Auto/health insurance $ _____
8. Savings $ _____
9. Monthly fees (e.g., ISP, athletic club) $ _____

    Service fees _____

              _____

              _____

10. Loan payments (including credit card debt) $ _____
11. Disposable income (e.g., clothes, entertainment, gifts) $ _____
12. Miscellaneous (e.g., clothing) $ _____
13. Other expenses $ _____

                    Total $ _____

                    Net Gain/Loss $ _____

                    Your Discretionary Income $ _____ /month

EXERCISE 9.3: The Time-Crunch Questionnaire

Please answer the following questions as you are (not how you would like to be) regarding your time management skills.

       1 = Rarely   **2 = Sometimes**   **3 = Often**

Add up the numbers you circled and check the questionnaire key to determine your level of time management skills.

1. I tend to procrastinate with projects and responsibilities.	1	2	3
2. My bedtime varies depending on the workload I have each day.	1	2	3
3. I am the kind of person who leaves things until the last minute.	1	2	3
4. I forget to make or refer to "to do" lists to keep me organized.	1	2	3
5. I spend more than 2 hours watching television each night.	1	2	3
6. I tend to have multiple projects going on at the same time.	1	2	3
7. I tend to put work ahead of family and friends.	1	2	3
8. My life seems to be full of endless interruptions and distractions.	1	2	3
9. I tend to spend a lot of time texting on my smartphone and talking to friends.	1	2	3
10. Multi-tasking is my middle name. I am a great multi-tasker.	1	2	3
11. My biggest problem with time management is prioritization.	1	2	3
12. I am a perfectionist when it comes to getting things done.	1	2	3
13. I never seem to have enough time for my personal life.	1	2	3
14. I tend to set unrealistic goals to accomplish tasks.	1	2	3
15. I reward myself *before* getting things done on time.	1	2	3
16. I just never have enough hours in the day to get things done.	1	2	3
17. I can spend untold hours distracted while surfing the Internet.	1	2	3
18. I tend not to trust others to get things done when I can do it better myself.	1	2	3
19. If I am completely honest, I tend to be a workaholic.	1	2	3
20. I have been known to skip meals in order to complete projects.	1	2	3
21. I will clean my room, garage, or kitchen before I really get to work on projects.	1	2	3
22. I will often help friends with their work before doing my own.	1	2	3
23. I tend to spend time on less important but more satisfying things at the cost of being efficient.	1	2	3
24. I end up wasting a lot of time with technology and gadgets (texting, videogames, Facebook, etc.).	1	2	3
25. I often find it hard to get motivated to get things done.	1	2	3
TOTAL SCORE			

EXERCISE 9.3: The Time-Crunch Questionnaire cont....

Questionnaire Key

75–51 points = Poor time management skills (time to reevaluate your life skills)

50–26 points = Fair time management skills (time to pull in the reins a bit)

0–25 points = Excellent time management skills (keep doing what you are doing!)

EXERCISE 9.4: Time Management Idea Exchange

1. List five reasons why people don't manage their time effectively (including time robbers). Which ones apply to your current lifestyle?

a._____

b._____

c._____

d._____

e._____

2. Explain the feelings of stress when your time isn't managed as well as you'd like it to be.

a._____

b._____

c._____

d._____

e._____

3. List the most beneficial time management techniques that you find helpful to manage your time effectively and keep on schedule, and then explain why they are beneficial to you.

a._____

b._____

c._____

d._____

e._____

4. Think up five new ways to manage your time more effectively.

a._____

b._____

c._____

d._____

e._____

5. What steps can you take to implement one or more of these time management techniques?

a._____

b._____

c._____

d._____

e._____

EXERCISE 9.5: The Importance of Prioritization

The following are two methods of improving your organizational skills for effective prioritization and time management.

ABC Rank-Order Method

A Highest Priority	B Moderate Priority	C Low Priority
1. _____.	1. _____.	1. _____
2. _____	2. _____	2. _____
3. _____	3. _____	3. _____
4. _____	4. _____	4. _____
5. _____	5. _____	5. _____

Important vs. Urgent Method

	High Importance	Low Importance
High Urgency	I: a._____ b._____ c._____	III: a._____ b._____ c._____
Low Urgency	II: a._____ b._____ c._____	IV: a._____ b._____ c._____

EXERCISE 9.6: Time Mapping

The following exercise invites you to chart out your day by clearly identifying how each 15-minute block of time is spent. You can also simply record your daily activities to observe where time robbers are stealing your time.

7:00 a.m. _____

7:15 a.m. _____

7:30 a.m. _____

7:45 a.m. _____

8:00 a.m. _____

8:15 a.m. _____

8:30 a.m. _____

8:45 a.m. _____

9:00 a.m. _____

9:15 a.m. _____

9:30 a.m. _____

9:45 a.m. _____

10:00 a.m. _____

10:15 a.m. _____

10:30 a.m. _____

10:45 a.m. _____

11:00 a.m. _____

11:15 a.m. _____

11:30 a.m. _____

11:45 a.m. _____

12:00 noon _____

12:15 p.m. _____

12:30 p.m. _____

12:45 p.m. _____

1:00 p.m. _____

1:15 p.m. _____

1:30 p.m. _____

1:45 p.m. _____

2:00 p.m. _____

2:15 p.m. _____

2:30 p.m. _____

EXERCISE 9.6: Time Mapping cont....

2:45 p.m. _____

3:00 p.m. _____

3:15 p.m. _____

3:30 p.m. _____

3:45 p.m. _____

4:00 p.m. _____

4:15 p.m. _____

4:30 p.m. _____

4:45 p.m. _____

5:00 p.m. _____

5:15 p.m. _____

5:30 p.m. _____

5:45 p.m. _____

6:00 p.m. _____

6:15 p.m. _____

6:30 p.m. _____

6:45 p.m. _____

7:00 p.m. _____

7:15 p.m. _____

7:30 p.m. _____

7:45 p.m. _____

8:00 p.m. _____

8:15 p.m. _____

8:30 p.m. _____

8:45 p.m. _____

9:00 p.m. _____

9:15 p.m. _____

9:30 p.m. _____

9:45 p.m. _____

10:00 p.m. _____

After you have written down the events or plans in the course of your day, what observations can you make from this exercise?

_____

EXERCISE 9.7: Execution of Tasks

Lacking some motivation to get some things done? One way to fan the fires of inspiration is to provide some incentive to accomplish big or arduous tasks by giving yourself a reward. Although the real reward is the accomplishment of the deed, a little incentive may be just the thing needed to get it done on time. Remember, not all rewards have to be material possessions. A phone call to a close friend at the end of the day can be as rewarding as a vacation to Tahiti in some cases. Remember, rewards are meant to decrease stress, not increase it.

Objective   **Reward**

1. _____   _____

   _____   _____

2. _____   _____

   _____   _____

3. _____   _____

   _____   _____

4. _____   _____

   _____   _____

5. _____   _____

   _____   _____

6. _____   _____

   _____   _____

7. _____   _____

   _____   _____

8. _____   _____

   _____   _____

9. _____   _____

   _____   _____

10. _____   _____

    _____   _____

EXERCISE 9.8: Practicing the Art of Subtraction

Does your life feel cluttered with too much stuff? Are your garage and basement filled with things that you haven't used (or seen) in years? Are there people in your life who are so emotionally needy that when you see them, you want to run and hide? Are there things in your life that at first seem to simplify life but now they seem to complicate it? If so, you might want to consider engaging in the art of subtraction (also known as "editing your life").

I. Clutter! Walk through your house or apartment and make a list of five things that fall into the category of personal clutter (this can include equipment, clothes, books, or anything laying on the floor).

1._____

2._____

3._____

4._____

5._____

II. People! Are there people in your life who take up time rather than contribute to your quality of life? Take inventory if you have any "friends" who seem to drain your emotional energy. The next question to ask yourself is this: Do you drain other people's energy? Do you give as well as take in your relationships and friendships?

1._____

2._____

3._____

III. Simplicity vs. Complexity. We tend to bring things into our lives out of both interest and fear. What things are in your life right now that may have begun out of interest but now you are ready to let go of? Another way to phrase this question is to ask yourself what things in your life tend to add complexity rather than simplicity. Once you have identified three things, begin to ask yourself what you can do to subtract these things to bring your life back into balance.

1._____

2._____

3._____

Expressive Art Therapy

"The mind is a place of living images and our hearts are the organs that tell us so."
— Anonymous

The Ageless Wisdom of Art Therapy

If we only used words to share our thoughts and emotions, we would find this expression of communication to be extremely limiting. There is a world of thoughts, feelings, and emotions that simply cannot be expressed in words, all of which begs for another outlet. With the realization that holistic stress management is the collaboration, not separation, of the conscious and unconscious minds, one must remember to utilize the powerful nonverbal aspects of the unconscious mind when looking for answers to resolve issues of stress. As has been mentioned many times in this book, the unconscious mind holds a wealth of information and insights begging to be shared through a powerful combination of colors, symbols, and images.

Art therapy is a coping technique that not only taps into this wealth of information from the unconscious mind, but also, when given the chance, becomes integrated with the verbal aspect of the conscious mind to work toward a peaceful resolution of problems, challenges, concerns, and issues.

It's uncertain how long humankind has used art as a form of artistic expression, but if the prehistoric artwork found in caves in Lascaux, France, is any indication, then art as a form of self-expression may indeed be one of the oldest methods of therapy.

The roots of art as a recognized form of therapy date back to the work of both Freud and Jung. After World War II, art therapy became respected as a viable modality of healing, as both a means of catharsis and a window into the unconscious mind. Today art therapy is used in a number of settings as a tool to help people unlock the means of expression that cannot be found in words alone. War veterans, anorexics, rape victims, prisoners, abused children, college students, corporate executives, and senior citizens have all engaged in the practice of art therapy as a means to resolve stress. Like a key that unlocks a door to a whole new world, the results, in many cases, have been nothing less than astounding.

You don't have to be Picasso, Rembrandt, or Georgia O'Keefe to engage in the practice of art therapy. It doesn't matter how well you draw, paint, or sculpt. Talent has nothing to do with the message of the work. Instead, the power of art therapy is based on the nature of what is drawn, the colors used, and the symbols represented pictorially. Everything has meaning!

 are examples of emotional expression through art therapy.

The Interpretation of Art in Art Therapy

Exercise 10.1 ("The Human Butterfly") and Exercise 10.2 ("Beyond Words") offer you several artistic themes for this technique.

Drawing, painting, sculpting, or any other artistic means to reveal the secrets of the unconscious mind are only part of the process of art therapy. Taking the time to verbally interpret the artwork is as important as composing the piece of artwork itself. Just as dreams are best left to the dreamer to fully comprehend the meaning, the artist (with a little bit of training) is the best qualified to uncover the meaning of what was expressed and represented artistically because the artist knows his or her

FIGURE 10.1 This illustration depicts a migraine headache. The theme he drew was how he felt when he gets angry. Notice the absence of the mouth.

FIGURE 10.2 This illustration depicts a recurring dream a person drew. As he described it, he is reaching for the apple, but can never grab it. It just hangs in mid air.

mind better than anyone else does. Perhaps because pastels and colored pencils/crayons are the most accessible materials, they have become the most common media of art therapy. Each color used in an art therapy session holds significance. Based on the initial work of Jung and his many followers who went on to develop the field of art therapy, a key of archetypal colors is now available to help interpret one's drawing (see Exercise 10.2).

Art Therapy and Chronic Illness

One of the most recognized benefits of art therapy was discovered 30 years ago by Carl Simonton, who used art therapy with other coping modalities as an integrated approach to treating cancer patients. Patients began to draw themselves, their tumors, and other aspects of their lives that often gave insight into the disease and in many cases the best way to treat it. Today art therapy is used as an integrative healing modality for several types of chronic diseases, including hypertension, irritable bowl syndrome, lupus, migraine headaches, coronary heart disease, and rheumatoid arthritis.

How to Incorporate Art Therapy into Your Life Routine

It has often been said that there is no wrong way to do art therapy. Although this may be true, you can take certain steps to enhance the process so that you gain as much from the experience as possible. The following are some tips that may augment your art therapy experience:

1. Drop all inhibitions about your artistic abilities. Art therapy is not about being an artist, as much as it is about simply drawing, as best you can, your thoughts and feelings.

2. Consider having on hand a good selection of art supplies, including pastels, crayons, colored pencils, and large sheets of white paper.

3. Give yourself about 20–30 minutes to draw one or more themes. Sometimes having some quiet instrumental music playing in the background helps to engage the right (creative) side of the brain.

Chapter 10

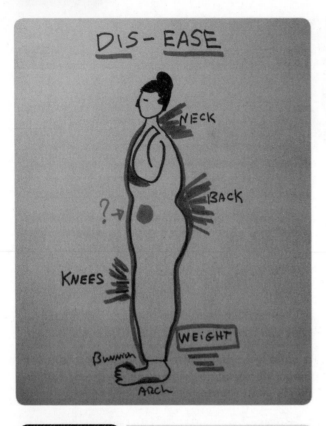

FIGURE 10.3 A woman drew a series of health issues in her neck, back, knees, and feet, all related to stress, titling the art piece, Dis-ease.

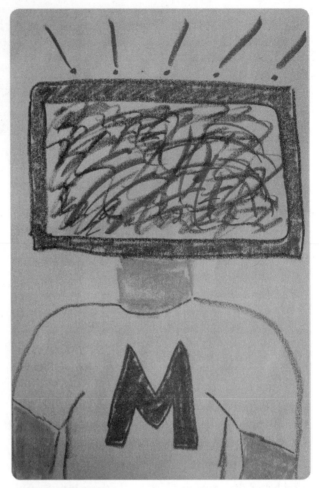

FIGURE 10.4 A student at a Midwestern university illustrates his life with a computer/tablet screen for a head. He added that he feels like his whole life revolves around the Internet and he cannot escape it.

4. It's important to remember to use whatever colors you wish. If you are doing these exercises in a large group and you need a blue pastel and cannot find it, call out. Laziness is not a good excuse during art therapy.

5. Working alone on a picture may lessen one's inhibitions, but doing this activity together with a small group of friends can really add to the experience, particularly when it comes time to articulate your interpretation. In the process of explaining to others what you have drawn, you help yourself process this experience as well.

6. Consider hanging your artwork on the refrigerator, bathroom mirror, or your home office corkboard for several weeks so that you can see it regularly. Often a deeper meaning may surface after several days of looking at your piece.

Best Benefits of Art Therapy

Art therapy appears to hold both immediate and long-term benefits as a tool for holistic stress management. The immediate effects can be summed up in the word *catharsis*, an emotional release. The long-term effects are more subtle than the short-term cathartic release is, but often more powerful. When art therapy participants elect to post their pieces of artwork where they can be seen regularly, the unconscious mind continues its work to reveal more messages of information. It is not uncommon for people to say that after looking at their art therapy work for several days they begin to see new meaning in the piece. With new meaning and deeper interpretation comes a shift in consciousness, allowing either greater insight into problems (a means toward a faster resolution) or simply a different perspective.

Chapter Summary

- Art therapy is an effective coping skill to express oneself nonverbally. Nonverbal communication is a significant aspect of the power of the unconscious mind. Art therapy also serves as a healthy catharsis for unresolved issues.

- Everything within the expression of art has meaning: colors, shapes, and so on. Interpretation of art therapy is best done by the person who created it.

- The cathartic nature of art therapy has been known to help those who suffer from chronic illnesses such as cancer and lupus.

- There are many ways to incorporate art therapy as an effective coping skill, from doodling to many forms of expressive art.

- The benefits of art therapy are many, including the inner peace associated with the resolution of stressors.

Additional Resources

Edwards, B. *The New Drawing of the Right Side of the Brain* (2nd ed.). New York: JP Tarcher; 1999.

Farrelly-Hansen, M. *Spirituality and Art Therapy*. Philadelphia: Jessica Kingsley Publishers; 2001.

Malchiodi, C. *The Art Therapy Sourcebook* (2nd ed.). New York: McGraw-Hill; 2006.

Silverstone, L. *Art Therapy Exercises*. London: Jessica Kingsley Publishers; 2009.

EXERCISE 10.1: The Human Butterfly

Theme: The butterfly is a symbol of transformation—to rise above life's issues and problems and move on. The words *butterfly* and *soul* are synonymous in Greek.

Activity: Spread out some colored crayons or pastels on a table or floor area where you can easily access them. If you are doing this with others, please remember to share! Allocate about 10–15 minutes to color in the wings of your butterfly.

As an additional phase of the human butterfly exercise, consider writing in the butterfly wings those inner resources or muscles of the soul (e.g., humor, patience, forgiveness, creativity, optimism) that you use to effectively cope with problems. If there are inner resources that you feel you would like to have be a stronger part of who you are (to enhance your coping skills), then write those attributes on the outside of the butterfly and draw an arrow from the word into the wing of the butterfly. By doing so, you send a direct message to your unconscious mind to begin to utilize these inner resources more often.

Interpretation: If you do this exercise in a small group, take turns showing your butterfly illustration and explain to the group your best interpretation from an archetypal meaning (see the art therapy color code in Exercise 10.2). You cannot help but be impressed if for no other reason than how unique each butterfly is when colored.

Consider hanging your butterfly on the fridge or office wall as a means to remind you both consciously and unconsciously of your inner resources.

EXERCISE 10.2: Beyond Words: Drawing for Emotional Relief

Art Therapy Themes: There are several themes to choose from when trying this exercise in art therapy. The following is a list of popular themes in the field of art therapy from which to choose.

1. Draw an expression of how you feel when you are either angry or afraid.
2. Draw a sketch of yourself (how you see yourself).
3. Closing your eyes, draw a line on the paper. Then open your eyes and slowly rotate the paper around until an image appears from which to continue and finish the sketch.
4. In the theme of healing, draw an actual or representational illustration of a part of your body that is not whole (e.g., disease or illness). Then draw a second image where healing has occurred.
5. Draw a mandala (a circular-shaped personal coat of arms with four quadrants depicting four aspects of your life that are important to you).
6. Draw your favorite animal.
7. Draw a dream (or recurring dream image).
8. Draw a significant event in your life.
9. Draw a house (one you live in or perhaps one you wish to live in).
10. Draw whatever you wish!

Instructions: Please read through the list of ten themes and then select one and begin to create your piece of artwork, spending about 15–20 minutes on this exercise. If time permits, you might consider selecting a second theme, which then allows you to choose which to share when done as a group activity.

Interpretation: If you do this exercise in a small group, take turns showing your illustration and explain to the group your best interpretation, including the interpretation of colors selected. Remember that the person best qualified to interpret his or her drawing is the person who drew it. If you do this as a group activity, it's highly recommended that you not interpret other people's work.

ART THERAPY COLOR CODE

Although there are exceptions, there is a consensus among art therapists (and even psychologists) that regardless of gender, nationality, or ethnic upbringing, each color used in art therapy represents an archetypal meaning. Typically, the color selection, as well as the objects drawn (house, tree, etc.), often parallel expressions of one's mental/emotional health. The absence of a color does not mean a lack of something; rather, the colors used express that which the unconscious mind wishes to covey at the time of the drawing. The following suggests associations between colors and their archetypal meanings:

Red: Passionate emotional peaks (from pleasure to pain). It can represent either compassion or anger.

Orange: Suggests a life change (big or small, typically more positive than negative).

Yellow: Represents energy (usually a positive message).

Green and Blue: Suggest happiness and joy (blue may even mean creativity). These colors also suggest a strong sense of desire for groundedness and stability in your environment.

Purple, Violet, or Pink: Suggest a highly spiritual nature, unconditional love.

Brown (and earth tone colors): Suggest a sense of groundedness and stability.

Black: Can represent either grief, despair, fear, or a sense of personal empowerment.

White: Can mean either fear, avoidance, cover-up, or hope.

Gray: Typically represents a sense of ambiguity, uncertainty about some issue you are working on.

Consider hanging your art piece on the fridge or office wall; often more subtle aspects of interpretation take a while to surface toward conscious recognition.

Chapter 11

Creative Problem Solving

"If your only tool is a hammer, you'll see every problem as a nail."
— Abraham Maslow

The Ageless Wisdom of Creativity

Invention, innovation, imagination, incubation, adaptation, and inspiration. These are but a few of the many words that come to mind when one begins to articulate the revered concept known as creativity and the creative process in which the seeds of creativity take root. One cannot help but stand in awe of such creations as da Vinci's *Mona Lisa*, Beethoven's *5th Symphony*, or Peter Jackson's film adaptation of J. R. R. Tolkein's *The Lord of the Rings*. Less venerated, but no less important, are inventions such as the weaving loom, automobile, jet airplane, and laptop computer. It has been said that it is the creative mind of the human species that separates us from all other species.

Necessity, it is said, is the mother of invention. Although necessity is not the same thing as stress, pushed to the limits, it can elicit the stress response very quickly. It's no secret that many creative moments come under duress, to make the unworkable work and the immovable move. Stress can prove to be a force of inspiration, which, in turn, results in some rather amazing inventions and works of art. If necessity is the mother of invention, then play certainly commands a paternal role in this unique process. Many of the world's finest creations, inventions, and innovations didn't occur in stressful episodes but rather in relaxed moments of tinkering (playing) in the garage.

By most accounts, human beings are the only species on the planet earth that employ the dynamics of creativity. Structures, songs, drawings, and mechanical devices are just some of the many things that humans, for better or worse, leave as a legacy to the rest of the world. Ironically, in a country known for its "American ingenuity," creativity is not cultivated as a human resource skill in the education system, whereas critical thinking is encouraged and highly praised. Interestingly, today American business leaders are in search of creative talent from other parts of the world. Given the rapid rate of change today in our personal lives, as well as the changes (both large and small) in the global village, it's no secret that creative problem solving will become one of the most sought after coping skills in all levels of human endeavors. For this reason, a review of these skills is essential in the paradigm of holistic stress management.

The Creative Process Revealed

The **creative process** has been inspected, dissected, and analyzed in the hope of revealing the secrets to such inventions as the light bulb, the telephone, and the Internet. Those who have cut open the proverbial goose to see how the golden egg is formed have all come to the same conclusion: Creativity is a multifaceted process combining imagination with organization, intuition with collaboration, and more recently, the right brain's functions with the left brain's skills. In his effort to understand the creative process, scholar and author Roger von Oech identifies, in a creative way, four distinct aspects that necessitate a more thorough understanding of the often illusive, yet always in demand creative process. Von Oech describes four aspects or roles of the creative process: the explorer, the artist, the judge, and the warrior. Let's take a closer look at these components.

The explorer: The first role of the creative process begins with a search for new ideas. To find ideas you have to leave the known and venture into the unknown. In other words, you have to venture off the beaten path. The **explorer** begins to look for ideas anywhere and everywhere. The farther you go off the beaten path, the more likely you will come up with one or more original ideas. In new environments, our sensory receptors are more open to new stimuli. Where do people go to explore new ideas? Art museums, hardware stores, greenhouses, travel magazines, and late night talk radio. Thomas Alva Edison was a big advocate of the exploration process: "Make a practice to keep on the lookout for novel and interesting ideas that others have used successfully. Your idea only has to be original in the adaptation to the problem you are working on." Nobel Prize Laureate Linus Pauling put it this way, "The best way to get a good idea is to get a lot of ideas." New ideas become raw materials for the next stage of the creative process. How does one sharpen his or her exploration skills? Creative experts suggest the following: Be curious, leave your own turf, break out of your routine, and don't overlook the obvious.

The artist: Once the explorer returns home with lots of raw materials to use, the **artist** grabs the relay baton and continues the creative process by incubating, manipulating, adapting, parodying, and connecting ideas until one idea surfaces as the best idea. In the role of the artist, you play with ideas. In the words of Pablo Picasso, "Every act of creation is first an act of destruction." An artist sheds all inhibitions to get his or her hands dirty by turning ideas upside down. The artist asks questions like, What if . . . ? After a given amount of time, the artist comes to a natural conclusion that one idea may stand out above the rest, yet presents all ideas to be judged.

The judge: The **judge** plays a very crucial, yet delicate role in the creative process. One must be flexible enough to validate the artistic abilities, but critical enough to make the best selection possible. As one shifts from the artist to the judge, one shifts from the right (imaginative) brain to the left (analytical) brain. The biggest hazard in the creative process is a reshuffling of these roles so that the judge begins the process. In every attempt when the mental processing begins with judgment, creativity is stifled. The role of the judge is to select the best idea of all the ideas gathered, then pass this idea to the warrior so the idea can take flight.

The warrior: A good idea that has no backing will die in the water. The role of the **warrior** is to champion the cause of the idea and make it a reality. To be a good warrior, you have to believe in yourself. Courage is a must, but so is tough skin because not everyone is going to be as crazy about your idea as you are. The warrior must overcome fear of failure, fear of rejection, and fear of the unknown. The warrior must be brave. Should he or she realize that the idea turned out to be less than ideal, then the creativity team reconvenes either to overhaul the first idea or scrap it entirely and select a new one.

Within you resides all four members of the creativity team—explorer, artist, judge, and warrior. Exercise 11.1, "The Roles of Creativity," highlights these roles as four aspects of your creative process by encouraging you to wear each of these hats. Exercise 11.2 entices you to shift from a left-brain analytical mind-set to a right-brain focus and get the creative juices going in preparation for your next creative endeavor.

Jonah Lehrer, author of the best-selling book *Imagine* and a contributing editor for *Wired* magazine, describes the creative process as anything but a straight line. In his examination of creativity, from various regions of the brain involved with imagination to companies like 3M, Apple, Google, and Pixar who foster a sense of creativity, Lehrer cites creativity as one of the most important inner resources of the 21st century, particularly with several problems (from the personal to the global) on our collective doorstep.

Unlocking Your Creative Powers

Everybody is creative, but not everyone chooses to use this inherent skill. When people are stuck in fear and anxiety, 10 times out of 10—not 9 or 8 times, but 10 times out of 10—fear becomes the motivating force, immobilizing people and inhibiting their creative skills. In the effort to understand the creative process, leaders in this field have come to understand that they must also address roadblocks that obstruct the creative process. The following, as outlined in Roger von Oech's best-selling book, *A Whack on the Side of the Head,* are a few of the more common **creative blocks** that must be dismantled before these valuable coping skills can allow us to reach our highest potential:

1. *Me? Creative?* The biggest block to the creative process is the belief that you are not creative. The roots of this belief typically sprout early in childhood when creative efforts are met by others with scorn rather than enthusiasm, and it sends a message of inadequacy. Rather than looking inept, most people simply forgo their creative skills and let this muscle atrophy.

    The truth is that everyone is creative, but creativity, like any other skill, takes practice. If you think you are not creative, you will fulfill your limitations. Instead, learn to see yourself as the creative genius you really are. Start with small projects such as cooking a fine meal or writing a poem. Then work your way up to bigger projects.

2. *No time for play.* Remember that play is a critical factor in the creative process. Kids love to play, but adults soon forget the freedom of play as more and more responsibilities invade their lives. Play is critical in the role of the artist, and play is always more fun when it includes others. So, consider inviting some friends to join you in playtime. Playtime can include anything from a mental health day of downhill skiing to wandering the aisles of Home Depot. For play to be effective, keep ego at home when you venture out!

3. *Perfection is stifling.* Nobody likes to make a mistake, and surely not in front of an audience. Rest assured that embarrassment and humiliation are forms of fear-based stress. Ironically, the truth is that the creative process involves mistakes. In the words of Woody Allen, "If you are not failing every now and then, it's a sign that you are not trying anything very innovative." And in the words of IBM founder Thomas J. Watson, "The way to success is to double your rate of failure." Edison failed with over 1,000 types of filaments for the light bulb before he found one that worked. We might still be in the dark if he gave up on number 900. Follow Edison's advice: Learn to focus on the positive, not the negative, and then keep going.

4. *But there's only one way, right?* The ego loves to be right and will do all it can to prove it is right. Ironically, in the creative process, there are many right answers. On occasion, there may be a best answer, but there are always many right answers. Looking for the right answer means stepping out of the box, exploring the unknown, and finding many answers from which to choose. In the words of French philosopher Emile Chartier, "Nothing is more dangerous than an idea when it is the only one you have." Learn to become comfortable with many right answers and many possible (viable) solutions to a problem.

5. *Fear of the unknown.* Creativity is certainly stifled in an age of specialization where professionals are kings of minutiae and the jack of all trades is nowhere in sight. Once again, in an effort not to look stupid, fear overrides the mental thought processes by claiming either ignorance or territorial turf issues and refuses to get involved. Learn to make every area your area by embracing the wonder of all aspects of life.

Are your creative efforts blocked by the fear that whatever you do might not be good enough? Exercise 11.3, "My Creativity Project," is an exercise to break through these blocks by delving into the creative process and coming out a victor. Enjoy!

There is no denying that Apple co-founder Steve Jobs was a creative genius. His biographer, Walter Isaacson, described Steve Jobs this way: "Some leaders push innovations by being good at the big picture. Others do so by mastering details. Jobs did both, relentlessly." In the words of Steve Jobs, "'You always have to keep pushing [outside the box] to be innovative." In his now famous *Think Different* commercial, the narrative ends with these words: "The people who are crazy enough to think they can change the world are the ones who do. Think Different."

From Creativity to Creative Problem Solving

The creative process is not a linear process with a direct route from problem to solution. If it were that easy, everyone would claim to be creative! Although the creative process isn't hard, it's not direct either. To use von Oech's metaphor of the four roles of creativity, most likely you will be switching hats often, from explorer to warrior, till it becomes obvious the problem is solved with complete satisfaction **Fig. 11.1 ▶**. The following is a tried-and-true method of **creative problem solving**. Once you have read through this process, Exercise 11.4 provides this same template to be used for any current problems you are facing that demand a creative solution.

1. *Describing the problem:* Take time to identify and describe the problem. Sometimes the answer can be found in how the problem is identified. Consider being playful in this first step, such as describing the problem as a child might see it, or as an alien might view it. Using the method of dividing and conquering, try breaking the problem down into smaller pieces.

2. *Generating ideas:* What to cook for dinner tonight? Come up with five selections. Where to take your next vacation? Come up with five possible ideas. How to pay for your college education? Come up with five viable solutions. Generating ideas is the fun stage of the creative problem-solving process. To do a good job generating ideas, learn to get comfortable stepping out of your comfort zone (the box) and venture out to search for great ideas.

3. *Selecting and refining the idea:* Once you have several ideas, you can begin to narrow the selection down to the best idea. To pick the best idea, consider playing the game What If. Try to imagine the idea already implemented and see how it

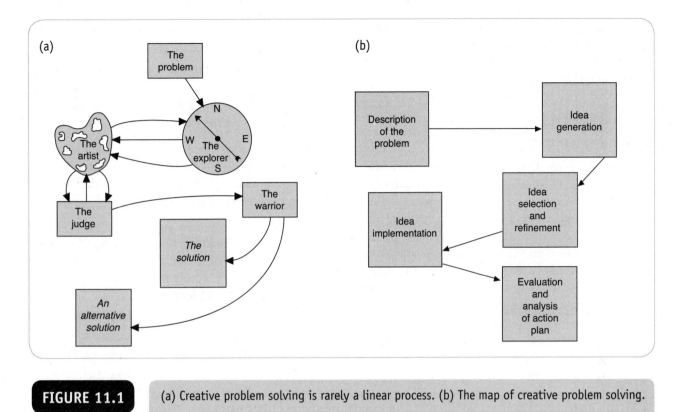

FIGURE 11.1 (a) Creative problem solving is rarely a linear process. (b) The map of creative problem solving.

works. Visualize it. Think the idea through to its desired result. Ask yourself what the pros and cons are. Although you won't know till you try, selection involves both intuition and imagination as well as good judgment skills.

4. *Implementing the idea:* Putting an idea into play can take minutes or weeks, depending on the problem begging to be solved. The implementation of every idea requires some risk as well as some faith that it will work. Implementation means taking the first step back into the unknown. It may mean making a phone call or getting in your car and driving somewhere. It may mean sitting down and talking with someone, and most likely it will mean participating in a collaborative effort to pull it off. Fear inhibits this stage of the creative process, but don't let it! Remember, face your fear and it will disappear!

5. *Evaluating and analyzing the idea:* When ideas work, and in this case, when the crisis is over, people tend to forget the magic that made it happen. But success begs to be highlighted by taking a good look so that the lessons can be learned

should they be needed again. It's a good habit to study successes as well as unmet expectations; valuable lessons can be learned from both ends of the creative process.

How to Incorporate Creative Problem Solving into Your Life Routine

The best way to incorporate creative problem-solving skills in your life routine is to follow the template in Exercise 11.4 for any and all problems. Reading books on creativity can help (and is strongly encouraged), but reading about doing something and actually doing it are two different things. Be on the lookout for how others solve their problems. Adaptation of ideas to your unique situation can prove to be very empowering!

The next best way to enhance your creative skills is to practice them, even in areas that are totally unrelated to problems begging for resolution. There is a wonderful transfer effect from the creative process with music, photography, cooking, or writing to the problems and dilemmas that face us each day. Engaging in small acts of creativity gives one the courage to try bigger things. When looking to initiate the creative problem-solving process, start small (e.g., what should I prepare for dinner tonight?).

Best Benefits of Creative Problem Solving

Everyone holds the keys to creativity; however, there are those who refuse to believe they are holding the keys in their hands. There are two kinds of people in this world: Those who think they are creative and those who don't. The people who believe they are creative are, indeed, very creative. Perhaps as no surprise, the people who don't believe they are creative are not creative. Creativity is a very empowering inner resource. Tackling a problem through ingenuity makes you feel like you can conquer the world. By engaging fully in the creative process you learn to let go of fears and anxieties that tend to hold you back, allowing you to sail ahead on the river of life.

Chapter Summary

- The creative process is very empowering as an effective coping technique for stressors, both big and small.

- The creative process is known to have four aspects; the first two (the explorer and the artist) are considered right brain, whereas the second two (the judge and the warrior) are considered left brain. The combined process is a whole brain activity.

- Ego-generated thoughts of fear combine to be the biggest impediment to the creative process.

Unlocking your creative powers first involves deactivating the ego.

- Creative problem solving takes the creative process and applies it to resolving stressful issues. There are five steps, from identifying the process to evaluating the solution.

- Incorporating the skills of creative problem solving begins with knowing the aspects of the creative process and then applying them to each problem that begs for resolution.

- Benefits of creative problem solving include empowerment and promoting high self-esteem.

Additional Resources

Gelb, M. *How to Think Like Leonardo da Vinci*. New York: Dell/Random House; 1998.

Issacson, W. *Steve Jobs*. New York: Simon & Schuster; 2011.

Lehrer, J. *Imagine: How Creativity Works*. Boston: Houghton Mifflin Harcourt; 2012.

McMeekin, G. *The 12 Secrets of Highly Creative Women*. Berkeley, CA: Conari Press; 2000.

Michalko, M. *Cracking Creativity*. Berkeley, CA: Ten Speed Press; 2004.

Thorp, T. *The Creative Habit*. New York: Simon and Schuster; 2003.

von Oech, R. *Creative Whack Pack*. New York: Warner; 1988.

von Oech, R. *A Kick in the Seat of the Pants*. New York: Perennial; 1986.

von Oech, R. *A Whack on the Side of the Head*. New York: Warner; 1983.

EXERCISE 11.1: The Roles of Creativity

Roger von Oech is right when he states that many hats are worn in the creative process. Review these four specific roles, and take some time to examine how you can integrate these creative aspects into your repertoire of skills. If you are like most people, you tend to see yourself wearing only one of these hats rather than all four. This is OK when projects or problems require more than one person to contribute their talents.

1. *The explorer:* To help you think outside the box, make a list of ten new places you can explore to find new ideas for any creative project, such as a hardware store, local museum, outdoor concert, or the Laundromat bulletin board. Next, make a list of five new resources to explore for any creative project.

_____

_____

_____

_____

2. *The artist:* Inside each and every one of us is an artist begging to play. Make a list of five new ways to engage in the art of play to enhance your creative skills.

_____

_____

_____

_____

3. *The judge:* How good are your judgmental skills? Are they *too* good? Are you the kind of person who judges first and asks questions later?

_____

_____

_____

_____

4. *The warrior:* The warrior is the legman in the creative process. A great idea without someone to market it and implement it is not really a great idea. How good are your warrior skills? What can you do to improve them?

_____

_____

_____

_____

EXERCISE 11.2: Getting the Creative Juices Going

Living in our left-brain culture tends to inhibit the creative process. The following exercises are provided to help you whack your way of thinking (from left brain to right brain) so that the creative problem-solving process may become just a bit easier.

I. Create two metaphors/definitions for an optimist and a pessimist:

a. An optimist is someone who . . .

1. _____

2. _____

b. A pessimist is someone who . . .

1. _____

2. _____

II. Describe two things that a cat and a refrigerator have in common:

_____

_____

III. Describe the following colors to a person who has been blind from birth:

a. Red _____

b. White _____

c. Blue _____

d. Green _____

e. Yellow _____

IV. Mind games: In the following line of letters, cross out six letters so that the remaining letters, without altering their sequence, will spell a familiar English word.

BSAINXLEATNTEARS _____

V. Create a metaphor for the meaning of life. Finish this sentence:

Life is like a _____

EXERCISE 11.3: My Creativity Project

"Imagination is more powerful than knowledge." — Albert Einstein

"My feeling is that the concept of creativeness and the concept of a healthy, self-actualizing human person seem to be coming closer and closer together and may perhaps turn out to be the same thing." — Abraham Maslow

This exercise is geared to help inspire the reader to take some initiative in starting and completing a project that requires some creative license. Initially, it was developed for a holistic health class to fully engage students in the creative process. Many students found this project to be the ticket to a new job. The purpose is to challenge you to exercise your creative talents to the limits you are most capable of. This project involves three aspects:

1. First, play the roles of the *explorer*, *artist*, *judge*, and *warrior*, respectively, to come up with a very creative idea and then bring it to reality. If you wish, you can use the template in Exercise 11.1.

2. Next, write up the experience, describing what you did (describe your experience in each of the four stages of creativity) and how you did it.

3. Finally, explain what you learned from this experience.

The area and magnitude of creativity are entirely up to you. I suggest, however, that you pick an area that is somewhat familiar, but not one in which you have a five-star command. Challenge yourself! Select a project that can range from art, to poetry, to cooking, to composing, to photography, to designing fashions, to writing a screenplay, to choreographing a dance, to anything. Start with a hobby or simply a burning desire. Build a dream from this. Consult your intuition and then come up with a finished product. Remember that the creative process cannot be rushed or demanded. This assignment will take some time, so please, plan accordingly.

Make the project manageable. In other words, do not, I *repeat*, do not try to build a re-creation of the Eiffel Tower in your back yard or compose the sequel to Handel's *Messiah* in 2 days. On the other hand, simply putting a new message on your voicemail is not the way to go either. Make the project a quality job and one you will be proud of.

The following are examples from previous students and workshop participants:

1. Producing a music video presentation for YouTube

2. Writing a family/neighborhood cookbook

3. Producing a short movie for a film festival

4. Planning a vacation around the world

5. Creating a holistic (mind-body-spirit) cancer treatment plan

6. Creating a flashmob dance experience and filming it for YouTube

7. Designing/planning a rose or perennial garden

8. Recording/producing a music CD

9. Designing a new iPhone app

10. Designing an app for measuring one's carbon footprint

EXERCISE 11.3: My Creativity Project cont....

My Creativity Project

How I did it:

_____

_____

_____

_____

_____

_____

_____

_____

_____

_____

_____

What I learned from this experiment:

_____

_____

_____

_____

_____

_____

_____

_____

_____

_____

_____

_____

_____

EXERCISE 11.4: Creative Problem Solving

There are many good ways to solve a problem. All we need to do is spend some time working at it from different directions until a number of viable solutions surface, and then choose the best one. The following is a time-tested strategic plan for creatively trying to solve problems and coming to a sense of resolution.

The problem: _____

1. Define the problem (please be as specific as you can):

_____

_____

_____

_____

2. Generate ideas (come up with at least four viable ideas and one zany one to bring out the play factor):

a. _____

b. _____

c. _____

d. _____

(z). _____

3. Select and refine the idea (pick the best idea from above and explain why you think this is the best idea):

_____

_____

_____

_____

4. Implement the idea (explain how you will put this idea into action; make a quick outline—four points of your action plan):

a. _____

b. _____

c. _____

d. _____

5. Evaluate and analyze the action plan (how did the idea work? what are some ways, if any, to improve on this idea should you decide to use it again?):

_____

_____

_____

_____

_____

Chapter 12

Communication Skills (in the Information Age)

"Any problem, big or small, within a family, always seems to start with bad communication. Someone isn't listening."
— Emma Thompson

It's no exaggeration to say that there is an explosive mass of information in the world today. In tandem with these tsunami waves of bits, bytes, words, photos, tweets, and YouTube video clips come hours and hours of communication—the ability to assimilate, digest, and when need be, share this information with others. Many people call this age we are living in the information age, but a more apt description is the "communication age." Ironically, face-to-face communication is becoming a rare event, if not a thing of the past for some as our global society progresses further into this social networking labyrinth. The price of convenience has been the greatly diminished quality of interpersonal communications, adding a whole new layer of stress to the human condition. The communication stressor affects the relationships among college roommates, friends, acquaintances, spouses, coworkers—nearly everyone!

Despite the many ways to communicate (and the number grows daily), our skills at conveying information, specifically in terms of our own thoughts and feelings, are considered to be poor at best, and diminishing. This chapter invites you to examine (perhaps reexamine) your assets and liabilities in terms of your ability to communicate, and then to work to improve these skills so you can minimize this aspect of stress in your life.

Miscommunication Again and Again

Perhaps the biggest problem that arises when two or more people communicate is that the message is not received as it was intended. As the expression goes, "Something was lost in translation." This issue is also known as *miscommunication*. This stressor can become an intense whirlpool of negativity, as stress increases among all parties involved, thereby magnifying feelings of anger and fear, many of which are left unresolved until the next communication episode, or perhaps indefinitely.

Miscommunication can be cited as an underlying cause in everything from divorces to world wars and a multitude of arguments and conflicts in between. Repeated miscommunication fans the flames of anger (frustrations, annoyances, etc.) and fear (anxiety, doubt, and insecurity). Although it might seem that advances in technology would decrease the level of miscommunication, we all know this not to be true. The vast majority of text messages and emails have no emotional intonation, often creating an air of doubt. (Is she/he mad at me?) Furthermore, dishonesty (a defense mechanism of the ego) arises when people claim to have an urgent phone call for a quick exit. (Have you ever noticed how so many calls or text messages are urgent?)

Although technology has changed dramatically over the eons, human nature, under the influence of the ego, has remained the same. Hence, age-old problems with the communication of information persist and now become magnified under a multi-faceted communications network. The need for excellent communication skills, as an effective coping technique in the age of high technology, is increasingly more important.

Decades ago the term *generation gap* was used to describe the communication chasm between parents and their teen children. Today the expression *technology gap* is used to explain the difference in technology preferences between people over and under 30 years of age. Generally speaking, people over 30 have a preference for phone calls over text messages and emails, whereas people under 30 favor most communication via texting. Tension arises when these communication preferences conflict, often with a little arrogance (from sarcasm to indifference) thrown in on both sides of the divide. Moreover, people under age 30 who have grown up in a world of immediate gratification tend to be more impatient when responses are less than instantaneous.

One of the main skills in face-to-face communication is eye contact. Scores of middle school and high school teachers across the nation cite an epidemic of students who prefer to look down rather than directly into the eyes of the person they are speaking to, a preference attributed to too much smartphone or computer screen time.

Anger and Fear Influences on Communication

Both fear and anger can cloud our ability to communicate effectively. Under the influence of anger, thoughts and feelings that might have been consciously filtered before leaving the mouth (or keypad) become verbal projectiles, often offending others, hurting some and ultimately leaving a mess to clean up afterward. Conversely, fear can add multiple layers of filters to one's thoughts and feelings. The result is that people often don't say what they really think or feel. For example, you might not like the new corporate organizational structure due to lost work hours, but directly conveying your thoughts and/or feelings may result in losing your job altogether. The inability to express one's thoughts and feelings compounds one's stress levels. Stated simply, poor communication skills amplify one's level of stress.

Smart Phones, Dumb Messagers

Before we explore some of the basics of good communication skills, it would be wise to give this topic more perspective with regard to the use of technology today and much of the stress it produces. The following are some of the more prevalent issues with regard to communication and miscommunication in the age of high tech information gadgets.

Communication Without Emotions

How many times have you received a text message or email and wondered if the sender was mad, upset, or less than ecstatic about something? Not having emotional cues to match the message can leave one in a cloud of doubt. Compelling word choice, punctuation, and the craft of an engaging writing style are what make reading a novel so enthralling. Rarely, if ever, are text messages and emails enthralling. When the emotional flavor is missing, the mind tends to fill in the blanks, often creating more stress, usually turning molehills into mountains.

Hiding Behind Technology

Technology has made avoiding some face-to-face situations quite easy, such as quitting your job with a text message, dumping a girlfriend/boyfriend with a public tweet or email, or subtly, even inadvertently humiliating a friend on Facebook with an unflattering photo. And although people have always found ways to avoid others they don't wish to talk to, technology (through the use of caller ID) has made it much easier to avoid communication.

Covering up the Truth

How many times have you said, "This call is urgent," when it really wasn't? Just like avoidance, lying has always been a part of the human condition, but technology allows people to add a whole new layer of deceit

by denying they received phone calls, voice messages, or text messages via dropped calls or technical glitches. As we all know, lying is a poor communication skill, and compromises the integrity of any relationship.

Absence of Body Language

Eons before verbal language was used as a form of communication, humans used body language as the primary means of personal expression. Body language, it is said, is hardwired into our DNA and often expressed unconsciously. By and large people will trust body language well over the spoken word, particularly when there is a "mixed message." As the expression goes, the body doesn't lie. Things are different now. Unless you're on Skype (and even then this is limiting), body language is basically irrelevant with the use of smartphones. Although some people may use emoticons (e.g., :)) at the end of a text, there is little to go on beyond the typed word or abbreviation (LMAO). Trust issues, wrapped in anxiety and frustrations, often ensue without the ability to fall back on body language.

Privacy Issues

Conversations between two people are no longer just between two people today. Like it or not, all phones are tapped and recorded, and all emails are searched for national security purposes. Employers often ask for Facebook passwords, and even if you think your Facebook settings are private with postings to just your friends, most likely they are not.

Communication/Information Overload

Years ago, people had healthy boundaries with the use of the home telephone (e.g., the no phone calls after 9:00 p.m. rule). Now that people carry their smartphones everywhere (including to bed), accessibility is constant. The fact that people can now access you 24/7 can lead to communication overload. Add to this the constant trolling for information on Facebook, Twitter, YouTube, or other means, and information overload becomes quite common.

Brevity vs. Integrity

The convenience of technology to communicate is nothing short of amazing, but convenience can carry with it carelessness. Carelessness, from typos to poor word choices in the brevity of communication, can lead to abundant miscommunication. Moreover, the spoken word has many intonations and nuances that are simply not there with text messages and emails (with the prevalent use of all caps and exclamation points to make a point). Although it may be true that attention spans have decreased dramatically in American culture, brevity in the expression of thoughts and feelings can promote misunderstanding to others and frustration to yourself as the recipient of these messages. Stated simply, brevity can compromise one's communication integrity. Short text messages and tweets cannot possibly convey the depth of one's consciousness.

Screen Time vs. Eye Contact

Admit it! It is hard to take your eyes off of a smartphone screen, tablet screen, and for that matter even a flat screen TV. The allure of the screen can be very addicting, particularly with high-resolution features. When speaking to someone face to face, the eyes are the most compelling feature. To paraphrase an expression, the eyes are the screen of the soul. So why has it become hard to make eye contact in the digital age? It's more difficult to lie to someone while making eye contact. In some Asian cultures, prolonged eye contact is considered rude, yet in the American culture, the lack of eye contact conveys not only rudeness, but dishonesty. Is abundant screen time changing the culture of face-to-face communication regarding eye contact? The answer appears to be yes, but not without an added stress component for many.

How to Incorporate Effective Communication Skills into Your Life Routine

Establish Healthy Boundaries

Break the myth! You do not have to be accessible 24 hours a day, every day of the week. Create blocks of time when you are free of the electronic leash of your smartphone and computer and stick to this schedule (e.g., no emails or text messages after 9:00 p.m., or no smartphones in the bedroom). Technology is supposed to serve you, not make you a slave to it. If you feel like you are always accessible, you need better boundaries. Additionally, communicate these boundaries to others so they know when you are available and when you are not, to help them avoid feeling frustrated.

Honor the Touch It Once Rule

If you open emails and read them but plan on responding later, most likely later will never come. The "touch it once" rule suggests that once you open an email or text, respond accordingly, even if it's a short message. Remember to honor your healthy boundaries as well.

Be Courteous

When you are talking to someone, no matter who it is, turn off your smartphone. Interrupting a face-to-face conversation to answer a phone call is simply rude. No exceptions. Being courteous also means being honest. This includes not indicating that every phone call or text message is urgent when it's really not.

Maintain Polite Eye Contact

When addressing someone face to face, make it a point to maintain polite eye contact. If you find your eyes glancing down, gently remind yourself to redirect your focus toward the eyes of the person with whom you are speaking.

Keep Personal Issues Private

Privacy is certainly an issue these days, but making a private argument public through various social media is simply immature. In the workplace, it is unprofessional. Avoid airing dirty laundry through social networking. It not only makes you look bad, it's inappropriate behavior.

Attack Issues, Not People

When you find yourself in the midst of a conflict, step back and look at the issues at hand. Rather than resorting to mud-slinging (attacking people), address the issue at hand. For example, rather than saying to some, "You're lying!" say, "I sense the issue here is honesty. Can we address this issue?"

Avoid Putting Others on the Defensive

When people are stressed, they tend to take things personally. Taking things personally is code for being on the defensive. When people are on the defensive, they don't hear words as they are meant to be expressed. Rather, they hear through the filter of ego, which tends to exaggerate one's insecurities. Two people who are stressed compound the degree of defensiveness, resulting in much miscommunication. Learn to disarm others by learning to avoid putting them on the defense. Equally important, learn to let down your defensive guard as well.

Learn to Be Tech Multi-lingual

If you are like most people, you probably have a preference in your communication styles (e.g., texting vs. using the phone). Remember that not everyone has the same preference. Some people prefer phone calls. Others prefer emails. Still others prefer live, face-to-face contact whenever possible. Learn to know what the preferred style is for the people with whom you communicate. If you are unsure, ask! Honor their preference when at all possible.

Avoid Information Overload

When the mind is flooded with information, mental processes are compromised, from concentration skills and memory to communication skills. The mind's ability to absorb and process information (both consciously and unconsciously) is extraordinary, but not without limits. Too much information is also known as sensory overload and burnout. Burnout is a code word for stress. How do you control the amount of information you take in through your eyes and ears? Once again, healthy boundaries are suggested.

Resolve Communication Problems When They Arise

It's a given that episodes of miscommunication and conflict will arise among people with whom you are connected. Avoidance (the flight response) may seem like an easy course of action, but ageless wisdom reminds us that ignoring problems only tends to make them worse down the road. When you find yourself in the midst of a communication meltdown, take time to resolve problems as soon as possible. Face-to-face communication is always the best way.

Best Benefits of Effective Communication Skills

Welcome to the full force of the information age, where the greater your communication skills are, the greater your chances are of reducing your stress levels, and most likely the stress levels of the people

around you. By establishing healthy boundaries with technology, learning to be multi-lingual with the various forms of technology, and being present when involved with face-to-face interactions, you will decrease miscommunication dramatically. Remember, communication skills are just that, skills. They require practice. Take time to practice the art of great communication skills, no matter what the latest advances in technology are.

Chapter Summary

- Various forms of technology offer many means of communication, yet people communicate using short messages and spend more time looking at various screens than using face-to-face interpersonal communications.

- All of these means of communication can lead to information overload, which compromises one's ability to communicate.

- People often use technology as an excuse for poor behavior (avoidance) or to give in to the urgency to answer a call or text message.

- Age-old communication skills that reinforce courtesy apply regardless of the type of technology one uses.

Additional Resources

Bartlett, L. Personal Conversation. Sunset Middle School, Longmont, CO. March 2012.

Flemming, C. *It's the Way You Say It*. Bloomington, IN: IUniverse; 2010.

Silberman, M. *PeopleSmart: Developing Your Interpersonal Intelligence*. San Francisco: Berrett-Koehler; 2000.

South, A. *Technology's Influence on Interpersonal Communication*, March 9, 2009. http://www.helium.com/items/1369744-technology-interpersonal-communication. Accessed July 17, 2012.

Thomas, M. The Impacts of Technology on Communication—Mapping the Limits of Online Discussion Forums. The University of Adelaide. http://online.adelaide.edu.au/LearnIT.nsf/URLs/technology_and_communication. Accessed July 17, 2012.

EXERCISE 12.1: Tech Communication Survey

Whether we like it or not, we are living in the high-tech, WiFi communication age, and we are all impacted by the use of technology and our means to communicate through it. The following survey invites you to probe your communication acumen (by taking an honest look at your current behaviors). Please answer the following questions as you behave (not as you wish you did).

1. I have been known to purposely not respond to phone calls or text messages.   YES   NO

2. I use the Facebook "Like" symbol as an easy way to communicate things I agree with.   YES   NO

3. I prefer texting to phone calls for the convenience of time or simply not actually talking to people.   YES   NO

4. I have unfriended/blocked some people on Facebook without telling them.   YES   NO

5. I find myself getting impatient when people don't respond quickly to text messages or emails.   YES   NO

6. I text over 25 times a day to family and friends.   YES   NO

7. I have been known to use text abbreviations in term papers, written notes, and other nontext media.   YES   NO

8. My spouse/significant other spends more time on the phone than talking to me.   YES   NO

9. My first communication preference is texting over phone calls or emails.   YES   NO

10. To be honest, my typical style of communication is usually quantity (brief messages) over quality (in-depth conversations).   YES   NO

11. I will typically answer a smartphone call or text message during a face-to-face conversation (e.g., at dinner, while watching TV, etc.) if it's urgent.   YES   NO

12. I am known to capitalize words and use exclamation points at the end of text and email messages.   YES   NO

13. I have been known to text and/or make smartphone calls from bed.   YES   NO

14. I typically use more than one Internet browser at a time.   YES   NO

15. I often find myself spending more time reading Facebook posts and tweets than talking face to face with friends and family.   YES   NO

16. I often interrupt my own work schedule to check emails and Facebook updates.   YES   NO

17. I post photos on Facebook to convey more than words can describe about my life experiences.   YES   NO

18 I have inadvertently sent text messages or emails to the wrong person.   YES   NO

19. I get most of my news and information from social media Web sites (Facebook, YouTube, Twitter, etc.).   YES   NO

20. I pretend to turn my smartphone off (and instead set it to vibrate) in the company of friends.   YES   NO

Key: If you answered more than seven questions with a Yes, then most likely you show signs of experiencing miscommunication with friends, relatives, and co-workers, leading to more stress in your life.

EXERCISE 12.2: What Did You Say?

Conversational skills may not seem like they belong in a stress management book, but nothing could be further from the truth. Poor conversational skills are often at the root of many stressful relationships. We are engaged in conversation from the moment we wake until the second we lay down our heads and enter the world of dreams. Whether it be family, friends, customers, clients, peers, colleagues, strangers, or even voices on the radio and television, our minds are programmed to listen and respond in conversation virtually every minute of the day.

A proverb states, "The three most important words to a successful relationship are communication, communication, communication." It's true! As social animals we gravitate toward others to engage in conversation. Good communication skills are essential to every aspect of our lives. The elements of conversation are rather complicated because we communicate with more than just words and voices. In fact, more of our communication skills are nonverbal than verbal.

1. How good are your communication skills, both verbal and nonverbal? Are you even aware of the messages you give to others with your clothing style, hair, eye movements, posture, hand gestures, and facial expressions?

2. What would you say is your body's silent message, that is, without dialogue? Why? Is this the message you wish to convey?

3. Listening skills are as important as the ability to articulate your thoughts and feelings. Yet, most people hear but seldom listen. More often than not, they begin to prepare what they are going to say within seconds of someone beginning to speak or respond. How good are your listening skills? What could you do to improve them?

4. Much research now suggests that men and women have different styles of communication. Have you ever noticed this? For example, have you noticed that when a woman says she'll call you tomorrow, she calls you tomorrow, whereas when a man says he'll call you tomorrow, most likely he will call you in a few days to a week. Although it may be true that men are from Mars and women are from Venus, we are both here on Earth, so we have to learn to be bilingual. What differences do you notice when talking to someone of the opposite gender? How are these differences magnified under stress? Please describe your thoughts on gender differences in communciation.

5. It has been said that when we speak we are very indirect, not really saying what we mean. We beat around the bush. Do you find that your verbal style is more indirect than direct? Do you tend to give mixed messages? After giving this some thought, can you think of ways to improve your verbal communication skills? Do you need to revise your nonverbal messages? How can you do this?

_____

_____

_____

_____

_____

_____

EXERCISE 12.2: What Did You Say? cont....

_____

_____

_____

_____

_____

_____

_____

_____

_____

_____

_____

_____

EXERCISE 12.3: Communication Skills 101

Gloria Estefan was right when she sang the hit song *Words Get in the Way*. They sure do, especially when we are stressed. As a rule, humans tend to be bad communicators when feelings of fear, anger, insecurity, intolerance, or even compassion (not wanting to hurt someone's feelings) cloud what we really wish to say to friends, roommates, spouses, children, and co-workers. Perhaps you've noticed. Below are several statements, questions, or comments that most likely have come out of your mouth on more than one occasion, resulting in miscommunication, hurt feelings, conflict, and perhaps even more stress. Read each comment and then take a moment to come up with a new and diplomatic way to rephrase these statements. Remember the first rule in conflict resolution: Attack issues, not people.

1. You really irritate me.

   _____

2. No, no. Everything is fine.

   _____

3. Oh, we always go there. Let's go here instead.

   _____

4. You want me to do *what*?

   _____

5. Why are you being so difficult?

   _____

6. You do this every time!

   _____

7. OK, can we just talk about this tomorrow?

   _____

8. I can't take this anymore!

   _____

9. Why can't you do it like this?

   _____

10. I need this done by 4:00 p.m. sharp.

   _____

11. Because we've always done it this way before!

   _____

EXERCISE 12.3: Communication Skills 101 cont....

12. Oh, nothing. It's nothing.

_____

13. I am sick and tired of this!

_____

What expressions do you hear from friends, family, and co-workers that mean something different from what the actual words indicate?

1. _____

2. _____

3. _____

4. _____

Additional Coping Skills

"God gave us two ends. One to sit on and one to think with. Success depends on which end you use. Heads, you win. Tails, you lose."
— Anonymous

There are literally dozens of effective coping techniques in the field of holistic stress management. To be effective, however, each technique must help increase awareness of the cause of the problem and assist you in your effort to work toward a peaceful resolution. The following are some additional coping techniques that merit attention and might be quite useful to you as you augment your repertoire of effective coping skills for the duration of your life journey.

Journaling: The Art of Soul Searching

The mind can quickly become a flurry of thoughts and feelings that, like a tempest wind, rushes around the inside of your head at dizzying speeds. Without a release, the pressure can build up dramatically to a point that eventually clouds your vision and ultimately inhibits clear thinking. One way to release this pressure is to get your thoughts and feelings down on paper, and that's the purpose of journal writing.

As a coping technique, **journaling** serves several purposes. First, it provides the means for a healthy catharsis, a way to release pent up thoughts and feelings from your head onto paper. It has long been believed that thoughts and frustrations can eventually become **toxic** if they are not allowed to flow freely out of your system. In fact, research now shows that people who keep a regular journal actually have a healthier immune system. Not only is there a cathartic effect to journaling, but writing your thoughts and feelings down on paper, or perhaps in a computer document, seems to provide insights on possible solutions to a host of problems.

Perhaps nowhere is this more evident than with therapists working with soldiers returning from the conflicts in Iraq and Afghanistan with post-traumatic stress disorder (PTSD), who use journaling as a healthy catharis.

Aside from a healthier immune system, journaling also has some long-term benefits. By rereading journal entries you can begin to see certain behavior patterns emerge that you might not notice with an occasional journal entry. In its simplest form journal writing is nothing less than soul searching, and there are many themes that can be used as vehicles for self-exploration, including writing poetry (making order out of the chaos of your mind), composing letters (a message of resolution), or simply making lists to organize your thoughts. Exercise 13.1 is a journal theme that actually helps to provide insights about personal goals and lifetime dreams using a seed as a metaphor.

Support Groups: Friends in Need

In 1989, a landmark study was conducted to show that **support groups** did nothing to promote the longevity of cancer patients. When it came time to analyze the data, David Spiegel, MD, was stunned. The message was clear: Support groups enhance the quality and length of lives. Without a doubt, those patients who partook in support group activities significantly outlived those who did not.

By and large, human beings are social animals. We need the companionship and company of others, if not for physical survival, then at least for moral support on our own human journey. Having a few close friends or colleagues with whom to share time and common interests provides a sense of belonging, a factor long thought to be critical for health and longevity. Sociologists call this the "buffer theory," suggesting that friends, family, and peers help minimize stress by simply being there to lend a helping hand or an ear to listen when needed. In many cases friends can offer objective insights or opinions that can widen your perspective of the problem at hand.

A strong support group means more than accruing friends on Facebook and posting updates. It means meeting up with close friends for a walk, nine holes of golf, lunch, or shopping. It means cultivating these close friendships with personal face-to-face time.

In this age of high technology, our society has become increasingly fragmented. People spend more time in front of a computer screen or television and less quality time with friends and family. Research based on the "tend and befriend" theory underscores the importance of support groups for women; however, men certainly benefit from this coping skill as well. Connectedness is essential for health and well-being. Exercise 13.2 challenges you to build stronger support groups as a buffer to stress.

Social Orchestration: Taking the Path of Least Resistance

Avoidance is the number one coping skill to deal with stress. Avoidance is also the number one *ineffective* coping skill to deal with stress. For this reason, avoidance is never advocated unless your life is in physical danger.

Social orchestration is often called the path of least resistance—side-stepping potential obstacles that might later create more stress. Social orchestration is not the same as avoidance. Social orchestration is a coping skill that enables you to organize and reorganize various responsibilities and events in your day or week to decrease feelings of being overwhelmed. Although some aspects of social orchestration, such as prioritizing and scheduling, are under the umbrella of time management, many give this coping skill a place of its own on the spectrum of effective coping techniques because it's that important.

One of the cautions of social orchestration is not to constantly rearrange your social contacts with friends, shortchanging both yourself and others. Be careful not to take advantage of your friends, or the foundation of your support group may start to crumble.

Hobbies and Outside Interests: Following Your Bliss

What do stamp collecting, golfing, and Akebono have to do with stress relief? When used as a diversion from the pressures of work, **hobbies** can provide a wonderful respite from the hassles of the 9–5 job or a stressful course load. Hobbies and outside interests not only provide balance to the mind, but also, in many cases, these activities of passion help you cope with problems in other aspects of your life by transferring the creative juices back to your job or career.

By and large, the process of hobbies such as gardening, photography, playing the guitar, and mountain climbing makes order out of some controlled sense of chaos. The conventional wisdom suggests that by mastering the skills necessary to generate a sense of organization and creativity, these same skills then transfer to other aspects of your life where chaos looms. Exercise 13.3 challenges you to explore this coping style further.

Dream Therapy: The Royal Road of the Unconscious Mind

Deep in the recesses of the unconscious mind lies a wealth of wisdom that is there simply for the asking, wisdom and guidance that offer keen insights and the means of resolution to a host of issues and problems that surface in the course of our daily lives. Unlike the conscious mind that shuts down while we are asleep, the unconscious mind is active and aware every hour of the day. There is a small catch to obtaining these nuggets of wisdom—they come in a coded language that has to be decoded before they can be utilized. Actually, the unconscious mind is multilingual through the language of dreams, symbols, Freudian slips, and a series of cognitive functions that are clearly associated with the right hemisphere of the brain (e.g., irrational thinking, nonlinear thinking, imaginative thinking, global thinking, intuitive thinking). It is the job of the conscious mind to decode the message of dream symbols. Unfortunately, most people never take the time to learn this language. Consequently, they wander aimlessly through a maze of problems and issues, unable to read the map provided by the unconscious mind, and hence stress is perpetuated.

Dream therapy is a process of taking the time to learn the symbolic language of the unconscious mind as presented in the dream state. Before dream interpretation can start, you first must make a habit of remembering your dreams. This can be done by programming your conscious mind to awake each morning and clearly remember your dreams or dream fragments. As you lay in bed, call to mind these dream passages. The next step is to take pen and paper in hand and record them as best you can. Analyzing your dreams is a process whereby the code of the dream symbols is broken. This can be done in a number of ways, including playing with the dream symbol and providing many interpretations until some tangible insight reveals itself.

Of great interest is the topic of recurring dreams, a message from the unconscious mind that, indeed, there is some problem begging for resolution. This avenue of dream therapy utilizes the power of lucid dreaming (similar to visualization, when you are awake and programming your mind to view a series of scenes). Then you finish the dream by visualizing and writing the script to a logical and peaceful conclusion. Exercise 13.4 takes you through this healing process, should you choose to do so.

Forgiveness: The Art of Moving on with Your Life

Anger is a survival emotion to be used long enough to get out of harm's way. Anger held longer than this brief moment in time turns toxic and becomes a control issue. You may tend to hold resentment against those who you feel have violated or victimized you, perhaps first as a protection but then as a type of revenge. Revenge, however, is an unhealthy style of mismanaged anger.

If anger becomes a toxin, then forgiveness is an antidote. The last thing people want to hear about in the face of violation is forgiveness, because it feels as if you received another slap across the face or kick in the butt. Surely, there must be adequate time for grieving. However, prolonged grieving can perpetuate mismanaged anger. Forgiveness is both the last stage of grieving and the first stage of celebration.

Here are some quick tips about the art of forgiveness:

1. *Forgiveness means moving on.* Realize that by forgiving someone of a misdeed, you are not doing him or her a favor. Rather, you are releasing yourself from the chains of anger so you can move on with your life. If unresolved anger is giving your power away, then acts of forgiveness mean reclaiming your personal power.

2. *Forgiveness does not mean the same thing as restitution.* Do not expect an apology through your act of forgiveness—you could be waiting a very long time. Most likely you will never receive one.

3. *Forgiveness starts within.* Forgiving someone of his or her misdeed requires that you must first learn to forgive yourself for those things you have done that have been less than stellar. Only by realizing your own misdeeds can you extend a sense of compassion to others, and true forgiveness (without any conditions) is compassion in action.

If you feel there is someone against whom you have been carrying a grudge or have kept their name on the top of your "S list," now is the time to resolve this stressor, make peace in your heart, and move on. Exercise 13.5 challenges you to engage in the act of forgiveness so that you can carry on with your life without carrying excess baggage.

The Healing Power of Prayer: Divine Connections

In times of stress it is not uncommon to turn to others for help. Sometimes we turn to friends and family.

Other times we turn to a greater source or higher power. If stress is indeed a perception of being cut off from the divine, then **prayer** is one means to reestablish this connection. Prayers come in many forms, from words of gratitude to calls for help (also known as intercessory prayer). Over the past decade, the topic of prayer has been of great interest, particularly intercessory prayer when used as a modality of healing in the field of complementary and alternative medicine. Regardless of one's spiritual background, religious upbringing, or lack thereof, the underlying premise of prayer appears to be the quality of intention put forth with request for help and assistance.

To gain the greatest benefit from the healing power of prayer, it's best to understand how to coordinate the efforts of both the conscious and unconscious mind. Based on the wisdom of luminary Sophy Burnham, the following are some aspects (nearly identical in nature to the template for visualization) to consider when using this modality as a coping technique.

1. *Present tense*: To the universal mind or divine consciousness, there is only one time zone: the present moment. Past memories and events as well as future events and aspects are all considered to be included in the present moment as well. Simply stated, divine consciousness appears not to understand events as anything other than now! Therefore, as you state your prayer, think in terms of bringing the image into the present moment as if you are experiencing it now.

2. *Focused concentration:* Prayer requires a clear transmission of intention. Maintaining a clear focus of your attention allows this to occur. Under duress, feelings of fear or anger act like static and tend to garble the message so that it is not heard clearly. Take time to quiet the mind and clear the static for a clear transmission of your request and intention.

3. *Positive thoughts and intentions:* Just as the unconscious mind understands only one time zone, it also understands only positive thoughts. Words expressed negatively are translated into a positive framework. Therefore, to coordinate both conscious and unconscious minds toward a unified goal, construct your prayer in a positive mind frame.

4. *Emotional vibration:* New research on visualization and prayer indicates that thoughts alone produce no lasting effect. What really galvanizes the power of visualization is the emotion (compassion) behind the thoughts. So as you begin to articulate your intention, generate a feeling of compassion with your request or expression of gratitude.

5. *Detached outcomes:* Placing an expected outcome on the desired intention of each prayer is analogous to throwing down an anchor on a boat that is about to set sail. It halts any progress. Although it's human to have expectations, this too becomes an emotional vibration that negates the intended outcome. The ego projects strong expectations. For prayer to have the greatest effect one must detach the ego from the outcome and simply let what happens, happen.

6. *Attitude of gratitude:* Upon the completion of the visualization offer an expression of gratitude for the experience. An honest expression of gratitude fills the sails of every prayer with wind to transport it to the intended destination, wherever that may be.

Times of stress can certainly elicit feelings of fear and anxiety, yet these same feelings can be counterproductive when the call for divine assistance is summoned. When fear enters the heart in the prayer process, there is no doubt that the message can be compromised. Exercise 13.6 guides you through this template to refine your prayer style for the best possible outcome. Remember, whatever the outcome, there is a bigger game plan than we can ever imagine, and answers to prayers come in their own time and way in accordance with this bigger picture.

Chapter Summary

- Journaling as a coping technique has both immediate (e.g., cathartic) effects and prolonged (e.g., clarity) effects for problem resolution.

- Close friends offer immeasurable and invaluable assistance in coping with stress.

- Social orchestration is a restructuring of one's daily responsibilities, also known as the path of least resistance.

- As a coping technique, hobbies provide both a healthy distraction away from problems and a transfer effect of creativity.

- The unconscious mind speaks in the language of dreams as a means to help solve issues in the waking hours. Dream therapy is a way to harness the meaning of dreams for personal gain.

- Forgiveness is a coping skill that helps deal with unresolved anger issues.

- Effective prayer is thought to employ four components: the use of the present tense, focused concentration, positive thoughts and intentions, and an emotional vibration of optimism and compassion.

Additional Resources

Baikie, K. A., & Wilhelm, K. Emotional and physical health benefits of expressive writing. *Advances in Psychiatric Treatment*, 11:338–346, 2005.

Burnham, S. *The Path of Prayer.* New York: Compass; 2002.

Delaney, G. *Living Your Dreams.* San Francisco: Harper SanFrancisco; 1996.

Dossey, L. *Healing Words.* San Francisco: Harper San Francisco; 1993.

Grason, S. *Journalution.* Novato, CA: New World Library; 2005.

Luskin, F. *Forgive for Good.* San Francisco: Harper SanFrancisco; 2002.

Metcalf, L., & Tobin, S. *Writing the Mind Alive: The Proprioceptive Method for Finding Your Authentic Voice.* New York: Ballantine; 2002.

Meyers, L. J. *Becoming Whole: Writing Your Healing Story* (2nd ed.). New York: Iaso; 2007.

Pennebaker, J. *Opening Up.* New York: William Morrow; 1990.

Pennebaker, J. W. *Writing to Heal: A Guided Journal for Recovering from Trauma and Emotional Upheaval.* Oakland, CA: New Harbinger Publications; 2004.

Seaward, B. L. *Managing Stress: A Creative Journal* (4th ed.). Burlington, MA: Jones & Bartlett; 2011.

EXERCISE 13.1: Journal Writing: The Seed

Begin this journal exercise with a seed (e.g., walnut, sunflower, tulip bulb, poppy). Hold the seed in your hand and close your eyes for a moment. Within your hand is a seed—the gift of life. Within this seed is a powerhouse of creation. From the tiniest seed grows the largest tree. From large seeds grow flowers, fruits, and an abundance of gifts that exult the five senses. The seed is the quintessential metaphor that represents a multitude of ideas or possibilities within each and every one of us. Inside each seed is the coded wisdom to manifest our intentions, whatever they may happen to be, but only if the right conditions exist.

If seeds are like ideas, intentions, or prayers that we cast out to the four winds in the hopes of them taking root, then our minds are similar to the fields of earth that await the collaboration of creativity. A seed that lands on unfertile soil is no different than an idea that finds its way into one's own inhospitable mind. Doubts, fears, frustrations, attachments, and conditional desires often sabotage the potential of each seed ready to germinate.

1. Using the seed as a metaphor, comb the recesses of your heart to come up with one intention that you truly wish to manifest in your life. Like the seed that you hold in your hand, describe it in fine detail.

2. Like the tree or flower from which the seed came, take a moment to reflect on the source of your inspiration. Where did your intention originate? By gaining clarity on this, you create a stronger bond of energy from source to seed, thereby ensuring a stronger outcome.

3. Just as there are many natural (and unnatural) things that can impede the growth of the seed that hits the ground, so too are there impeding thoughts within our own mind that can sterilize the strongest seeds. By recognizing what these factors are we can begin to take steps to cleanse the ground and refertilize it for the best effect. What thoughts inhibit the growth of your best intentions?

4. In the best words possible, visualize the realization of your intention—not only the roots, but also the branches and leaves. In essence, what fruit will this seed bear when it is fully grown?

EXERCISE 13.1: Journal Writing: The Seed cont....

EXERCISE 13.2: Defining Your Support Group

Support groups are vital to the quality and longevity of our lives. Support groups are composed of friends, colleagues, peers, neighbors, and perhaps most of all, family members. Your support group is made up of those people you feel closest to who are there to socialize with, give a helping hand, or cry on their shoulders when you feel like doing so. The following questions are to help you reinforce the foundations of your support group.

1. As best as you can, create what you think is the best definition of a friend.

_____

_____

2. Make a list of those people who you feel constitute your support group.

a. My closest male friends include: _____

_____

b. My closest female friends include: _____

_____

c. The friend(s) I know I can share any problem with, at any time, include: _____

_____

_____

d. The friends I can call to go play or go shopping include: _____

_____

_____

e. These friends energize me; they don't drain my energy: _____

_____

_____

f. Friends on whom I know I can call for a favor at any time include: _____

_____

_____

g. Friends who are mentors include: _____

_____

_____

h. Friends who expand my personal horizons with new ideas or activities are: _____

_____

_____

EXERCISE 13.2: Defining Your Support Group cont....

3. How has your support group changed over the years?

_____

_____

4. Some people in our support groups tend to drain our energy rather than replenish it. Do you have friends like this? _____

If so, how do you cope with them? _____

5. What factors in your life detract from your ability to "be there" for others in your support group?

_____

6. It has often been said that we can never have enough friends. Although this may be true, you cannot spend repeated quality time with everyone, because this weakens the integrity of true friends. What do you do to nurture the connections between you and your friends? In other words, how are you a good friend to others?

_____

_____

7. For a variety of reasons, friends tend to come and go in our lives. New friends can become a breath of fresh air in our lives. New friends are harder to make and keep as we age. It helps to continually foster new interests and hobbies. Make a list of three new places where you can begin to meet new people to add as possible members of your support group.

_____

_____

_____

_____

_____

_____

_____

_____

_____

EXERCISE 13.3: Hobbies and Outside Interests

Here is a question to consider: What would you do for a living if your career didn't exist? Here is another question: If money wasn't a factor in sustaining your desired lifestyle, how would you spend the rest of your life? Hobbies and outside interests provide a sense of balance to the long hours of work that tend to define who we are in this world. The truth is that you are not your job, your career, or even your paycheck. Yet, without claiming some outside interests as a significant part of your life, it becomes easy to see yourself as a passive victim in a rapidly changing world.

1. What are your current outside interests? Name three things or activities that you partake in on a regular (weekly) basis.

a._____

b._____

c._____

2. If you had a hard time coming up with three specific outside interests that qualify as true hobbies, or perhaps you are looking for some new interest to enter your life, what are some examples of things you have always wanted to do or get involved with, or groups or organizations you always wanted to become a member of that can get you started in this direction?

a._____

b._____

c._____

3. Playing the guitar, knitting a sweater, or making plans to remodel the kitchen are great things to do, but they require time. Making time for hobbies and outside interests requires some discipline. What steps do you take to ensure that you have the time to fulfill your passions of your personal outside interests?

_____

_____

_____

_____

4. Would you say that your involvement in one or more of your hobbies has a transfer effect in other aspects of your life? If so, how? Please explain:

_____

_____

_____

_____

EXERCISE 13.4: Dreams Revisited

Although we all have dreams, remembering them is not always easy. But there are occasions when a certain dream is replayed in our mind over the course of months, perhaps even years. These recurring dreams may have only a short run on the mind's silver screen, or they may last throughout the course of our lifetime. These dreams, perhaps foggy in detail, surface occasionally in the conscious state, and the story they tell is all too familiar.

It is commonly believed that recurring dreams symbolize a hidden insecurity or a stressful event that has yet to be resolved. They don't have resolved endings. Although there is much to the dream state that is still unknown, it is believed that dreams are images that the unconscious mind creates to communicate to the conscious mind in a language all its own. This form of communication is not a one-way street. Messages can be sent to the unconscious mind in a normal waking state as well.

Through the use of mental imagery, you can script the final scenes of a recurring dream with a happy ending. What seems to be the final scene of a dream is actually the beginning of the resolution process. The following is a true story: Once there was a young boy who had an afternoon paper route. One day, while the boy was delivering papers, a large black German shepherd jumped out of the bushes and attacked him. The owner called the dog back, but not before the dog drew blood. As the boy grew into adulthood his love for dogs never diminished, but several times a year he awoke in a sweat from a recurring dream he had had once too often.

The Dream: "It is dark and I am walking through the woods at night. Out from behind one of the trees comes this huge black dog. All I can see are his teeth, and all I can hear is his bark. I try to yell for help, but nothing comes out of my throat. Just as he lunges for me, I awake in a panic."

With a little thought and imagination, a final scene was drafted to bring closure to this dream story.

Final Scene: "I am walking through the woods at night with a flashlight, a bone, and a can of mace. This time, when the dog lunges at me, I shine the light in his eyes and spray mace in his face. He whines and whines, and then I tell him to sit. He obeys. I put the bone by his nose and he looks at me inquisitively. Then he licks the bone and starts to bite into it. I begin to walk away and the dog gets up to follow, bone in mouth. I stop and look back and he stops. He wags his tail. The sky grows light as the sun begins to rise, and the black night fades into pink and orange clouds. As I walk back to my house, I see the dog take his new find down the street. I open the door and walk upstairs and crawl back into bed." It has been 5 years, and this man has never had this dream again.

Ultimately, we are the creators of our dreams. We are the writers, directors, producers, and actors of our dreams. Although drafting a final scene is no guarantee that the issues that produce recurring dreams are resolved, it is a great starting point in the resolution process, a time for reflection that may open up the channels of communication between the conscious and unconscious mind. Do you have a recurring dream that needs a final scene to be complete? Write out your recurring dream and give it a final scene.

_____

_____

_____

_____

_____

_____

EXERCISE 13.4: Dreams Revisited cont....

EXERCISE 13.5: Sweet Forgiveness

"You cannot shake hands with a clenched fist." —Indira Ghandi

Every act of forgiveness is an act of unconditional love. If unresolved anger is a toxin to the spirit, forgiveness is the antidote, and where anger is a roadblock, forgiveness is a ladder to climb above and transcend the experience. For forgiveness to be complete and unconditional, you must be willing to let go of all feelings of anger, resentment, and animosity. Sweet forgiveness cannot hold any taste of bitterness because they are mutually exclusive. Victimization is a common feeling when one encounters stressors in the form of another person's behaviors. When we sense that our human rights have been violated, feelings of rage can quickly turn into feelings of resentment. Left unresolved, these toxic thoughts can taint the way we treat others and ourselves. To forgive those who we feel have wronged us is not an easy task. Often it's a process, and at times, a very long process at that. Yet turning the other cheek does not mean you have to let people walk all over you. Forgiveness is not a surrender of your self-esteem, nor is it a compromise of your integrity. When you can truly forgive the behavior of those whom you feel violated by, you let go of the feelings of control and become free to move on with your life. Resentment and grudges can become roadblocks on the human path. Forgiveness turns a hardened heart into an open passageway to progress on life's journey. Think for a moment of someone who might have violated your humanness. Is it time to let go of some toxic thoughts and initiate a sense of forgiveness?

To begin this exercise, write the name of that person or those persons toward whom you feel some level of resentment. Beside each name write down what action or behavior it was that offended you and why you feel so violated. What feelings arise in you when you see this person, or even hear his or her name? Next, make a note of how long you have felt this way toward this person. Finally, search your soul for a way to forgive the people on your list, even if it means just to acknowledge their human spirit. Then practice the act of forgiveness as best you can, and let the feelings of resentment go.

_____

_____

_____

_____

_____

_____

_____

_____

_____

_____

_____

_____

_____

_____

EXERCISE 13.6: The Healing Power of Prayer

Regardless of one's religious background, or lack thereof, prayer is a commonly used coping technique that is used in times of duress. To seek help in times of need is considered a savvy strategy in overcoming problems, no matter what size. Although prayer can be a very personal behavior, we now know that there are certain steps to ensure a clear transmission for divine intercession. Consider using the outline below as a personal template to refine the healing power of prayer.

1. *Present tense:* State your prayerful intention in the present tense below.

_____

_____

_____

2. *Focused concentration:* Clear your mind by using the space below to write down any distracting, negative thoughts as a means of releasing them.

_____

_____

_____

3. *Positive thoughts and intentions:* State your intention in the most positive way.

_____

_____

_____

4. *Emotional vibration:* Call to mind the most favorable emotion you can feel. If it helps, write down the experience and feelings to help re-create this feeling now.

_____

_____

_____

5. *Detached outcomes:* Write down any fears, anxieties, or desires that need to be released to make the prayer really fly.

_____

_____

_____

6. *Attitude of gratitude:* Take a moment to write a few words of thanks here for what you are grateful for as this happens.

_____

_____

_____

Part 3

Effective Relaxation Techniques

The Art of Calm: Relaxation Through the Five Senses

"If you are looking for fast acting relief, try slowing down."

— Lily Tomlin

The Ageless Wisdom of Physical Relaxation

A quick study of ancient Greece reveals that hot baths, muscle massage, aromatic fragrances, melodic music, and scrumptious food were only a few of the several methods used to achieve balance from the cares and worries of the day. The Greeks weren't alone in their efforts to promote relaxation. Similar means to seek balance among mind, body, and spirit can be found in the cultures of ancient civilizations around the world, from Egypt to Polynesia. Ageless wisdom emphasized the importance of achieving balance between hard physical work and relaxation.

In their wildest dreams, citizens of ancient civilizations could never have conceived of the high-tech, fast-paced global village we live in today. Laptop computers, airplanes, iPods, and microwaves never even entered their imagination, yet in many ways, their lives were no different than ours today. Stress has always been and always will be a part of the human landscape. What citizens of previous generations did know was the importance of taking time to relax, something that we often fail to remember. Indeed, there is an art to relaxation, an art to the mastery of calmness and tranquility in a stress-filled world. Ironically, like the basis of most stress, this mastery is cultivated through the perceptions of the five senses. The art of calm is derived from knowing how to turn off the negative input and replace it with positive sensations.

Sight. Sound. Smell. Taste. Touch. These five senses are the portals through which information enters the brain so the mind can determine threat from non-threat, friend from foe. Just as information comes into these five senses to detect danger, these same portals of sensory information are receptive to any and all information that calms the mind and body. Massage therapy, aromatherapy, music therapy, and hydrotherapy are but a few of the contemporary examples of ageless methods employed to return to a sense of calm through one or more of the five senses.

As the planet turns faster and faster into a world of rapid change and high technology, the human spirit yearns for a sense of stability garnered through the wisdom of time-proven methods of rest and relaxation. Muscle massage, aromatherapy, hydrotherapy, good food, good music, slow deep breathing, and peaceful images to seduce the mind into a state of tranquility

are more than fads or popular trends. By all accounts, these are time-honored practices. So it's no secret that references to all of these modalities of "healing" can be found in the texts and lifestyles of ancient Greece, Egypt, Polynesia, Australia, and the Mayan peninsula. These ancient traditions remind us of what we so often forget: to take time to balance the rush of life with frequent rest-filled pauses. The art of calm reminds us that we are human beings, not human doings, and as such, we need to take frequent breaks to simply be.

An often-asked question about relaxation techniques is this: Isn't sleeping as good as or better than meditation, yoga, or any other relaxation technique? The simple answer is *no*! Sleeping does not produce the same effects, because during sleep, the unconscious mind works to resolve issues from the previous day. Stress-based emotions that were suppressed or left unresolved tend to show up while sleeping in a variety of ways, including high blood pressure, muscle tension, and TMJD. What makes every effective relaxation technique unique when compared to nocturnal sleep (where the conscious mind is inactive) is the *conscious intention* to relax. The act of sleep is involuntary whereas these techniques are voluntary, meaning that there is a conscious effort to achieve homeostasis. By doing so, rather than acting as adversaries, both the conscious and unconscious minds work in unison for the integration, balance, and harmony of mind, body, spirit, and emotions.

Sense of Sight

As humans, we are, above all else, visual animals. Approximately 70 percent of sensory information is processed through our eyes. Another 20 percent is garnered by the ears, and the remaining 10 percent is taken in by the other three senses. As such, it makes sense to believe that if we close our eyes, if only momentarily, our stress levels should drop dramatically. Perhaps this is why people who choose to relax by using diaphragmatic breathing, listening to music, or receiving a massage close their eyes rather than keep them open. Using the sense of sight to relax may be an oxymoron, because in many cases the sense of sight is quite literally turned off. In other cases, however, a calming image is used to replace a stressful scene. When asked to name a calming image, most people turn their eyes toward nature—mountain vistas, ocean beaches, lush primeval forests—the grandeur of nature that brings all problems into perspective. Using the sense of sight to promote relaxation can instill a deep sense of inner peace.

Sense of Sound

Sounds can rile your nerves and sounds can tame the wildest of beasts. Like all information that is processed through the five senses, one's perception makes the difference between tranquility and annoyance—in this case, between melody and noise. Sounds that promote a sense of calm are endless and can include soft rippling waterfalls, rhythmic ocean waves caressing the sandy beach, and wind chimes. Music therapy is the name given to the use of music to promote a sense of deep relaxation through the principle of entrainment. Classical, jazz, new age, and scores of other types of music that include ocean waves, dolphin songs, and rain are just some of the many soothing sounds that can calm one's nerves.

Sense of Smell

Fragrances have long been held in esteem by people the world over as a means to lift one's spirits and calm one's mind. There appears to be a universal agreement that flower scents (e.g., roses, star lilies, orchids) as well as many herbs (e.g., peppermint, rosemary, allspice) can diffuse the meanest temper. For some, pine trees hold the same properties, as does the smell of the ocean, and of course most everyone's attention is swayed by a wide selection of food scents.

Sense of Taste

It's been said that 80 percent of taste is smell. Those who have experienced a cold might tell you that food simply doesn't taste as good when they are sick. The tongue's taste buds are divided into five specific regions: sweet, bitter, salty, sour, and a fifth region for savoriness, called umami. For some, taste also includes the feel of the morsels of food as they pass over the tongue and roof of the mouth and down the throat. It would be fair to say that taste involves a little bit of touch as well.

Sense of Touch

Humans not only crave touch, but research now reveals that without it, our health diminishes greatly. Human contact through touch is critical to the health of each newborn baby. Without it they die. The skin is the largest organ of the body, and with so many neural endings at the periphery of muscle and skin the sense of touch is by far the most delicate sense. Muscle massage in all its many forms is not the only means to relax through the power of touch. Hot baths, saunas, furry cats and dogs, kneading bread, holding hands, walking barefoot on cool grass, hot showers, and making love are just a few of the many ways that touch exalts the human spirit to deeper levels of relaxation.

The Divine Sense

There are some experiences that simply cannot be summed up by one of the five senses. In fact, many experiences involve a synergistic effect of two or more sensory cues that tip the scales toward utter delight. Then there are some events or experiences that rise above the five senses to simply delight the human spirit at the soul level—the feeling that you have touched the face of God. Each of these experiences will vary from person to person, but the unique quality they share is that they bring the individual out of his or her personal experience to become one with something greater than the self.

How to Incorporate Relaxation Techniques into Your Life Routine

Every technique for relaxation is a skill, and skills require not only practice, but also the discipline to practice. Just like learning to type on a computer keyboard, shoot baskets, hit a golf ball, or speak a foreign language, every relaxation technique has a learning curve, meaning that the more you practice, the more efficient you become at it.

Although the end result of each technique is the same—homeostasis—every technique has its own nuances and amount of time needed to achieve the best results. For example, diaphragmatic breathing can be done in as little as 5 minutes a day, whereas a full body massage requires about 90 minutes. Regardless of which technique you employ, the ideal approach is to do something every day to unwind.

By and large, relaxation techniques are simple and cost effective (free). It doesn't take much time or money to sit quietly, close your eyes, and breathe. Yet in this fast-paced life, some techniques are better suited to a classroom setting, such as yoga, tai chi, and cardio exercise. Massage therapy is in a category all by itself. (Although massaging your muscles feels good, nothing beats a full body massage by a certified massage therapist.) If you are the kind of person who needs some encouragement, discipline, or perhaps just camaraderie, then you might consider choosing a relaxation technique where coaching is encouraged and there is an added sense of community. Exercises 14.1 and 14.2 guide you through the awareness of relaxation using the five senses.

Developing Your Mastery of Relaxation Techniques

There is no one way to calm the mind, body, and spirit. How you choose to return to homeostasis is entirely up to you, but regardless of which technique you use, it will involve one or more of the five senses. Some techniques will prove their effectiveness immediately (e.g., muscle massage) whereas others (e.g., meditation) may take repeated exposure before you sense the profound impact they can truly have.

Perhaps it's human nature to be a creature of habit, but most people tend to gravitate toward one, maybe two relaxation techniques. The holistic approach suggests cultivating the power of all senses. Therefore, it's to everyone's advantage to have a repertoire of at least five personal favorites, ideally one from each sense. If that seems overwhelming, consider simply becoming adept at one or two techniques. The rest of this book highlights many tried-and-true relaxation skills.

Stress Relief and Chronic Pain

Nearly every relaxation technique is useful in the effort to decrease **chronic pain**. Physical relaxation is the perfect antidote for all stress: mental burnout, physical exhaustion, emotional distress, and the absence of inner peace. Most, if not all, techniques for physical relaxation help to minimize the symptoms of chronic pain.

Best Benefits of Physical Relaxation

When the body is aroused for fight or flight, even at low intensities during periods of chronic stress, every organ in the body is at risk of becoming a target of neural or hormonal activity or both. Our muscles are the most frequently hit target organ. In fact, it's fair to say that muscle tension is the number one symptom of stress. Although muscle tension doesn't necessarily place people in the hospital, other organs targeted for stress surely will. The heart, the stomach, the skin, the adrenal glands, and the ovaries all become at risk for what Hans Selye called the general adaptation syndrome: excessive wear and tear on the body due to a lack of homeostasis.

Each technique for relaxation has one aim: to return the body to a state of homeostasis. In our current 24/7 society where fast-food lifestyles and virtual relationships are the norm, the body not only craves homeostasis, but also requires it on a daily basis. Although most, if not all, of these techniques are used as a preventive measure against disease and illness, it is not uncommon to see people who, caught in the grips of chronic disease, use one or more of these techniques for relief from chronic pain. In many cases, various techniques have been known to reverse the damage caused by the disease and the symptoms of stress associated with it.

The cost of not returning to a state of homeostasis is potentially lethal. Remember that the body is the battlefield for the war games of the mind. Simply stated: Stress kills! When the body is not given the chance to return to a baseline level of rest, organs targeted by the emotional consequences of stress will certainly be affected. This fact cannot be understated. Therefore, it stands to reason that the need to relax is as important as taking a daily shower or brushing your teeth. It's that important.

Specific Benefits

What are the specific benefits of habitual periods of rest and relaxation? They include, but are not limited to, the following:

- Decreased resting heart rate
- Decreased resting blood pressure
- Decreased respiration cycles
- Decreased stress hormone activity
- Decreased fatigue levels
- Decreased sense of anxiety
- Decreased muscle tension
- Increased sleep quality

- Increased integrity of the immune system
- Increased digestion
- Increased mental concentration and attention span
- Increased sense of self-esteem
- Increased sense of well-being

- The purpose of relaxation techniques is to intercept stressful stimuli through one or more of the five senses and promote a sense of homeostasis. The benefits of relaxation techniques, from a resting heart rate to better-quality sleep, are numerous.

Chapter Summary

- We take in countless stimuli from our five senses, many of which promote stress. We can also take in stimuli that promote relaxation through these same five senses.

Additional Resources

Matthews, A. M. *The Seven Keys to Calm.* New York: Pocket; 1997.

Seaward, B. L. *The Art of Calm.* Deerfield, FL: Health Communications; 1999.

EXERCISE 14.1: The Art of Calm: Relaxation Through the Five Senses

Please list five ideas for relaxation for each of the five senses. Note that a sixth category, the "divine" sense, has been added for any ideas that might be a combination of these or perhaps something beyond the five senses (e.g., watching a child being born). Describe each idea in a few words to a sentence. Be as specific as possible, and be creative!

The Sense of Sight

1. _____

2. _____

3. _____

4. _____

5. _____

The Sense of Sound

1. _____

2. _____

3. _____

4. _____

5. _____

The Sense of Smell

1. _____

2. _____

3. _____

4. _____

5. _____

The Sense of Taste

1. _____

2. _____

3. _____

4. _____

5. _____

The Sense of Touch

1. _____

2. _____

3. _____

4. _____

5. _____

The "Divine" Sense (Beyond the Five Senses)

1. _____

2. _____

3. _____

4. _____

5. _____

EXERCISE 14.2: Relaxation Survival Kit

A **relaxation survival kit** is like your personal first-aid kit for stress. Keep it well stocked with things that nurture or sustain your personal sense of homeostasis, in this case, homeostasis that comes from pleasing one or all of the five senses. Just like a first-aid kit, please be sure to replace any items that have been used—like chocolate (taste)—so that in the event of another personal disaster, or day from hell, you can pull out your kit and put yourself back on the path toward inner peace. To start this process, begin by making a list of the items you wish to include in your relaxation kit, and then use this list as a means of keeping inventory.

Sight

1. _____

2. _____

3. _____

4. _____

5. _____

Touch

1. _____

2. _____

3. _____

4. _____

5. _____

Sound

1. _____

2. _____

3. _____

4. _____

5. _____

Smell

1. _____

2. _____

3. _____

4. _____

5. _____

Taste

1. _____

2. _____

3. _____

4. _____

5. _____

Additional Items

1. _____

2. _____

3. _____

4. _____

5. _____

The Art of Breathing

> *"There are over 40 different ways to breathe."*
> — Ancient Chinese proverb

The Ageless Wisdom of Breathing

There is an ancient proverb that is often cited to students learning the art of self-discipline. It states, "There are over 40 ways to breathe." If you are like most people, you might laugh or perhaps even smirk at this notion. After all, most people think there is only one way to breathe—a combination of inhaling and exhaling. The ageless wisdom of this proverb, however, suggests that the art of breathing opens the mind and body to a profound sense of relaxation. Although there is no one-size-fits-all relaxation technique that works for everyone, there is one that comes close. If you look closely at the plethora of relaxation techniques, from hatha yoga to tai chi to autogenics and meditation, you will see that **diaphragmatic breathing** is used in all of these. Indeed, of the many ways to breathe that promote relaxation, most if not all place the emphasis of the breath on the lower abdomen. The beauty of this technique is that it can be done anywhere and anytime.

By and large, Americans are thoracic breathers, meaning that we tend to breathe with our upper chest. Diaphragmatic breathing, also known as belly breathing, places the emphasis of each breath on the lower abdominal area. If you were to watch anyone breathing while they sleep, you would notice that this is the only way they breathe; this is the way that you breathe when you sleep, because in a resting state, the body tries to maintain the greatest level of homeostasis.

The Breath Cycle

There are four specific phases of each breath cycle. They include:

- *Phase 1:* The inhalation of air, also called the "in-breath"

- *Phase 2:* A very slight pause before you exhale

- *Phase 3:* The exhalation of air, also called the "out-breath"

- *Phase 4:* A very slight pause before you inhale again

You should remember not to hold your breath during phases 2 and 4 but to merely acknowledge that indeed there is a pause between the in-breath and the out-breath. In a normal resting state, the average person has between 14–16 breath cycles per minute. Under situations of stress this number can double, as breathing becomes more rapid and shallow. There are, however, those who tend to hold their breath when under stress (being stuck in phase 2 or phase 4). Holding one's breath tends to increase heart rate and blood pressure, thus being counterproductive to relaxation. When people are VERY relaxed, they may breath as few as 3–6 breath cycles per minute.

It should be noted that some people who take 3–6 breaths per minute are anything but relaxed. These are people who are more commonly known as "breath-holders" (they forget to breathe properly). In adopting this habit of breathing, they place undue pressure on their central nervous system, invoking a low-level stress response.

How to Incorporate the Art of Conscious Breathing into Your Life

Exercises 15.1 ("Breathing Clouds Meditation") and 15.2 ("Dolphin Breath Meditation") guide you through the steps of diaphragmatic breathing. The best way to incorporate breathing as a relaxation technique is to practice belly breathing every day, even if it's only for 5 minutes each day—and we all have 5 minutes. Here are some suggestions:

- When you wake up in the morning, before you get out of bed, take five comfortably slow, deep breaths.

- While in the shower, with your hands at your side, take five comfortably deep breaths.

- On the way to work or class, turn off the radio or iPod for 5 minutes and consciously breathe.

- Close the door for 5 minutes and sit quietly and simply breathe.

- Take five deep sighs on the way home from work or class.

- Take five deep sighs waiting in line at the campus center, grocery store, post office, or bank.

- As you close your eyes to fall asleep, take five comfortably slow, deep breaths.

Developing Your Mastery of Diaphragmatic Breathing

Believe it or not, this is one technique you have already mastered. At this point all you need to do is practice what you already know. Simply place the emphasis of each breath on your lower abdomen. This sensation may feel awkward at first, but soon it will feel quite comfortable and normal. Exercises 15.1 and 15.2 are just two of the "40" techniques available that can help you develop your mastery of diaphragmatic breathing. Another breathing technique in Exercise 15.3 invites you to relax the whole body in this manner.

Stress Relief and Chronic Pain

Breathing can become quite short and shallow during high-pressure situations, which is why body wisdom generates a long, deep sigh every now and then. Long, deep breaths begin to reverse the physical effects of a stressful moment. Many pain centers incorporate breathing techniques as a complementary modality for chronic pain. One technique specifically invites the individual to imagine breathing into the area where there is pain as a means to reduce the tension in this area, often with great results.

Best Benefits of Diaphragmatic Breathing

If you were to sit in the presence of a meditating yogi and count the number of his breath cycles per minute, you might find that he can comfortably breathe one breath cycle (inhaling and exhaling) per minute. If you were to count the number of breaths you take per minute in the course of any given day, most likely you would count between 14 and 16 breath cycles per minute. When people get stressed they tend to breathe more frequently per minute, with each breath being more shallow. The benefits of breathing may seem simple, but they have a profound influence on other aspects of human physiology, including decreasing resting heart rate, resting blood pressure, and muscle tension.

Stop reading for a moment and take a long, deep sigh. Notice how you feel when you exhale. Relief! The breathing cycle is actually a cycle of slight tension or expansion (inhalation) followed by a phase of complete relaxation (exhalation). This is why the exhalation phase is considered to be the most relaxing phase of the breathing cycle. Diaphragmatic breathing works the same way as a deep sigh.

Chapter Summary

- Diaphragmatic breathing is the most relaxed way to breathe (as opposed to thoracic breathing).

- There are four phases of each breath cycle: 1) inhalation, 2) very slight pause, 3) exhalation, 4) very slight pause.

- In a normal resting state, we tend to breathe about 14–16 breath cycles per minute. When stressed, this number can double. When relaxed, this number can be as low as 3–6 breaths.

- The exhalation phase (phase 3) is believed to be the most relaxing phase of breathing.

- Diaphragmatic breathing is known to help relieve chronic pain.

Additional Resources

Farhi, D. *The Breathing Book*. New York: Owl; 1996.

Hendricks, G. *Conscious Breathing*. New York: Bantam; 1995.

Iyengar, B. K. *Light on Pranayama*. New York: Crossroad; 1981.

Lewis, D. *Free Your Breath, Free Your Life*. Boston: Shambhala Press; 2004

Lewis, D. *The Tao of Natural Breathing*. Berkeley, CA: Rodmell Press; 2006.

Rosen, R. *The Yoga of Breathing: A Step by Step Guide to Pranayama*. Boston: Shambhala; 2002.

EXERCISE 15.1: Breathing Clouds Meditation

The words *spirit* and *breath* are synonymous in virtually all cultures and languages. So important is the breath as a means to achieve inner peace that it is *the* hallmark of nearly every meditation practice. Breath is the life force of energy. If you have ever been aware of your own normal breathing style, you may have noticed that when under stress, your breathing becomes more shallow. You may also come to realize *just how good* a deep sigh really feels. *This* is the underlying message of the breathing clouds meditation: to instill a wonderful sense of inspiration with each inhalation, and total relaxation with each exhalation.

Ancient mystics have said that there are more than 40 different ways to breathe. What they mean by this is that the breath serves as a powerful metaphor for releasing thoughts and feelings and cleansing the mind, thus promoting a deeper level of contemplation, as well as achieving a profound sense of inner wisdom. Although there are many ways to achieve this goal, conscious breathing—that which unites mind, body, and spirit—offers a direct *and* unencumbered path toward inner peace.

This meditation/visualization exercise is deeply rooted in the Eastern culture, a world rich in metaphor. The implied message here is to release, detach, and let go of any and all thoughts and feelings that no longer serve your highest good. This powerful image of breathing clouds is a vehicle to do just that.

As with any type of visualization exercise, please feel free to augment, edit, and embellish the suggestions given in this exercise, to make them vivid *and* the most empowering for you.

Primarily with this meditation, there are two images: The first is of white clouds, which represent the inhalation phase of the breathing cycle. The second is of dark clouds, which symbolize the exhalation phase. The white clouds symbolize clean, fresh air. The dark clouds represent stressful thoughts, lingering anxieties, nagging problems, issues, or concerns that trouble you or simply add weight to an already busy mind.

The goal of this meditation is to clear any and all pressing issues, those unresolved feelings, those negative thoughts, or perhaps even excess energy, so that your mind becomes clear of thought and your body becomes completely relaxed.

This breathing exercise includes 12 breathing cycles, with each cycle composed of one inhalation (breathing in through your nose) and one exhalation phase (breathing out through your mouth). As we come to the 11th and 12th cycles—with your mind cleared of mental chatter—you may notice that the air you exhale has become as clean and clear as the air you inhale. This is the goal: homeostasis!

Once again, remember that as you follow the suggestions of this meditation please follow a breathing cycle that is most comfortable for you.

Instructions

- To begin, find a comfortable place to sit or lie down where there are no interruptions; a time and place for you, and for you alone. Take a moment to adjust any clothing to enhance your own comfort level.

- Then close your eyes and take a comfortably slow, deep breath. Breathe in slowly, and as you exhale, feel a sense of calm throughout your *entire* body. Please repeat this casual normal breathing cycle about four more times, making each breath comfortably slow and comfortably deep. Should your mind wander, know that this is OK, but gently guide your attention back to your breath.

As you do this, feel your abdominal area expand as you inhale, and then contract as you exhale.

EXERCISE 15.1: Breathing Clouds Meditation cont....

1. After several comfortable breath cycles, when you feel ready, imagine that the next breath that you take in (inhaling through your nose) is drawn from a beautiful cloud of pure white air—clean, fresh air! As you slowly breathe in this cloud of clean air through your nose, feel it circulate up to the top of your head and down the back of your spine, to where it resides at the *base* of your spine. Then, when you are ready to exhale, feel the air move up from your stomach area, into your lungs, and out through your mouth. As you *slowly* exhale, visualize that the air you breathe out is a dark cloud of dirty air—this symbolizes any stress and tension you may be feeling. As you begin to exhale, call to mind a problem or issue that has occupied your thoughts for the past several days. Then, allow this thought or feeling to leave as you exhale through your mouth.

2. Once again, using your mind's eye to focus on a beautiful white cloud, breathe in clean, fresh air through your nose, and feel it circulate throughout your body.

When you are ready to exhale, breathe slowly out through your mouth; as you do, once again visualize a cloud of dark air leaving your body, symbolic of any thoughts and feelings that at one time may have served you, but now no longer do. To hang on to these thoughts and feelings only weighs you down and holds back your highest potential.

3. On the next inhalation, slowly breathe in a white cloud of clean, fresh air through your nose, and again feel it circulate throughout your body and, this time, cleanse every cell in your body.

When you are ready to exhale, breathe slowly out through your mouth, and once again as you do, visualize a cloud of dark air leaving your body. Again, this represents any frustrations, anxieties, or anything that needs to be released.

4. Slowly now, inhale clean, fresh air through your nose. When you're ready, slowly exhale dark, dirty air through your mouth.

5. Inhale.   Exhale.

6. Inhale.   Exhale.

7. Inhale.   Exhale.

8. Inhale.   Exhale.

9. Inhale.   Exhale.

10. Inhale.   Exhale.

11. Slowly inhale clean, fresh air though your nose, and as you do, feel the air slowly circulate up to the top of your head. As it begins to move down the back of your spine, feel this clean, pristine air move into every cell in your body, to cleanse and invigorate the entire cell, clear down to the structure of your DNA.

As you begin to exhale, once again, breathe out slowly through your mouth, and as you do this, notice that the air you breathe out is nowhere near as dark as the air you first exhaled moments ago. Continue exhaling through your mouth, and observe the air you exhale.

12. Inhale clean, fresh air through your nose once more, and as you do, feel the air slowly circulate up to the top of your head. As it begins to move down the back of your spine, feel this clean, pristine air move into every cell in your body. Allow it to cleanse and invigorate the entire cell, including the strands of your DNA.

As you slowly begin to exhale, breathe out, once again through your mouth, and notice that the air you breathe out has become as clear as the air you have been breathing in. This symbolizes a deep sense of inner peace. Continue to exhale through your mouth and observe the air you breathe out.

EXERCISE 15.1: Breathing Clouds Meditation cont....

13. Now begin to notice that as you become more and more relaxed, more calm, and more energized by the clean, fresh air circulating through your body, your body is completely relaxed, and your mind is wonderfully calm and clear.

As you return to normal breathing, think to yourself this phrase as you begin to exhale: "I AM calm and relaxed." (Repeat!)

14. Now, with your next breath, slowly bring yourself back to the awareness of the room you are in. Become aware of the time of day, the day of the week, and what you have planned after you have completed this relaxation session.

15. When you feel ready, slowly open your eyes to a soft gaze in front of you. If you'd like, go ahead and stretch your arms and shoulders. Notice that although you feel very relaxed, you don't feel tired or sleepy. You feel fully energized and ready to accomplish whatever goals you have planned, fully realizing that now you are renewed and refreshed to once again feel the power of relaxation, as it energizes your whole being.

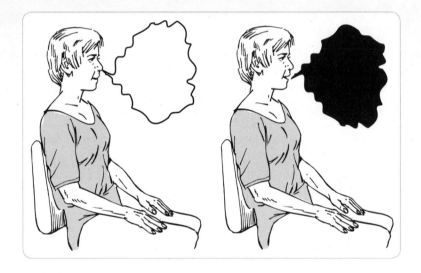

EXERCISE 15.2: Dolphin Breath Meditation

Breathing is, perhaps, the most common way to promote relaxation. Taking a few moments to focus on your breathing, to the exclusion of all other thoughts, helps to calm mind, body, and spirit. By focusing solely on your breathing, you allow distracting thoughts to leave the conscious mind. In essence, clearing the mind of thoughts is very similar to deleting unwanted emails, thus allowing more room to concentrate on what is really important in your life: that which really deserves attention.

In a normal resting state, the average person breathes about 14–16 breath cycles per minute. Under stress, this can increase to nearly 30 breath cycles per minute. Yet in a deep relaxed state, it is not uncommon to have as few as 3–6 breath cycles in this same time period. The breathing style that produces the greatest relaxation response is that which allows the stomach to expand, rather than the upper chest. (This is actually how you breathe when you are comfortably asleep.) Take a few moments to breathe, specifically focusing your attention on your abdominal area. If any distracting thoughts come to your attention, simply allow these to fade away as you exhale.

Sometimes, combining visualization with breathing can augment the relaxation response. The dolphin breath meditation is one such visualization.

Instructions

Imagine, if you will, that like a dolphin, you have a hole in the crown of your head with which to breathe. Although you will still breathe through your nose or mouth, imagine that you are now taking in slow, deep breaths through the opening at the top of your head.

As you do this, feel the air, or energy, come in through the top of your head, down past your neck and shoulders to reside momentarily at the base of your spine.

Then, when you feel ready, very slowly exhale, allowing the air to move back out through the dolphin spout, the opening situated at the top of your head. As you slowly exhale, feel a deep sense of inner peace reside throughout your body.

Once again, using all your concentration, focus your attention on the opening at the top of your head. Now, slowly breathe air in through this opening—comfortably slow, comfortably deep. As you inhale, feel the air move down into your lungs, yet allow it to continue farther down, deep into your abdominal region. When you feel ready, slowly exhale, allowing the air to move comfortably from your abdominal region up through the top of your head.

Now, take three slow, deep dolphin breaths; each time you exhale, feel a deep sense of relaxation all throughout your body.

1. Pause . . . Inhale . . . Exhale.

2. Pause . . . Inhale . . . Exhale.

3. Pause . . . Inhale . . . Exhale.

Just as you imagined a hole in the top of your head, now imagine that in the sole of each foot, there is also a hole through which you can breathe. As you create this image, take a slow, deep breath and through your mind's eye visualize air coming in through the soles of each foot. Visualize the air moving in from your feet, up through your legs, past your knees and waist, to where it resides in your abdominal region. When you feel ready, begin to exhale slowly, and allow the air to move back out the way it came, out through the soles of your feet.

EXERCISE 15.2: Dolphin Breath Meditation cont....

Using all your concentration, again focus your attention on the openings at the bottom of your feet and once again breathe in air through these openings, comfortably slow, comfortably deep. As before, feel the air move up your legs and into your abdominal region as your lungs fill with air. Then, when you feel ready, exhale, allowing the air to move slowly from your abdominal region, back through your legs, and out the soles of your feet.

Once again, please take three slow, deep breaths, this time through the soles of your feet; each time you exhale, feel a deep sense of relaxation all throughout your body.

4. Pause . . . Inhale . . . Exhale.

5. Pause . . . Inhale . . . Exhale.

6. Pause . . . Inhale . . . Exhale.

Now, with your concentration skills fully attentive, with your mind focused on the openings in *both* the top of your head and the soles of your feet, use your imagination to inhale air through both head and feet.

As you do this, slowly allow the passage of air entering from both head and feet to move toward the center of your body, where it resides in the abdominal region, until you exhale. Then, when you feel ready, slowly exhale and direct the air that came in through the top of your head to exit through the dolphin hole, while at the same time, directing the air that entered through the soles of your feet to leave from this point of entry as well. Once you have tried this, repeat this combined breath again three times, and with each exhalation, notice how relaxed your body feels.

7. Pause . . . Inhale . . . Exhale.

8. Pause . . . Inhale . . . Exhale.

9. Pause . . . Inhale . . . Exhale.

When you're done, allow this image to fade from your mind, but retain the sense of deep relaxation this experience has instilled throughout your mind, body, and spirit.

Then take one final slow, deep breath, feeling the air come into your nose or mouth, down into your lungs, and allow your stomach to extend out and then deflate as you begin to exhale. Again, feel a deep sense of calm as you exhale.

When you feel ready, allow your eyes to open slowly to a soft gaze in front of you, and bring your awareness back to the room where you now find yourself. As you bring yourself back to the awareness of the room you are now in, you feel fully energized, recharged, revitalized, and ready to accomplish whatever tasks await you.

EXERCISE 15.3: The Circle Breath

According to many Asian wisdom keepers, there are over 40 different ways to breathe. This breathing exercise is practiced in many parts of the world, including Tibet, Hawaii, and Peru, and goes by many names and variations. Some call it the "protection breath"; others call it the "healing breath." We will simply call it the circle breath. Please read the instructions and then follow the five easy steps several times each day to relax and keep yourself grounded in the course of living in a busy and fast-paced world. Although throughout the entire exercise you will be breathing in through your nose or mouth, this exercise invites you to use your imagination and begin the exercise by feeling yourself breathe air in through your heart space (the center of your upper chest).

1. Take a long, slow, deep breath in through your heart space and draw this air (or energy) up to the crown of your head as you inhale.

2. As you slowly exhale, allow the air (energy) to gently cascade down from the top of your head, down the back of your spine to where it resides at the base of your spine.

3. Slowly inhale. As you do, draw this air (energy) from the base of your spine up to your heart space. As you lift the air from the base of your spine through your stomach area, become aware of a sense of balance in your mind, body, and spirit.

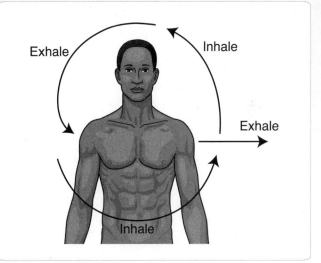

4. Slowly exhale out through your heart space in the direction of the sun (some people exhale to the sea, others to the mountains—whatever works for you). As you exhale, direct any distracting thoughts, nervous energy, or wandering thoughts from your heart space outward.

5. Repeat steps one through four 5 times.

Chapter 16

The Art of Meditation

*"Meditation—
it's not what
you think!"*
— Anonymous

The Ageless Wisdom of Meditation

Welcome to the age of information overload and sensory bombardment! It's here with a vengeance and growing stronger each day. Waves upon waves of information (some via entertainment, most through one's smartphone screen) can flood the mind to a point where ultimately you cannot think straight. Even if you think you can think straight, your friends will argue otherwise. Signs of an over-stimulated mind (and the mind's storage unit called the brain) include, but are not limited to, forgetfulness, rudeness, sarcasm, ego-self-righteousness, and general fatigue. The mind craves sensory stimulation, but the mind also craves sensory downtime to make sense of (process) all the bits and bytes of facts, perceptions, opinions, and perspectives. What is the secret to downtime? Actually, it's no secret at all. It's called meditation.

So important is the practice of **meditation** that every culture since the beginning of time has included it as a fundamental practice of living. Historically, credit was given to the Asian continent as the birthplace of meditation; however, a closer look reveals that the practice of centering or "quieting the mind" is a time-honored practice of inner peace among all the world's indigenous peoples.

The premise of meditation is simple. By quieting the mind from both external noise and internal chattering, one begins to gain greater clarity about important aspects of life. In 2003, *Time* magazine's cover story on meditation revealed that more than 25 million Americans meditate regularly. What was once considered to be a passing fad promoted by the Beatles after an exposure to Maharishi Mahesh Yogi (the founder of Transcendental Meditation) in India has now become a mainstay in U.S. culture. Moreover, magnetic resonance imaging (MRI) technology has been used to research the activation of various brain tissues during meditation, revealing that, much like the wisdom keepers have said for eons, the practice of meditation rewires the neural circuitry to promote calmness throughout the brain and body.

Although Freud coined the term *ego* about a hundred years ago, the concept of the conscious mind's censor is ageless. In many Eastern cultures the ego, as we understand it, is referred to as the self or false self. The purpose of meditation is to quiet the voice of the false self so that the inherent wisdom from the higher self or the true self can be accessed. Perhaps this is best explained by an ancient Chinese proverb, which states, "When the pupil is ready, the teacher will come." We are both the pupil and teacher. This proverb suggests that when we take the time to quiet the mind of the mental chatter that tends to distort clear thinking, we become receptive to insights (simple and profound) that give clarity and direction on the human path. For this reason, the fruits of meditation are often described as enlightenment.

You don't have to be watching CNN or accessing your favorite news app to know that the information age has taken off with a vengeance. Smartphones, laptops, microcomputer chips, and the Internet all spew bits and bytes of information incessantly in a 24/7 world. Everyone and everything seems to have instant accessibility. This means there is very little downtime to simply sit and relax without being bombarded with information. And even if you turn off the computer, your mind—under the control of the ego—picks up the slack and continues the babble. Because the mind is such an abstract concept, it and the practice of meditation are often explained in terms of metaphors. Before the introduction of computers, meditation was described as being like a broom that sweeps away the dust of the mind or ocean waves that wash away footprints in the sand. In the high-tech information age, a newer, perhaps more apt metaphor is used to explain meditation as a process similar to deleting old unwanted emails.

Types of Meditation

Although there are many hundreds of ways to meditate, all varieties of centering tend to fall into one of three categories: exclusive meditation, inclusive meditation, and mindfulness (which some people consider a form of inclusive meditation). Let's take a closer look at these various forms of centering as well as examples of each.

Exclusive Meditation

To hold one thought in the focus of your concentration, at the exclusion of all other thoughts, is the premise of **exclusive meditation**. A busy mind can race from thought to thought in milliseconds and become easily distracted. The consequence of a distracted mind is mental distortion, which is the antithesis of increased awareness; it is often called "clouded thinking." Various means to promote a focused concentration include sensory cues such as a verbal mantra (e.g., repeating the word *om*), a visual

226

object (e.g., looking at a mandala), an audio mantra (e.g., listening to ocean waves), or a tactile object (e.g., rosary beads). The premise behind exclusive meditation (also called restrictive meditation) is that by training the mind to focus on one thought, all other thoughts are compelled to evaporate from the conscious mind, thus allowing for increased awareness. The various forms of mental cleansing (e.g., mantra) act like a metaphoric wind that blows away the clouds or distractions produced by the ego. Transcendental Meditation, Deepak Chopra's Primordial Sound meditation, and Herbert Benson's Relaxation Response are all examples of exclusive meditation.

The most common mantra used in exclusive meditation is to focus on one's breathing. To do this one sits quietly with eyes closed, and through the mind's eye observes the continuous inhalation and exhalation of each breath. If distracting thoughts appear to divert attention, they are metaphorically exhaled on the out breath. So common is the breath as a mantra and so symbolic is the breath as a tool for cleansing that it is used in conjunction with nearly every relaxation technique known. Exercise 16.1, "Rainbow Meditation," is an exercise that uses a series of affirmations and visualizations with breathing to allow a clearing of the body's major energy centers (chakras).

Inclusive Meditation

Imagine that you are observing yourself, watching yourself engaged in the thinking process. **Inclusive meditation** is the ability to step outside your thoughts, detach from your stream of consciousness, by looking and observing but not judging your thoughts and emotions. Rather than excluding thoughts, inclusive meditation invites the practitioner to observe all thoughts, but not cast judgment on any thoughts or emotions. By pursuing a practice of inclusive meditation one begins to honor the discipline of detaching the ego's desires and the expectations we hold for others and ourselves. Some practices of inclusive meditation include the contemplation of an imponderable puzzle, also known as a Koan (e.g., How many angels can dance on the head of a pin? What is the sound of one hand clapping?). Zen meditation, various forms of Buddhist meditation, contemplative meditation, and centering prayer all serve as examples of inclusive meditation where the higher states of consciousness are attained from the observed becoming the observer.

Mindfulness Meditation

To be fully present with each and every activity that you do is the hallmark of **mindfulness meditation**. Rather than multitasking and having your mind ricocheting all over the place at every moment of each waking day, mindfulness meditation invites the practitioner to be fully present with each and every activity he or she does. For example, when washing the dishes, one would focus one's attention by feeling the water and soap over the hands, then feel the shape of the dish as it is handled and cleaned. Similarly, when walking outside, be mindful of the air temperature, the position of the sun, the smell of the earth, and so on. Mindfulness also includes maintaining a sense of gratitude for all the many great blessings in life, rather than ego-driven thoughts of feeling victimized by a series of personal injustices. A classic exercise in mindfulness is to pick up an apple, smell it, feel it, look at its color and texture, and feel the weight in the palm of your hand. Be mindful of where it was grown and how it nourishes the body when eaten, then take a bite to savor the taste of the apple, with each bite being mindful of all of these aspects.

Insightful Meditation

Insightful meditation isn't so much a type of meditation as it is an effect of cleansing the mind to unveil new thoughts, intuitive thoughts, insights, or what some people call enlightenment. Theoretically speaking, once the mind is still it begins to reflect a deep-seated wisdom contained in the fathoms of the unconscious mind, or as Carl Jung suggested, the collective unconscious. As the expression goes, you cannot demand enlightenment. You must trust that insights will, indeed, come when you are truly ready. Insights shouldn't be considered the goal of any meditation practice, because goals are accompanied by desires and desires are, for the most part, deeply rooted in ego. The primary goal of meditation is to calm the mind, even if nothing shows up once this state is reached. In other words, it's nice if it happens, but it doesn't always happen. There are ways, however, to encourage the ego to be still long enough that, given the chance, deep insights may appear. Exercises 16.2, "Crystal Cave Meditation," and 16.3, "Celestial Heavens Meditation," are examples of meditation/visualization exercises that augment the process of clarity by removing mental and emotional obstructions to allow a greater sense of insight regarding personal issues and one's human potential.

Meditation and Cognitive Function

It has long been held that the practice of meditation increases awareness by helping to access regions of the unconscious mind that are often deemed inaccessible by the censorship of the ego. Although the unconscious mind and the right hemisphere of the brain are not the same thing, it appears that cognitive functions of the unconscious mind are very similar to functions associated with the right hemisphere of the brain. In fact, the right side of the brain may be the specific organ of choice for the unconscious mind to do its work. The overall effect of meditation appears to be to allow both hemispheres of the brain to work in unison. Under stress, left brain skills tend to dominate our thinking patterns, thus promoting a less than holistic approach to mental, emotional, and spiritual well-being. **Table 16.1 ▾** is a short list of recognized right and left brain cognitive functions.

Meditation and ADD

It's no secret that attention deficit disorder (ADD) has become a national epidemic in the United States. The inability to focus one's attention on anything for a specific period of time has become a societal norm. There are many reasons for this, ranging from poor diet (lack of omega-3 fatty acids and an abundance of aspartame) to the oscillations of repeated television broadcast signals (not to mention commercial camera shots and angles). Add to this the obsession with voice mails, emails, instant messages, and the newest technology device about to hit the market, and it's a wonder anybody gets anything done at all with the proliferation of technological distractions. Despite the push for medications, we can safely assume that people do not have a Ritalin deficiency.

Zen masters laugh at the notion of ADD. Not because it's funny; rather, they are of the opinion that *everybody* with an ego has ADD. They believe that meditation is the means to train the mind to focus. More specifically, meditation is the way to domesticate the ego from wandering all over the conscious map. Meditation is the age-old tool of consciousness to increase attention and sharpen one's focus.

There are many people who claim that because they have been diagnosed with ADD, they cannot (and perhaps never will be able to) meditate. Nothing could be further from the truth! Although it may be hard at first (and to be honest, initially it is hard for everyone to learn to meditate), stay with it. It will get easier. It would be a good idea to learn to minimize distractions

TABLE 16.1	Left and Right Brain Cognitive Functions

Left Brain Thought Processes	Right Brain Thought Processes
Analytical skills	Synthesis skills
Judgment skills	Accepting, receptive nature
Time consciousness	Not time conscious
Verbal acuity	Symbolic thought processes
Linear thought progression	Nonlinear thought processes
Math acuity	Irrational thought processes
Logical thought processes	Highly intuitive nature
Sequential thought processes	Highly imaginative nature
Literalness	Humor/playfulness
Concrete/fact orientation	Metaphorical thought processes
Skepticism	Spontaneity
Cautiousness	Music appreciation
Working well with things	Working well with people

such as smartphone use and to eat healthier, too, by avoiding foods that negatively affect brain chemistry.

How to Incorporate Meditation into Your Daily Routine

The best way to begin and maintain a practice of meditation is to dedicate time to sit (or lay) quietly for a short period of time each day. Like taking a shower or brushing your teeth, meditation is best adopted as a daily practice or ritual, not a casual leisure activity when time permits. Most people claim not to have time in the day to sit quietly, yet the practice of meditation, or centering, need only take 5 minutes a day to start. Select a time of day (morning is often suggested as the best time to ground you for the rest of the day, but any time will work). Next select a specific place (either home or work) that is designated as your meditation place, such as a corner of the bedroom or den. By designating a place to do this (as you do with eating or brushing your teeth) you create a healthy boundary for this purpose. The next step is to minimize all distractions. The purpose of meditation is to minimize distractions generated from the ego to gain insight from the depths of your unconscious mind. Because the ego is so easily distracted by external stimuli, it defeats the purpose of meditation (particularly when you are starting this practice) to have external distractions, such as blaring televisions, stereos, radios, or smartphones going off in the midst of deep concentration.

Suggestions for Meditation

1. First, it is highly recommended not to meditate on a full stomach. This tends to promote drowsiness or sleeping, which does not lend itself to full awareness.

2. Second, turn off all smartphones and high-tech devices. Establish your meditation space as a tech-free zone. Go so far as to not even bring the device into the space so as not to be tempted to look and see who might be trying to get in touch. A healthy boundary with technology is essential for meditation.

3. Select a time in the day (mornings are thought to be best, before breakfast, or you could choose evenings well after dinner) and keep this time as a regular part of your daily schedule.

4. Keeping your spine straight is the optimal position for meditation, because it not only produces minimal neural discharge, but also offers a clear and unobstructed path for the energy of the spine (known as Kundalini energy) to move to the crown of the head.

5. If you prefer, consider playing some soft music (as white noise) to promote a deeper sense of awareness. Some people also prefer to burn a candle or incense. The use of relaxing sensory stimuli really helps to create a calm environment conducive for a sound meditative practice.

6. Boredom is a common experience in the initial stages of a meditative practice and, some say, is a necessary stage in the realms of higher consciousness. Obsession with boredom is the ego's way of manipulating the mind to abandon meditation as a practice. Rather than giving in, it's best to sit through this phase until the ego is fully domesticated. Having said that, some meditative practices tend to lose their appeal after a prolonged period (for some people, it's months; for others, years). Should you find that your meditative practice has become flat and predictable and is not allowing you to cross that threshold of insight, consider varying your practice by using different music, a different mantra, or perhaps shifting entirely from exclusive to inclusive (or vice versa).

7. Meditation CDs also serve as a means to either enhance or provide variety with one's meditative practice. There are many different types of meditation CDs with a host of different meditation themes. If you find that it is really difficult to minimize distractions (e.g., intrusive family members), you may wish to consider listening to a selection from a meditation CD with headphones to help strengthen the mind.

8. As a variation to your meditation practice, consider inviting like-minded friends or colleagues to do a group meditation (e.g., for world peace). Additionally, meditation groups meet regularly in community and church settings, and this too might offer a means to enhance your meditation practice or add some variety to it.

9. Sometimes it's nice to begin a meditation session by reading a short passage from a daily meditation book. There are many books to choose from, including *365 Tao*, *Promise of a New Day*, and, of course, the Bible.

Developing Your Mastery of Meditation

If you are interested in starting a meditation practice, you don't need to travel miles away to an Indian ashram or Buddhist temple. The practice of meditation can be done anywhere you can find or make a quiet space. Like all other techniques in this book, meditation is a skill that serves you best with regular practice, in this case, every day. Developing a mastery of meditation does not mean that you will be able to levitate, bi-locate, or become psychic. What a mastery of meditation does provide is the ability to stay centered and grounded in the midst of change, to hold a place of inner peace in the heart, which ultimately is what centering means.

Stress Relief and Chronic Pain

Ageless wisdom reminds us that meditation is essential for stress relief. Mindfulness meditation is perhaps the most common form of meditation used by those suffering from chronic pain, as revealed by the work of Jon Kabat-Zinn. Focusing on your pain might seem like the last thing you wish to do; however, the practice of mindfulness meditation often allows one to achieve deeper insights into the mind–body connection, which in turn, is shown to minimize and maybe even heal the source of pain.

Best Benefits of Meditation

By all accounts, the benefits of meditation for both mind and body are quite impressive. A short list includes, but is not limited to, the following:

- Increased attention span
- Increased imagination and creativity
- Increased patience
- Increased tolerance
- Increased intuitive awareness
- Decreased resting heart rate
- Decreased resting blood pressure
- Increased immune system strength
- Increased quality of sleep
- Combined brain hemispheric lateralization

Chapter Summary

- Meditation is best defined as "increased concentration that leads to increased awareness."

- The purpose of meditation is to clear the mind of ego-based thoughts, which then promotes clear thinking.
- Meditation falls into two categories: exclusive and inclusive. Mindfulness meditation is a type of inclusive meditation. Ultimately, all types of meditation can promote personal insights.
- Insights gathered from insightful meditation are from the deep-seated wisdom of the unconscious mind.
- Meditation is thought to improve cognitive functions and reduce the symptoms of ADD.
- Incorporating meditation into your daily routine is suggested as a powerful strategy for stress management. Even five minutes a day helps.
- Meditation, specifically mindfulness meditation, is known to decrease the effects of chronic pain.

Additional Resources

Books

Benson, H. *Beyond the Relaxation Response.* Berkeley, CA: Berkeley; 1994.

Benson, H. *The Relaxation Response.* New York: Morrow Press; 1975.

Dyer, W. *Getting into the Gap* (with CD). Carlsbad, CA: Hay House; 2003.

Hahn, T. N. *Peace Is Every Step.* New York: Bantam; 1992.

Kabot-Zinn, J. *Wherever You Go, There You Are: Mindfullness Living in Everyday Life.* New York: Hyperion; 1994.

Rofe, R. *Meditation.* Charleston, SC: Create Space; 2012.

Salzberg, S. *Quiet Mind: A Beginner's Guide to Meditation.* Boston: Shambhala; 2008.

Seaward, B. L. *Quiet Mind, Fearless Heart.* Hoboken, NJ: John Wiley & Sons; 2005.

Tolle, E. *The Power of Now.* Novato, CA: New World Library; 1999.

Weiss, B. L. *Meditations* (with CD). Carlsbad, CA: Hay House; 2002.

Meditation CDs

Miller, E. *Letting Go of Stress.* www.DrMiller.com. 1.800.528.2737.

Seaward, B. L. *A Change of Heart.* Inspiration Unlimited; 2002. 303.678.9962

Seaward, B. L. *Sweet Surrender.* Inspiration Unlimited; 2002. 303.678.9962

Seaward, B. L. *A Wing & a Prayer.* Inspiration Unlimited; 2003. 303.678.9962

EXERCISE 16.1: Rainbow Meditation

From a metaphysical/spiritual perspective, there are seven regions of the body that need to be constantly revitalized with universal energy to maintain optimal wellness. These same seven areas also correspond to seven major endocrine glands. Perhaps by no coincidence, there are seven notes to the harmonic scale and seven colors to the rainbow. This mental imagery exercise brings to mind these seven areas and the colors associated with them. Each area is represented as a circular window through which energy passes. This window goes by the name of "chakra," a Sanskrit word to describe a spinning wheel. Each color has a series of meditational phrases that can be repeated to yourself as you visualize this image. When first learning this exercise it is best to try it lying down, if possible. And, as with any guided mental imagery exercise, feel free to modify these suggestions to augment the strength of the image for you.

Instructions

THE BASE OF THE SPINE: *RED*

Imagine a beam of light emanating from the base of your spine: a laser beam of red light. This area and color are metaphorical symbols representing your being grounded to the earth. To be grounded means to feel stable and securely rooted in your environment, both physically and emotionally. Take a slow, deep breath and as you exhale, see this beam of red light and say the phrase to yourself, "I feel grounded." Take one more deep breath and repeat this phrase again.

NAVEL (AN INCH BELOW THE BELLY BUTTON): *ORANGE*

Now, focus your attention on the center of your body. If you are like most people, this point is approximately 1–2 inches below your belly button. Imagine that from this point emanates an orange beam of light outward toward infinity. This area of your body represents both the literal and figurative center of your body. To become centered means to focus inward and to maintain a personal balance. To be centered also means to feel self-confident and worthy of high self-esteem. Think what it is like to have a strong sense of self-confidence and self-esteem. Now, take a slow, deep breath, and as you exhale see this beam of orange light and say this phrase to yourself, "I feel centered" or "I have confidence." Take one more deep breath and repeat this phrase again.

THE UPPER STOMACH: *YELLOW*

From here, bring your attention to your upper stomach. This area is often referred to as the solar plexus. From this area imagine a beam of brilliant yellow light emanating outward toward infinity. This area and color are symbolic of several factors, including self-empowerment and the ability to receive love from family, friends, and all elements of the universe. Like the previous area, it too is related to self-esteem. Take a slow, deep breath, and as you exhale, focus on this beam of yellow light and say the following phrase to yourself: "I feel loved." Take one more deep breath and repeat this phrase again.

THE CENTER OF THE UPPER CHEST: *GREEN*

The upper chest houses the heart, perhaps the most important organ in the body. The heart is symbolic of the emotion love, for it is through the heart that we share compassion with our fellow human beings and creatures of the planet, even the planet itself. Like a window, the metaphorical heart can be opened to share love or it can be closed. The latter is often compared to a "hardened heart." Open the window of your heart and imagine an emerald green beam of light shining forth. This region of your body and this color represent your ability to share your feelings of warmth, happiness, compassion, and those aspects that comprise the emotion of love.

EXERCISE 16.1: Rainbow Meditation cont....

Take a slow, deep breath, and as you exhale, focus on this color green and say to yourself, "I choose love unconditionally." Take one more deep breath and repeat this phrase again.

THE THROAT: *LIGHT BLUE*

Bring your attention to your throat. Imagine a soft blue beam of light emanating from your throat area and extending toward infinity. This area and this color represent your meaningful purpose in life or your life mission. For a moment, ponder what you think this might be for you right now. It may be very general yet profound or it may be a short-term goal you wish to accomplish. Think of the willpower and the drive necessary to accomplish this mission. Know that you have this resource within you. Focus on this mission and at the same time focus on the color blue. Take a deep breath, and as you exhale, repeat this phrase, "I have a meaningful purpose to my life and I can do it." Take one more deep breath and repeat this phrase again.

THE CENTER OF THE FOREHEAD: *INDIGO BLUE*

This area of the forehead is sometimes referred to as the third eye. This area symbolizes wisdom and intuition. More clearly it symbolizes wisdom from the balance between the right and left hemispheres of the brain and the conscious and unconscious minds and the ability to access all mental faculties. Focus your attention on this area, just above your nose, in between your eyes. Using your imagination see the color indigo blue emanate as a laser beam of light shooting straight toward infinity. As you see this color blue, think of your ability to balance your thinking skills to access your deepest wisdom. Take a slow, deep breath, and as you exhale, repeat the phrase to yourself, "I feel balanced" or "I have inner wisdom." Take one more deep breath and repeat this phrase again.

THE CROWN OF THE HEAD: *VIOLET*

Imagine a violet or lavender beam of light coming from the crown of your head. Regardless of which position your head is resting in, this beam of light always directs itself upward toward the heavens. During the Renaissance period, this chakra was depicted as a halo over the head. This body region and the color associated with it represent your connection to the divine consciousness of the universe. To feel connected is a very important aspect of one's well-being. Focus on this color and think what it is like to feel a sense of connectedness and belonging. To be aware of this connection is to feel at one with the universe, to feel at peace with yourself. Take a slow, deep breath, and as you exhale visualize this color and say to yourself a phrase that reinforces a feeling of connectedness. (It might be something like "I am one with the world," "I am at peace with myself," or "I am one with God.") Take one more deep breath and repeat this phrase again.

Finally, allow all these beams of light to grow in all directions so that soon they all merge together and you find yourself surrounded by a ball of brilliant white light.

EXERCISE 16.2: Crystal Cave Meditation

There is an ancient proverb that says, "When the student is ready, the teacher will come." In truth, we are both the student and the teacher. To be "ready" means to quiet the mind. More specifically, it means to still the voice of the ego, so that the wisdom from the teacher can make itself known.

Seeking council from your intuition, the collective unconscious, or your higher self need not be a complicated process. It's simply an exercise in discipline *and* patience. The following exercise is a tool to be used when trying to gain clarity on an issue or become more grounded with any decision-making process. The crystal cave represents a *magical* metaphor of that still place in your mind, where the teacher's wisdom can be heard clearly above the static noise of the conscious mind.

Instructions

To begin this exercise, first focus your awareness on your breathing:

1. Feel the air come into your nose or mouth and travel down deep into your lungs. Feel your stomach extend out, then return, as you exhale. As you repeat this cycle of slow, deep breathing, become aware of how relaxed your body is with each exhalation.

2. Now, take a very slow, deep breath, as slow and as deep as you possibly can. Comfortably slow, comfortably deep. Then, follow that with one more breath, even slower and even deeper than before.

As you continue breathing comfortably . . .

3. Imagine that you are standing at the bottom of a short set of marble stairs, about 10 steps in all. At the bottom, where you are, it is somewhat dark, but at the top of the stairs you see a brilliant radiant light reaching down toward you. As you look up, you are immediately attracted toward the light, and . . .

4. You feel compelled to walk up the stairs, toward the light. But because the steps are rather large, you find that you can take only one step at a time. As you walk up the first step, you begin to feel a sense of inner peace within yourself, that you have not felt for a long time. All judgments about yourself are suspended and you begin to accept yourself for *all* that you are. Now, take a slow, deep breath and exhale, and feel yourself step up to the next level.

5. As you move up toward the second step, you begin to feel a sense of inner peace between you and all of your family members. Whatever differences may exist, allow yourself to realize that *they* are unimportant now. So leave whatever frustrations you may have behind, as you progress up the next step. Once again, take a slow, deep breath, and as you exhale feel yourself step up to the next level.

6. On the third step you begin to gain a sense of peace and resolution among all your friends and acquaintances. On this step, there is no resentment, no animosity—only compassion for everyone you have ever met, and this feels so good. Once again, leave whatever frustrations you have behind as you progress up the next step. As you do this, take a slow, comfortable, deep breath, and as you exhale, confidently feel yourself move up to the next level.

7. The fourth step brings a sense of calm and serenity within you and your higher self. As you continue up the stairs, you begin to notice that you feel yourself becoming much lighter. With each step toward the light, you feel your body become lighter and more relaxed. With this sense of lightness and peace, you almost feel yourself floating up the remaining steps, toward the top.

EXERCISE 16.2: Crystal Cave Meditation cont....

8. As you appear on the top step, you find yourself surrounded by a brilliant golden-white light. Almost immediately, you feel yourself floating up into the light. Each cell in your body radiates with this brilliant golden-white light, and this feels wonderful. In a moment's recognition, you immediately sense that you cannot distinguish yourself from the light. And once again, you feel an incredible sense of love, support, and nurturing from this source of radiance.

Take a nice, slow, deep breath and breathe this light into your body.

9. Now, surrounded in light, you feel yourself floating down a hall of crystal, and the light that resides in you, and all around you, shines through the crystal, so that tiny rainbows appear everywhere—brilliant reds, deep oranges, bright yellows, lush greens, azure blues, and intense purples. The colors of these rainbows make you smile and you feel a sense of warmth, wonder, and awe as you float effortlessly through this hall toward what appears to be an opening into a crystal cave.

10. As you continue to float peacefully through this hall of crystal, you come upon a large room, and you notice that it, too, is constructed of crystal prisms, each filled with tiny rainbows slowly dancing all around the room. As various colors of the rainbow filter through the crystal, you see an area off to the left that has a sunken floor. You are drawn immediately to this area, and you soon find yourself sitting on a comfortable cushioned step, once again surrounded by the beauty of warm, dancing light all around you.

11. As quick as the mind can travel, you find yourself transported to this room in search of an answer. Deep in your heart there is a question, begging to be asked. There is some morsel of wisdom you yearn to have, to help you on your quest for self-improvement. This is why you have come here. Take a slow, deep breath and again feel a sense of warmth and comfort as you exhale.

12. Now, take a moment to look around the room. Intuitively, you feel the presence of someone nearby. As you gaze around, you notice that sitting next to you is a wise and friendly sage. It may be someone you fondly recognize immediately (male or female), or it may be someone you have never seen before, yet know and trust deep in your heart. Look into the person's face and deep into his or her eyes, and as you do, notice that you feel an immediate sense of recognition, an immediate sense of comfort and compassion coming from within this person directly toward you.

13. After you exchange smiles, you remember the question to which you seek an answer. The essence of wisdom on the face of this sage radiates through to your mind. All you need do is think the question, and your voice will be heard. Now once again, take a slow, deep breath and find peace and comfort in the stillness. Then, listen very carefully for the answer. It will come as one of your own thoughts. Yet, at a deep level you will know that this insight has come from a place beyond the limits of your conscious mind. Sometimes, the answer comes quickly. Other times it is planted as a seed to germinate and grow at the most appropriate time of receptivity. With the questions now posed, trust that the wisdom you seek is both accepted *and understood* at the deepest level. Take a moment to quiet your mind now, and listen for the answer.

14. Now, when you feel ready, thank this person with a thought, a smile, or perhaps even a wink, and as you do, you find yourself floating on a beam of light back through the hall of prism glass with multicolored rainbows. You enter through the passage of brilliant golden-white light and you come to the place where you now sit or lay.

EXERCISE 16.2: Crystal Cave Meditation cont....

15. Take a deep breath and relax, contemplating the message you have received. Take one more slow, comfortable, deep breath, and as you exhale bring yourself back to the awareness of the room in which you now find yourself. Become aware of the time of day, the day of the week, and perhaps what you have planned after you have completed this relaxation session.

16. When you feel ready, open your eyes to a soft gaze in front of you. If you wish, begin to slowly stretch your neck and shoulders, and then think to yourself about how great this sense of peace from the wisdom you have gained feels throughout your mind and body. And with confidence, you are ready to begin a new day.

EXERCISE 16.3: Celestial Heavens Meditation

Imagine that this evening is a warm summer night—neither hot, nor humid, but comfortably warm. You step outside the back door and feel a slight breeze in the air, and it feels really nice against your face.

The sun has set, but it's still somewhat light. You look up in the sky and it is full of clouds—big, billowy clouds. The sun's last rays light up the clouds on the western horizon, and this light turns the gray clouds pink and orange for a few lingering moments. Tonight, the sky looks so inviting.

As you stand at the back door, you think to yourself how nice it would be to grab a blanket and lie under the stars for a few hours. Then you think to yourself, "Hey, why not?" So you go back inside and grab a blanket, perhaps even a pillow, and then head back outside again.

After meandering a ways, you find a nice comfortable spot, far away from any city lights—your own private place to lie down and relax. You spread the blanket out and then lie down. Notice how good it feels to connect with the earth, and again you feel the summer breeze upon your face, and it feels good, too.

From the time you first looked outside tonight to this very moment, you noticed that the sky has filled with more clouds, but you also notice that the winds have picked up and they quickly move the clouds from west to east across the night sky. Every now and then you see what looks like an evening star peeking through the clouds. You look closely, but your mind begins to wander, and the star hides again.

Metaphorically speaking, clouds are like thoughts in your mind, and tonight these clouds represent the multitude of thoughts racing through your mind. The purpose of this meditation, this time looking up in the sky, is to clear your mind of excess thoughts; persistent, nagging thoughts; and random thoughts so that your mind becomes as clear as the clearest night sky.

Specifically, these clouds overhead, these big, billowy clouds, are symbolic of any thoughts, issues, problems, or conflicts that you are facing in your life right now. As you see a cloud overhead, label it with whatever thought comes to mind, take a nice deep breath, and as you exhale, let it go as you watch the wind carry the cloud away. In doing so, you allow yourself to detach from this thought or concern long enough to gain a better sense of clarity. Once again, take a nice, slow, deep breath and allow each cloud above to slowly disappear from view over the eastern horizon.

Every now and then you glimpse a star twinkling through the clouds. The first stars to appear in the night sky are typically our neighboring planets. Take a moment to focus on a star, but then notice it is quickly covered up as another cloud comes into view. As you see this next cloud come into view, bring to mind another stressor, some frustration or anxiety, label the cloud with it, and then watch it move across the horizon, fading from view. Once again, take a nice, slow, deep breath, and allow this cloud and the thought it represents to slowly disappear from view, over the eastern horizon.

Every cloud that comes into view represents some problem or issue, but tonight, the cool wind acts like a broom to sweep away all these thoughts and concerns, leaving your mind clear and still. Allow the wind to carry your thoughts and concerns away off to the horizon and beyond. Notice that as these clouds begin to move away from your field of vision, your body and mind become more and more relaxed. Once again, take a nice, slow, deep breath, and allow the cloud overhead to slowly disappear from view over the eastern horizon.

Concentrate and look up in the sky. Tonight, and every night, the sky serves as a metaphor for your mind. As you gaze up to the heavens, you notice that above the layer of thick, billowy clouds, there is a very thin layer of clouds as well, so thin that you can faintly see the brightest stars shine through. This layer of clouds is also being pushed by the wind from west to east, and it moves high above your head. This layer of clouds represents any lingering thoughts, any random thoughts, or perhaps any excess energy that distracts your attention

EXERCISE 16.3: Celestial Heavens Meditation cont....

away from the celestial sea that it veils. Take a nice, deep, slow breath, and allow this thin layer of clouds to slowly disappear over the horizon.

Above you now the sky is clear, and the stars are so near you can practically reach out and touch them. As you gaze upward, you see in front of you the Milky Way stretched thick and wide across the sky, as if someone took a paintbrush across the sky. As you focus on the stars, you begin to recognize familiar constellations: the Big Dipper, Orion, or perhaps the Pleiades.

Stars in the night sky are points of light that convey brilliance and wisdom. Take a moment to pick one star and focus your entire awareness on it. Once again, take a nice, deep, slow breath, and as you exhale, feel a sense of deep peace throughout your mind and body, as deep as the celestial sky. Take one more slow, deep breath, and this time as you exhale, allow your eyes to wander until they find another star to focus on. Again feel a deep sense of inner peace.

When you feel ready, close your eyes to this image and bring your awareness back to your body. Once again take a nice, slow, deep breath and feel a profound sense of relaxation throughout your mind and body.

Imagine yourself sitting up on the blanket, then standing up and picking up the blanket and turning toward the direction of home. Soon you find yourself back on your back porch and then in the blink of an eye, you are lying comfortably on your bed. Become aware of how relaxed you are, yet how energized you feel, refreshed and renewed.

When you feel ready, slowly open your eyes to a soft gaze in front of you, and bring yourself back to the awareness of the room you are now in.

Remind yourself that although you feel relaxed, you do not feel sleepy or tired. In fact, you feel reenergized and renewed. On your next breath as you exhale, think to yourself the phrase, "I am reenergized and renewed and inspired to continue whatever projects await me today."

Chapter 17

The Power of Mental Imagery and Visualization

"All this or something better now manifests for me in totally satisfying and harmonious ways, for the highest good of all concerned."

— Shakti Gawain

The Ageless Wisdom of Imagery and Visualization

Plato once said that no thought exists without an image to accompany it. This insight is as true today as it was at the time he first said it over two millennia ago. The power of the mind is nothing less than phenomenal. When combined with the power of the human spirit, nothing, it seems, is impossible. Take, for example, Joe Simpson, who after falling several hundred feet only to shatter his right leg, descended single-handedly down Siula Grande in the Peruvian Andes and lived to tell about it in his book and subsequent movie, *Touching the Void*. By imagining himself moving painstakingly slowly from point to point, he did the impossible and survived. Simpson is not alone in his efforts to harness the power of visualization, but his story is certainly one of the most dramatic ever told.

Just as the mind can create positive images to accomplish the impossible, it can also manufacture images to immobilize our human potential. Perhaps with the proliferation of television and visual media to be found everywhere, visual images abound, thus accentuating each person's ability to create images (real or imagined) in his or her mind. The power of the mind to create images that can either heal or hurt is well founded throughout the history of humanity. Perhaps as no surprise, people unknowingly practice the art of visualization all the time, particularly imagining a series of worst-case scenarios with the anticipation of a stressful event. In the words of Albert Einstein, "No problem can be solved from the same consciousness that created it." Visualization and mental imagery require a different mind-set than the typical frenetic consciousness so prevalent today.

Visualization and Imagery

Although the terms **visualization** and **mental imagery** may seem like the same concept (and to many they are), those who specialize in the area of mind-body-spirit healing note a distinct difference, based on both the study of the mind and personal experience with scores of clients.

Visualization is the conscious direction of images on the screen of the mind's eye. Conscious intention is the hallmark of creative visualization. In the process of visualization, you are the writer, director, producer, and audience, all in one, which can become a very empowering experience. Conversely, mental imagery is best described as a series of images that bubble up from the unconscious mind without the ego's censorship. Mental imagery is often described as a spontaneous flow of thoughts originating from the unconscious mind. Uncensored spontaneity is the hallmark of mental imagery. Keeping in mind the wealth of wisdom contained in the depths of the unconscious mind, mental imagery can often prove to be far more effective than the work of the conscious mind alone.

The Art of Guided Visualization

Many people who find it hard to hold their concentration for prolonged periods of time find it easier to listen to someone else direct them through a visualization process. Focusing the mind for an intended period of time certainly requires discipline. Keeping your mind focused with the help of guided visualization CDs is one way to achieve the intended goal of relaxation or healing. Continued exposure to guided visualization CDs may also help you to augment your own imagination and creative abilities. As with any exposure to experiences that cultivate the powers of your mind, embellish all suggestions to your liking from the selected tracks and ignore any and all suggestions that you do not have a strong comfort level with.

Types of Visualization

Your imagination can take you wherever you wish to go, yet it seems that visualizations tend to fall into one of three categories.

- *Tranquil scenes:* The epitome of a tranquil scene is a sublime beach with waves of aqua blue water slowly edging toward the shore. Tranquil scenes range from primeval forests to thick snowflakes falling from the sky. And the sky is the limit when it comes to tranquil scenes. When looking to relax using this technique, imagine a scene that provides you with the deepest sense of relaxation. Exercise 17.1 is an example of using a tranquil image as a metaphor to promote relaxation.

- *Behavioral changes:* Mental imagery and visualization became mainstream several decades ago when coaches started using these techniques to enhance sports performance with their star athletes. Under the name of mental training, athletes would rehearse their events again and again in their mind to gain an edge over their competition. Since then, and perhaps even before, visualization has been used as a core technique in the area of behavior modification, including smoking cessation and changes in eating behaviors.

■ *Internal healing body images:* Perhaps nowhere else has the use of visualization been more dramatic than in the efforts to improve one's health status, from the repair of broken bones to the evaporation of tumors (both benign and malignant). Patients use both visualization and mental imagery to not only understand the illness, but also make peace with it. Exercises 17.2 and 17.3 are examples of employing visualization and mental imagery to promote physical healing.

The Essential Components of Visualization

Both visualization and mental imagery employ the faculties of both the conscious and unconscious minds, though visualization has a greater hand in the direction of the script. To gain the greatest benefit from guided visualization, it's best to understand how to coordinate the efforts of both the conscious and unconscious minds. The following are some aspects to consider to enhance this experience.

■ *Present tense:* To the unconscious mind there is only one time zone: the present moment. Past memories and events as well as future events and aspects are all considered to be included in the present moment. Simply stated, the unconscious mind appears not to understand events as anything other than now! Therefore, as you craft your image, think in terms of bringing the image into the present moment as if you are experiencing it now.

■ *Incorporate all five senses:* The stronger the image, the more real it becomes. Where appropriate, call to mind not only the power of your sense of sight, but also that of your sense of smell, touch, hearing, and taste, if possible. Make the image as real as you possibly know how.

■ *Positive thoughts and intentions:* Just as the unconscious mind understands only one time zone, it also understands only positive thoughts. Words expressed negatively are translated into a positive framework. Therefore, to coordinate both the conscious and unconscious minds toward a unified goal, construct your healing intention in a positive mind frame.

■ *Emotional vibration:* New research on visualization and prayer indicates that thoughts alone produce no lasting effect. What really galvanizes the power of visualization is the emotion behind the thought. So as you begin to create the desired image, whether it be for a sense of tranquility, a positive behavior change, or the restoration of healing, generate a feeling of compassion with the image or series of images.

■ *Detached outcomes:* Placing an expected outcome on the desired intention of each visualization is analogous to throwing down an anchor on a boat that is about to set sail. It halts any progress. Although it's human to have expectations, this too becomes an emotional vibration that negates the intended outcome. The ego projects strong expectations. For visualization to have the greatest effect one must detach the ego from the outcome and simply let what happens, happen.

■ *Attitude of gratitude:* Upon the completion of the visualization, offer an expression of gratitude for the experience. An honest expression of gratitude fills the sails of every visualization with wind to transport it to the intended destination, wherever that may be.

How to Incorporate Imagery and Visualization into Your Life Routine

Although the practice of visualization can be as varied as the person doing it, here are some suggestions to get the most out of this process, in addition to the template previously mentioned that includes using the present tense, positive thoughts, detached outcomes, and the expression of an attitude of gratitude. If you intend to use this relaxation skill, you will find that like any other skill, the more you practice it, the better it will serve you. The beauty of visualization is that the practice can be done practically anywhere you can sit or lay quietly with your eyes closed for several minutes.

The following are some time-honored aspects of the creative visualization process that can help augment your experience to the fullest extent.

Step 1: Relaxation: The brain's right hemisphere is at its strongest in the presence of total relaxation. This means to create a desirable image, the mind must be clear of mental chit-chat and ego-based distractions. Loosen any tight-fitting clothing and find a comfortable place to unwind. Once you have minimized or eliminated all distractions, begin by taking a slow, deep breath and let all random thoughts leave your mind as you exhale.

Step 2: Concentration: A focused mind is a clear mind. Using your powers of concentration, focus your attention toward your breathing as a means to ensure a clear mind. If your mind wanders with distractions, acknowledge these thoughts and feelings and then focus your attention entirely back to your breathing.

Step 3: Visualization: Next, combine a desired image with an intention and focus on this for several minutes. If you find your mind wandering (and this will happen from time to time), merely redirect your attention back to the desired image with a comfortable, slow, deep breath.

Step 4: Affirmation: Metaphorically speaking, a positive affirmation used in tandem with visualization is the postage needed to properly deliver the intended message. Combining an image with a word or phrase unites the energies of both the right and left brain hemispheres for the best desired result.

Stress Relief and Chronic Pain

Visualization holds the potential to offer immediate satisfaction for stress relief, by simply closing your eyes to the outside world. For this reason and many others, both mental imagery and visualization have been used extensively to help treat chronic pain. With the understanding that chronic pain is more than a physical ailment, mental imagery helps translate the language of the unconscious mind to provide insights for healing and restoration in areas such as the lower back, neck, shoulders, or even cancer. Visualization empowers the conscious energy to create a new vibration of healing for whatever area of the body seeks it.

Best Benefits of Imagery and Visualization

In its simplest sense, visualization is like taking a mini vacation, leaving all your cares and worries behind to get to a place of inner peace. The effects of visualization and mental imagery range from being mildly relaxing to profoundly enlightening, depending on the particular image used, the frequency employed, and the conditions under which the visualization was experienced. Everyone can gain significant benefits from a single experience of guided visualization.

Chapter Summary

- Visualization is the conscious direction of images on the screen of the mind's eye. Mental imagery describes specific images that bubble up from the unconscious mind.

- The three most common types of visualization for relaxation and healing are 1) tranquil scenes, 2) behavioral changes, and 3) internal healing body image.

- To get the most out of visualization one should 1) use the present tense, 2) use all five senses, 3) use positive thoughts and intentions, 4) use positive emotions, 5) have no expectations of the outcome, and 6) include an attitude of gratitude.

- Both mental imagery and visualization have been used to help decrease chronic pain.

Additional Resources

Dyer, W. *Getting into the Gap.* Carlsbad, CA: Hay House; 2003.

Epstein, G. (Ed.). *Encyclopedia of Mental Imagery.* New York: ACMI Press; 2012.

Gawain, S. *Creative Visualization.* New York: Bantam; 1978.

Katra, J., & Targ, R. *The Heart of the Mind.* Navato, CA: New World Library; 1999.

Locke, S. *The Healer Within.* New York: Mentor; 1986.

Roman, S. *Spiritual Growth: Being Your Higher Self.* Tiburon, CA: H. J. Kramer; 1989.

Simonton, O. C. *Getting Well Again.* New York: Bantam; 1978.

Targ, R., & Katra, J. *Miracles of Mind.* Navato, CA: New World Library; 1998.

Thondup, T. *The Healing Power of Mind.* Boston: Shambhala; 1996.

EXERCISE 17.1: Solitude of a Mountain Lake

Imagine yourself walking alone in the early morning, along a path of a primeval forest, through a gauntlet of towering pine trees. Each step you take is softly cushioned by a bed of golden-brown needles. Quietness consumes these surroundings and then is broken by the melody of a songbird. As you stroll along at a leisurely pace, you focus on the sweet, clean scent of the pines and evergreens, the coolness of the air, the warmth of the sun as it peeks through the trees, and the gentle breeze as it passes through the boughs of the pines and whispers past your ears.

Off in the distance, you hear the rush of water cascading over weathered rocks, babbling as it moves along. Yards ahead, a chipmunk perches on an old decaying birch stump along the side of the path, frozen momentarily to determine its next direction, then in the blink of an eye, it disappears under the ground cover and all is silent again. As you continue to walk along this path you see a clearing up ahead, and you notice your pace picks up just a little to see what is there. First boulders appear ahead, then behind them, a deep blue mountain lake emerges from beyond the rocks. You climb up on a boulder to secure a better view, and you find a comfortable spot carved out of the weathered stone to sit and quietly observe all the elements around you.

The shore of the lake is surrounded by a carpet of tall green grass and guarded by a host of trees: spruce, evergreen, pine, aspen, and birch. On top of one of the spruce trees, an eagle leaves his perch and spreads his wings to catch the remains of a thermal current, and gracefully glides over the lake. On the far side of the lake, off in the distance, dwarfing the tree line, is a rugged stone mountain. The first snows of autumn have dusted the fissures and crevasses, adding contrast to the rock's features. The color of the snow matches the one or two puffy white clouds and morning crescent moon that interrupt an otherwise cloudless day. A slight warm breeze begins to caress your cheeks and the backs of your hands as you direct your attention to the surface of the mountain lake.

The slight breeze sends tiny ripples across the surface of the lake. As you look at the water's surface, you realize that this body of water, this mountain lake, is just like your body—somewhat calm, yet yearning to be completely relaxed, completely calm. Focus your attention on the surface of the water. These ripples that you observe represent or symbolize any tensions, frustrations, or wandering thoughts that keep you from being completely relaxed. As you look at the surface of this mountain lake, slowly allow the ripples to dissipate, fade away, and disappear. To enhance this process take a very slow, deep breath and feel the relaxation this brings to your body as you exhale. And as you exhale, slowly allow the ripples to fade away, giving way to a calm surface of water. As you continue to focus on this image, you see the surface of the lake becoming more and more calm, in fact very placid, reflecting all that surrounds it.

Feel how relaxed you feel as you see the surface of the lake remain perfectly still, reflecting all that is around it. The water's surface reflects a mirror image of the green grass, the trees, the mountain face, even the clouds and crescent moon. Your body is as relaxed as this body of water, this mountain lake. Try to lock in this feeling of calmness and etch this feeling into your memory bank so that you can call it up to your conscious mind when you get stressed or frustrated. Remember this scene so that you can recall the serenity of this image that you have created to promote a deep sense of relaxation, and feel your body relax just by thinking of the solitude of this mountain lake.

EXERCISE 17.2: The Body Flame

Imagine, if you will, that the energy that you burn all day long is not just physical energy (such as calories), it's mental and emotional energy, as well. Imagine that this source of energy, which invigorates *every* cell, resides in the center of your body. The Japanese call this reservoir of energy the *hara*. The Chinese refer to it as the *dan tien*. Although it cannot be measured by Western science at this time, this energy is essential to *your* well-being.

Take a moment now to locate the center of your body, and feel where this is, your center of gravity, the center of your entire body. As you begin to focus on this area, realize that this is about an inch or two below your belly button.

It is believed that when this energy is too excessive (perhaps from a flurry of thoughts or unresolved emotions) you begin to feel frantic and overwhelmed, sometimes just plain exhausted.

The body flame meditation is a way to help clear your mind of excess thoughts and excess energy and return your mind–body to a profound sense of inner peace. As you do this meditation, as with all meditations, call to mind the power of your five senses, and the power of your imagination and memory, to draw forth the power of this visualization.

To begin this meditation, the best position is to lie comfortably flat on your back, keeping your spine aligned from your head straight down to your hips. If you choose to sit, this will work as well.

Next, concentrate on your breathing by making each breath comfortably slow and comfortably deep. If your mind should happen to wander, gently guide it back to the focus of your breathing.

If your eyes are not already closed, go ahead and close your eyes and, once again, locate the center of your body; then, using your mind's eye, call to mind an image of a flame hovering over this part of your body.

Metaphorically speaking, this flame is a symbol of your state of relaxation. It feeds off your body's energy. When your body has an abundance of energy—perhaps nervous thoughts or negative feelings—this flame will be quite tall. Perhaps even like a blow torch.

When you are completely relaxed, your flame will be quite small. This small flame is called the "maintenance flame." It's like what you would see as a pilot light in a gas stove. This is the desired size for complete relaxation.

So now, focus with your mind's eye, and take a look at the size of your body's flame. See its size relative to your body's level of energy. So, what does your flame look like? How big or small does it seem to you right now?

As you place all of your attention on the flame of your body, look at its color. Your body flame may be an intense, brilliant yellow/white color. As you look at this image, what color does your flame hold?

Once again with your mind's eye, take a look at the *shape* of your body's flame. Direct your attention to the base of the flame and notice, is the bottom round or oval? How does it appear to you?

Then, as you focus your eyes toward the tip of the flame, notice that it comes to a jagged point.

You may even notice that your flame dances around a bit or perhaps it remains still. As you look at this flame, *feel* it feed off the excess energy in your body, and let it burn off any excess energy that you wish to release to return to a complete sense of relaxation.

EXERCISE 17.2: The Body Flame cont....

Take a deep breath and let your flame burn off any excess energy you feel detracts from your ability to relax.

Once again, if you find your mind is distracted by wandering thoughts that pull your attention away from the image of the flame, gently redirect your attention back to this image, and then allow your mind to send these thoughts and feelings from your head to your body's center and up through the flame.

As you continue to watch this image of the flame, feel your body slowly become more calm and relaxed. And to help this out, take a nice, slow, comfortable, deep breath. As you exhale, feel a greater sense of calm throughout your body.

Now look once again at the image of your flame; as your body becomes more tranquil, notice the flame decrease in height. Soon you will notice that your flame decreases in size, to about a quarter to one-half inch tall.

As you focus on the image of your body flame, once again notice the color, shape, and size. And as you see the flame decrease in size, feel your body relax, as you draw your attention to the relaxation effect of the maintenance flame.

There are times when this flame can be used to aid in the healing process of your physical body. Place the flame over a specific part of your body, an area that is sore or experiencing pain, and allow the flame to feed off the excess energy of this area and restore a sense of peace to the organ or physiological system that is yearning for wholeness.

Now, take several slow, deep breaths, and as you exhale, allow your body flame to return a sense of peace to this area. As you do this, feel peace reside here. When you feel ready, slowly return the image of the flame back to the center of your body.

Now, continue to focus your mind's eye on your body flame. When you feel completely relaxed, with your flame very small, notice how still it is. Then, when you feel you are at a point of complete relaxation, slowly allow this image to fade from your mind, but retain this feeling of relaxation, knowing that your mind is now clear with fewer and fewer distractions.

To augment this relaxation process, please take one more slow, deep breath and then slowly bring yourself back to the awareness of the room you are in. Become aware of the time of day, the day of the week, and what you have planned after you have completed this relaxation session. When you feel ready, very slowly open your eyes to a soft gaze in front of you. If you would like, go ahead and stretch your arms and shoulders. Notice that although you feel relaxed, you don't feel tired or sleepy. You feel fully energized and revitalized, ready to do whatever you have planned for the rest of the day.

EXERCISE 17.3: Body Colors and the Healing Light

The human body craves wholeness, and given the chance, the body will do all it can to return to a place of optimal health. In all its splendor, the body's innate ability to return to wholeness is a wonder to behold.

The word *health* comes from the root word *hal*, which means to be whole or holy. When we call upon the strength of the human spirit to work in unison with our mind and body, wholeness, expressed through inner peace, is achieved.

This meditation/visualization exercise calls upon the unconscious mind to awaken the innate healing powers of mind, body, and spirit so that you may return to that place of wholeness, that place of inner peace, wherever you may be.

As you do this meditation, as with all meditations, call to mind the power of your five senses and the power of your imagination and memory, to draw forth the power of this visualization.

As with any type of visualization exercise, please feel free to augment, edit, and embellish the suggestions in this exercise, to make them vivid *and* the most empowering for you.

Imagine yourself lying in a warm, shallow pool of clear blue water. Visualize, through your mind's eye, that as you float effortlessly, your internal body reflects just one color—a brilliant white, as if you are observing a white silhouette in a pool of turquoise blue water. As you visualize this image, clearly picture a complete outline of your body, the contents of which are illuminated by the color white.

Now, focusing on this white silhouette, take a moment to carefully examine all parts and regions of your body, from your head down to your toes. As you do this, search for any specific locations or regions of your body that feel tense, active, or perhaps express a sensation of pain. This can include any muscles, joints, organs, physiological systems (like the immune system or cardiovascular system), or any part of your body that seems less than whole, yet *craves* wholeness. For some, this might even include your mind, if by chance you find that a multitude of thoughts are constantly racing through your mind, with each thought competing for your attention.

Through this systematic scanning process, please locate one or perhaps several areas that are under stress and strain and have not been allowed to fully relax to the same capacity as the rest of your body.

For the moment, let's refer to these "active" areas as "hot spots," because typically they *are* more metabolically active than all other areas that are more relaxed. As you locate a specific area of tension, allow yourself to envision that this area is symbolized by a strong, pulsating red light. Symbolically, the color red indicates a higher metabolic level of arousal or energy state, and here the same meaning can be quite literal.

Invite yourself to take a slow, deep breath, and as you do, imagine that you are slowly inhaling *and* exhaling through an opening in this area. Follow this breath with one more, even slower, even deeper breath. As you breathe once more through this area, feel the flow of energy move through this region, as if a logjam floating on a river has been set free.

As you envision your body represented by these two colors—a mass of white, with one, two, or perhaps several red pulsating areas—take a moment to specifically focus on the red pulsating lights. As you do this, through your conscious intention, invite these areas to become calm, as calm as the rest of your body.

With your mind's eye, imagine that this hot spot *slowly* begins to change color, transforming from a bright, pulsating red light to a bright, but less intense orange color. Then take a nice, slow, deep breath, and as you exhale watch the color change to orange. As you observe the color transform from red to orange, so too does the intensity of pulsation change to a slower rate—symbolizing that indeed, the area *is* becoming more calm.

EXERCISE 17.3: Body Colors and the Healing Light cont....

Once again, take a slow, deep breath, and as you do, imagine that you are once again inhaling and exhaling through the region of your body acknowledged with a small pulsating orange light. Please follow this breath with one more, even slower, even deeper breath. Once again, as you breathe once more through this area, feel the flow of energy move through this region like a slow, yet strong flowing river of water.

Observe closely: As you look at and feel this area of tension or pain, once again become aware of the color orange and feel a deeper sense of calming beginning to occur in this region. The color orange is symbolic of change. The intention of this meditation *is* change, changing any areas of tension to a calm, tranquil sense of homeostasis, from stress to inner peace.

Now, with this calming sensation taking hold, begin to see the orange-colored light transform from bright orange to the color yellow. Once again take a slow, deep breath, and note the change as you exhale. The color yellow is symbolic of energy. In this case, a healing energy that enables the area in question to slowly return to homeostasis. As you observe the yellow color, note that the yellow light pulsates very infrequently, if at all. This means that this focus of your attention really is becoming more relaxed.

At your leisure, take a slow, deep breath, and as you do, imagine that you are inhaling and exhaling *through* this area. Follow this with one more even slower, even deeper breath. As you breathe once more through this area, feel the flow of energy move effortlessly through this region of your body.

Now, as you observe the area, symbolized by a yellow light, you sense and feel that this area you have focused your attention on is much more relaxed, more calm. Notice, as you observe the white silhouette of your body, that now all areas begin to match the sensation of calmness that you feel in the rest of your body.

As you look at this image of your entire body, you notice a beautiful reflection of white light. Once again, take a slow, deep breath, and as you exhale, observe that the yellow area is now blending to become white with the brilliant white color that your internal body reflects. As you continue to look at this image you have created, you now see that your entire internal body image is one color—a brilliant white, radiating a calm light all around it. This color is symbolic of your level of complete relaxation and optimal health, and this image is one that you can recall to your consciousness at any time to invoke a sense of personal tranquility.

Take a slow, deep breath, and as you exhale, think to yourself this phrase, "I am calm and relaxed. I am whole!"

Now, once again, imagine your body lying comfortably and effortlessly in a shallow pool of warm water. Directly overhead, suspended about 4–5 feet above you, is a crystal bowl, filled with beautiful rays of light. These rays cascade down, like a fountain of water, over you. This crystal bowl contains an unending supply of golden-white light, a source of dynamic life force and energy. As this light pours over your body, it has the ability to stimulate and augment the healing process that *you* have initiated with your own ability to heal—through the color transformations from red to orange to yellow.

Using the power of your mind, slowly move this waterfall of luminescent energy over a specific part of your body that you feel needs the reinforcement of deep healing. With the power of intention, allow the crystal bowl to tip its contents over this specific region of your body. Feel the warmth of this healing light as it continually pours into your body. More and more, allow the warmth of the healing light to move to the desired location and feel your body absorbing the light where it needs it the most.

As you do this, see the image of golden-white light within you and all around you. Take a moment to sense what this really feels like. Then, take a slow, deep breath and feel a deep sense of relaxation throughout your entire body. Once again, repeat to yourself the phrase, "I am calm and relaxed. I am whole."

EXERCISE 17.3: Body Colors and the Healing Light cont....

Notice now that you feel calm and relaxed, yet at the same time you feel wonderfully energized.

Take one final slow, deep breath, and as you exhale, feel the sensation of relaxation envelop your whole body.

At your leisure, when you feel ready, slowly open your eyes to a soft gaze in front of you. Take a moment to familiarize yourself with your surroundings, by thinking about what you have planned once you finish this meditation. Realize that although you feel relaxed, you don't feel tired or sleepy; you feel fully energized and revitalized and ready to accomplish whatever task awaits you today.

Soothing Sounds: Music to Relax By

"Music is a moral law. It gives a soul to the universe, wings to the mind, flight to the imagination, a charm to sadness, gaiety and life to everything. It is the essence of order, and leads to all that is good, just and beautiful."
— Plato

The Ageless Wisdom of Music Therapy

On a large drum lay several thousand fine grains of sand. Positioned around the drum sit approximately 20 people, each facing toward the center of the circle where the drum is positioned. Upon the command of the leader, the entire group begins to chant a sacred Sanskrit mantra, a vibration known to instill a sense of harmony to all living things in its presence. The sound of "OM" resonates throughout the room, and as it does so, the fine grains of sand laying randomly on the surface of the drum began to move. Like atoms in a molecule, the stationary position becomes a dance. As they move they begin to form a pattern, a beautiful mandala-shaped labyrinth. With each repetition of the "OM" chant, the pattens become clearer.

The vibration of the chant "OM" proves itself to be more than a cute new-age exercise. The tone of healing reveals it holds the power to create order from chaos, symmetry from randomness, harmony from discordance. All of this with the intention to heal, from one note of a musical scale. Long ago, mystics and healers held the inherent wisdom that indeed, music has a very special power to restore a sense of wholeness to any individual in need of tranquility, from the stressed to the infirm. Even Plato suggested the merits of music as a panacea to ill health. Those who watched the 2012 London Olympic saw that swimmers Michael Phelps, Ryan Lochte, and Nathan Adrian used music (via ear buds and noise canceling headphones) in preparation for their gold medal performances.

In 1960, Hans Jenny was so intrigued by the concept of **sympathetic resonance**, he began to study the relationship of sound to nearby objects. He coined the term *cymatics* to describe this science, and his research can be viewed through the collection of films he made to observe the effects of sound on a variety of substances, from water to oil. The images he recorded are nothing less than astonishing. It doesn't take much to make the leap from the effects of sound on sand particles or water droplets to the effects of sound on cell physiology. All living things are affected by sound vibrations. Music is the most obvious means to use vibrations to promote feelings of tranquility.

Sound is energy made audible. Unpleasant sound is commonly called noise. Sounds pleasing to the ear may fall in the category of music: a progression of musical tones that affects mind, body, spirit, and emotions. The field of physics (renowned for its interest in energy) lends great credence to the ageless wisdom of sound vibrations. Quantum physics reminds us that everything is energy, hence the effect of vibrations on anything can be powerful. The power of music's healing (or harming) abilities goes far beyond the receptivity of the eardrum to convert sound waves into biochemical properties for the nervous system to respond to.

Cultures from every corner of the world have recognized the effect music has on people. Music can arouse a call to arms (marches by John Philip Sousa come to mind) as easily as slow peaceful melodies (such as Mozart's concerto in C minor) can soothe the savage beast. Today, **music therapy** often conjures up images of people lying on a couch with headphones, their minds far away from the rest of the world. Yet by and large, music therapy includes a more active than passive role. Playing an instrument or singing is as much a part of good vibrations as simply listening to someone else make the music.

Over the years, several studies have been done to determine the most popular means to promote relaxation. The act of listening to music ranks at the top every time.

The Physics of Health: Entrainment and Sympathetic Resonance

Centuries ago, a young man set out to design a clock that used a pendulum and counterbalance as mechanical components for telling time. Although the first clock was impressive, it was during the creation of the second pendulum clock that Christian Huggans discovered more than a new way to build a mechanical clock. He discovered a new law in physics called **entrainment**. As it turned out, the motion of the two pendulums initially was not set in synch, but in a short period of time, they began to sway in motion like twin clocks. Entrainment is defined as the mutual phase locking of similar vibrations. When two objects are in close proximity, the object of weaker vibration will match or entrain to the object of stronger vibration. Entrainment is referred to in the field of physics as the law of the conservation of energy, and examples abound in nature, including the menstrual cycles of women who live and/or work together. Entrainment is also referred to as sympathetic resonance. Energy vibrations hold a greater influence over us than most people realize. Ancient shamans knew this and often used the power of the drum beat to evoke entraining vibrations for more than just a healing intention.

Every cell in our bodies maintains a vibration, as do many organs such as the brain and heart. Some vibrations are difficult to measure, but the vibrations of the heart are easily detected through an EKG. Under ideal conditions, there is harmony among all vibrations housed in the human body, and this harmony is depicted as optimal health. Scientists know that cancer cells oscillate at a different (usually faster) vibration than normal healthy cells.

According to both physicists who study energy and experts who study the healing properties of sound, the vibration of homeostasis is identical to the vibration known as the Schumann resonance. The Schumann resonance, which is 7.8 hertz (Hz), is calculated by multiplying the circumference of the earth by its electromagnetic field. Perhaps it is no coincidence that 7.8 Hz is the same frequency detected in many sounds in nature such as whale and dolphin songs and waterfalls. It would appear that, like dolphin songs, music that is composed with this vibration instills a sense of relaxation that is unequalled by other methods.

As one might imagine, not all vibrations are healing. Some vibrations can be downright hazardous. As outlined in his landmark book *Cross Currents*, physician Robert Becker highlights the problems with ELFs (extremely low frequencies) and their consequences on human health. Powerful vibrations that are not in a harmonious chord with the 7.8 Hz frequency can entrain cells, organs, and living organisms into a level of dissonance with devastating consequences. This underlies the problem encountered by people who live near high-tension power lines who contract cancer or the rising rate of brain tumors found in frequent smartphone users.

Good Vibrations: Music . . . Without Words

By some accounts, there are only two kinds of music in this world: those with words (lyrics) and those without words. In studies that have looked at the cognitive functions of either the right or left hemisphere of the brain, it has been revealed that each hemisphere

specializes in a host of thought patterns and sensory stimulation processing.

The left hemisphere of the brain is the seat of analytical, rational, verbal, and linear thought processes. The right hemisphere of the brain, now well known for being the receptive, intuitive, and imaginative half, is most greatly influenced by music without words. Studies show that music without words produces a greater calming effect. The reason appears to be that when music with words is introduced, the analytical mind becomes activated by associating thoughts and memories with the interpretation of the lyrics. Rather than relaxing, this type of music is known to raise resting heart rate and blood pressure rather than lower them. For this reason, music without words is the recommended choice to promote the greatest level of relaxation. There is no shortage of instrumental music in this classification, including but not limited to classical, jazz, new age, and what is now being called lifestyle music.

Tuning Out Bad Vibrations

Music therapy goes beyond simply turning on your CD player or iPod and flopping down on the couch for a few minutes. When you consider that all sound is vibration, then all vibrations lend themselves to the potential of either promoting relaxation or inhibiting the process completely. We can never get away from all sounds into complete silence. However, there are some sounds (noise) that can become quite irritating, whether it's a loud muffler on the car driving behind you or the cacophony of noise from blaring radios and televisions all over the house. You surely can minimize noisy disturbances that tend to add to a stressful mind. One way is by taking a proactive stance by closing windows, turning off equipment, or simply removing yourself from the area for a while. There is another option; it's called white noise. White noise is any sound that you use to balance out the irritating noise that causes you stress, and music can do this quite nicely.

How to Incorporate Music Therapy into Your Life Routine

The easiest way to incorporate music therapy as a relaxation technique is to place a CD of calm, relaxing music into a CD player and either sit or lie down with your eyes closed and let the melody transport you to that magical place where troubles are not allowed. To do this most effectively it's best to minimize all other distractions. The most simple way is to use headphones to block out all other noise (just be careful not to play the music too loud and damage your hearing). To have a more profound experience, close your eyes and allow yourself to float freely on a river of musical notes and watch on the screen of your mind's eye where each song takes you. Exercise 18.1 invites you to take the next step in incorporating music therapy as a means to promote relaxation. If you are looking for new suggestions for relaxing music, consider the following.

Top Ten Recommended CDs of Relaxing Music

I am often asked to make recommendations of relaxing music. The ten CDs listed in Table 18.1 ▾ are what I (and many others) consider to be *the* classics to soothe the savage beast, breast, or anything else that's stressed in your house. This is slow music for fast times. All of these can be found in iTunes. Consider making your own compilation as your personal music Rx.

Developing Your Mastery of Music Therapy

Of all the qualities that are used to determine the effectiveness of music as a means to promote relaxation, one's perception of the music (like or dislike) is at the top of the list, because what is the most calming music to one person is akin to fingernails on a chalkboard to another set of ears. Developing your mastery means taking the time to cultivate your tastes and build a music collection that nurtures that sense of peace in you. If you are like most people, you may find that over time your taste in music expands to include types of music that at an earlier age you wouldn't have been caught dead listening to. The bottom line is that it doesn't matter what the experts think or recommend, it only matters what you prefer. One commonality among people looking to add music therapy to their collection of relaxation techniques is a hunger to add more music to one's library.

Stress Relief and Chronic Pain

Music as vibration has a tremendous influence on mind, body, spirit, and emotions. The right music (your perception is a key factor) can melt stress away, and stress aggravates chronic pain. Music as vibration also holds

TABLE 18.1   Top Ten Relaxing CDs

Artist	CD Title	Instrumentation
EverSound Series	*One Quiet Night**	Various instruments
Jim Wilson	*Northern Seascapes*	Solo piano
Michael Hoppé	*The Poet*	Solo cello
Michael Hoppé	*The Dreamer*	Solo flute
Secret Garden	*White Stones*	Violin and piano
Bruce Becvar	*Forever Blue Sky*	Solo guitar
David Lanz	*Christophori's Dream*	Solo piano
Chris Spheeris	*Eros*	Solo guitar
Yanni	*In My Time*	Solo piano
Deuter	*Sun Spirit*	Various instruments

One Quiet Night is a compilation from the EverSound Music collection that I was invited to compile as a sample of the best relaxation music on this label. It has received rave reviews as wonderful music to promote relaxation.

the potential for coping with and minimizing chronic pain in ways that people still don't understand. The answer appears to be through the power of entrainment.

Best Benefits of Music (Sound) Therapy

Living in the digital age of MP3 technology (and whatever else may come onto the scene shortly), it becomes easy to forget that for millennia music was the sole creation of live performances by people playing a variety of instruments. Music therapy is so much more than simply listening to music; it also includes playing a musical instrument and singing as well.

The benefits of music therapy are many, but two stand out among the rest. First, listening to music has the potential to act as a diversion tactic to steer the focus of your attention away from that which stresses you to a distant place where thoughts and worries are left far behind. Music, like a magic carpet, can transport you to distant lands and memories. Anyone who has listened to a Mozart concerto or Beethoven's *Fifth Symphony* knows the power that music has to shift one's focus of attention. In the words of contemporary composer Michael Hoppé, "Music lifts the veil of anxiety to view a place where love is stored."

The other benefit of music, although initially more subtle, becomes more dynamic well after the music has ended. As sound vibrations, music imparts a healing vibration that returns mind, body, and spirit to a deeper level of homeostasis. In either case, the healing power of music allows one to pause in the midst of stress long enough to catch one's breath.

Chapter Summary

- Music can both excite and relax the central nervous system.
- Research suggests that we relax through the entrainment of musical vibrations and sympathetic resonance.

- The most effective type of music to relax by is music without lyrics; this engages the left hemisphere of the brain, which is the side used when stressed.
- White noise is any sound used to balance irritating ambient noise.
- There are many ways to incorporate music therapy into your daily routine, from making iPod playlists to listening to the sounds of a natural waterfall or ocean waves.
- Music therapy often is used to reduce the symptoms of chronic pain.

Additional Resources

Becker, R. *Cross Currents*. New York: Tarcher/Putnam; 1999.

Campbell, D. *The Mozart Effect*. New York: Avon; 1997.

Campbell, D. *Music: Physician for Times to Come*. Wheaton, IL: Quest; 1991.

Campbell, D. *The Roar of Silence*. Wheaton, IL: Quest; 1989.

Gaynor, M. *The Healing Power of Sound*. Boston: Shambhala Press; 2002.

Goldman, J. *The Seven Secrets of Sound Healing*. Carlsbad, CA: Hay House; 2008.

Halpern, S. *Sound Health*. New York: Harper & Row; 1985.

Hoppé, M. Personal communication. June 15, 2009.

Merritt, S. *Mind, Music & Imagery*. Santa Rosa, CA: Aslan; 1996.

Ortiz, J. *The Tao of Music: Sound Psychology*. San Francisco, CA: Red Wheel Weiser; 1997.

Sachs, O. *Musicophilia, Tales of Music and the Brain*. New York: Vintage Books; 2008

Spear, D. Z. *Ears of the Angels*. Carlsbad, CA: Hay House; 2002.

EXERCISE 18.1: Good Vibrations Playlist: From Sound to Music

The following are some exercises to engage more fully in the practice of music therapy.

1. **Make (Mix) Your Own iPod/MP3 Playlist:** Today's technology makes it very easy for you to compile your favorite instrumental songs onto a playlist. Here is a suggestion: Make a list of 12–16 of your favorite instrumental pieces. Be sure to include not only a variety of styles (e.g., classical, new age, jazz) but also a variety of instrumentation (e.g., piano, guitar, violin, cello). Listen to your playlist in the car when you get stuck in traffic, at the office when things there go haywire, and at home, to help you unwind late at night.

2. **Finding the Lost Chord:** Not everyone is blessed with a great singing voice, but you don't have to have one to do this exercise. Remind yourself of the location of the chakras, find a nice quiet place (preferably where no one will hear you), and simply voice the word OM (Ohhmmmmmmmmm). Carry the note for about 30 seconds, starting with the root chakra, then taking a slight pause, and then moving up through the line of chakras. (This may feel really weird, but that's why you have closed the door.) Try repeating this cycle about three to four times. You can also find CDs with the OM chant and merely sing along. (Synchronicity has an "OM" CD [call them at 1.800.926.2033], as does Jonathan Goldman, whose CD is called *Chakra Chants*.)

A variation of this exercise is to sing the scale (doe, ray, mee, fah, so, la, tee, doe), starting with the lowest note and continuing up the scale through each of the seven notes (seven notes—seven chakras).

3. **Music and Visualization:** For this exercise, find a CD with instrumental music. Those listed as new age work the best (two suggestions: John Serrie's *And the Stars Go with You* or Raphael's *Music to Disappear In*). Hit the play button, turn the lights down low, lie down on your back, and close your eyes, listening to the piece (or pieces) of music that you have selected. Allow your mind to wander and begin to observe whatever images appear on the screen of your mind's eye. Note the colors, symbols, energies, and so on, and merely observe where your mind takes you. Allow the music to help you paint a picture. As you do this, it's essential not to judge what you visualize, but rather to simply observe and enjoy! Another option is to listen to a hemi-sync CD (from the Monroe Institute), a specially designed instrumental music CD that entrains the theta waves of each brain hemisphere for the ultimate music therapy experience (www.hemi-Sync.com).

4. **The Musical Sounds of Nature:** Nature provides an incredible soundtrack. In this exercise, you are invited to listen to the actual sounds of nature (e.g., a thunderstorm, waterfall, ocean surf, bird songs) or find a CD with these recorded sounds. Give yourself about 30 minutes to listen to the natural sounds and simply allow your mind to wander wherever it will, without any judgment or reservations.

EXERCISE 18.1: Good Vibrations Playlist: From Sound to Music cont....

5. **My Top Instrumental Cuts of Calming, Relaxing Music Are:**

a. _____

b. _____

c. _____

d. _____

e. _____

f. _____

g. _____

h. _____

i. _____

j. _____

k. _____

l. _____

m. _____

n. _____

o. _____

6. **The Top Five Energizing Songs That Lift My Spirits Are:**

a. _____

b. _____

c. _____

d. _____

e. _____

Massage Therapy and Bodywork

"Without adequate tactile input, the human organism will die. Touch is one of the principal elements necessary for the successful development and functional organization of the central nervous system, and is as vital to our existence as food, water, and breath."

— Ken Dychtwald

The Ageless Wisdom of Massage Therapy

Although tense muscles don't necessarily place people in the hospital like cancer and heart disease do, muscle tension is the number one symptom of stress. At the mere hint of stress, the nervous system releases epinephrine and norepinephrine to prepare the body for fight or flight. Every muscle responds to the call, resulting in various levels of muscle contraction. Whether the muscles tense for seconds, minutes, or days, the effects can be pronounced. You don't have to be on the run to experience soreness. Muscles can easily tense in a sitting position in front of a computer screen, behind a steering wheel, or even standing in line at the grocery store. Over time, slight contractions lead to an imbalance in opposing muscles resulting in poor posture, structural imbalance, lower back pain, and a host of other problems.

As I was lying on a massage table, Dan began the process of deep tissue massage. With low lighting, a scented candle burning, and soft instrumental music playing in the background, the environment exuded relaxation. Curious about the types of people he works on, I asked what percentage of his clientele comes to him because of stress. His reply: "100 percent! All of them."

According to historical records, the practice of **massage therapy** dates back to ancient Egypt, but most likely muscle massage is as old as time itself. Throughout the ages the demands of strenuous physical work resulted in extreme muscle soreness, stiffness, and pain. Muscle massage offered an obvious answer to an age-old symptom. Even a life of leisure has its moments of stress, and the pampering of kings, queens, and various leaders was not without its practice of muscle massage either. A quick glance at the names of various types of massage indicates the worldwide appeal of this technique.

Today muscle massage is one of many modalities in the family of massage therapy known as bodywork, including Swedish massage, Thai massage, shiatsu, Rolfing, and many, many others. Interestingly, one needn't actually be touched to experience the effects of muscle relaxation. Additional "touch" therapies include pet therapy, hydrotherapy, stone therapy, aromatherapy, and energy healing.

Massage therapy is now a bona fide therapeutic practice certified through the American Massage Therapy Association (AMTA). Asian bodywork styles, such as shiatsu and Thai massage, are certified through the American Organization for Bodywork Therapies of Asia (AOBTA). Certification typically requires a 6-month program with over 500 hours of classroom instruction in an approved school and 3 years of professional experience. Since the inception of AMTA in 1943, massage's popularity has mushroomed, particularly in the past decade. There are now over 250 approved massage therapy schools nationwide and more than 58,000 certified members. Students are taught a variety of massage styles, and then typically specialize in one or two as they begin their practice.

Let's take an in-depth look at the family of modalities that constitute the field of bodywork:

Types of Bodywork

- *Swedish massage:* **Swedish massage** is the most commonly known type of massage in the United States. Created decades ago by gymnast Peter Heinrik Ling, this style of massage emphasizes both decreased muscle tension and increased circulation to the muscle group worked upon. Swedish massage includes a number of movements including effleurage (long stroking), petrissage (rolling or squeezing), and friction (deep kneading), all of which attempt to relax the specific muscle fiber. As with most types of massage, the therapist greets you and then leaves the room so that you may disrobe and lay comfortably under a sheet on the massage table. Upon reentering the room, the therapist may begin at the head or feet to begin the session.

- *Shiatsu:* Based on the Oriental concept of energy or chi, **shiatsu** (also known as accupressure) is a massage style that works to unblock the flow of chi or life force energy that travels through the body's energy meridian system. Direct pressure is placed on a specific meridian point to release, unblock, or decongest the flow of energy, thus bringing the body's flow of energy back into balance. The word *shiatsu* translates to mean "finger pressure"; however, fingers, knuckles, and even elbows may be used in this process. Although the method of shiatsu is used as a means to promote relaxation, it is also known to help relieve sinus problems, TMJD, tension headaches, and nausea. Some dentists now use various shiatsu points for their patients.

- *Rolfing/structural integration:* Muscles may contract, but it's the fascia that holds the muscles together. Fascia, the connective tissue of your body that is composed primarily of collagen, can become restricted due to chronic muscle tension resulting in a distortion to one's spine and skeletal structure. Structural integration is known in the field of bodywork as deep tissue massage. The purpose is to help realign the body in its most correct posture by working to release the constriction of fascia.

- The concept of structural integration was first put forth by cell biologist Ida Rolf in the early 20th century. In a technique she developed to realign the body's ideal skeletal structure, called **Rolfing**, the massage therapist applies deep pressure along the lines of muscle tissue to release constricted fascia. Those who have had a single session (or the entire 10-session treatment) will tell you that while it's being done, this type of deep tissue work is anything but relaxing. In fact, it can be downright painful. However, these same people will also tell you that the effects of Rolfing are phenomenal as chronic pain disappears with deep tissue work. It should be noted that deep tissue work is also done with a style of bodywork called myofascial release and some types of osteopathic manipulation.

- *Sports massage:* Amateur and professional athletes alike spend a lot of time flexing and contracting muscles. It's the nature of their work. In the quest for the elusive gold medal, Olympic coaches searched for ways to quicken the pace of recovery and muscle restoration from extended bouts of arduous training. Muscle massage was proven to be one way to augment the recovery process, by flushing out waste products (lactic acid) and increasing circulation to tired muscles in the recovery stage postexercise. **Sports massage** developed as a combination of a few other types of massage including the kneading motions of Swedish massage, the deep tissue work of structural integration, and the finger pressure of shiatsu. The treatment of sports massage is not exclusively for Olympic athletes. Anyone can benefit from a good sports massage, including the weekend warrior.

- *Reflexology:* At first glance, **reflexology** appears to be nothing more than a simple foot massage. Looks can be deceiving. The art of reflexology dates back to ancient Egypt, and what appears to be a foot massage is really a means to provide relaxation to the entire body. The science of reflexology is based on the concept of a hologram where the foot is a template for the entire body. Virtually all the body's organs are mapped out on the foot's imprint including the toes, sole, and heel. The purpose of reflexology is not only to massage the muscles of the foot, but also to provide a reciprocal healing to various organs that correspond to the areas of the foot being massaged. However, you don't have to understand (or believe in) the holographic concept of reflexology to appreciate a good foot massage.

- *Thai massage:* **Thai massage** is believed to date back over 2,500 years ago, often credited to Shivago Komarpaj, the Budda's personal physician. Legends aside, Thai massage, as it is known and practiced today, is thought to be a combination of bodywork influences from India, China, and Southeast Asia that integrate traditional medicinal practices with wellness lifestyle habits. Although techniques and practices vary from region to region, the style that has migrated to the West includes a complex sequence of soft tissue pressure (massage) combined with stretching, twisting, and joint manipulations. Pressure is used with the manipulations to achieve stretching and twisting, which requires several different positions to achieve the desired result of alignment, flexibility, and relaxation. Proper leverage is essential for this style of bodywork, and typically a small effort by the practitioner results in a large effect for the client. It is not uncommon for the body worker to twist, pull, push, and rotate segments of body parts and joints for the optimal effect.

- The session is typically divided into zones (e.g., feet and legs, legs and back, chest and abdomen, arms and hands, neck and face) and during the session the client will both lie down and sit. It is also not uncommon for the body worker to use his or her hands, elbows, feet, and knees for the specific leverage desired. Like acupressure, Thai massage acknowledges working with the body's energy patterns to establish a correct alignment for the optimal energy flow. Each technique in Thai massage is designed to stimulate and access the flow of intrinsic (subtle) energies by allowing the release of blocked energies that inhibit a sense of balance for mind, body, and spirit. Although it may look and feel painful, the peaceful nature of Thai massage is based on the principles of Buddhist compassion, and like a good yoga session it actually feels quite refreshing.

Other Touch Therapies

Not all touch therapies involve a massage therapist, nor do they involve muscle manipulation. Interestingly, they can produce the same end result. The following are just a few of the more common examples of touch therapy; unlike most modalities of bodywork that may require a therapist, some of these can be self-directed.

- *Stone therapy:* **Stone therapy** is a type of bodywork where smooth river stones are either heated or, in some cases, cooled and placed on various regions of the body to promote a deep sense of relaxation. These regions align with the energy centers of the body known as chakras. Some types of stone therapy go one step further and are used by the therapist as a tool to augment deeper or harder muscle contact.

- *Pet therapy:* Rubbing the stomach of a dog or the head of a cat may seem like a far cry from a full body massage, but the connection to an animal can be equally profound and relaxing. Research studies reveal that pet owners appear to have less stress, showing signs of decreased resting heart rate, blood pressure, and muscle tension. Soft fur or even feathers are not only soothing to the touch for human skin, but also appear to decrease the firing of muscle neurons, which in turn decreases muscle tension. What never seems to be mentioned in the clinical studies involving **pet therapy** is the emotional component. Unconditional love is also known to allay the worst frustrations and anxieties.

- *Hydrotherapy:* If you have ever stepped into a hot bubbling Jacuzzi and lingered for several minutes, then you know how relaxing **hydrotherapy** can be. Warm water draws blood from the body's core to the periphery. Because the muscles of the arms and legs are part of this periphery they become engulfed in blood. Unlike during a bout of exercise, where working muscle capillaries are rich in blood as a means to provide nutrients for energy metabolism, in a resting state the muscles become very relaxed, in essence experiencing the same effect as a muscle massage. Even without the air jets, a warm bath can produce the same effects.

- *Aromatherapy:* Like the name suggests, **aromatherapy** combines the smells of pleasant fragrances to promote a sense of relaxation. Lavender. Peppermint. Rose. Vanilla. Specific fragrances target the olfactory nerve to decrease the neural firing in muscles, replacing it with the parasympathetic response associated with relaxation. Although the essential oils from plants and flowers have been used for eons, they have taken on a new appeal with the broad interest in complementary medicine. Lavender is often used in maternity wards when mothers are going into labor. The scent of vanilla is often used to relax people who are nervous entering the tunnel of the MRI machine. Some massage therapists combine aromatherapy with their practice of bodywork to produce a deeper sense of relaxation, in some cases applying a scented lotion directly on the skin.

- *Energy work:* Therapeutic touch, Healing Touch, Reiki, polarity healing, zero balancing, **qi gong**, and bio-energy are all types of **energy work** that combine the use of the human energy field, chakras, and meridians to promote a balance in one's life force of energy. Ironically, with most of these therapies there is no direct touching at all. The work is done at the more **subtle energy** levels of the human energy field, yet changes produced through the subtle energy systems are quite profound. Initially one might feel a sense of heat to a particular region, but generally what most people feel is an improved sense of well-being.

How to Incorporate Massage Therapy into Your Life Routine

The following are some suggestions that may help you include this incredible relaxation technique in your stress management repertoire.

Selecting a Massage Therapist

Although the art of self-massage (see next page) can feel good, nothing beats having a full body massage, which typically takes about 1½ hours. Across the country, the cost of a massage varies from $50 to $125 per session, depending on the locale. One might think that all massages are similar; however, no two massage therapists are alike. Before you make an appointment, determine which type of massage you prefer. Some like deep tissue work, others don't. The best way to select a massage therapist is to ask your friends and colleagues for a recommendation. Shop around to see who is good and who is available. Really good massage therapists tend to be booked up; however, you might consider asking to be called for their first cancellation.

As more and more massage schools open up across the country and more people consider massage therapy as a new vocation, these students need practice. Massage therapy schools offer massage therapy sessions at reduced rates so their students can learn the trade. It's my opinion based on personal experience that students tend to be more attentive when they are learning a skill, and for this reason do an excellent job.

The Art of Self-Massage

Giving yourself a massage can be a welcome relief to tired, achy muscles overworked from sitting all day at a computer station or completing a strenuous workout. Performing a variation of a Swedish massage (kneading and stroking on your shoulders, quads, or calves) can prove quite effective in reducing muscle tension. If you have a friend, spouse, roommate, or partner who can help you with the neck and shoulders, consider asking that person for help with the promise of returning the favor. Exercise 19.1 can guide you through the basics of a muscle self-massage while Exercise 19.2 leaves room for a self-assessment.

Stress Relief and Chronic Pain

With muscle tension being the number one symptom of stress, bodywork of any kind is desirable. Its popularity over the millennia speaks of its effectiveness. Not all chronic pain is structural (muscles, fascia, ligaments, and bones), but a large percentage is. For this reason, bodywork in the form of muscle massage is considered to be paramount in the effort to reduce the symptoms of chronic pain. Different types of massage (e.g., deep tissue, sports massage, acupressure) will vary as to their long-term effectiveness, yet all forms of bodywork are considered beneficial.

Best Benefits of Massage Therapy and Bodywork

The benefits of any type of bodywork can be felt immediately. Specific changes include decreased muscle tension and increased relaxation. In an age of high-tech virtual communication, more and more people have less direct contact with others. The consequence can be feelings of isolation and depression. Human touch is proven unequivocally to be essential for health and well-being. The long-term effects go well beyond the time spent lying on a massage table.

Chapter Summary

- Bodywork is a term used to describe many types of massage, including Swedish massage, shiatsu, Rolfing, sports massage, reflexology, Thai massage, and others.

- The need for human touch is considered essential.

- Muscle tension is the number one symptom of stress, which is why bodywork of all kinds has become so popular.

- Other types of touch therapy include aromatherapy, stone therapy, pet therapy, hydrotherapy, and various types of energy work (e.g., healing touch, therapeutic touch, Reiki).

- Perhaps more than any other modality, bodywork is known to help relieve the symptoms of chronic pain.

Additional Resources

Lundberg, P. *The Book of Massage.* New York: Fireside; 2003.

Shcatz, B. *Soft Tissue for Pain Relief.* Charlottesville, VA: Hampton Road Press; 2001.

Stone, V. *The World's Best Massage Techniques.* Lions Bay, BC, Canada: Fair Winds Press; 2010.

Widdowson, R. *Head Massage.* London: Sterling; 2003.

Wills, P. *The Reflexology Manual.* Rochester, VT: Healing Arts Press; 1995.

EXERCISE 19.1: Muscle Self-Massage

Ideally, the best massage you can receive is one performed by a licensed massage therapist who is both trained and experienced in many types of bodywork. The muscles that produce the greatest amount of stress and tension are located on the back side of your body—the hardest parts to reach! Fear not, however, because help is on the way, even if it's from your own set of hands. The following is a description of a few strategic areas that are prone to muscle tension and ways to relieve this tension with your own hands, beginning with the head, neck, and shoulders and continuing with the hands, legs, and feet. Enjoy!

HEAD

The temples, scalp, and eyes can be the target of significant muscle tension. Begin by taking your hands along the sides of each of your temples and, using your fingertips, start to make small circles along the sides of your head above your eyes. After a series of 5–10 circles moving in a clockwise direction, apply a bit more gentle pressure and reverse direction, going counter-clockwise. Next, using your nondominant hand, extend your reach over the crown of your head and begin to knead the scalp in a clockwise direction, starting with gentle pressure on the right side of the head, then moving toward the back of the head, and finally working the left side of your head. Feel free to change hands, switching to the dominant hand. Then, place both hands over the crown of your head and, with your fingertips, massage the scalp with gentle pressure until you feel a slight tingling in your scalp. Be sure to take a slow, deep breath to promote good blood circulation. Relax your hands, and then reverse direction and repeat. When finished, close your eyes and take several comfortably slow, deep breaths.

FACE

Your face repeatedly uses hundreds of muscles in the course of a day. A soft touch to these muscles always feels great. Begin by using the tips of your index and middle fingers of each hand by making small circles under and around each eye. Then progress by making small circles, first around the forehead, then around the cheekbones, and finally moving down the sides of the jaw and chin, continuing with small circles with the fingertips for several moments. Relax your hands by your sides and take three slow, deep breaths.

NECK

In the age of laptops and desktop computers, it is not uncommon to experience a stiff neck, aching shoulders, and even headaches. As the midpoint between the head and shoulders, the neck deserves attention and muscular relief. Begin with both hands resting alongside the neck, and then, leaning your head to the left, support your neck with your left hand and begin to knead the right side of your neck with your right hand. After several moments, lean your head to the right side and knead the left side of your neck with the opposite hand. Next, using the fingertips of each hand, gently make small circles along the sides of the neck. Then, taking your dominant hand, begin to knead the muscles of the back of neck, reaching from the base of the neck and slowly moving up toward the crown of the head, with the palm of your hand resting on the crown. Change hands when needed and repeat.

SHOULDERS

Continuing where the neck and shoulders meet, place your wrists along the sides of your neck with your hands cupping the point where the neck and shoulders join. From here, begin a gentle kneading action at the center of your upper shoulders by applying gentle pressure alongside the spinal column. Then, with your nondominant hand, reach to the back of your dominant shoulder and continue the kneading action with your fingertips, again alongside the spinal column. Finally, work your way over to where the shoulder and arm connect by kneading the deltoid muscles. Relax your nondominant arm and take a few deep breaths. Then, using your dominant hand, repeat this process on the opposite side to your nondominant shoulder.

EXERCISE 19.1: Muscle Self-Massage cont....

HANDS

Your hands may not seem like the place to hold much tension, but given all the work they do, from typing at the computer keyboard to hundreds of other daily tasks, the hands also deserve significant attention. With your dominant hand, begin by making strong stroke motions from the base of the palm of your non-dominant hand toward where the fingers connect to the hand. Then work your thumb and fingers along the sides of each of the fingers in your nondominant hand. Finally, take the fingers of your dominant hand and stroke the back side of your nondominant hand from wrist to where the fingers attach. After several moments, release and relax both hands. Take a few comfortably slow, deep breaths, and then repeat this process using the opposite hand to massage your dominant hand.

LEGS

Hold the left side of your left leg with your left hand. Then, using the palm of your right hand, apply gentle pressure with your thumb on the top of your left leg from the midthigh to the knee. Continue this stroking action along the inside of the upper leg as well for a few moments. Next, using both hands on the left leg, with your thumbs on the top (or sides) and the fingertips underneath, alternate kneading the hamstrings with first the right hand, and then the left. Relax and take a few slow, deep breaths. Then, with one hand, reach for your calf muscle and knead this with your hand, squeezing and releasing the calf muscle between your thumb and fingertips. After several moments, release, relax your leg, and take several slow, deep breaths. Then repeat this technique with the opposite leg.

FEET

Considering all the work the feet do, from standing and walking to supporting your entire frame, both feet deserve much needed comfort. Begin by placing your right foot on your left knee (or extending your reach to your right foot). Using both thumbs, begin to stroke the sole of the foot, from the heel to the ball of the foot. After several moments take a slow, deep breath and repeat. With your fingertips, begin to work the area where the toes connect to the foot. Next, cup the heel of your foot with your left hand. With the fingers of your right hand, knead the tops of your foot, including the toes. Relax your foot back on the floor, rest your hands, and then repeat this procedure with the other foot.

EXERCISE 19.2: Self-Assessment: Bodywork

1. Have you ever had a session of massage therapy?   YES   NO

2. If so, what type(s) of bodywork did you have?

_____

3. Have you ever had a session of energy work?   YES   NO

  Reiki   YES   NO

  Healing touch   YES   NO

  Therapeutic touch   YES   NO

  Polarity therapy   YES   NO

  Reflexology   YES   NO

  Myofascial release   YES   NO

  Cranio-sacral therapy   YES   NO

  Bio-energy healing   YES   NO

Can you describe what one or more of these techniques felt like?

_____

_____

_____

_____

4. If you have not had a session of massage therapy, what is the primary reason (e.g., money, time, feelings of discomfort about the technique, not sure who to try)? Please explain.

_____

_____

5. Do you own a pet?   YES   NO

6. Have you experienced the benefits of pet therapy?   YES   NO

7. Have you experienced the benefits of aromatherapy?   YES   NO

If so, what are some of your favorite aromatherapy scents?

_____

_____

_____

8. Do you have any additional thoughts on massage therapy, pet therapy, or aromatherapy?

_____

_____

_____

Chapter 20

Hatha Yoga

"You have to learn to listen to your body, going with it and not against it. You will be amazed to discover that, if you are kind to your body, it will respond in an incredible way."
— Vanda Scaravelli

The Ageless Wisdom of Yoga

One of the most ancient practices of stress management comes from the Asian continent and is often described as a 6,000-year-old science of self-mastery. The Sanskrit word *yoga* means union. Specifically, yoga refers to the integration, balance, and harmony of mind and body. Patanjali is given credit for recording the specific postures, known as *asanas* (ah-san-ahs) that assist in the process of augmenting this union of mind (*ha*) and body (*tha*). Although there are many types of yoga, including karma yoga and kundalini yoga, **hatha yoga** is by far the most popular style in the Western world. The fact that today hatha yoga is practiced by millions of people throughout the world indicates how ageless the wisdom of this union really is, and is a recognition of the importance of maintaining this union in an increasingly stress-filled world.

What appears to be a series of simple flexibility exercises that work the lower legs, lower back, neck, shoulders, and arms is really a progression of conscious movements, in combination with one's breath, to discipline the mind and ego. The purpose is to fully integrate a higher sense of conscious awareness in all movements, actions, and behaviors throughout the course of any given day. The subtle theme of hatha yoga is that by learning to become more flexible with your physical body, in turn, you become more flexible with your thoughts and emotions in each and every situation that you encounter in your environment.

The Omega Institute, well respected for decades among health educators for offering adult education classes in all aspects of mind-body-spirit healing, cites yoga as a powerful psychospiritual discipline that has the intention of integrating all aspects of one's human experience. Practitioners of hatha yoga would certainly agree, saying that a simple practice appears to transform the human body into a vessel capable of great vitality and longevity. Practitioners would also be the first to tell you that although hatha yoga is derived from the Hindu culture, it is not, repeat not, a religion; it's merely a philosophy of living your life in balance.

Since the beginning of the 21st century, yoga (primarily hatha yoga) has been studied extensively as a means to improve one's overall health status, suggesting that age-old claims of improved vitality and stress reduction are, indeed, quite valid. Proponents assert that the repeated daily series of selected asanas promotes longevity and facilitates homeostasis of mind, body, and spirit. By their very nature, researchers have focused on the more measureable physiological outcomes. Claims regarding muscle strength and flexibility have been substantiated, and reports about increased aerobic capacity to one's cardiovascular system also appear positive. Hatha yoga is now recognized as a suitable complementary healing modality for many chronic health-related issues such as breast cancer as well as a multi-modal approach to stress management.

Many, if not all, yoga practitioners acknowledge a sense of mental enjoyment from the habitual physical practice of asanas. Now science has begun to back up these claims. Results from a 3-month study revealed that, indeed, subjects noted this stress management modality caused a dramatic decrease in anxiety levels.

The popularity of hatha yoga has now fully exploded in U.S. culture, to the point where styles and instructors have become very territorial (e.g., certifications, trademarks, patents, precision in postures), which is the antithesis of this "egoless" practice. The result has made the practice of hatha yoga more technical (and ego-based) than it needs to be. In fact, hatha yoga practiced in the United States is a far cry from its roots in India. Bluntly stated, hatha yoga has gone corporate, and with it, mass marketing to the ego: yoga capitalism. Today, yoga has become very ego-centric, with expensive yoga accoutrements, yoga competitions (an oxymoron), even arrogant yoga instructors who brag about the number of followers they have. First and foremost, yoga is about non-ego, but sadly this aspect is virtually missing in American hatha yoga classes today. The upshot of all this is that finding a quality yoga instructor is quite easy. However, not all hatha yoga classes are created equal (**Table 20.1 ▶**). If possible, it would be a good idea to sample a class (e.g., use a one-day pass) to determine if the instructor's teaching style (everything from the use of props to augmenting comfort level) and health philosophy are compatible with your own. Even if you only do a few asanas each morning before you begin your working day, this would be a good start. Many asanas also can be done (briefly) in the course of a day (e.g., stepping away from the computer, before or after exercise).

TABLE 20.1 **Yoga Chart**

Type	Method	Advantages	More Info
Ashtanga Yoga	Intense class that synchronizes breathwork with a high-speed series of asanas	Considered a "serious" workout for muscles and cardiovascular system	Ashtanga.com
Power Yoga	Hatha yoga with intense muscle power asanas	Americanized yoga, very demanding for muscular strength	Power-yoga.com
Bikram Yoga	Yoga practiced in 105-degree heat to replicate the climate of India	Heat brings its own challenge; said to provide a cleansing feeling	Bikramyoga.com
Iyengar Yoga	Focus is placed on the specifics of each asana, while holding each posture for a relatively long time	Good for beginners who are not flexible; props (blocks) are often used	Iyengar-yoga.com

Pranayama: The Art of Breathing

In the practice of hatha yoga, conscious breathing plays a vital role in the process of uniting mind, body, and spirit. Breathing, or *pranayama,* influenced by the diaphragm, is the current of life force that circulates the flow of universal energy throughout the body. The word *prana* means breath, and the word *yama* translates to pause. Unlike the common practice of thoracic (upper chest) breathing, the pranayama invites a conscious effort of the entire pulmonary system including the nose, throat, lungs, intercostal muscles, and diaphragm.

Each yoga asana is composed of a contraction phase and a release phase, where muscles in a specific region of focus are slowly stretched and relaxed. As the muscles are stretched, air is drawn into the lungs by the diaphragm. As the muscles begin the relaxation phase of the asana, one exhales. When first learning these positions, trying to coordinate the pranayama with the asanas may seem challenging, but with practice, the coordination becomes second nature.

The Art of Conscious Stretching

Desk work, computer work, prolonged driving, and even walking in high-heeled shoes tend to promote an unnatural state of contracted muscles. Eventually the body adapts to these positions and various muscles remain contracted, causing stiffness and soreness. Moreover, tensed muscles tend to distort one's posture along the spinal column, which eventually leads to chronic pain in the lower back, hips, and shoulder region. The asanas used in the practice of hatha yoga are designed to help provide a full range of motion to all joints and promote correct posture in the vertebral column.

The art of conscious stretching is a practice to stretch the intended muscle group, without pain, long enough to allow for the full restoration of one's structural integrity. Conscious stretching means to complete the posture without ego. Most, if not all, asanas have Sanskrit names with Western counterparts, such as *Tadasana* (mountain pose) or *Matsyasana* (fish pose). Without a doubt, *shavasana* (corpse pose) is by far the most relaxing posture, and the one everyone cannot wait to do at the end of yoga class.

How to Incorporate Hatha Yoga into Your Life Routine

Exercise 20.1, "Salute to the Sun," guides you through a short series of yoga asanas to try on your own. The following are some tips and suggestions to consider when incorporating this relaxation technique into your lifestyle routine:

- Maintaining a practice of hatha yoga on your own is possible, and those who make it a practice tend to do some routine (long or short) nearly every day. Motivation and time can run low in a busy day, which is why yoga classes have become very popular in this country. If you choose to attend a class, ask around to find the best fit for your schedule and personality. Despite the new certification requirements, no two yoga classes are exactly alike. Many yoga studios offer a drop-in fee that is an excellent way to sample various classes.

- Hatha yoga means to unite mind and body. The ultimate goal of yoga is to do so by lowering the walls of the ego (the censor of the conscious mind). Whereas most athletic endeavors have a competitive edge to them, hatha yoga does not. It doesn't matter that your attempts at an asana don't equal those of an instructor, classmates, or pictures in a book. Pain is not a goal in yoga. Although reaching and stretching are encouraged, pain is not. Know your limits and avoid pain.

- It is best not to perform any yoga asanas on a full stomach. Yoga instructors suggest that you allow 1–2 hours between eating and a yoga workout, particularly if you attend a Bikram yoga class where the room temperature is intentionally set high.

- Wear loose-fitting clothing and avoid wearing jewelry (e.g., watches, earrings, necklaces, bracelets).

- Find a quiet place to practice. A well-lit, well-ventilated room is ideal. A thin yoga mat is recommended for several standing positions but is not necessary.

- Early morning is believed to be the preferred time for conscious awareness; however, afternoon and evening are when the body is most limber. Yoga postures tend to have a greater relaxation effect after a long busy day. Find a time that best fits your schedule.

- The underlying premise of hatha yoga is balance. It is highly recommended that when a posture is done on one side of your body (e.g., right knee to chest), that you repeat it on the other side (e.g., left knee to chest) to maintain a sense of balance.

- Many yoga sessions begin with the Salute to the Sun (Exercise 20.1). If you are new to yoga, this might be a great practice to incorporate into your session.

- Breathing is a central part of hatha yoga. Practice your breathing (pranayama) and try not to hold your breath at any one point.

- Meditation is not a requirement of yoga, but it's a nice complement to a yoga session. Most classes end with you lying on your back on the floor in shavasana (corpse pose), which is the relaxation pose. Some instructors will offer a contemplative meditation at this time. You can do this on your own as well.

Stress Relief and Chronic Pain

Hatha yoga, for most people, is considered primarily a preventive and maintenance health exercise; however, it has long been recognized for its ability to restore a sense of peace and tranquility to the most hectic lifestyle. Moreover, the nature of hatha yoga is to provide balance to musculature on each side of the body, providing symmetry to muscle groups that are often imbalanced from stress, leading to chronic pain, particularly lower back, back, hip, neck, and shoulder pain. Many case studies report tremendous success in the cessation of chronic pain through a regular practice of yoga.

Best Benefits of Hatha Yoga

Hatha yoga is more than stretching your muscles and feeling limber. It is a philosophy of life: a means of living your life in balance and harmony. This philosophy goes beyond postures to include healthy eating, a practice of meditation, maintaining a strong ethical nature, and treating all people with respect.

One session of yoga can make your body feel great! Tight muscles become more flexible, and closing a session in the corpse pose is always a nice way to feel relaxed. People who maintain a regular practice of yoga (three or more times per week) find themselves to be not only more flexible with their body, but also more flexible in their thinking. They claim to sleep better, eat better, have less emotional mood swings, and maintain an overall positive sense of well-being. When honoring the aspects of balance and integration through a progression of asanas, hatha yoga is believed to help augment the balance and integration of the brain's right and left hemispheres, thus promoting a sense of relaxed awareness. More recently, hatha yoga has been used by many to help alleviate chronic problems from lower back, neck, and shoulder pain to carpal tunnel syndrome.

Over the last decade many types of hatha yoga have developed, each with its own focus and specialization. Please complete Exercise 20.2 after reading this chapter.

Chapter Summary

- There are many types of yoga. Hatha yoga is the most commonly practiced yoga in the world.

- Hatha yoga means to unite mind and body.

- More than simple muscle stretches, hatha yoga is a metaphor for living your life in balance.

- Breathwork, known as pranayama, is essential with the coordination of the yoga asanas (postures).

- Hatha yoga is an activity that does not engage the ego.

- Hatha yoga has proven quite effective in reducing the symptoms of chronic pain.

Additional Resources

Devi, N. J. *The Healing Path of Yoga*. New York: Three Rivers Press; 2000.

Farhi, D. *The Breathing Book*. New York: Owl; 1996.

Finger, A. *Introduction to Yoga*. New York: Three Rivers Press; 2000.

Francina, S. *The New Yoga for People over 50*. Deerfield Beach, FL: Health Communications; 1997.

Iyengar, B. K. S. *Light on Life*. Emmaus, PA: Rodale Press; 2005.

Norberg, U. *Hatha Yoga*. New York: Skyhorse; 2008.

Rosen, R. *The Yoga of Breath*. Boston: Shambhala; 2002.

Ward, S. W. *Yoga for the Young at Heart*. Navato, CA: New World Library; 2002.

Weintraub, A., & Cope, S. *Yoga for Depression*. New York: Broadway; 2003.

EXERCISE 20.1: Salute to the Sun (*Surya Namaskar*)

The Salute to the Sun is a very symbolic series of asanas. It is traditionally performed at the beginning and end of each yoga session. *Surya namaskar* began as a form of meditation worship wherein one would start the day by facing east and performing the series of movements in order to maintain harmony throughout the day. Today it is recognized as an excellent exercise to stretch and limber muscles throughout the entire body, but particularly the spine and legs. Runners and joggers may recognize a few of these stretches, because they are excellent flexibility exercises for hamstrings and calf muscles.

The Salute to the Sun should be performed slowly, and every effort should be made to maintain balance through each posture. Once the movements become more natural, the exercise can be done more rapidly. Each posture is counterbalanced in the next asana. A complete Salute to the Sun consists of two sequences. In the first cycle, lead with the right foot in position 4, and in the second, lead with the left. It makes no difference what direction you face when doing this exercise; however, facing east marks symbolic awareness of the beginning of the life of each new day.

Pre-position: Stand with your feet shoulder-width apart, spine completely aligned, and weight evenly distributed on both feet. Hold hands straight above head, palms facing out, with arms fully extended.

Position 1 `Fig. 20.1 ◀` `Fig. 20.2 ◀`: Raise your arms in a wide circular motion over your head and then slowly bring them down in front of your face to the midpoint of your chest. Hold palms together and exhale.

FIGURE 20.1   **FIGURE 20.2**

Position 2 `Fig. 20.3 ▶`: Raise your arms directly over your head, pushing from the waist, keeping legs straight and back slightly arched. As you do this, slowly inhale and look up to the sky.

FIGURE 20.3

EXERCISE 20.1: Salute to the Sun (*Surya Namaskar*) cont....

Position 3 [**Fig. 20.4** ▶]: Leading with your hands, reach to your toes, exhaling as you lower your head to your knees. Keep your back comfortably straight and knees slightly bent. (Tight hamstrings will decrease the length of your reach. Reach only as far as it is comfortably possible.)

FIGURE 20.4

Position 4 [**Fig. 20.5** ▶]: Place your palms on the floor, then bring your right foot between your hands. Extend the left leg behind you, and lower your knee to the floor. Inhale as you extend the leg, arch your back, and look up to the sky.

FIGURE 20.5

Position 5 [**Fig. 20.6** ▶]: Bring the right foot back to meet the left, and exhale. Raise your hips and buttocks high, keeping your head down and eyes directed toward your feet. Arms should be fully extended.

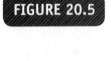

FIGURE 20.6

Position 6 [**Fig. 20.7** ▶]: Lower your knees to the floor, followed by your chest and then your forehead. Hips should be slightly bent and raised off the floor. Breath is slowly exhaled throughout.

FIGURE 20.7

EXERCISE 20.1: Salute to the Sun (*Surya Namaskar*) cont....

Position 7 `Fig. 20.8 ◀`: Bring your hips to the floor, fully extending your legs behind you. Then inhale while placing your hands directly beneath your shoulders and raising your chest. Look up to the sky, and arch the head and back slightly.

FIGURE 20.8

Position 8 `Fig. 20.9 ◀`: Raise hips and buttocks high off the floor, keeping your palms and feet flat on the floor. As you do so, exhale. Keep your head down, eyes directly toward your feet, and your arms fully extended.

FIGURE 20.9

Position 9 `Fig. 20.10 ◀`: Place your left foot between your hands, extend your right leg back and place the knee on the floor as you inhale. Arch your back and head slightly, looking up to the sky.

FIGURE 20.10

Position 10 `Fig. 20.11 ◀`: Bring your feet together, with arms extended and hands reaching toward feet. Keep your back straight and knees slightly bent. As you bring your head to your knees, exhale.

FIGURE 20.11

EXERCISE 20.1: Salute to the Sun (*Surya Namaskar*) cont....

Position 11 **Fig. 20.12 ▶**: Reach with your hands overhead, and slowly inhale. Extend your head back to look up to the sky, arching the back slightly.

FIGURE 20.12

Position 12 **Fig. 20.13 ▶**: Lower your arms to midchest height, palms touching, and exhale.

FIGURE 20.13

Now repeat the entire exercise, this time leading with the left foot in position 4. Upon completion, turn your attention inward to observe any and all physical sensations.

EXERCISE 20.2: Hatha Yoga Revisited

Hatha yoga has been around as a mind-body exercise for generations. Its popularity has increased dramatically over the past decade, making hatha yoga more popular today than cardiovascular exercise in many parts of the country. More than just basic stretching, hatha yoga is a practice of achieving balance within the body's structure as well as a union of mind, body, and spirit. This worksheet serves as a means to refresh your memory regarding some of the basics of hatha yoga as well as to have you articulate how this means of relaxation, whether it was a one-time experience or a regular part of your daily routine, has felt for you personally.

Hatha Yoga Review

Please answer the following questions in a sentence or two:

1. What does the word "hatha" mean?

_____

2. What does the word "yoga" mean?

_____

3. List two other types or styles of yoga.

_____

4. What is the "Salute to the Sun"?

_____

5. What is the "pranayama"?

_____

6. What is the "shavasana"?

_____

Mind-Body Processing

1. Describe in a few sentences what your body feels like right after a hatha yoga session.

_____

2. In your own words, what do you feel is the essence of hatha yoga?

_____

3. What has the yoga done for you mentally, physically, and emotionally?

_____

4. How does hatha yoga help alleviate pain or chronic pain?

_____

5. Please share any other comments you have regarding hatha yoga here:

_____

_____

_____

Chapter 21

Self-Hypnosis and Autogenics

"Open your mind to the power of self-suggestion."
— Johannes Schultz

The Ageless Wisdom of Self-Hypnosis

For decades, if not centuries, Western science held the belief that the mind, as powerful as it is, could not control the autonomic nervous system. Aspects of human physiology including heart rate, blood pressure, breathing, blood distribution, and other parameters were thought to be totally under the influence of brain regions that were not influenced by conscious thought. All of this changed dramatically in the early 20th century when Western scientists traveled to the Himalayan region of India to observe yogis who appeared to display mystical powers of human physiology. The ability to sit comfortably on a bed of nails paled in comparison to the ability to control one's breathing, heart rate, and blood flow.

The average person breathes 14–16 times per minute. When completely relaxed, the average person can take as few as 6 breaths per minute. These yogis could comfortably breathe less than once per minute. Moreover, they could decrease their heart rates to less than 20 beats per minute. For all intents and purposes they appeared dead. These feats were thought to be humanly impossible. Perhaps even more amazing was the demonstration of certain yogis to redistribute the flow of blood entirely to the right side of the body, leaving the left side stone cold. Punctures to the skin produced no bleeding.

In the 1960s, Elmer and Alyce Green, from the Menninger Clinic, traveled to India to conduct scientific investigations of these talented yogis. They even convinced one yogi, Swami Rama, to come back and be studied under laboratory conditions. Results revealed that these changes were neither magic nor the ploy of some adept conjurer. These yogis, who had cultivated a wealth of mental discipline, were indeed able to defy the autonomic nervous system and consciously influence a host of physiological parameters. They not only redefined the word *homeostasis,* but also opened the door to a view of consciousness that had only been hinted at as an illusion before, and sowed the seeds for a new field of study: psychoneuroimmunology.

It's well known that in a relaxed state, the mind is more receptive to suggestions—either those one gives to oneself or those one hears from someone else. The receptivity to the power of suggestion is more commonly known as hypnosis. Most likely, everyone has seen or heard of people volunteering to be hypnotized on stage by an entertainer. Through the use of hypnosis, participants perform ludicrous acts that appear to defy reality. However, centuries before some magician thought to use hypnosis as part of his Las Vegas act, the power of suggestion through the use of guided hypnosis was used. In the late 1700s, Anton Mesmer combined the use of hypnotic suggestion with magnets as a means to heal people of a host of serious diseases. Today the word *mesmerized* is used to suggest a trance-like state of bewilderment.

In 1939 two German physicians, Johannes Schultz and Wolfgang Luthe, combined the use of hypnosis and relaxation to create what is commonly known today as **autogenic training** or self-regulation: the ability to follow a series of self-suggestions to promote a deep sense of relaxation. The technique of autogenics did not go unnoticed by magicians either. Houdini, and many others who followed in his footsteps, was known for using the power of self-suggestion and self-regulation to perform many of his escape tricks and illusions. It goes without saying that you would have to be very relaxed to be handcuffed in a straightjacket and submerged under water and escape unscathed!

The Power of Suggestion

Some people shudder at the mention of hypnosis, and for that matter **self-hypnosis**, but in truth, people give themselves suggestions all the time. Usually it's the ego doing the suggesting, directing people to watch out for this or avoid that. The ego is a master at the power of suggestion and becomes even more so during times of stress. The real power of human potential comes not from the ego, however, but a deeper source of strength hidden in the unconscious mind often censored by the ego. In a relaxed state, the ego is disarmed. Self-guided suggestions (or even those provided by others such as a therapist on a guided imagery CD) allow you to unite the power of the conscious and unconscious minds to achieve states of physiological homeostasis that are not possible when the ego is standing guard. As a rule, people are most open to the power of suggestion when they are relaxed. This is the promise of self-regulation.

The Art of Self-Regulation

The secret to autogenic training is to make your arms, hands, legs, and/or feet feel comfortably warm and heavy. The warmth and heaviness come from the flow of blood that you consciously direct to whatever region you focus your awareness on. In a resting state, the majority (80 percent) of your body's blood resides in your gastrointestinal (GI) tract. The other 20 percent circulates throughout the body to provide oxygen and a host of nutrients for metabolic functions. By consciously directing the flow of blood from your body's core to your arms and hands or your legs and feet, you begin to send a message to the autonomic nervous system to constrict the blood vessels in your stomach area and dilate the blood vessels in either the arms or the legs, thus allowing the movement of blood to these areas.

Because muscles are not normally saturated with blood in a resting state, the autogenic effect is very relaxing (similar to the feelings when sitting in a Jacuzzi). To initiate this technique, all you need to do is give yourself a series of suggestions to have either your arms and hand, or legs and feet (some even suggest trying the back of your head) feel warm and heavy. If you wish, you can add to this suggestion a visualization of blood flowing to the desired areas. Turn to Exercise 21.1 to begin the process of this new mind-set.

How to Incorporate Autogenics into Your Life Routine

Lie on your back in a comfortable position, with your arms by your side. Take a moment to focus your awareness on your breathing, following the flow of air in through your nostrils and down deep into your lungs. As you exhale, simply relax. This is the first stage of autogenics. Exercise 21.2 guides you through an entire autogenics session.

Many people who use autogenics feel that it is a great technique to use to fall asleep at night. For this reason, autogenics is a technique to use late at night, or perhaps on weekend mornings when there is no rush to get out of bed. When done properly, this technique takes about 15–30 minutes, and like most skills, the more you practice it, the easier it becomes. It is an easy technique to use for muscle soreness. It has also been used by patients (with the help of their physicians) who are undergoing surgery. They experience fewer complications with healing. Exercise 21.3 leads you through an additional contemplation of the autogenic technique.

Developing Your Mastery of Autogenic Training

To begin the practice of autogenic training, please consider following these guidelines:

1. Be sure to minimize all distractions such as blaring radios, televisions, and smartphones.

2. Find a quiet place to lie down. (It's best to try this technique lying down, but it can be done sitting.)

3. Get comfortable, loosening any tight-fitting clothing. Begin to focus on your breathing. Pay close attention to your body's physiology and your heart rate.

4. Follow the directions in Exercise 21.2. You can read through these directions first and then call to mind the progression of steps with either the arms, legs, or head.

Stress Relief and Chronic Pain

When people take the time to learn the premise of autogenic training, they find it to be one of the most powerful means of relieving the symptoms of physical stress. It also is a favorite for people with insomnia and people suffering from Raynaud's disease. Autogenics is often used in tandem with clinical biofeedback and is found to be very useful as a means to control not only sensations of pain, but also, in some cases, the causes of it.

Best Benefits of Autogenics

The immediate effects of autogenics are similar, in some ways, to a muscle massage. Like a dry sponge, tight muscles have very poor blood flow due to constricted blood vessels and capillaries. The practice of autogenics allows for a greater distribution of blood flow to the intended area, helping to saturate the muscles with blood, and in a sense, massaging them from the inside. Metaphorically speaking, the dry sponge becomes saturated, making the tissue more pliable and relaxed. The neural endings in the muscles decrease their firing, which, in turn, sends a message to the brain to relax. The long-term effects of autogenic training give one a sense of profound relaxation through autosuggestion. It also provides a sense of empowerment knowing that there are some things you truly have control over, and this tends to carry over into other areas of your life.

Chapter Summary

- Autogenic training means self-regulation, referring to the ability to self-regulate your body's physiological systems.

- In simple terms, autogenic training teaches one to relax by making various body parts (e.g., hands, arms, legs) feel warm and heavy (like an internal muscle massage).

- Autogenic training is based on the concept of self-hypnosis, the ability to talk yourself into a relaxed state.

- Many people swear by the effects of autogenic training for deep relaxation and easing chronic pain.

Additional Resources

Alman, B., & Lambrou, P. *Self-Hypnosis: The Complete Manual for Health and Self-Change*, 2nd ed. New York: Brunner/Mazel; 1991.

Blair, F. R. *Instant Self-Hypnosis*. New York: Sourcebooks; 2004.

Green, E., & Green, A. *Beyond Biofeedback*. New York: Delacorte Press; 1977.

EXERCISE 21.1: The Power of Self-Suggestion

The following is a brief exercise to assist you in uniting the powers of your conscious and unconscious minds by giving yourself your own suggestions to follow as a means to promote a deeper sense of relaxation. Please first create and then read through your own suggestions so that you have a strong comfort level with them. Then assume a comfortable position and talk yourself through each of these suggestions. Remember that in a relaxed state you are open to the power of suggestions, particularly those that you give yourself. After giving some thought to one or more of these behaviors you might wish to change, write these down as well, so they can be used in a relaxed state.

Suggestions for Relaxation

Example: "My body is calm and relaxed."

1. _____
2. _____
3. _____
4. _____

Suggestions for Self-Improvement and Confidence

Example: "I can do anything!"

1. _____
2. _____
3. _____
4. _____

EXERCISE 21.2: The Direct Approach of Autogenics

Autogenic training has both a direct and an indirect approach to relaxation. The direct approach is a more detailed visual interpretation than simple general instructions to feel warm and heavy. In this exercise, a slight variation on the original technique offers added instructions for those who need more understanding of how the physiological changes occur. In the direct approach, the specific mechanisms involved in warmth and heaviness are focused on to initiate a stronger sense of relaxation. Here, you start out with diaphragmatic breathing to induce relaxation. When mind and body become relaxed through this technique, the mind becomes more receptive to additional thoughts (warmth and heaviness), and thus the selected awareness process is enhanced.

The length of time required for this approach will vary. To begin, you may want to work on only one body region, such as the arms and hands. With proficiency, you can add to the duration of each session. The following instructions can be read prior to your session, or they can be read to you by a friend while you are performing this technique. Assume a comfortable position and become as relaxed as possible.

Instructions

1. First, concentrate on your breathing. Feel the air come in through your nose or mouth, down into your lungs, and feel your stomach rise and then fall as you exhale the air through your mouth.

2. Take a comfortably slow, deep breath, feeling the air enter the lower chambers of your lungs. Feel your stomach rise slowly with the intake of air, and then slowly descend as the air leaves your lungs. Repeat this, making the breath even slower and deeper. With each exhalation, feel how relaxed your body has become.

3. Focus on your heartbeat. Listen to and feel your heart beating in your chest. As you concentrate on this, allow a longer pause after each heartbeat. Just by allowing the thought of your heart relaxing, you can make it do so. Allow a longer pause after each beat. Now, to help relax the heart muscle, take one more slow, deep breath, and as you exhale feel how relaxed your heart has become. Again, consciously choose to place a longer pause after each heartbeat.

4. Take a moment to realize that in the resting state you are now in, your body's core receives the greatest percentage (80 percent) of blood, most of it going to the gastrointestinal tract. While the body's core is receiving a great supply of blood, the periphery—arms and legs—receive only a maintenance supply.

5. Be aware that when your muscles are saturated with blood, they become very relaxed and pliable, like a wet sponge. Now, think to yourself that you would like to re-create the feeling of relaxation in the muscles of your arms and hands.

EXERCISE 21.2: The Direct Approach of Autogenics cont....

6. Allow the blood to move from the body's core up to your shoulders and down toward your arms and hands. As you think and desire this, you will begin to constrict the blood vessels of your stomach area while at the same time dilating those of your arms and hands.

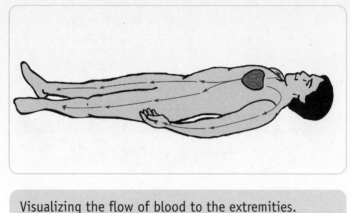

Visualizing the flow of blood to the extremities.

7. With each breath you take, with each beat of your heart, allow the flow of blood to move from your stomach area to your arms and hands.

8. You will begin to notice that as you allow this movement of blood from your core to your arms and hands, they begin to feel slightly heavy. They feel heavy because they are not quite used to the sensation of additional blood flow to this region. You will also notice that your arms and particularly your hands feel warm, especially your palms and fingers, because they have the greatest number of temperature receptors.

9. With each breath and each beat of your heart, allow the blood to continue to move from your stomach area toward your arms and hands. Feel how comfortable your arms and hands have become. They feel warm and heavy, and very relaxed. As the muscles become saturated with blood, stiffness dissipates and relaxation ensues.

EXERCISE 21.2: The Direct Approach of Autogenics cont....

10. Soon you will notice that your arms feel increasingly heavy, so much so that should you want to move them you couldn't because they feel immobilized. You feel as if they are making indentations in the floor or chair frame. Your arms and hands feel so relaxed they just don't want to move.

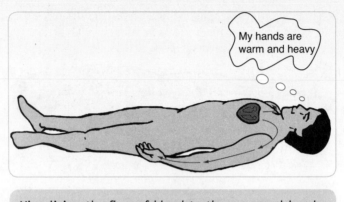

Visualizing the flow of blood to the arms and hands, the breath becomes even slower and deeper. With each exhalation, feel how relaxed your body has become.

11. With each breath and each beat of your heart, continue to send the flow of blood to your arms and hands. Feel the warmth spread from your arms all the way down to your palms and fingers.

12. Take a long, slow, deep breath and gauge how relaxed your whole body feels as you exhale. Sense how relaxed your arms and hands feel.

13. Now, take one more slow, deep breath, and as you exhale allow the flow of blood to return to your stomach area. Reverse the flow of blood from your arms and hands back to your body's core. By thinking this, you now allow the blood vessels of the arms and hands to constrict, shunting the blood back to the GI tract. At the same time, you allow the blood vessels of the stomach area to dilate and receive the flow of blood you have sent to it.

14. As the blood returns, you may notice that your arms begin to feel a little lighter, but the sensation of warmth still lingers.

15. With each breath you take, with each beat of your heart, allow the flow of blood to return to where it came from.

16. Again, concentrate on your breathing. Feel the air come in through your nose or mouth, down into your lungs, and feel your stomach rise and then descend as you exhale the air through your mouth.

17. Now, take a comfortably slow, deep breath and feel the air enter the lower chambers of your lungs. Feel your stomach rise slowly with the intake of air, and slowly descend as the air leaves your lungs. Do this again, making the breath even slower and deeper. With each exhalation, become more aware of how relaxed your body has become.

EXERCISE 21.2: The Direct Approach of Autogenics cont....

18. Next, focus again on the beat of your heart. Listen to and feel your heart beating in your chest. As you concentrate on this, allow a longer pause between heartbeats. Just by allowing the thought of your heart relaxing you can make it do so. Think to allow a longer pause between beats. To help relax the heart muscle, take one more slow, deep breath, and feel how relaxed your heart has become as you exhale. Again, place a longer pause after each heartbeat.

19. Again, take a moment to realize that in the resting state you are now in, your body's core contains the greatest percentage of your blood supply, roughly 80 percent.

20. Think to yourself that when your muscles are saturated with blood, they become very relaxed and pliable like a wet sponge. Now become consciously aware that you desire to re-create that feeling of relaxation in the muscles of your legs and feet.

21. Allow the blood from your stomach area to move down toward your legs and feet. As you think and desire this, the blood vessels of your stomach area will begin to constrict, while at the same time those of your legs and feet will begin to dilate. This constriction process in your body's core will begin to shunt blood to your thighs, hamstrings, calves, and feet, where the dilating vessels will be able to receive more blood.

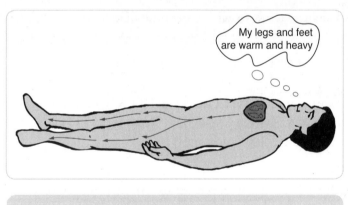

My legs and feet are warm and heavy

Visualizing the flow of blood to the legs and feet.

22. With each breath you take, with each beat of your heart, allow the flow of blood to move from your stomach area down toward your legs and feet.

23. You will begin to notice that as you allow this movement of blood from your body's core to your legs and feet, both your legs and feet begin to feel slightly heavy. This heaviness increases with each breath and each heartbeat. They feel very heavy because muscles in this region are not used to the sensation of additional blood flow. You will also notice that your legs and particularly your feet feel warm, especially the heels of your feet and your toes, because they have the greatest number of temperature receptors.

EXERCISE 21.2: The Direct Approach of Autogenics cont....

24. With each breath and each beat of your heart, allow the blood to continue to move from your stomach area to your legs and feet. Feel how comfortable your thighs and calves are. They feel warm, comfortably heavy, and very relaxed. As the muscles become saturated with blood, stiffness dissipates and relaxation ensues.

25. Be aware that your legs now feel increasingly heavy, so much so that you want to move them but they feel immobilized. You feel as if each leg has sunk under its weight into the floor. Your legs and feet feel so relaxed they don't want to move.

26. With each breath and each beat of your heart, continue to send the flow of blood to legs and feet. Feel the warmth spread from your stomach area all the way down to your toes.

27. Take a long, slow, deep breath and gauge how relaxed your whole body feels as you exhale. Feel how relaxed your legs and feet feel.

28. Now, take one more slow, deep breath, and as you exhale allow the flow of blood to return to your stomach area. Reverse the flow of blood from your legs and feet back to your body's core. By thinking this, you allow the blood vessels of the legs and feet to constrict, shunting the blood back to the GI tract. At the same time, you allow the blood vessels of the stomach area to dilate and receive the flow of blood you are sending to it.

29. As the blood returns, you will notice that your legs are beginning to feel a little lighter, but the sensations of warmth linger, especially in your feet and toes.

30. With each breath you take, with each beat of your heart, allow the flow of blood to return to where it came from.

31. As your body returns to a resting state, feel the sensation of relaxation throughout. Although you feel relaxed, you don't feel tired or sleepy. You feel alert and energized.

32. When you feel ready, open your eyes and stretch the muscles of your arms, shoulders, and legs.

EXERCISE 21.3: Autogenic Training

Please listen to the Autogentic Training exercise on the CD that accompanies this textbook, and then write your impressions in response to the following questions:

1. What were your first impressions when completing the audio session of autogenic training? How did it make you feel? Did this exercise make you more aware of how slight or even dramatic changes in perceptions of warmth and heaviness can make various body parts feel?

_____

_____

_____

2. How did this technique compare to your experience with massage therapy, progressive muscular relaxation (PMR), guided mental imagery, music therapy, or any other type of relaxation session you have had?

_____

_____

_____

3. Are you someone who suffers from chronic pain? If so, how does a session of autogenic training affect the sensations for chronic pain (either directly in the affected muscle group or indirectly)?

_____

_____

_____

4. Muscles are like sponges. When they are filled with blood they are less tense (more pliable) than when there is little circulation. Dry muscles, like dry sponges, are very stiff. This technique is a great exercise to do before you fall asleep (insomniacs take note). If you have problems falling asleep at night, try this exercise and then write your impressions of how this worked below.

_____

_____

_____

5. Please share any other comments you have regarding autogenic training here:

_____

_____

_____

Nutrition: Eating for a Healthy Immune System

"We got a chance to see exactly what the major food industry groups want for American customers. They want ignorance."

— Editorial, *New York Times*

The Ageless Wisdom of Healthy Eating

Since the beginning of time, food has played an essential, if not critical, role in the survival of the human species. Over the ages, food was hunted, gathered, and grown, not only for nutrients and energy, but also for health and the restoration of health from disease and illness. Plants in the form of fruits, vegetables, legumes, and herbs were critical to one's diet. Additionally, food (specifically "comfort foods") is a great pacifier, and there is no denying that certain foods can exalt the senses to a state of euphoria in a way that no other means can. Combined with great company, eating is known as one of the greatest means of happiness.

For all these reasons, it's not an understatement to say that nutrition used to be taken very seriously, because life depended on it. In essence, eating food was considered to be the first course of action to take to maintain health and well-being. Ironically, today much of the food available is the cause of many diseases and illnesses, rather than a means to prevent a decline in one's health. At no time in the history of the United States have food choices been so great, yet the quality of food so questionable. For millennia nutrition was first and foremost a health issue; however, today health concerns are grossly outweighed by economic and political concerns. One only need be reminded how cows (known herbivores) became mad in the first place. They were fed rendered parts of other cows, lambs, and chicken feces, all mixed in with their grain cereal.

In the past few decades a large uncontrolled experiment has been conducted on the American population through the introduction of synthetic substances into food production. With the introduction of synthetic hormones, antibiotics, pesticides, herbicides, fungicides, fertilizers, artificial sweeteners, artificial fats, food brighteners, and most recently genetically modified foods, Americans have seen a corresponding rise in a variety of chronic diseases. Some foods contain so many chemicals that there is literally no place for them on the "MyPlate" recommendations, yet people consume vast quantities of these every day. A case in point occurred in 2001 when Kellogg's Corn Flakes and Taco John taco shells were recalled due to the amount of pesticides found in them. The year 2004 saw the first case of mad cow disease in the United States, something Americans were assured would never happen.

In 1995 the American Cancer Society (ACS) stated that although the death rate due to cancer had decreased due to early detection, one out of every three people would contract cancer in their lifetime. They also stated that 60 percent of all cancer could be eliminated if people would choose a healthier diet. Apparently, people's appeals for good taste have won out over their concern for health in the 24/7, fast-paced American lifestyle. The ACS might as well have been shouting in the wind, because its warning seems to have gone unheeded.

In an effort to promote shelf life and increase profits, the major food corporations concoct ingenious ways to keep food looking and tasting fresh. We now know that chemical preservatives, hydrogenated fats, and scores of other synthetic components used in the process of food production certainly prolong shelf life, but appear to do absolutely nothing to promote health. Instead, they compromise it. Today synthetic food is a stressor to the body, specifically, the immune system.

Even if there weren't such an influx of synthetic foods, there are a series of problems that occur regarding nutrition and stress. Each problem itself is easy to rectify; however, as these problems mount, their combined effects pose a greater danger to the integrity of your health. Metaphorically speaking, there are four dominos that tumble in a progression of a stressed lifestyle, the result of which significantly compromises one's physiology.

- *Stress domino #1:* Under the physiological demands of the stress response, the body's requirement for energy increases, regardless of whether the actions of fight or flight are used. In simple terms, more glucose is released into the bloodstream as a source of immediate energy. Then, more free fatty acids are released, just in case they are needed for long-term energy. The net result of these and other metabolic reactions to the stress response is a depletion of both macronutrients (carbohydrates, fats, and proteins) and micronutrients (vitamins, minerals). As the micronutrients are depleted the efficiency of their metabolic response becomes compromised until they are replaced.

- *Stress domino #2:* Sadly, as a rule, when people are stressed, good eating habits are the first thing to go in a hectic schedule. Home-cooked meals are replaced with convenient fast foods. As was noted in the book *Fast Food Nation*, these foods are processed for taste, not nutrition. The vast majority of these foods contain what are known in nutrition circles as "empty calories," meaning they have little or no nutritional value. The consequence of bad eating habits is that the nutrients depleted during prolonged periods of stress are not replaced. Hence, the body's physiological systems operate less efficiently. Many systems are compromised including the immune system and the reproductive system. Under compromised conditions, the body tries to compensate, but over time even these backup systems fail. The end result is a host of physiological problems that lead to poor health.

- *Stress domino #3:* As if it's not bad enough that valuable nutrients are depleted during prolonged stress, and many of these nutrients are not replaced, many fast foods, junk foods, and convenience foods contain substances that act on the nervous system to keep the stress response elevated. These include:

- *Caffeine:* Coffee, tea, soda pop, and chocolate contain a constituent found in caffeine called methylated xanthines, a substance known to trigger the release of epinephrine and norepinephrine, which in turn increase heart rate, blood pressure, and other metabolic activities in the preparation for fight or flight.

- *Refined sugar:* Research suggests that refined or bleached sugar can have a similar effect on the nervous systems as caffeine. It's no secret that processed foods are high in refined sugar. High fructose corn syrup and table sugar are two examples of refined sugar.

- *Refined flour:* As with refined sugar, refined flour appears to affect the nervous system and, in some cases, the adrenal (stress) glands.

- *Salt (sodium):* Salt is known to cause the body to retain water. Water retention tends to increase blood pressure. Although only one teaspoon of salt is recommended per day, processed food is loaded with salt to appease the taste buds.

- *Stress domino #4:* A new term has entered the American lexicon regarding the proliferation of toxic chemical residues found in the body: *bio-*

burden. It describes the amounts of toxic chemical substances that are found in the body's blood and tissue samples, including mother's milk. Not only do processed foods contain a plethora of chemicals, but the skin also absorbs chemicals from make-up, shampoos, hair dyes, deodorants, sun block, and other substances applied topically to the skin. The effects of these substances on humans are not conclusive, but in animal studies the results are disturbing. Suffice to say that even in trace amounts these chemical residues become a stressor to the body's physiology and immune system, challenging the integrity of one's overall health and well-being. Please turn to Exercise 22.1 and evaluate your stress-related eating behaviors.

A Few Words About Water

Although it contains no calories, water is often acknowledged as being the most important nutrient. In simple terms, we would die quickly (in a matter of days) without it. Although the average person does drink a fair amount of beverages, most people do not consume enough water. Instead coffee, teas, and soft drinks act as diuretics, resulting in a moderate state of dehydration. As the rule goes, if you are thirsty, most likely you are already showing signs of dehydration.

Signs of dehydration include sluggishness, fatigue, headaches, low energy, and poor appetite. This not only stresses the body's physiology, but also may increase emotional stress regarding other life issues. Many proponents of rehydration suggest drinking eight glasses of water per day, but the real test to see if you are drinking enough water is to check the color of your urine. Near clear urine is the goal. One good goal is to drink a glass of water soon after you awake because the body has gone roughly 8 hours without any fluids.

Best Benefits of Healthy Eating

The benefits of healthy eating are too numerous to mention, but suffice to say that sound nutritional practices play a crucial role in nearly every aspect of health, from eyesight to kidney function. Moreover, poor nutritional habits only add to the critical mass of stress that people face each day. The human body has an amazing ability to adapt to the stress placed on it. For this reason, poor eating habits tend to result in chronic illnesses rather than acute problems. The good news is that the body, by and large, has the great gift of resiliency, meaning that by making healthy changes in your diet, your body has a better chance to begin and sustain the healing process. Today, healthy eating requires a slight sense of vigilance with regard to the food industry; however, at the same time, you could drive yourself nuts trying to avoid all the potholes in the national food chain. For this reason it's best to be cautious, but not neurotic about your food choices.

How to Incorporate the Practice of Healthy Eating into Your Life Routine

Hippocrates, the father of modern medicine, once said, "Let food be your medicine and let medicine be your food." Unfortunately today, rather than eating food as medicine, the vast majority of people eat food as poison. Like toxins dumped into a river, the human body can take only so much before signs of disease and illness manifest. The following is a list of suggestions to tip the scale back to balance and promote a sense of health and well-being:

1. *Consume a good supply of antioxidants.* Antioxidants fight the damage of free radicals that destroy cell membranes, DNA, RNA, and mitochondria. Antioxidants can be found in foods containing beta-carotene, vitamin C, vitamin E, and the mineral selenium. If you were to take a look at the eating habits of indigenous tribes around the world, you would notice that the greatest amount of calories in their diet comes from vegetables. Vegetables not only contain a rich supply of vitamins, minerals, and fiber, but also contain a wonderful supply of antioxidants, nature's antidote to free radicals. Research in the field of nutrition has begun to reveal that antioxidants can be found in a variety of natural food sources, including vegetables, fruits, and herbs.

2. *Consume a good supply of fiber (30–40 grams/day with* **organic** *vegetables).* Fiber helps clean the colon of toxic materials that might otherwise be absorbed into the bloodstream. The average American eats about 5–8 grams of fiber daily, far below the recommended amount. There is not a lot of fiber in iceberg lettuce, but there is plenty to be found in dark green leafy veggies, citrus fruits, and legumes. Fiber also helps regulate the elimination process of your bowels. Under the best conditions, typical transit time from mouth to rectum is about 12–18 hours. Experts suggest that there should be one bowel movement per meal. For the average person who eats three meals a day, this would mean three bowel movements; however, many people confide to their physicians that their average is more like one per day. Waste that doesn't get removed becomes toxic to the colon and affects the whole body. Colon cancer is the third most prevalent type of cancer in the United States.

3. *Drink plenty of fresh, clean (filtered) water.* As was mentioned earlier, water acts as a transport system to remove toxic waste produced by each cell to the kidneys, where it can be excreted. Dehydration tends to compromise the body's ability to remove toxic waste. Toxins that are not flushed out cause damage of all kinds at the cellular level.

An article in *National Geographic* stated that only 1 percent of the world's water is drinkable. News reports suggest that fresh water will become the issue of the decade. (The United Nations has even suggested that wars will be fought over water.) Toxicologists have noted that agricultural runoff from industrial farms into our national waterways has infiltrated our water supply. Moreover, water specialists have noted an increase in pharmaceutical by-products (e.g., Zoloft, Prozac, birth control pills) in our drinking water, which may be related to a score of health problems. As you can see, water safety is already an issue. In addition, water filtration plants use huge amounts of chlorine and fluoride in their water treatment procedures, all of which end up in your tap water. For this reason it is a great idea to install your own water filtration system as a means to purify the water you drink. Bottled water may sound like a good idea, but supplies of bottled water are stored in warehouses for prolonged periods of time, allowing the chemicals from plastic residue to seep into the water. Water stored in hard (nonbendable) plastic is the only recommended water product, suggesting you may wish to bring your own bottled water with you. A good goal to determine if you are drinking enough water is the excretion of near-clear urine.

4. *Decrease consumption of pesticides, fungicides, and herbicides.* These are toxic and many are carcinogenic. Eat organic food whenever possible. Current research reveals that we consume large amounts of synthetic estrogens from the foods we eat. Synthetic estrogens are used in a host of agricultural products such as fertilizers, pesticides, fungicides, and herbicides. (They are also found in animal food products where these substances are used in their feed.) These toxins are not simply found on the exterior of fruits and veggies to be washed off; they are also taken up by the root system and deposited in the stems, leaves, and fruits of these plants. Once consumed, it's the role of the liver to filter out toxins, but the liver can do only so much, and those chemicals that slip back into the bloodstream are transported to fatty tissue. Long before the word *organic* was introduced to the American lexicon, the word *natural* conveyed a sense of the pristine nature of foods that were undisturbed by the agricultural complex. Today the word *natural* has become a marketing term, and rarely does it mean what the word originally described. Today, the difference between organic and natural is this: 100 percent organic means that the soil in which the plants are grown must be clean of synthetic chemicals and pesticides for a period of 3 years and that the crops grown on the soil must be exposed to only natural fertilizers (such as seaweeds). In 2001, Congress passed legislation requiring that certified organic food be labeled as such. Be sure to read your food labels.

5. *Consume an adequate amount of complete proteins.* White blood cells are composed of amino acids from protein sources. To ensure the intake of all essential amino acids it is necessary to consume complete proteins. There are eight amino acids that the body cannot produce and must be obtained from outside food sources. Foods such as meats, fish, poultry, and eggs contain all the essential amino acids (hence the term *complete*), whereas many grains and legumes do not. If you are not a vegetarian, this really isn't a concern; but if you are, it is important to know how to complement your protein sources to ensure you are getting all the essential amino acids. Because amino acids are used for the production of enzymes, hormones, and the entire family of white blood cells, it is imperative to consume adequate amounts of protein in your diet. Again, 100 percent organic is the preferred source.

6. *Decrease consumption of all processed foods (e.g., junk food, fast food).* Here are two little-known facts: Not only does most food travel a distance of at least 1,500 miles from farm to store, but the average amount of time that packaged food remains on the grocery store shelf is about 3–6 days, depending on your locale. If you were to check the expiration date on these packages, however, you would find that the suggested shelf life is projected in years. What allows these products to endure this long? If you read the labels, you would find a long list of preservatives composed mainly of chemicals. Once again, the role of the liver is to filter these out of the system, but the liver can do only so much. Most people's livers are overtaxed. Many of these chemicals enter the bloodstream to wreak havoc on the body. Once in the bloodstream, it becomes the job of the immune system to destroy or remove them, but an overtaxed immune system can do only so much as well. For this reason, it is best to minimize or avoid processed foods altogether. As the expression goes, "think outside the box," particularly with processed foods, to avoid overconsumption of additives and preservatives that your body really doesn't need.

7. *Decrease/avoid the consumption of antibiotics and hormones.* Perhaps it's no coincidence that the rise in cancer corresponds to the rise of many unnatural chemicals found in our foods today. One topic of concern is the proliferation of pharmacological drugs found in our protein sources today. To stop the spread of disease among cattle, chicken, turkey, and even fish farmed in hatcheries, these animals are given massive amounts of hormones and antibiotics. Although some pass through, many of these chemicals are stored in the animals' muscle tissue, which is then eaten by unsuspecting consumers, whether it's bought in the grocery store or served on a plate in a restaurant. Antibiotics can have an adverse effect on the intestinal flora in your GI tract (killing the much-needed friendly bacteria called acidophilus). A significant decrease in acidophi-

lus lays the groundwork for the yeast infection called *Candida*. *Candida*, it should be noted, is suggested by some to be the underlying cause of fibromyalgia and chronic fatigue syndrome.

8. *Consume a good supply and balance of omega-3s (cold water fish and flaxseed oil) and omega-6s (vegetable oils).* There are two **essential fatty acids** that the body cannot produce and must be consumed from outside sources. Ironically, there is no mention of these two essential fatty acids on the 2010 MyPlate dietary guidelines. Although the merits of omega-3 oils have been known for decades, surprisingly few people are aware that omega-3 is used in the synthesis of prostaglandins, whose primary role is as an anti-inflammatory agent. Long ago, cold-water fish was considered brain food. What was once considered an old wives' tale now turns out to be quite true, because omega-3s are considered an essential aspect of brain tissue (which is composed mostly of fatty tissue). The American diet is heavy in omega-6s and virtually nonexistent in omega-3s. The suggested balance between these two is a ratio of 2:1 (omega-6:omega-3).

9. *Decrease intake of saturated fats (meat and dairy products).* Current research suggests that a diet high in saturated fat is associated with higher levels of cholesterol. But here is another interesting fact: When fats are digested and transported to the liver, they cannot travel via the bloodstream until they get to the liver. Instead, they have to be transported via the lymphatic system. In his book *Spontaneous Healing*, Andrew Weil states that a diet high in fats tends to preoccupy the immune system with energy devoted to this delivery, thus decreasing the efficiency of the immune system. Balance is the key.

10. *Decrease/avoid intake of transfatty acids (partially hydrogenated oils).* Fats that are liquid at room temperature are called lipids. Lipids are prone to becoming rancid when they are subjected to heat and light. Researchers figured out a way to decrease rancidity by changing the molecular structure of lipids to make them solid at room temperature. The process is known as hydrogenation, and today these fats are known as partially hydrogenated oils or transfatty acids. Transfatty acids are anything but natural. The current joke about transfatty acids is that the reason that they prolong shelf life is that bacteria won't go near them. We should be as smart. Trans-fatty acids tend to destroy cell membranes by blocking the gates that allow nutrients to go in and waste products to leave. When cells become toxic, cancer is not far behind. Transfatty acids, found in most baked goods such as cereal, cookies, and tortilla shells, are associated with both coronary heart disease and cancer, and perhaps scores of other diseases we don't know about yet. These act like free radicals and should be avoided at all costs.

11. *Eat a variety of food colors (fruits and vegetables with bioflavonoids).* The Eastern traditions suggest eating foods (fruits and veggies) with a wide variety of colors. Not only does food provide energy, but the colors also provide energy to the body's core energy centers (chakras). Known as the "rainbow diet," food colors are thought to play an important role in the vitality and health of the organs associated with each chakra region: cranberry juice for urinary tract infection, tomatoes for prostate health, bilberries for the eyes, and so on. In the mid to late 1990s, food researchers discovered that **bioflavonoids**, non-nutrients associated with food color, contain an active ingredient to help prevent cancer. The real message here is to eat a good variety of fruits and vegetables (organic whenever possible). Consider Exercise 22.2 as an invitation to evaluate your food color intake.

12. *Consume a good balance of foods with proper pH.* The body's acid/alkaline balance is very delicate. Although it is assumed that by the time food particles have been digested for absorption they do not disturb this balance, this assumption is now being questioned because recent discoveries suggest that cancerous tumors are more likely to grow in an acidic environment. Many processed and pasteurized foods are acidic, thus tipping the scales toward a body more prone to cancer. Proponents of raw foods (fruits and veggies) suggest that this type of diet helps the body regain its balance toward the magic number 7 on the acid/alkaline scale. This might be something to consider for those people who have cancer.

13. *Replenish nutrients consumed by the stress response.* The stress response (fight or flight) demands energy, in the form of both carbohydrates (glucose) and fats (lipids). If you are experiencing chronic stress, more than likely you are using and possibly depleting a host of essential nutrients. A whole series of metabolic reactions that require vitamins and minerals is necessary to have these nutrients available for use. The following are believed to be involved with energy metabolism and thus need to be replaced on a regular basis under stress: B complex vitamins (B_6, B_{12}), vitamin C, magnesium, calcium, chromium, copper, iron, and zinc.

14. *Decrease consumption of simple sugars.* It is believed that the average person consumes 2–3 times his or her body weight in refined sugar each year. Perhaps it's human nature to have a sweet tooth, but as the saying goes, everything in moderation. A diet high in refined sugar sets the stage for many health problems. Aside from overtaxing the pancreas to regulate blood sugar levels with the release of insulin, it is suggested that cancer cells thrive on a high simple-sugar diet. Some reports suggest that refined sugar also decreases white blood cell count. All of this implies that a diet high in refined sugar is a threat to your immune system.

15. *Decrease/avoid "excitotoxins."* As noted in the critically acclaimed book *Excitotoxins*, aspartame (Nutrasweet) and monosodium glutamate (MSG) inhibit brain function by crossing the blood–brain barrier, thus affecting cognitive functions including response time, decision making, attention span, and memory. Pilots for several national airlines are forbidden to drink any beverage or food (even gum) with aspartame. Current research reveals that when not refrigerated, the two amino acids that combine to form this artificial sweetener go through a chemical reaction resulting in the formation of formaldehyde. In laboratory studies, formaldehyde is shown to compromise the integrity of the immune system. MSG is also cited as an excitotoxin. Due to agreements made with the FDA, MSG is not listed on food labels as monosodium glutamate; rather, it is simply listed as "spice." Read the labels and avoid excitotoxins!

16. *Moderate your consumption of alcohol.* A high intake of alcohol (more than two glasses a day) is said to compromise liver and immune function. Current studies reveal that excessive alcohol consumption decreases the efficiency of the immune system, thus making one more vulnerable to the effects of bacteria, viruses, and other pathogens that make their way into the body. Although studies show that red wine can increase levels of HDLs (the good cholesterol) in your blood, moderation is the key to good health.

17. *Prepare food in the best way possible.* Even though you may think you are getting an adequate amount of vitamins and minerals, you may be losing these nutrients depending on how you cook your foods. Many vitamins are destroyed with high amounts of heat, which is why microwave ovens are not recommended. Veggies should be steamed, not cooked in water, because the water-soluble vitamins and minerals are leached out and then thrown down the drain when they are boiled. A new health food trend these days is the raw food diet, which advocates eating vegetables and fruits uncooked so that the full array of vitamins, minerals, and enzymes is available to the human body for absorption.

18. *Eat organic and free range meats whenever possible.* Due to the increasing presence of hormones and antibiotics in beef, chicken, and other animal products it is highly recommended to eat organic and free range animal products. The term *free range* was introduced to convey a sense that animals were free to roam and eat natural vegetation. Check with your butcher, because this is not always the case. With the introduction of mad cow disease and chronic wasting disease in the past few years, eating organic has taken on a whole new importance. Buffalo is a good meat choice, because to date, this is one animal that hasn't been tinkered with.

19. *Avoid* **genetically modified organisms (GMOs**, *also known as Frankenfoods), which are known to promote allergy problems.* For centuries farmers have experimented with plants through grafts and cross-fertilization to come up with new variations of species of plants, from fruits (seedless oranges) to flowers (the variegated tulip). It wasn't until the late 1990s when scientists began to pull genes from one species (e.g., flounder) and place them in the DNA of another (e.g., tomato), hence playing God with our food supply. We now have super tomatoes that can withstand a cold frost. The problem comes when people with an allergy to one food (nuts) find themselves having an acute allergic reaction to food they previously were able to eat (corn) because of genetic engineering. A dramatic rise in food allergies has been linked to a corresponding influx of genetically modified foods. Current estimates suggest that over half of the food bought in your local grocery store is genetically modified, yet due to political pressure by food corporations, you will never see this on a food label. GMOs are a burden to the immune system, which doesn't recognize this unnatural concoction. Allergic reactions are a message from your immune system that something is terribly amiss. Again, organic foods are your safest bet.

20. *Use herbal therapies to boost your immune system.* Long before the Bayer company patented aspirin, herbs were (and in many countries still are) the primary source of healing to bring the body back to a sense of homeostasis. Today pharmaceutical companies are spending millions to replicate the active ingredients of various herbs, yet traditional herbalists will tell you that the best results occur by going directly to the plant itself. If that's not possible, consider tinctures or teas. Herbs and spices that are known to help boost or activate the immune system include astragulus; shiitake, maitake, and rishi mushrooms; tumeric; osho; and echinacea. Milk thistle is also good for helping the liver cleanse toxins from the body, and in this day and age, everyone could use milk thistle. Linda Whitedove is a traditional herbalist in Boulder, Colorado, and a former consultant for Home Grown Herbals. She is the first herbalist hired by her local hospital in the department of integrative medicine to work alongside physicians. As a guest speaker in my nutrition course, Linda had this to say about the connection between herbs and chronic illness: "Not long ago, people used many herbs and spices when preparing foods, such as rosemary, oregano, thyme, coriander, cilantro, and basil. It was the essential oils in these plants that contain many healing properties. Today most people eat out, or eat processed foods. The only natural additive they're getting is sodium and that's not even a spice. My recommendation is to cook more of your own meals and reintroduce the use of more fresh spices."

Best Benefits of Sound Nutritional Habits

After reading this chapter you may wonder if any food is safe to eat. The answer is yes! In today's market, organic foods offer the best source of healthy nutrients for the body. Remember, the body is resilient and desires a state of wholeness. Given the chance, it will do all it can to return to a state of wholeness. This means that you can still enjoy an ice cream cone every now and then. If, however, you or a loved one is diagnosed with a chronic disease, you may wish to pull in the reins and guide your eating habits with several of these suggestions. Here is a final tip to help keep your body in balance: Consider eating one meal a day for your immune system.

Chapter Summary

- This chapter highlights a metaphor of stress dominos: 1) stress depletes nutrients, 2) poor eating habits don't replace needed nutrients, 3) some foods actually trigger the stress response, and 4) many foods negatively impact the immune system.

- Water is an essential nutrient, and one many people don't get enough of.

- Stress can compromise the immune system, as can many foods. However, many foods and specific eating habits can enhance the immune system.

- Consider eating at least one meal a day for your immune system.

Additional Resources

Blaylock, E. *Excitotoxins: The Taste That Kills*. Santa Fe, NM: Health Press; 1994.

Hick, M., & Campbell, C. *Healthy Eating, Healthy Living*. Dallas, TX: Benbella; 2011.

Kessler, D. *The End of Overeating*. New York: Rodale; 2009.

Lyman, H. *The Mad Cowboy*. New York: Scribner; 2001.

Margel, D. *The Nutrient Dense Eating Plan*. Laguna Beach, CA: Basic Health; 2005.

Nestle, M. *What to Eat*. New York: North Point Press; 2007.

Ornish, D. *The Spectrum*. New York: Ballantine; 2008.

Pollan, M. *In Defense of Food*. New York: Penguin; 2008.

Roberts, P. *The End of Food*. New York: Mariner; 2009.

Robins, J. *The Food Revolution*. Berkeley, CA: Conari Press; 2001.

Rountree, R., & Colman, C. *Immunotics*. New York: Putnam; 2000.

Scholsser, E. *Fast Food Nation*. Boston: Houghton Mifflin; 2001.

Simon, C. *Cancer and Nutrition*. Garden City, NY: Avery; 1994.

Somer, E. *Food and Mood*. New York: Henry Holt; 1995.

Teitel, M., & Wilson, K. *Genetically Engineered Food*. Rochester, VT: Park Street Press; 1999.

Weil, A. *Eating Well for Optimal Health*. New York: Knopf; 2000.

Weil, A. *Spontaneous Healing*. New York: Knopf; 1995.

EXERCISE 22.1: Stress-Related Eating Behaviors

Please read the following statements and circle the appropriate answer. Then tally the total to determine your score from the key below.

4 = Always   3 = Often   2 = Sometimes   1 = Rarely   0 = Never

1. I tend to skip breakfast on a regular basis.	4	3	2	1	0
2. On average, two or three meals are prepared outside the home each day.	4	3	2	1	0
3. I drink more than one cup of coffee or tea a day.	4	3	2	1	0
4. I tend to drink more than one soda/pop per day.	4	3	2	1	0
5. I commonly snack between meals.	4	3	2	1	0
6. When in a hurry, I usually eat at "fast-food" places.	4	3	2	1	0
7. I tend to snack while watching television.	4	3	2	1	0
8. I tend to put salt on my food before tasting it.	4	3	2	1	0
9. I drink fewer than eight glasses of water a day.	4	3	2	1	0
10. I tend to satisfy my sweet tooth daily.	4	3	2	1	0
11. When preparing meals at home, I usually don't cook from scratch.	4	3	2	1	0
12. Honestly, my eating habits lean toward fast, junk, processed foods.	4	3	2	1	0
13. I eat fewer than 4–5 servings of fresh vegetables per day.	4	3	2	1	0
14. I drink at least one glass of wine, beer, or alcohol a day.	4	3	2	1	0
15. My meals are eaten sporadically throughout the day rather than at regularly scheduled times.	4	3	2	1	0
16. I don't usually cook with fresh herbs and spices.	4	3	2	1	0
17. I usually don't make a habit of eating organic fruits and veggies.	4	3	2	1	0
18. My biggest meal of the day is usually eaten after 7:00 p.m.	4	3	2	1	0
19. For the most part, my vitamins and minerals come from the foods I eat.	4	3	2	1	0
20. Artificial sweeteners are in many of the foods I eat.	4	3	2	1	0
TOTAL SCORE					

Score: A score of more than 20 points indicates that your eating behaviors are not conducive to reducing stress. A score of more than 30 suggests that your eating habits may seriously compromise the integrity of your immune system.

EXERCISE 22.2: The Rainbow Diet

Food color is more important than just having a nice presentation on your dinner plate. Each color holds a specific vibration in the spectrum of light. When this is combined with the nutrient value of food, it can help to enhance the health of the physical body. In the science of subtle energies, each of the body's primary chakras is associated with a specific color (see chart below). It is thought that eating fruits and vegetables associated with the color of various chakras provides healthy energy to that specific region. For example, women with urinary tract infections (root chakra) are encouraged to drink cranberry juice (red). Diabetics with macular problems are recommended to eat blueberries and take the herb bilberry (blue). Recent research suggests that the active ingredients in fruits and vegetables that give them their color are called bioflavonoids, and these are now thought to help prevent cancer. Even Dr. Oz promotes the rainbow diet. Regardless of Eastern philosophies or Western science, the bottom line is to eat a good variety of fruits and vegetables. The following list identifies the seven chakras, their respective body regions, and the color associated with each chakra/region. List five fruits, veggies, or herbs for each color.

<u>Chakra</u>	<u>Body Region</u>	<u>Color</u>	<u>Food Choices</u>
7. Crown	Pineal	Purple	_____
6. Brow	Pituitary	Indigo	_____
5. Throat	Thymus	Light Blue	_____
4. Heart	Heart	Gree	_____
3. Solar Plexus	Adrenals	Yellow	_____
2. Navel	Spleen	Orange	_____
1. Root	Gonads	Red	_____

Additional Thoughts: _____

_____

_____

_____

Physical Exercise: Flushing Out the Stress Hormones

"How much happiness is gained and how much misery escaped by frequent and challenging exertion of the body."
— Anonymous

The Ageless Wisdom of Physical Exercise

We begin this chapter with a news alert: The health of Americans is in serious decline. We are eating more and exercising less. We are so fixated on computer screens throughout each waking hour of each day that we don't get outside. If we do, it's only where there is WiFi access. Humans have created an information-based society that their bodies cannot adapt to. As a consequence, many Americans (and all those planetary citizens to whom we have exported this lifestyle) are in grave danger of being overweight or obese and contracting a serious chronic disease, creating a lifetime of discomfort combined with emotional and financial hardship. Fact: Human beings were not designed to sit in front of computers or television screens, yet this describes the majority of U.S. citizens today.

The field of exercise physiology is relatively new as an academic discipline when compared to the fields of mathematics and physics, yet the information garnered from over seven decades of research has proven to be invaluable with regard to physical health and longevity. The bottom line is that physical exercise is essential for health and well-being.

In the early 1970s coronary heart disease made headline news as the nation's number one killer. Sadly, more than four decades later, coronary heart disease is still ranked as the number one killer in the United States. At times, it appears that Americans have grown numb to the statistics. Today, exercise formulas can be found on cereal boxes and in infomercials, yet despite the best efforts by health care educators and practitioners, not only has coronary heart disease remained the leading cause of death, but Americans have grown fatter and more sedentary, and have contracted a whole host of chronic diseases that were unknown 30 years ago, such as Epstein-Barr (chronic fatigue syndrome) and fibromyalgia.

What we now know about exercise is that the body needs periodic bouts of physical stress to maintain a proper level of health in every physiological system including the cardiovascular system, the immune system, the nervous system, and the digestive system. Ironically, physical exercise is a form of stress: In no uncertain terms, physical exercise is the fulfillment of the fight or flight response. In the course of exercise, there is an increase in heart rate, blood pressure, respiration, perspiration, and muscle tension. The physical demands for energy metabolism initiate a cascade of hormones and enzymes for energy production.

Physical exercise isn't the fountain of youth, but it does do something that other relaxation techniques don't do as well. Under stress your body produces a flood of stress hormones including cortisol, vasopressin, and aldosterone. Because these same hormones are produced during exercise, they are used for their intended purpose rather than causing ultimate wear and tear on the body. Furthermore, upon the completion of your workout, exercise acts to flush these hormones out of the body. Perhaps the best effect of exercise is what is known as the parasympathetic rebound effect—after exercise, your heart rate, blood pressure, and breathing cycles return to a lower resting rate than before you exercised. In a day and age when physical threats are few and far between, the actual need to run or fight may seem rather antiquated. Nothing could be further from the truth. Mental, emotional, and spiritual stressors have replaced physical stressors, and although you cannot really run away from these problems, cardiovascular exercise has proven to be a valuable means to deal with these kinds of problems as well. Simply by bringing the body back into balance (homeostasis) the other wellness components are positively affected.

Energy Balance

It is hard to walk by the checkout stand at the local grocer and not notice the latest fad diet grabbing the headlines. Low protein, high protein, low carb, low fat, high density, low toxins, low calories—the list is nearly endless. Quite frankly, there is no one diet for everyone, and research reveals that diets have a rather poor success rate. This much we know about diets: To maintain your weight, the number of calories consumed must equal the number of calories expended. Weight loss results from less calories eaten than expended and weight gain results from more calories eaten than burned. This is the science behind what is referred to as **energy balance**. The body in all its amazing wonder and wisdom knows enough to store calories that may be needed later for fight or flight.

The simple truth is that excess carbohydrates that are not broken down into glucose and used for energy are stored as fat (adipose tissue, or what some people refer to as cellulite). Moreover, protein that is not used for refurbishing cell structure and other metabolic demands such as hormone and enzyme synthesis is also stored as fat. Fats and lipids that are not needed for metabolic demands are stored as adipose tissue. Given the "super-size" mentality of our fast-food nation and the sedentary lifestyle of the couch potato culture, it's no wonder that obesity is such a problem. The bottom line is that there is a huge imbalance in the energy balance.

Cortisol and Weight Gain

Is there a connection between chronic stress and obesity? Perhaps. There is new speculation that cortisol, a hormone released from the adrenal gland during the stress response, may be related to the steady accumulation of body fat in one's lifetime. Given the amount of chronic stressors each American has today, and the incredible rate of obesity, there may indeed be a connection. Cortisol is responsible for a number of metabolic activities for fight or flight including ensuring the release of glucose and free fatty acids into the blood for short- and long-term energy. If a person chooses not to fight or flee (anaerobic or aerobic exercise), watching hours of television instead, then the body may redistribute these energy nutrients as adipose tissue (fat). Additional speculation suggests that cortisol may be a principle hormone to regulate appetite under stress, to ensure that there is an adequate supply of both short- and long-term energy. It is well known that stress (acute and chronic) raises blood sugar levels of Type II diabetics, hence making an exercise program all the more important for this target population.

A training program that includes regular cardiovascular exercise helps to ensure that the hormones synthesized and released as a result of chronic stress are used for their intended purpose and then flushed out of the system with other metabolic waste products. Exercise also burns calories, making this a desired health package for everyone. It's no secret that the marketplace is becoming flooded with drugs and herbal products intended to minimize or block the effect of cortisol on appetite and weight gain. However, drugs and supplements can have several side effects, throwing your body's biochemistry out of balance. When performed correctly, the short- and long-term effects of exercise restore balance to mind, body, and spirit with no harmful side effects—and it's free.

The Mind-Body-Spirit Connection

From cereal boxes to infomercials, physical exercise is promoted as the best way to maintain physical fitness. Although this is quite true, there is a whole other side to exercise that receives far less notoriety, yet is equally important: the impact of exercise, specifically cardiovascular exercise, on the mind. Ask anyone who has maintained a cardiovascular fitness program for any length of time and they will tell you that what first began as a fitness regime soon became a mental health program. Rhythmic activities such as running, swimming, walking, or bike riding not only allow for emotional catharsis, but also become a type of meditation. The continuous deep breathing cycle, repetitive physical motion, or perhaps both act as a mantra for increased concentration and awareness, thus giving the mind a sense of peace as well. With greater mental clarity comes greater access to the right brain cognitive skills. Imagination, acceptance, receptivity, intuition, and other right brain functions are highly accessible, making an aerobic activity session truly a holistic modality.

There are even more additional benefits. When the term *runner's high* was first coined, nonrunners thought this was a marketing strategy to win them over. It took science a while to catch up with psychology, but evidence now reveals that the brain produces a series of neurochemicals called neuropeptides that have an opiate-like quality. Beta-endorphin was found to be the primary chemical agent that produced a euphoric sensation when running, swimming, walking, or performing any other activity with the proper intensity, frequency, and duration.

How to Incorporate Physical Exercise into Your Life Routine

In simple terms, there are two types of exercise: anaerobic and aerobic. Although these terms have become household words to some, a quick review is necessary. Anaerobic exercise involves short, intense bursts of energy that typically last no longer than a few minutes, usually less. Because the supply of both blood and oxygen are deficient, muscle contractions are the result of stored energy in the muscle by way of a chemical compound known as adenosine diphosphate (ADP). The word *aerobic* means "in the presence of oxygen," and the energy demands from this type of work require oxygen, delivered by the blood, for muscle contraction. Because the redistribution of blood from the body's core (GI tract) to the periphery (arms and legs) takes about 5 minutes, the first part of an aerobic workout involves some anaerobic work.

Examples of anaerobic work include weight lifting, sprints, and isometric exercises. Aerobic exercise, also referred to as "cardio" exercise, includes jogging, walking, swimming, cycling, spinning, and any other activity where the supply of oxygen meets the demand of the work involved. Using a stress metaphor, anaerobic work is used in the fight response, whereas aerobic work is employed in the flight response.

To incorporate physical exercise into your life routine, begin by setting some reasonable goals for yourself. Do you wish to lose some (fat) weight? Do you wish to lower your resting heart rate and blood pressure? Perhaps you would like to decrease your percentage of body fat and increase some muscle tone, or maybe you wish to celebrate your 30th, 40th, or 50th birthday by deciding to run a 10K road race or marathon. Select a reasonable goal, decide what type of exercise (aerobic or anaerobic) is best suited for this goal, and then begin to map out a workout strategy to help you accomplish this goal. Determine the right components for fitness (read the all-or-none principle below) as well as ways to chart your progress. Remember that some goals may require you to seek a trained professional (e.g., marathon coach). Finally, start small and slow and work your way up to a greater challenge. Ideally, a well-balanced or holistic exercise program includes a combination of both anaerobic work (muscle strength) and aerobic work (cardiovascular endurance). Exercises 23.1 and 23.2 are provided to assist you in putting together a cardiovascular fitness program.

The All-or-None Conditioning Principle

It's no secret that laziness is a force to be reckoned with in the American lifestyle. Given the chance, most people would rather sit and rest than get up and exercise. Mark Twain once said, "When I feel the urge to exercise, I lay down till it goes away." Sadly, his thought on this matter is not unique. Perhaps for this reason, researchers in the field of exercise physiology have studied the dynamics of exercise to determine what is the minimal amount required to gain the coveted health benefits. The dynamics involved include four factors: intensity, frequency, duration of exercise, and mode of exercise. To gain the benefits of exercise, one must employ all of these or receive none of the benefits, hence the name **all-or-none conditioning principle**.

- *Intensity:* Intensity is the challenge placed on the specific physiological system being worked (e.g., cardiovascular, musculoskeletal). Intensity of exercise is typically expressed as one's target heart rate for cardiovascular work (75 percent of one's maximal heart rate) whereas pounds, reps, and sets are used to determine the level of intensity for muscle strength.

- *Frequency:* Frequency is determined by the number of workouts per week. The minimum recommended number of workouts per week is three, with usually a day of rest in between each workout.

- *Duration:* Duration is measured by the amount of time spent exercising. The minimum duration per workout is about 20–30 minutes if you add a 5-minute warm-up and a 5-minute cool down.

- *Mode of exercise:* Different types of exercise are designed to challenge different physiological systems of the body. Weight training will not enhance one's cardiovascular endurance very well, nor will jogging develop muscle strength, although it will help tone muscles. The mode of exercise is specific for the benefits you wish to gain.

Phases of a Workout

Regardless of which mode of exercise you choose to do, experts agree that every workout should follow the progression of these three steps:

1. *Warm-up:* A period of 5–10 minutes where blood flow is allowed to redistribute to the large muscle groups followed by light stretching. When you start breaking a sweat, then a proper warm-up has been achieved.

2. *Stimulus period:* A period of 20 minutes (or more) where the intensity of the activity is reached and maintained for the duration of the exercise period.

3. *Cool down:* A 5–10 minute period of decreased intensity that allows for a gradual shift in the flow of blood from the large muscle groups to the body's core. Most exercise physiologists insist that this is as crucial as the stimulus period, because without a proper cool down, complications may arise with the cardiovascular system.

A Word About Soreness and Injuries

In exercise circles there are two kinds of pain, good pain and bad pain. Good pain (a dull pain) occurs when muscles are sore, but the soreness comes from the lack of use and typically disappears within hours to a day or so. Bad pain (sharp pain) is a sensation generated from the joints and doesn't lessen in a few hours. Sprains, strains, and fractures fall in this category. This type of pain may require medical attention.

Additional Tips for a Successful Exercise Program

- *Start cautiously and progress moderately with your exercise routine.* The biggest problem with exercise programs is when people do too much too soon, resulting in injuries. For this reason, sage advice reminds us to start slow and work our way up to the routine we wish to maintain. Most people begin exercise programs not to keep their heart or bones healthy, but to lose weight. Although this is a great means to lose weight, the simple truth is that pounds don't disappear overnight. The recommended speed of weight loss, so that it stays off, is about 1–2 pounds per week. Typically anything more than this is water loss, which will return with rehydration.

- *Select an activity you really enjoy.* Because obesity is such a concern in the American culture (not to mention coronary heart disease), the focus of attention is on cardiovascular exercise, and for good reason. The good news is that there are many different types of cardiovascular exercise, including walking. It's best to pick an activity that you like or think you like and begin with that. It's also important to have a backup activity in the event that an injury prevents you from continuing or you simply get bored with the sport. Most people quit their exercise programs out of boredom, so variety is also a good aspect to consider.

- *Select a specific time of day to exercise.* A routine is essential for maintaining a healthy exercise program. Selecting a specific time each day to exercise (even if you only do it three times per week) creates healthy boundaries. Some people consider exercise a lower priority than work and hence when work piles up, the workout gets cancelled at a time when it's probably the most important. Establish healthy boundaries with your exercise routine and stick to it.

- *Exercise with the best clothes and equipment.* You don't have to spend a lot of money for exercise equipment (although many people do). Perhaps the most important piece of equipment is a good pair of workout shoes. Although spending $100 on a pair of running shoes may seem outrageous, consider that a pair of good shoes is really an insurance policy against injuries. It's worth the extra money to ensure that you don't get hurt during a workout. If you begin to get sharp joint pain, the first thing to consider is a new pair of exercise shoes.

- *Initiate an exercise support group.* Let's face it, exercise is work and it's easy to quit work when you're working out by yourself. It's harder to back out when you have made a commitment with others to do it together. Working out with a friend makes the time go by quicker, and camaraderie can be a great motivation to stay with your program. If you are having a hard time getting/staying motivated, consider inviting some friends to join you.

- *Set personal fitness goals for yourself.* Even the best exercise routines can become monotonous without a goal to reach for. Some people use road races as personal goals. Others set personal health goals (e.g., lower cholesterol, lower resting heart rate). Having a personal goal serves as great intrinsic motivation to get out of the house when other things seem to distract you from exercising.

- *Care and prevention of injuries.* An injury can become a stressor quite quickly. If you are using exercise to reduce stress, this is the last thing you want to have happen. If you feel joint soreness at any time during an exercise period, this is the time to stop. If you feel a general soreness after a workout (this is to be expected), then give yourself a day's rest before starting back again.

Your Body's Natural Rhythms

Your body runs on a natural clock. Science calls this clock your circadian rhythm, and it has been the topic of much interest over the past 100 years. We know that the body not only craves exercise and relaxation, but also craves a routine schedule. Apparently, changes (big or small) in eating, sleeping, engaging in physical exercise, and other lifestyle habits tend to throw off the body's clock. When the clock is thrown off, our health suffers, sometimes dramatically. Exercise 23.3 invites you to check in with your circadian rhythms to determine whether they promote or detract from your health status.

In the midst of experiencing chronic pain, the last thing you may wish to do is exercise, but in fact, some types of exercise may be the best thing for you. Overtraining in any sport, whether it be running, cycling, or swimming, can lead to an overuse syndrome, which can precipitate chronic joint or muscle pain. Physical exercise can exaggerate a difference in leg length or knee stability issues. One type of exercise that may indeed help chronic pain is Pilates. Developed by Joe Pilates several decades ago as a series of exercises to strengthen the core muscles of the body's frame, Pilates was originally used by dancers and athletes for both prevention and rehabilitation of athletic injuries. Today, like hatha yoga, Pilates classes are commonly taught at fitness clubs and Pilates centers around the country.

Developing Your Mastery of Exercise as a Relaxation Technique

Exercise as a relaxation technique is one of the best ways to bring balance back into your life. Walking is the most underrated activity, and nearly everyone can walk. Any other sports require some skill, yet skills increase with practice. Although the benefits of a single bout of exercise can be felt almost immediately, research shows that it takes about 6–8 weeks to notice more significant changes, such as weight loss, decreased cholesterol, and so on. To really gain the full effects of physical exercise, your exercise routine must be as much a part of your life as taking a shower and brushing your teeth.

Best Benefits of Physical Exercise

If you could take all the benefits of physical exercise and manufacture them in a pill, it would be the most popular pharmaceutical in the world. But you cannot. Our bodies were designed for exercise. They were not designed to sit in front of a computer screen all day or a television all night. Physical exercise is actually good stress for the body; the body requires it to keep things in balance. By not exercising, the cardiovascular system becomes less efficient, bones begin to demineralize, energy balance is compromised, and several other metabolic processes become unbalanced.

The benefits of exercise have to be gained from the actual work of exercise, and exercise is work, but the payoffs are incredible.

Here is a short list of the beneficial effects of regular exercise:

1. Increased immune system function

2. Increased quality of sleep

3. Decreased resting heart rate and blood pressure

4. Increased mental alertness and concentration skills

5. A decrease of the aging process

Chapter Summary

- Physical exercise is stress to the body, but in proper amounts, exercise is good stress that the body needs to maintain a healthy balance for optimal living.

- Physical exercise helps regulate one's energy balance.

- The stress hormone cortisol is associated with weight gain; exercise can help regulate cortisol.

- Exercise may be good for the body, but it's also good for the mind, from helping to induce the "runner's high" to creative problem solving.

- For exercise to be beneficial it must include the right aspects of intensity, frequency, and duration.

- A proper exercise routine must include an adequate warm-up, stimulus period, and cool down period.

■ Your body runs on a 24+ hour clock known as your circadian rhythms. For optimal healthy living, it is suggested to eat, sleep, and exercise at about the same time every day to honor these rhythms.

Additional Resources

Anderson, B. *Stretching* (20th anniv. ed.). Bolinas, CA: Shelter; 2000.

Bingham, J. *No Need for Speed: A Beginner's Guide to the Joy of Running*. Emmaus, PA: Rodale Press; 2002.

Green, B. *Get with the Program*. New York: Simon & Schuster; 2002.

Kowalchik, C. *The Complete Book of Running for Women*. New York: Pocket; 1999.

Meyers, C. *Walking: A Complete Guide to the Complete Exercise*. New York: Ballantine; 1992.

Pelletier, K. *The Best Alternative Medicine: What Works? What Does Not*. New York: Simon & Schuster; 2000.

Ratey, J. *Spark. The Revolutionary New Science of Exercise and the Brain*. New York: Little Brown & Co.; 2008.

Reynolds, G. *The First 20 Minutes: Surprising Science Reveals How We Can: Exercise Better, Train Smarter, Live Longer*. New York: Hudson Street Press; 2012.

EXERCISE 23.1: Determining Your Target Heart Rate

Using the formula below, calculate your estimated target heart rate. Typically, target heart rate is 75 percent of your maximal heart rate. The number 220 is a constant estimate for everyone. If your fitness level is poor, consider an initial target heart rate to be 65 percent. Once you have estimated your target heart rate for your cardiovascular workout, check your heart rate by taking your pulse on the ulna (wrist) or carotid (neck) artery to see if you are within the target range of intensity that will produce the beneficial effects of regular rhythmic exercise.

Predicted Target Heart Rate Formula

220   (constant #)

− _____   (your age)

= _____   (your predicted maximal heart rate)

× .75   (% intensity)

= _____ (your predicted target heart rate for cardiovascular exercise)

(divide by 6 for a 10-second count)

Example

220 − 20 = 200 × .75 = 150 beats/min

divided by 6 = 25 beats for a 10-second count

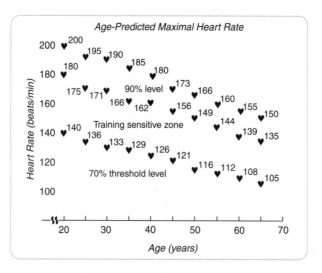

EXERCISE 23.2: Personal Fitness Program Training Log

Week of: _____

Target heart rate: _____

Exercise Schedule	Sun	Mon	Tue	Wed	Thu	Fri	Sat
Date							
Time							
Exercise mode (e.g., cardio, weights, flexibility, stretching)							
Warm-up period (minutes)							
Warm-up exercises							
Intensity (e.g., heart rate)							
Duration of exercise period							
Cool-down period							
Cool-down exercises							
Personal comments							
Other							

EXERCISE 23.3: Your Circadian Rhythms

Your body runs on a 24+ hour clock, based on the earth spinning on its axis around the sun. Research shows that people who keep to a regular schedule tend to be healthier (e.g., fewer colds, flus) than those whose life-style behaviors tend to be more erratic because these tend to stress your body. In this exercise you are asked to monitor your lifestyle behaviors based on the time of day that the following behaviors occur for one full week.

Week of: _____

Circadian Rhythms	Sun	Mon	Tue	Wed	Thu	Fri	Sat
1. Time that you awake each morning							
2. Time that you go to bed							
3. Time that you fall asleep							
4. Time that you eat breakfast							
5. Time that you eat lunch							
6. Time that you eat dinner							
7. Times that you snack							
8. Times of bowel movements							
9. Time that you exercise							
10. Time that you have sex							
11. Other regular activities							

What observations can you make from charting your body functions?

_____

_____

_____

_____

Chapter 24

Additional Relaxation Techniques

"That the birds fly overhead, this you cannot stop. That the birds make a nest in your hair, this you can prevent."

— Ancient Chinese proverb

Tai Chi

There is a life force of subtle energy that surrounds and permeates us all. This energy goes by many names; the Chinese call it *chi*. To move in unison with this energy is to move as freely as running water. A congestion or distortion of one's life energy ultimately leads to disease and illness. Therefore, the goal in life is to be in harmony with the flow of chi, because this promotes tranquility and a sense of being one with the universe. This is the essence of tai chi, a moving meditation that dates back to ancient China and provides a means to create and maintain this harmony and balance with the vital life force of universal energy and the natural world of which we are very much a part.

The words *tai chi* can best be translated to mean the "supreme ultimate," a symbolic representation of balance, power, and enlightenment. Although it is often called the softest of the martial arts, those who study this art form know that above all else, it is a discipline that unites mind, body, and spirit. The art of self-defense comes much later, if at all. Mental, emotional, and spiritual stress can block the flow of chi through the body. It is the progression of moves consciously executed with precision and finesse in the practice of tai chi that works to unblock and regulate the life force of universal energy, hence restoring health. To see tai chi practiced by a master is nothing less than poetry in motion, which is why it is often called a moving meditation. The majority of people who practice tai chi perform it not as a means of self-defense, but rather as an exercise to promote health and vitality.

The underlying premise of tai chi is to learn to move with the flow of energy rather than fight or resist it. In everyday life this philosophy translates to the concept of going with the flow of things you cannot control, rather than wasting or depleting your personal energy. The philosophy of tai chi is based on the Taoist concept of yin/yang, where opposites come together to form a whole (e.g., soft/hard, masculine/feminine, hot/cold). Exercise 24.2 leads you through a pattern of opposites to understand the concept of balance. However, any good tai chi instructor will tell you that the Taoist path is not one of extremes, but rather the middle road where one strives to live in balance and harmony with all aspects of one's life.

To learn this relaxation technique correctly, it is best to find a teacher whose philosophy of tai chi matches yours (e.g., self-defense vs. healthy vitality). Books or videos may serve as a good supplement, but they rarely provide a sound method of quality instruction. As any good tai chi instructor will tell you, once you have learned the sequence of steps, it will take years, if not decades, to fully master them. If you have an interest in or curiosity about this technique, consider checking your yellow page directory, newspaper community listings, or the Internet for classes in your area. When you find a course, ask if you can observe or participate in one class to get a feel for the instructor and decide from there if you wish to continue.

Progressive Muscular Relaxation

Nearly all relaxation techniques, from massage and meditation to yoga and tai chi, trace their origins back to the ancient cultures of Asia. One exception is the technique known as progressive muscular relaxation (PMR), which was created by an American physician several decades ago. As a physician, Edmund Jacobson noted that virtually all his patients who were sick appeared to have one common symptom: muscle tension. So concerned was he about this phenomenon that he decided to create a muscle relaxation technique that would help alleviate tense muscles and possibly restore people to health.

Jacobson designed a systematic approach to reducing muscle tension whereby a person begins at the top of his or her head and isolates a specific muscle group. He or she then begins a process of tensing and relaxing each muscle group, moving from head to toe, so that the individual can recognize the difference between tension and relaxation. By doing so, the desired effect is to be aware of muscle tension that may exist and work to release it through progressive relaxation. Progressive muscular relaxation has proven to be a beneficial technique for people with insomnia, TMJD, and even those who wish to quit smoking. Exercise 24.1 is a modified example of this technique.

Clinical Biofeedback

The mind holds an incredible power to influence the body—in both positive and negative ways. Clinical biofeedback is a technique that enhances the mind's power of healing with the assistance of technology that simply amplifies one or more of the body's physiological parameters so the mind can get a better picture of what is going on inside. Through the wonderful complexities of biochemistry the human body gives off a number of vibrations of electrical impulses. Monitoring various physiological indices such as heart rate, blood pressure, muscle tension, brain waves, body temperature, and blood flow allows technology to mirror specific aspects of human physiology. In doing so, the mind can intercept these stress-prone areas (e.g., muscle tension) and help the body return to a deeper state of homeostasis.

Through the use of electrodes, transducers, a television monitor, and a certified biofeedback specialist, an individual is taught to observe an aspect or area of his or her body and then, through self-regulation, consciously decrease activity in this area with the help of the television monitor (or stereo speakers).

Clinical biofeedback has been very instrumental in helping people treat and heal a range of physical problems caused by stress, such as tension headaches, migraine headaches, lower back pain, TMJD, hypertension, Raynaud's disease, and many, many others. For this reason it is regarded as one of the premier modalities of complementary medicine. If this is something you wish to explore, consider locating a certified biofeedback specialist in your area.

Chapter Summary

- Tai chi is known as a moving meditation, a simple exercise to help regulate the flow of chi through your body. The practice of tai chi is a metaphor to "go with the flow."

- Progressive muscular relaxation is a technique to help reduce muscular tension by learning (and practicing) the regulation of muscle tension throughout the body.

- Clinical biofeedback is a relaxation technique in which a person uses a machine to amplify one or more body functions (e.g., heart rate, temperature, muscle tension) and learns to control these for optimal relaxation.

Additional Resources

Chen, T. *Step-by-Step Tai Chi with Tiffany Chen* (DVD). West Chester, OH. Acacia. 2008.

Freeze-Frames (a biofeedback program). The HeartMath Institute. Boulder Creek, CA. www.heartmath.org.

Huang, A. *Complete Tai Chi*. Boston: Tuttle; 1993.

The Journey to the Wild Divine: The Passage (a biofeedback video game). The Wild Divine Project. 1.866.594.WILD, www.wilddivine.com.

EXERCISE 24.1: Progressive Muscular Relaxation

The following is a slight variation of Jacobson's original technique, which divides muscle contractions into three intensities—100, 50, and 5 percent—for 5 seconds' duration, followed by the relaxation phase of 5–10 seconds' duration after each contraction. By sensing the differences between muscle contraction intensities, you become more aware of your muscle-tension levels over the course of a day. The instructions below were written to be read yourself before you perform the technique, or to be read out loud by a friend or colleague. Included here are three muscle groups (the face, neck and shoulders, and hands); however, you can expand this to include your abdominal area, upper legs, buttocks, calf muscles, and feet as well. Before you begin, find a comfortable position (preferably on your back on a carpeted floor); loosen any restrictive clothing; kick off your shoes; take several slow, comfortable, deep breaths; and simply begin to unwind in the starting position.

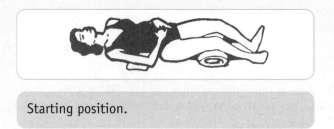

Starting position.

1. *Face.* Tense the muscles of the forehead and eyes, as if you were pulling all your facial muscles to the center of your nose. Pull really tight, as tight as you can, and hold it. Feel the tension you create in these muscles, especially the forehead and eyes. Now relax and exhale. Feel the absence of tension in these muscles, how loose and calm they feel. Try to compare this feeling of relaxation with the tension just produced. Now, contract the same muscles, but this time at 50 percent of the intensity, and hold it. Then relax and exhale. Feel how relaxed those muscles are. Compare this feeling to that during the last contraction. This comparison should make the muscles even more relaxed. Finally, contract the same facial muscles slightly, at only 5 percent intensity. This is like feeling a slight warm breeze on your forehead and cheeks. Hold it. And relax. Take a comfortably slow and deep breath and, as you exhale, feel how relaxed the muscles are.

EXERCISE 24.1: Progressive Muscular Relaxation cont....

2. *Shoulders.* Concentrate on the muscles of your shoulders and isolate these from surrounding neck and upper arm muscles. Take a moment to sense the muscles of the deltoid region. Notice any degree of residual tension. (The shoulder muscles can also harbor a lot of undetected muscle tension, resulting in stiffness. Quite literally, your shoulders carry the weight of all your thoughts, the weight of your world.) Now consciously tense the muscles of your shoulders really tight, as tight as you can, and hold it, even tighter, and hold it. Now relax these muscles and feel the tension disappear completely. Sense the difference between how these muscles feel now and how they felt during contraction. Once again, contract these same muscles, but this time at half the intensity. Hold the tension, keep holding; and now completely relax these muscles. Sense how relaxed your shoulder muscles are. Compare this feeling with what you felt at 100 percent intensity. Finally, contract these same muscles at only 5 percent, only just sensing clothing touching your shoulder muscles. Hold it, keep holding, and relax. Release any remaining tension so that these muscles are completely loose and relaxed. Feel just how relaxed these muscles are. To enhance this feeling of relaxation, take a comfortably slow, deep breath and sense how relaxed your shoulder muscles have become.

3. *Hands and forearms.* Concentrate on the muscles of your hands and forearms. Take a moment to feel these muscles, including your fingers, palms, and wrists. Notice the slightest bit of tension. Now consciously tense the muscles of each hand and forearm really tight by making a fist, as tight as you can, and hold it as if you were hanging on for dear life. Make it even tighter, and hold it. Now release the tension and relax these muscles. Feel the tension disappear completely. Open the palm of each hand slowly, extend your fingers, and let them recoil just a bit. Sense the difference between how relaxed these muscles feel now compared with what you just experienced at 100 percent contraction. They should feel very relaxed. Now contract these same muscles at a 50 percent contraction. Hold the tension, keep holding, and relax again. Sense how relaxed these muscles are. Compare this feeling of relaxation with what you just felt. Now, contract these same muscles at only 5 percent, like holding an empty eggshell in the palm of your hand. Now hold it, keep holding, and relax. Release any remaining tension so that these muscles are completely relaxed. Feel just how relaxed these muscles have become. To enhance this feeling of relaxation, take a comfortably slow, deep breath and sense how relaxed your forearm and hand muscles have become.

When you are done, lie comfortably for several moments and sense how your body feels. Take several slow, deep breaths and begin to retain this feeling of deep relaxation all throughout your body. When you feel ready, slowly make yourself aware of your surroundings. Then open your eyes to a soft gaze in front of you. If you wish you can begin to stretch your arms and hands. When you feel ready, sit up and bring yourself back to the full awareness of the room where you find yourself.

EXERCISE 24.2: The Yin/Yang of Life

Tai chi is based on the Taoist concept of seeking balance and going with the flow. The yin/yang symbol represents the balance of life where two opposite aspects come together, not in opposition but in union of the totality of the whole. The yin/yang symbol represents the balance of life.

1. Take a moment to fill in the blanks of the table below

Yin	Yang
_____	heaven
moon	_____
autumn, winter	_____
_____	masculine aspects
cold, coolness	_____
_____	brightness
inside, interior	_____
_____	things large and powerful
_____	the upper part
water, rain	_____
_____	movement
night	_____
_____	the left side
the west and north	_____
_____	the back of the body
exhaustion	_____
_____	clarity
development	_____
conservation	_____
_____	aggressiveness
contraction	_____

EXERCISE 24.2: The Yin/Yang of Life cont....

2. Assuming you have tried or currently practice the art of tai chi, please describe your impressions of this type of exercise as a means to promote relaxation.

_____

3. How do you see the effects (philosophy) of tai chi carrying over into other aspects of your life?

_____

_____

_____

4. The concept of balance is crucial to life, yet in this 24/7 society, balance seems to be a rare commodity. List five things you can do to bring balance to your life.

a. _____

b. _____

c. _____

d. _____

e. _____

5. Please share any other comments regarding tai chi here:

_____

_____

_____

Part 4

Designing Your Personal Relaxation Program

Chapter 25

Designing Your Personal Relaxation Program

"To know and not to do, is not to know!"
— Anonymous

There is an old joke shared among behavioral psychologists that goes like this: "How many psychologists does it take to change a light bulb?" Answer: "One, but the light bulb really has to want to change." Making changes in our lives, whether they be small corrections or a complete about-face, requires more than just an exposure to the concepts—it requires a burning desire and steady discipline, so that the changes become permanent and not just a passing fancy. Experts who study behavioral change note that although people may want an immediate complete makeover, changes that really last begin one habit at a time, until it is fully mastered and incorporated into one's daily routine. This approach may take a little longer, yet the results are more successful because they become a part of who you are.

By now, you most likely have a pretty good idea of what aspects of your life need fine-tuning to bring you back to a place of balance. Although you may have already started on some aspects of reducing stress in your life and working to resolve issues that trigger feelings of anger or fear, it's always a good idea to look at the bigger picture. Exercise 25.1, "Mandala for Personal Health," invites you to organize your stress relief habits so that all aspects—mind, body, spirit, and emotions—are equally addressed in your strategy to maintain personal balance and optimal well-being.

Additional Resources

American Holistic Medical Association. www.holisticmedicine.org.
American Holistic Nurses Association. www.ahna.org.
Institute of Noetic Sciences. www.noetic.org.
National Wellness Institute. www.nationalwellness.org.
The Omega Institute. www.eomega.org.

Energy Healing

Eden, D. Energy Healing. Innersource. 1.800.835.8332
Hurwitz, W., MD. Medical Intuitive. 212.877.2031
Wirkus, M., & Wirkus, M. BioEnergy Healers. 303.652.1691

EXERCISE 25.1: Mandala for Personal Health: Your Holistic Stress Management Strategy

This mandala exercise invites you to use this symbol of wholeness as both a reminder of your true self and a compass to help get you there, should you lose your way in the course of daily events or circumstances that tend to cloud your vision and perspective. Using the mandala below, first write your name in the center. Next, keeping in mind that many activities cross the lines between these quadrants, write in each respective quadrant your ideas, skills, techniques, exercises, and habits that allow you to achieve inner peace through the integration, balance, and harmony of mind, body, spirit, and emotions. For example, let's take the quadrant for physical well-being. You might consider writing down ideas for your personal exercise program, new or improved eating habits, sleep habits, perhaps even acupuncture and a massage. List those things that you either currently do or wish to include in your life routine. When you finish, place the mandala somewhere you can see it regularly, to serve as a reminder to guide you to your optimal health potential. You may also consider doing a larger version by cutting out color photographs and words from magazines to bring this mandala to a whole new level.

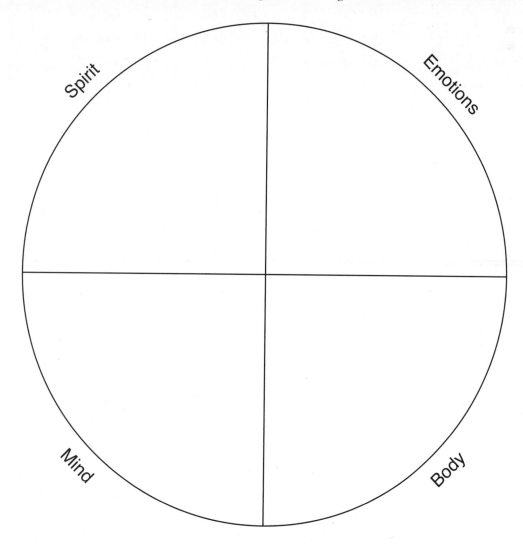

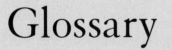

Glossary

Absurd/nonsense humor: This type of humor is best exemplified by Gary Larson's *The Far Side*, and all the many cartoonists who have followed in his footsteps. The humor of comedian Steven Wright also is a prime example.

Acute stress: Distress that is very intense (pounding heartbeat) but short-lived, usually about 15–20 minutes.

Agnostic: Individuals who do not know if there is a higher source.

Alarm reaction: Considered to be the first stage of the general adaptation syndrome, when stimuli are recognized as a threat and the body goes into fight-or-flight mode.

All-or-none conditioning principle: A concept that says one needs the right intensity, frequency, and duration to produce the benefits of exercise, such as muscle toning, oxygen uptake, and weight loss.

Alternative (complementary) medicine: Encompasses over 600 healing modalities, ranging from acupuncture to zero balancing. Every healing modality is geared to promote homeostasis among mind, body, and spirit. Every technique for stress management falls into this category.

Aromatherapy: A collection of fragrances, such as lavender and vanilla, that are used to promote relaxation.

Art of subtraction: An expression created by the author to help the reader put into play a behavior that begins to eliminate responsibilities, things, and even relationships rather than accumulate them.

Art therapy: A nonverbal coping technique that helps the individual access insights and information from the unconscious to help increase awareness of various life aspects. Art therapy also is a powerful means of catharsis.

Artist, the: Von Oech's second phase of the creative process, wherein the person plays with the raw materials brought back from the explorer's journey.

Assertiveness: The ability to have and hold healthy boundaries. People who are not assertive tend to feel like victims.

Atheist: Individuals who do not believe in a higher source.

Autogenic training: Giving oneself a series of suggestions to promote relaxation by focusing on a specific body part (e.g., hands, arms, legs). Typically the suggestion relates to warmth and heaviness of the specified area, which promotes a deeper sense of relaxation.

Autoimmune diseases: Diseases that occur due to an overactive immune system that "attacks" the body. Examples include lupus and rheumatoid arthritis.

Bathroom humor: Often described as vulgar, crude, and tasteless, bathroom humor gets its name from the use of various body functions known to occur in the privacy of the bathroom. Examples of bathroom humor are found in movies such as *Borat, Dumb and Dumber,* and *Bridesmaids.*

Belly breathing: Please see *diaphragmatic breathing.*

Bioecological influences: Factors that may induce stress in the mind, body, or spirit. Examples might include solar flares, seasonal changes, and weather influences.

Bioflavinoids: Nonnutrients found in foods (fruits and vegetables) that contain antioxidants and seem to provide a means to fight cancer and other illnesses. Bioflavinoids provide the colors in foods.

Black humor: Not ethnic humor, but humor about death. Also called gallows humor, black humor is often described as a flirtatious brush with death.

Calculated risk taker (Sensation Seeker): Also called the Type R personality, these people do things to the extreme (e.g., sports). They look at all of their options carefully and then proceed forward.

Calculated risks: One of five characteristics used to promote self-esteem; this characteristic highlights the need for critical thinking combined with assertiveness to achieve personal goals.

Campbell, Joseph: Renowned mythologist credited with coining the term *the hero's journey* and discovering the importance of reacquainting ourselves with the works of mythology as a compass for our lives.

Cannon, Walter: Renowned Harvard physiologist who coined the term *fight or flight.*

Centering process (autumn): A time to go inside and do some serious soul searching, cultivating one's internal relationship.

Chakras: The word *chakra* (pronounced SHOCK-ra) is a Sanskrit word meaning spinning wheel. There are thought to be seven primary chakras located from the crown of the head to the base of the spine, each associated with an endocrine gland or region of the body.

Chronic pain: Neural pain typically generated from muscles, joints, bones, or fascia that robs your attention from everything else because you can focus only on the pain, which lingers for weeks, months, or years.

Chronic stress: Distress that is not as intense as acute stress, but lasts a long time—days, weeks, months, or even years.

Circadian rhythms: The biological rhythms in your body based on the internal 24–25 hour clock that the body runs on. Sleep cycles and eating cycles are based on circadian rhythms.

Codependent personality: Based in the drug and alcohol recovery movement with ties to the enabler, the codependent traits include perfectionism, approval seeking, and victimization, all of which perpetuate the stress process.

Cognitive distortion: In simplest terms, this expression says it all: Making a mountain out of a molehill.

Connectedness: One of five characteristics used to promote self-esteem with an emphasis on support groups—those people to whom we feel connected.

Connecting process (summer): A realization that we are all connected and the connection is made and nurtured through love.

Cortisol: The stress hormone produced in the adrenal gland that is responsible for many metabolic functions related to blood sugar and triglyceride levels in the blood.

Creative blocks: A host of ego-driven attitudes and perceptions that limit one's creative abilities.

Creative problem solving: A term that highlights five steps for creative strategies to solve problems, issues, and concerns. The steps begin with identifying the problem and conclude with an analysis of the solution.

Creative process, the: There are four phases to the creative process and they must be followed in this order to see the best results: the explorer, the artist, the judge, and the warrior.

Daily life hassles: A term coined by Richard Lazarus to depict the small stressors that tend to add up over the course of a day or two. Unlike chronic stressors that last weeks or months, daily life hassles are little events (like locking your keys in your car) that, when combined with many other little hassles in the course of a day, create a critical mass of stress.

Defense mechanisms: A series of thoughts and behaviors created and used by the ego to protect itself from pain and to promote pleasure. Examples include rationalization, denial, and projection.

Depression: A period of pronounced unhappiness, as if a cloud of darkness looms overhead. From a holistic perspective, depression is thought to be directly tied to anger issues (depression is anger turned inward). The mechanistic paradigm insists that depression is a chemical imbalance.

Descartes, René: A 17th-century scientist/philosopher who is credited with the reductionist method of Western science (also known as the Cartesian principle). Descartes is equally renowned for his influential philosophy of the separation of mind and body as well as the quote, "I think therefore I am."

Diaphragmatic breathing: Also called belly breathing or abdominal breathing, this popular relaxation technique invites the individual to place the emphasis of breathing on one's stomach area rather than the upper chest.

Distress: The unfavorable or negative interpretation of an event to be threatening that promotes continued feelings of fear or anger. Distress is more commonly known simply as stress: a perceived threat (real or imagined) to one's mind, body, spirit, or emotions.

Divine mystery: Sometimes called the fourth pillar of human spirituality, the divine mystery is the culmination of all things that cannot be explained by the Cartesian model of reality, yet certainly exist through personal experience. Examples might include apparitions of the Virgin Mary, crop circles, stigmata, and spontaneous healings.

Divinity theory: Most theologians think that humor is a gift from God, hence this theory. The origin of the clown is said to be from healers and shamans doing God's work.

Double entendre: A joke that has two meanings, with one usually of a sexual nature, but not always. Disney cartoons are filled with humor for kids and adults, often using the same joke.

Dream therapy: The ability to remember and record one's dreams, which contain a wealth of information from the unconscious mind, that in turn helps one navigate the course of daily events. As a coping technique, dream therapy is particularly helpful with stressful recurring dreams.

Dry humor and puns: Perhaps the opposite of quick-witted humor, puns are based on word play that often gets a groan rather than a laugh, though some people really like these.

Effective coping skills: These include any and all coping skills that help one increase awareness of a problem and/or help resolve an issue. Alcoholism may be a coping technique, but it's not an effective one. Reframing, time management, art therapy, journaling, and creative problem solving are all examples of effective coping skills.

Ego: A term coined by Freud naming the part of the psyche that not only triggers the stress response when threatened, but also defends against all enemies (defense mechanisms) including thoughts and feelings generated from within.

Einstein, Albert: World-renowned theoretical physicist who revolutionized perceptions of reality with the equation $E = MC^2$, suggesting that everything is energy. His later years focused on a spiritual philosophy including pacifism.

Emotional well-being: The ability to feel and express the entire range of human emotions, but to control them, not be controlled by them.

Empowerment: One of five characteristics used to promote self-esteem, highlighting aspects that make you feel special and outstanding.

Emptying process (winter): Also known as the dark night of the soul and the winter of discontent, the emptying process is a time to release, detach, and let go of thoughts, attitudes, perceptions, and beliefs that no longer serve you.

Energy balance: The difference between calories consumed (meals and snacks eaten) and calories burned (exercise and basal metabolic rate).

Energy psychology: Describes how subtle energy (chakras, meridians, and the human energy field) and subtle anatomy combine with consciousness to either enhance or detract from one's health.

Energy work: Encompasses a wide array of healing modalities. Various forms of energy work include, but are not limited to, healing touch, therapeutic touch, Reiki, bio-energy, acupuncture, acupressure, music therapy, zero balancing, and even pet therapy. In essence, all forms of therapy and relaxation involve some aspect of energy and entrainment.

Entrainment: A term from the field of physics that is used to explain the behavior of energy. Entrainment is the mutual phase locking of vibrations, allowing the object of lesser (weaker) vibration to match the object of greater (stronger) vibration. Entrainment is thought to be the primary reason why we find music to be relaxing.

Essential fatty acids: Fatty acids that the body cannot produce and hence that must be consumed from outside sources. Omega-3 (linolenic) acids can be found in flaxseed oil and cold-water fish. Omega-6 (linoleic) acids can be found in various vegetable oils.

Eustress: A sense of happiness or euphoria. Eustress is considered to be "good" stress. Abraham Maslow called this a peak experience. Examples include falling in love or meeting a movie star or sports hero.

Excitotoxins: A name coined by the brain surgeon Russell Blaylock specifically identifying aspartame and MSG as chemical substances that affect brain function because they cross the blood–brain barrier and cause headaches, memory loss, and impaired cognitive function.

Exclusive meditation: The ability and practice of focusing all of your thoughts on one aspect (e.g., a mantra) to the exclusion of all other thoughts. Transcendental Meditation (TM) is an example.

Execution (action plan): A term in time management referring to when personal responsibilities are executed or carried out to personal satisfaction.

Exploder: The exploder erupts like a volcano, spewing the hot lava of intimidation to control others. This type of mismanaged anger style tends to make the news headlines. Road rage is perhaps the most common example of this style.

Explorer, the: The first stage of von Oech's creative process, wherein the person goes out and looks for ideas. The explorer is someone who learns to think outside the box.

Fight-or-flight response: The body's natural response to stress, activated by a perceived threat that cascades from the brain to the adrenal glands for quick movement that allows one to survive.

Forgiveness: A coping technique that assists one in learning to let go of feelings of anger and animosity toward others whom we feel have violated us.

Freud, Sigmund: Considered the pioneer in the emerging field of psychology, laying the groundwork 100 years ago that is still considered to be the cornerstone of psychology. Freud coined the terms *ego*, *defense mechanisms*, and many others, forming the basis of contemporary psychology with a strong focus on anxiety (stress).

General adaptation syndrome (GAS): A term coined by renowned stress researcher Hans Selye, describing the three phases in which stress takes its toll on the body.

Genetically modified organisms (GMOs): Food that has been genetically altered by splicing DNA from other species (e.g., the gene of a flounder fish into tomatoes). GMOs are related to many food allergies and are considered to be a stress to the body.

Grounding process (spring): Once room has been made from the emptying process, new insights may be revealed to assist a person to move from point A to point B. The grounding process is the vision of the vision quest.

Hardy personality: Three traits comprise the hardy personality: challenge, control, and commitment, all of which combine to help this type of person to overcome any adversity.

Hatha yoga: A relaxation technique that offers balance (union) between mind and body. More than simple flexibility exercises, hatha yoga is a progression of conscious movements in combination with one's breath designed to discipline the mind and ego.

Healthy boundaries: A term used to describe appropriate behavior for a less stressful lifestyle. Examples include no smartphones in movie theaters and not watching television during weeknights (or at all).

Healthy emotions: Healthy emotions are commonly thought of as joy and happiness, but all emotions are healthy when expressed correctly.

Helpless-hopeless: A stress-prone personality type developed from repeated failures and misfortune (e.g., child abuse, sexual abuse, spousal abuse, destitution).

Hero's journey: A term coined by mythologist Joseph Campbell outlining the classic template of the human journey with three stages: departure, initiation, and return.

Hobbies: Interests outside one's professional life that serve as a healthy distraction from the stress of daily responsibilities. Making order out of chaos seems to have a transfer effect from one's personal to professional life.

Holistic medicine: A healing approach that honors the integration, balance, and harmony of mind, body, spirit, and emotions to promote inner peace. Every technique used in stress management is considered to support the concept of holistic medicine. Also called alternative medicine.

Homeostasis: A term coined by Claude Bernard to represent the body's condition at complete rest.

Human energy field: Also known as the electromagnetic field around an object and as a colorful aura. The human energy field is thought to be composed of layers of consciousness that surround and permeate the physical body.

Humor therapy (comic relief): The ability to use humor and laughter to even out the emotions and bring some joy and happiness back into one's life.

Hydrotherapy: The use of hot tubs, Jacuzzis, and flotation tanks to promote relaxation.

Immune system–related disorders: Health issues that arise from either an underactive (e.g., colds, flus, cancer) or overactive immune system (e.g., lupus, rheumatoid arthritis), each of which is affected by stress.

Inclusive meditation: The ability and practice of observing all of your thoughts without any emotional attachment. Zen meditation serves as an example.

Incongruity theory: A theory that states the reason we laugh is because when two concepts come together in our head and they don't make sense, we get a chuckle.

Insightful meditation: When done properly, all forms of meditation (inclusive and exclusive) offer insights that might not normally be detected when the ego is dominating the mind.

Irrational fears: An overwhelming feeling of anxiety based on a false perception (making a mountain out of a molehill).

Journaling: A coping technique that allows the individual to review and explore thoughts, attitudes, beliefs, and behaviors that contribute to personal stress. Short-term benefits include a cathartic release of emotions; long-term effects include insights and analysis of personal growth.

Judge, the: Von Oech identifies the role of the judge as the third stage of the creative process, but one people typically place first, thus compromising the entire process.

Jung, Carl: Twentieth-century physician who, under the initial tutelage of Sigmund Freud, forged a new premise of psychology honoring the importance of the human spirit, becoming the second greatest influence in the field of psychology.

Lazarus, Richard: A renowned psychologist who coined the term *daily life hassles*.

Life-change units: A unit of stress as determined by the number of stressful life episodes one has had at a certain point in one's life.

Massage therapy: The manipulation of muscle tissue and fascia to relieve soreness and tension. Also called bodywork, massage relieves the number one symptom of stress: muscle tension.

Mechanistic model: A theory that suggests that just as the universe operates like a big grandfather clock, so, too, does the body. This model denies the existence of the human spirit.

Meditation: An ageless technique for both mental and physical relaxation. Meditation is best defined as an increased concentration that leads to increased awareness. In essence, meditation is the ability to quiet the mind by domesticating the ego. There are hundreds of ways to meditate but they generally fall into one of three categories: exclusive, inclusive, and mindfulness.

Mental imagery: A series of images that bubble up from the unconscious mind with neither intent nor ego censorship. Often used as a healing modality with cancer patients and people with chronic diseases.

Mental well-being: The ability to gather, process, recall, and communicate information. Also called intellectual well-being.

Meridians: First described by Chinese medicine, a meridian is a river of energy that runs through the body. Humans have 12 major meridians, and each meridian has a pulse. Blocks or congestion at any point in the meridian are typically addressed using an acupuncture needle (or shiatsu).

Mindfulness meditation: Being fully present (mindful) of all of one's actions. An example would include being mindful of eating an apple. Some people see mindfulness as an extension of inclusive meditation.

Mismanaged anger styles: There are four styles of mismanaged anger: the somatizer, the exploder, the self-punisher, and the underhander. Each style is a method of control; however, by maintaining this anger style one really gives one's power away.

Muscles of the soul: This term encompasses a host of inner resources that help one deal with obstacles in one's life. They include, but are not limited to, humor, optimism, patience, curiosity, faith, humbleness, and persistence.

Music therapy: Using music to promote relaxation. This can be done in several ways, including listening to music (preferably instrumental music), playing an instrument, or even singing.

Nervous system–related disorders: Stress-related physical symptoms initiated by an overactive nervous system. These include, but are not limited to, headaches, irritable bowel syndrome, and hypertension.

Neuropeptides: Chemical compounds (perhaps as many as 600) not only secreted in the brain, but also now known to be manufactured by cells throughout the body. These chemicals have the unique ability to communicate to each other in a fashion not yet understood by Western science.

Neustress: Any kind of information or sensory stimulus that is perceived as unimportant or nonconsequential.

Newton, Isaac: A preeminent scientist and scholar greatly influenced by René Descartes who was instrumental in championing the mechanistic model of reality.

Organic foods: Foods that are certified to be grown in clean soil with no use of herbicides, pesticides, fungicides, or synthetic fertilizers.

Paradigm shift: A change of perception in how one sees or views the world. An example would be shifting from a mechanistic model of reality to a holistic model of reality.

Parody: A style of humor where something is made fun of. Self-parody is thought to be the best type of humor to reduce stress (as long as it doesn't bash one's self-esteem).

Pet therapy: Because most people touch (pet) their pets, pet therapy often falls in the category of massage work. People who own pets tend to be healthier than those who don't.

Physical exercise: Either aerobic (with the use of oxygen) or anaerobic (without the use of oxygen) work that develops the cardiovascular and musculoskeletal systems, respectively.

Physical well-being: The best or optimal functioning of all the body's physiological systems (e.g., cardiovascular, immune, musculoskeletal, endocrine, nervous, reproductive, digestive, pulmonary systems).

Positive affirmations: The ability to give oneself positive feedback in the midst of a bad situation so that one does not get sucked into the vortex of negativity. Positive affirmation is not a denial of a bad situation; rather, it is the ability to rise above it.

Prayer: A coping technique that invites help from a higher source (whatever you choose to call this) for guidance and assistance in daily situations.

Prioritization: A concept applied to first identifying and then ordering personal responsibilities.

Psychointrapersonal influences: Stressors that originate in the mind, either real or imagined. These are usually the result of ego-driven issues.

Psychoneuroimmunology (PNI): A term coined by Dr. Robert Ader in the 1970s to suggest that the brain, nervous system, and immune system collaborate or conspire against one's health.

Qi gong: A form of Chinese energy exercise and energy healing, where qi or chi is directed through the body as a means of balancing one's energy. Qi gong healing may involve a qi gong healer to facilitate the energy healing process.

Quick-witted humor: A style of humor that is based on a quick wit without using sarcasm. Quick-witted humor often involves clever wording or phrasing that catches you a bit off guard and leaves you impressed.

Examples include the works of Mark Twain and NPR's *Car Talk* radio show.

Reflexology: Not merely a foot massage, reflexology dates back to ancient Egypt as a means of promoting relaxation to the whole body, which is mapped out on the soles of the feet. Massaging the feet becomes a means to work on all aspects of the body.

Reframing: The ability to change one's perception from a negative to a more positive approach. Some would add it includes seeing the benefit from a bad situation.

Relaxation survival kit: A relaxation technique in which an individual collects various items that help promote relaxation through the five senses. Examples include chocolate/taste, Mozart/sound, bubble wrap/touch, and hand lotion/smell.

Release/relief theory: Freud's theory of laughter is based on his concept that all laughter is the result of suppressed sexual desire, expressed through laughter to release sexual tension.

Role models: One of five characteristics used to promote self-esteem including mentors and heroes who are looked up to for their accomplishments and the attributes that helped them achieve them.

Rolfing/structural integration: Also known as deep tissue work, this form of bodywork focuses primarily on the fascia that holds muscles in place. By working at this level, the spine becomes realigned.

Sarcasm: Thought to be the lowest form of humor, the word *sarcasm* means to tear flesh. Because sarcasm is a latent form of anger, it promotes rather than reduces stress. Avoid this type of humor at all costs!

Satire: Satire is said to be a written form of parody; however, satire can also be acted out. Examples include the works of Art Buchwald and George Carlin, the movie *Shrek*, and many skits on *Saturday Night Live*.

Scheduling: A term in time management to signify the coordination of personal responsibilities with the allocation of time in the course of each day.

Seasonal affective disorder (SAD): A condition brought on by the lack of direct sunlight (usually during the winter months) that affects one's production of melatonin and hence serotonin, resulting in symptoms of depression.

Seasons of the soul: There are four seasons of the soul: the centering process, the emptying process, the grounding process, and the connecting process.

Self-esteem: A personal perception of how highly you value yourself. People with high self-esteem tend to have little stress, because they let things roll off their back. People with low self-esteem appear to have lots of stress, feeling like a passive victim in a cruel world. Lance Armstrong is someone with high self-esteem.

Self-healing: The body's unique ability to restore a sense of homeostasis when not interrupted by stress, poor nutrition, and the like. An example is a fever, which is the body's way to kill off invading microbes.

Self-hypnosis: The ability to calm oneself with suggestions of relaxation. All forms of relaxation involve some sense of self-hypnosis; autogenic training would be at the top of this list.

Self-punisher: This style of mismanaged anger is where a person feels guilty for feeling angry and adopts one or more obsessive-compulsive behaviors, from excess eating, sleeping, and exercise to self-mutilation.

Self-talk: The perpetual conversation that occurs in the mind. Self-talk can be either directed by the ego and become self-defeating or directed by the conscience to build greater confidence and potential in one's life.

Shiatsu: Also called acupressure. The massage therapist places pressure on various meridian points to release the blockage of energy that in turn produces tension.

Slapstick: Also called a physical farce, slapstick humor comes to us from vaudeville. Getting a pie thrown in the face or slipping on a banana peel are examples of slapstick humor.

Social influences: Stressors generated from external sources such as traffic, urban sprawl, and ex-spouses.

Social orchestration: A coping strategy in which a person begins to rearrange his or her daily/weekly schedule to accommodate urgent responsibilities and daily interruptions so that stress is minimized. Often called the path of least resistance. Social orchestration is considered by some an aspect of time management.

Social Readjustment Rating Scale (SRRS): A scale developed by Holms and Raye using life-change units to determine one's level of stress.

Somatizer: A mismanaged style of anger whereby anger is not expressed; rather, it is suppressed. The result is damage to the body (*soma* means body). Examples include TMJD, lupus, rheumatoid arthritis, and migraine headaches.

Spiritual health: This term, coined by the author, represents the ability to put the muscles of the soul in play. Spiritual health is the cultivation and utilization of our inner resources to overcome any and all obstacles on the spiritual path.

Spiritual hunger: A term to illustrate the quest for understanding of life's biggest questions and of the bigger picture and how each of us fits into it.

Spiritual materialism: An ego-based behavior of people who pride themselves on attending countless spiritual retreats, workshops, or pilgrimages to distant holy lands, even yoga workouts on the path toward spiritual enlightenment.

Spiritual potential: A term coined by the author to explain the cadre of inner resources used to dismantle roadblocks on the spiritual path. Also called muscles of the soul, these inner resources include, but are not limited to, humor, faith, optimism, compassion, courage, patience, and forgiveness. The potential to use these muscles resides within all of us.

Spiritual well-being: The maturation of higher consciousness as developed through the integration of three facets: relationships, values, and a meaningful purpose in one's life. A fourth facet is the acknowledgment of the divine mystery of life.

Sports massage: This type of bodywork is considered to be a combination of Swedish massage, deep tissue work, and even some shiatsu, as a means of restoring health to muscle tissues after rigorous workouts.

Stage of exhaustion: The third stage of Selye's general adaptation syndrome, in which one or more organs targeted by excessive neural or hormonal activity goes into dysfunction.

Stage of resistance: The second stage of Selye's general adaptation syndrome, in which the body and all its organs try to return to homeostasis. If the stress persists, this may not be possible and the third stage begins.

Stone therapy: A type of bodywork where stones (hot or cold) are placed on various parts of the body (some place them on the chakra areas) to balance the body's energy. Sometimes the stones are used to aid in muscle manipulation.

Stress: Also called distress. This term has many different definitions, but most people agree that it is a perceived threat (real or imagined) to one's mind, body, spirit, or emotions.

Stress-prone personalities: A collection of personalities that promote stress rather than diminish it. These include the Type A personality, the codependent personality, and the helpless-hopeless personality.

Stress reaction: Any strategy that leads one back in the direction of homeostasis. Holistic stress management includes using both effective coping skills (mind) and relaxation techniques (body) to address both causes and symptoms, respectively.

Stress-resistant personalities: These are personality traits that allow a person to cope well with stress, giving the appearance that they are resistant to crisis. These include the hardy personality, the survivor personality, and the sensation seeker, also known as Type R.

Stress response: The same as the fight-or-flight response.

Stressor: Any issue, concern, or problem that is perceived to be a threat to one's mind, body, spirit, or emotions.

Subtle anatomy: Also called energy anatomy, subtle anatomy is composed of the human energy field (aura), the chakra system, and the meridian system of energetic pathways that supply energy (also known as chi or prana) to the organs and physiological systems with which they connect.

Subtle energy: Often described as a life force that surrounds and permeates everyone and everything.

Superiority theory: First coined by Plato to describe the reason why people laugh. Plato observed that we tend to laugh at other people's expense. Jokes about Tiger Woods or Martha Stewart and blonde jokes might fall in this category.

Support groups: A coping technique that allows an individual to let others offer comfort and support in times of need. Examples would include Alcoholics Anonymous and bereavement groups.

Survivor personality: A collection of personality traits that combine to enhance one's ability to survive stressful events from plane crashes to terminal cancer.

Swedish massage: Perhaps the most common type of massage known in Western culture. Swedish massage includes various strokes, kneading, and manipulations of muscle tissue to flush waste products out and restore a sense of calm to the entire body.

Sympathetic resonance: A term from the field of physics similar to entrainment where two objects, such as tuning forks, are in "like" vibration.

Techno-stress: A term coined to focus on the stress induced by the proliferation of technology from smartphones to upgrades, downloads to laptops.

Tend and befriend: A theory presented by Shelly Taylor which states that women who experience stress don't necessarily run or fight, but rather turn to friends to cope with unpleasant events and circumstances.

Thai massage: A type of bodywork that dates back many centuries but has gained new popularity in Western culture. Thai massage combines a kneading action with pulling of limbs and even some energy work for a combined effect of relaxation.

Tickler notebook: A means of collecting funny items (e.g., cards, letters, JPEG files, jokes) and reading or perusing these when you are having a really bad day, or even when you're sick in the hospital.

Time management: The ability to prioritize, schedule, and administrate personal responsibilities for personal satisfaction.

Time mapping: A term used in time management where a person plots out various responsibilities and their locations to make the most efficient use of their time.

Time robbers: Behaviors that steal valuable time away from a productive day. Examples might include watching television or spending lots of time with friends rather than studying.

Toxic thoughts: Thoughts and perceptions created by the mind (specifically, the ego) that chip away at one's self-esteem. Toxic thoughts perpetuate stress.

Type A personality: Initially called the worry sickness, Type A behavior is now regarded as the aggressive-based personality, with traits that are associated with coronary heart disease.

Underhander: The underhander's motto is, "Don't get mad, get even!" This is a common style of mismanaged anger at the worksite where passive-aggressive behavior becomes the norm for some people. Sarcasm is the most common form of this style.

Uniqueness: One of five characteristics used to promote self-esteem, highlighting aspects that make you feel special and outstanding.

Visualization: The conscious direction of images on the screen of the mind's eye. A relaxation technique.

Warrior, the: This is the fourth stage of von Oech's creative process, wherein the warrior takes the idea to the street (marketing and implementation).

Wellness paradigm: The integration, balance, and harmony of mind, body, spirit, and emotions leading toward optimal well-being.

Yerkes-Dodson principle: A concept that suggests that some stress (excitement or stimuli) is good to a point, then it becomes bad. Up to a point this enhances one's performance, past that point, it diminishes it. This "point" is different for everyone.

Index

Index

Photo Credits

Chapter 1
Page 20, © 2003 Ziggy and Friends Inc. Reprinted with permission of UNIVERSAL PRESS SYNDICATE. All rights reserved.

Chapter 7
Chapter Opener, page 119, © Creatista/ShutterStock; page 122, Bizarro (2007) © Dan Piraro. King Features Syndicate; page 123, © 2000 Ziggy and Friends, Inc. Reprinted with the permission of UNIVERSAL PRESS SYNDICATE. All rights reserved.

Chapter 9
Chapter Opener, page 143, © Photos.com.

Chapter 19
Chapter Opener, page 257, © Photodisc.

Chapter 20
Chapter Opener, page 265, © Kim Pin Tan/ShutterStock, Inc.

Chapter 25
Chapter Opener, page 319, © auremar/ShutterStock, Inc.

Glossary
Opener, page 323, © Photos.com